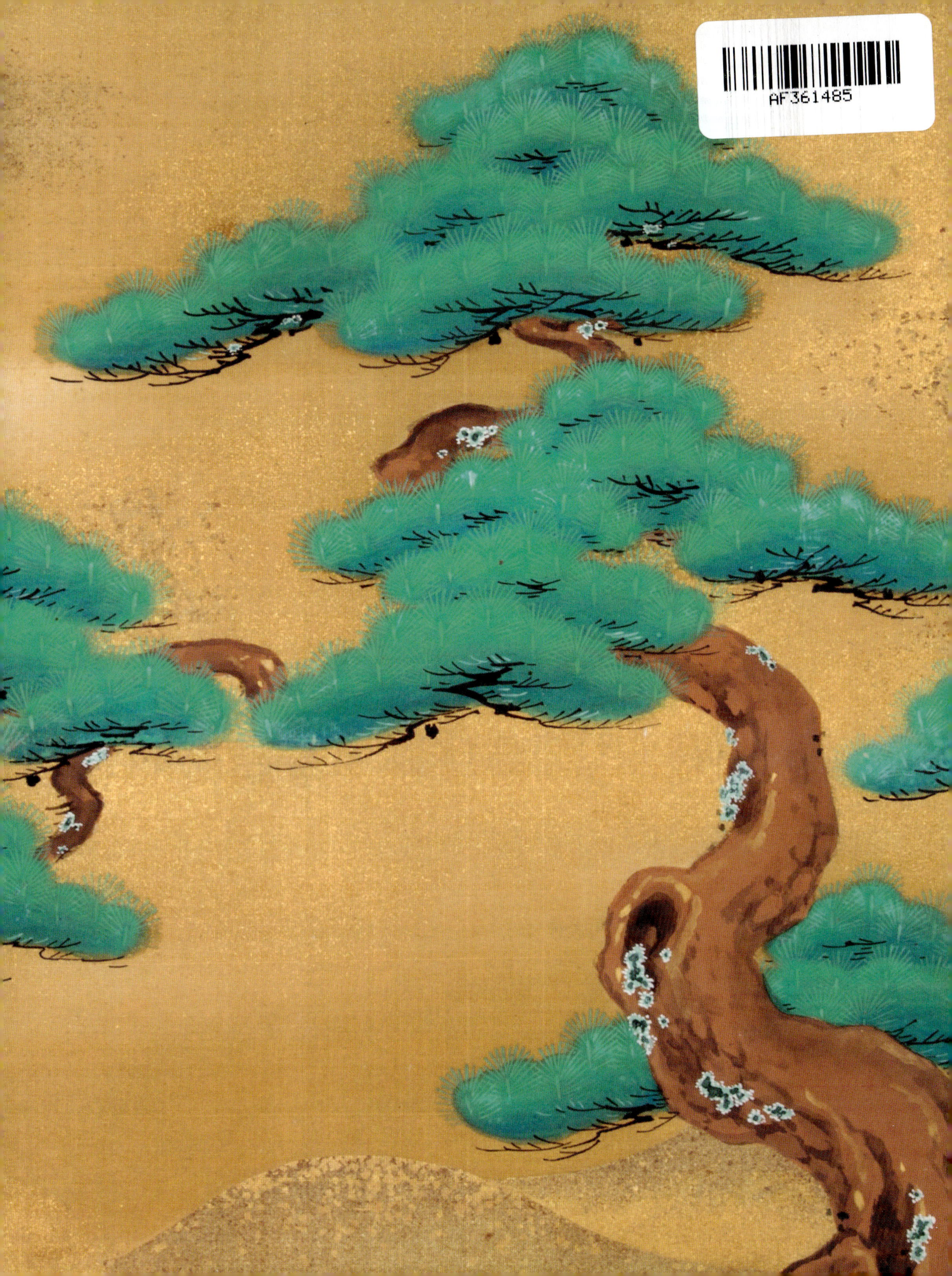

AF361485

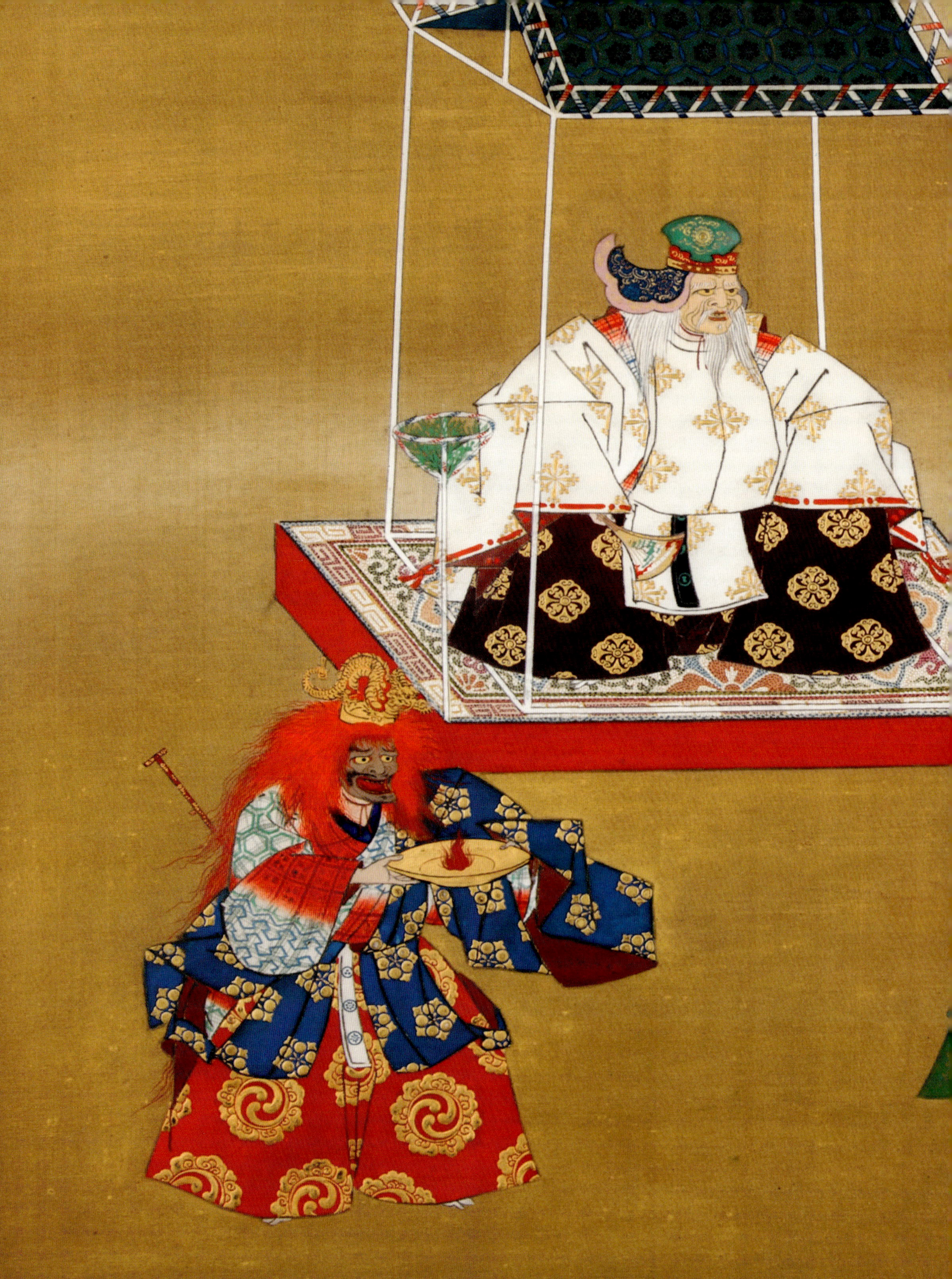

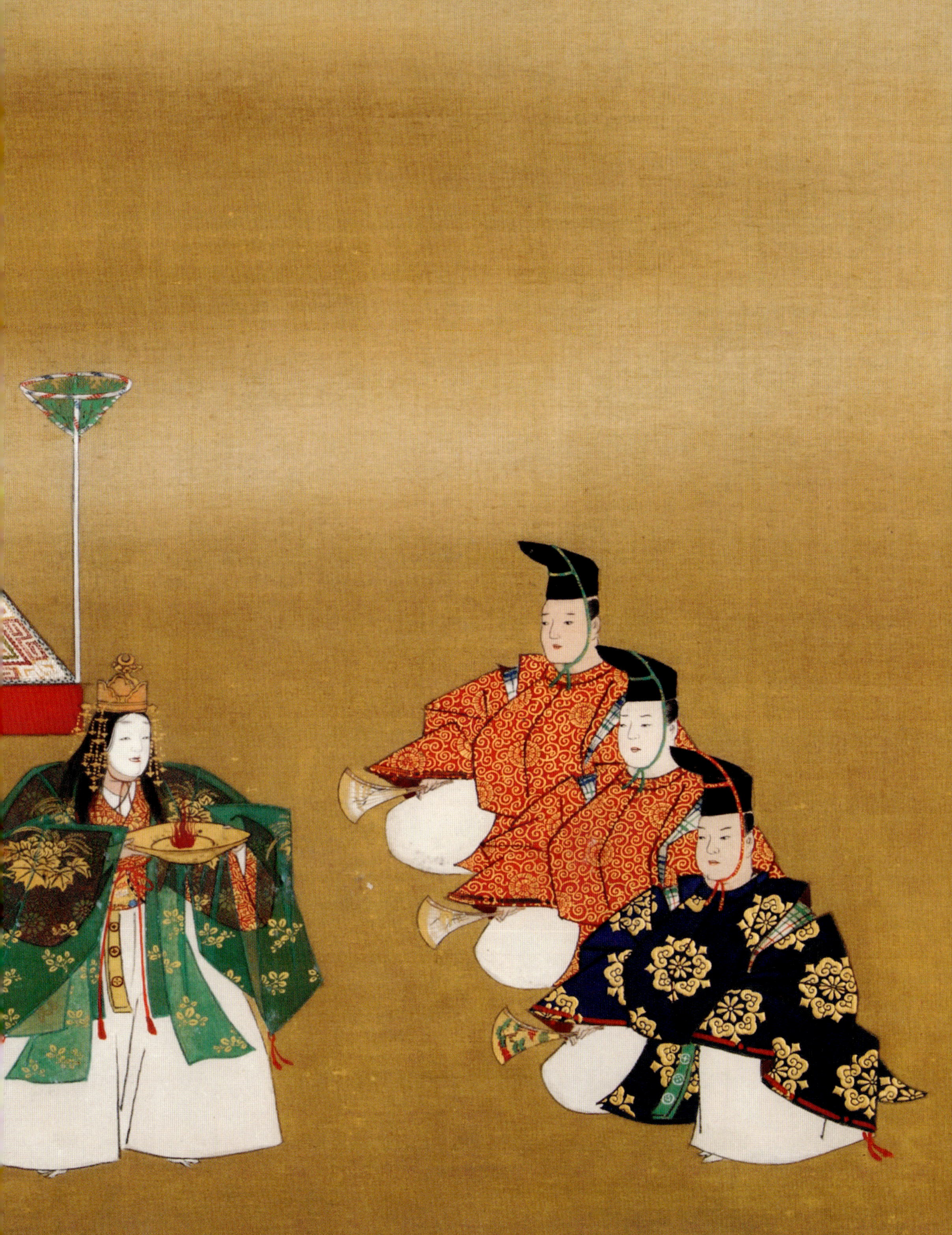

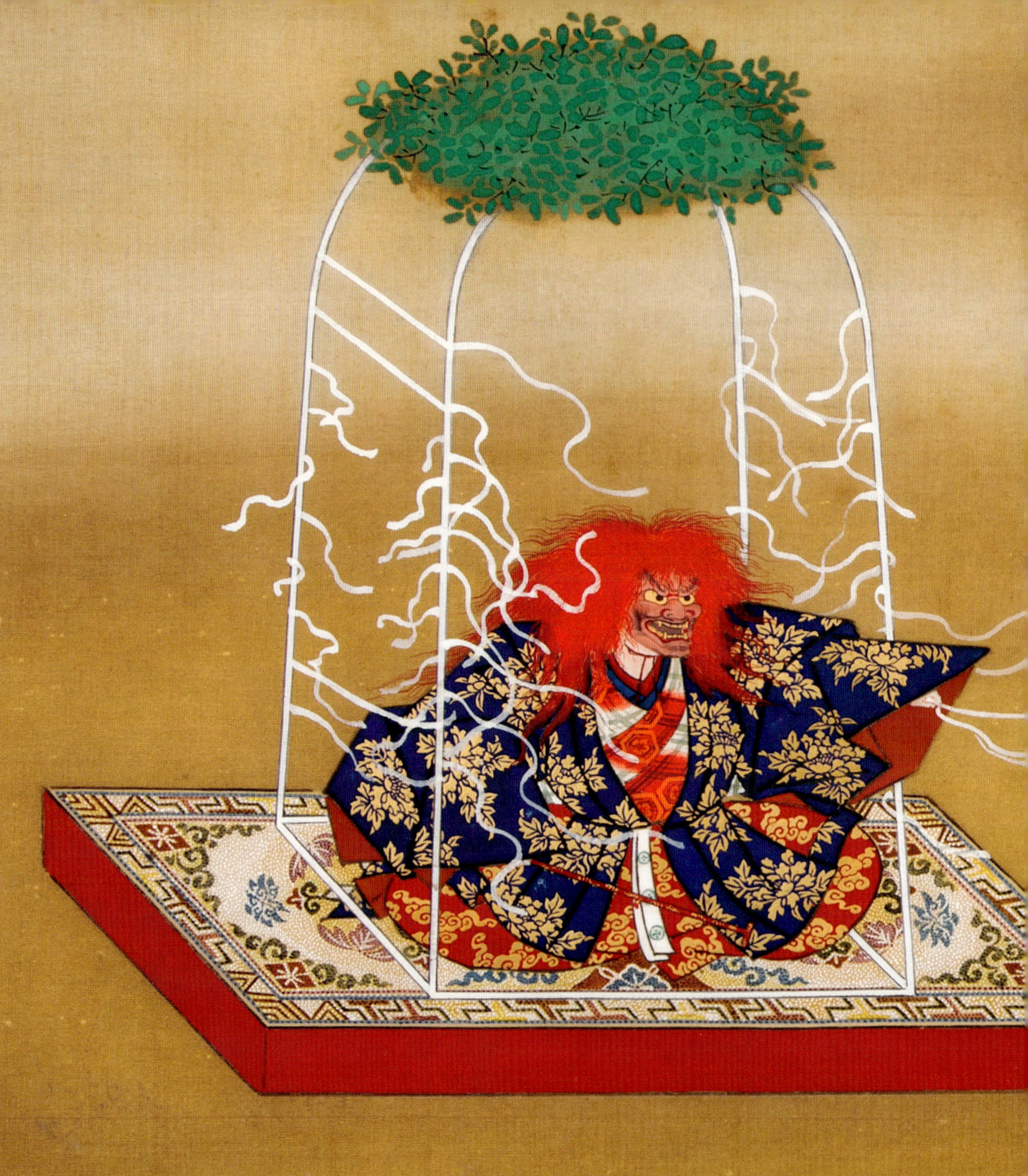

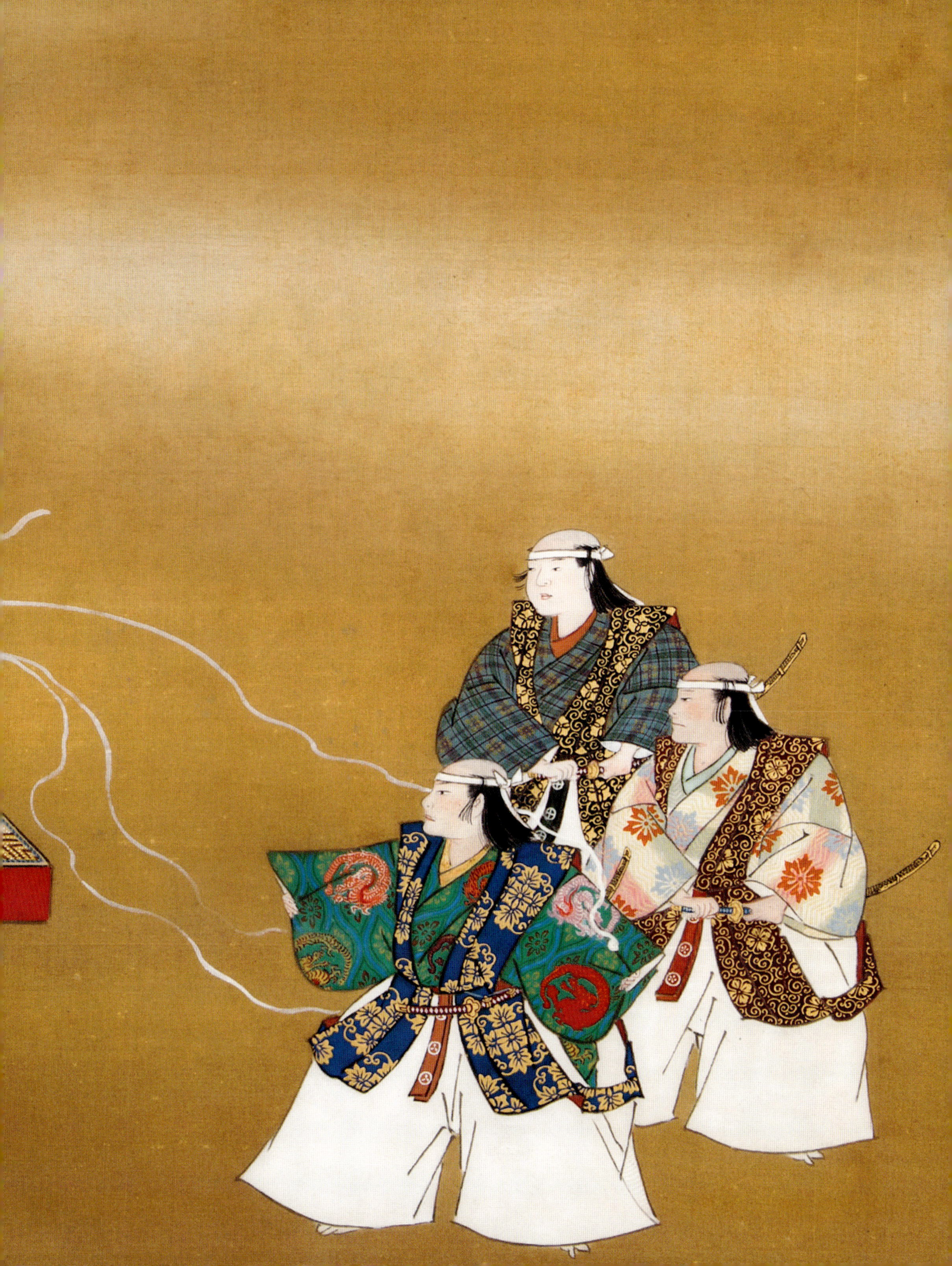

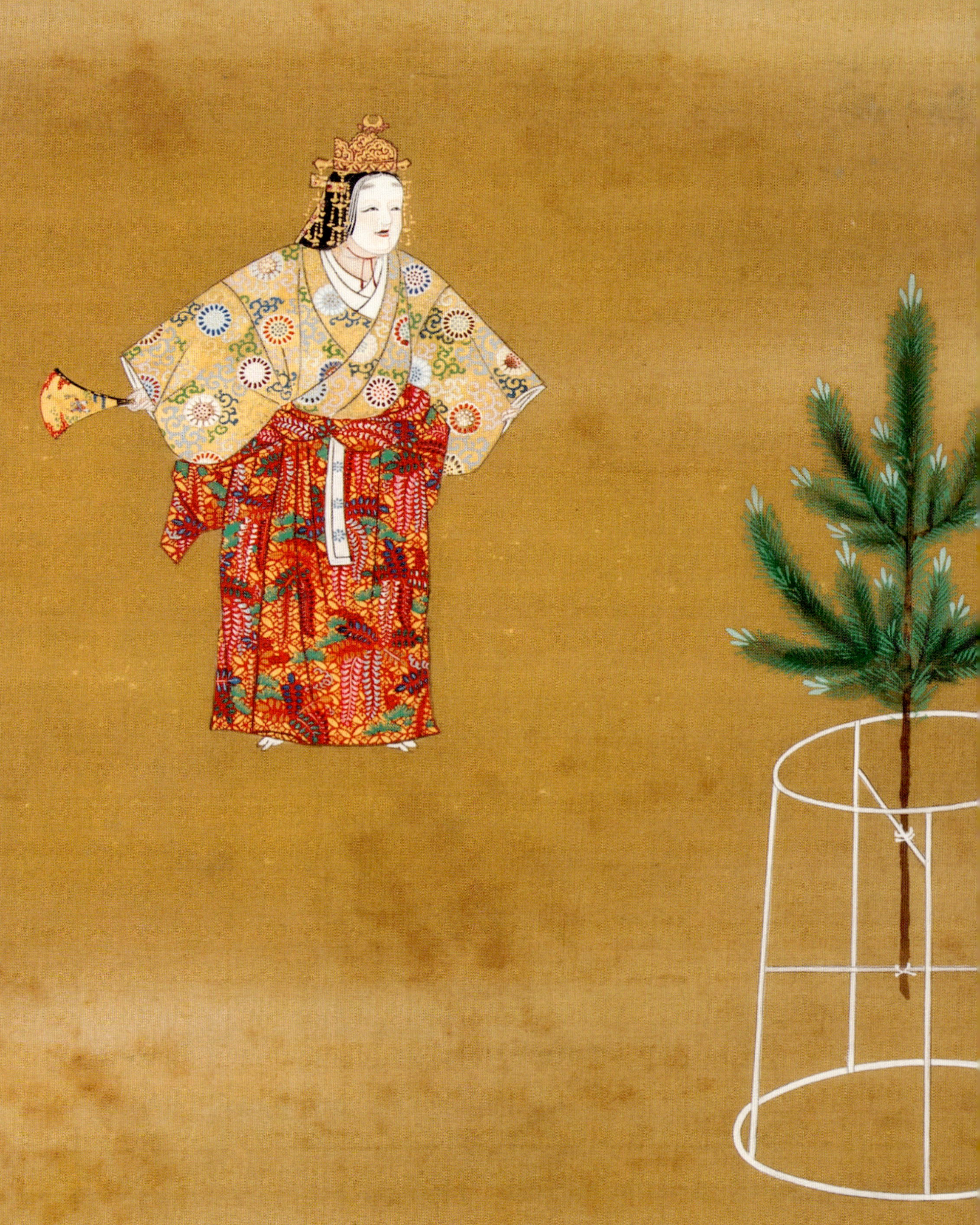

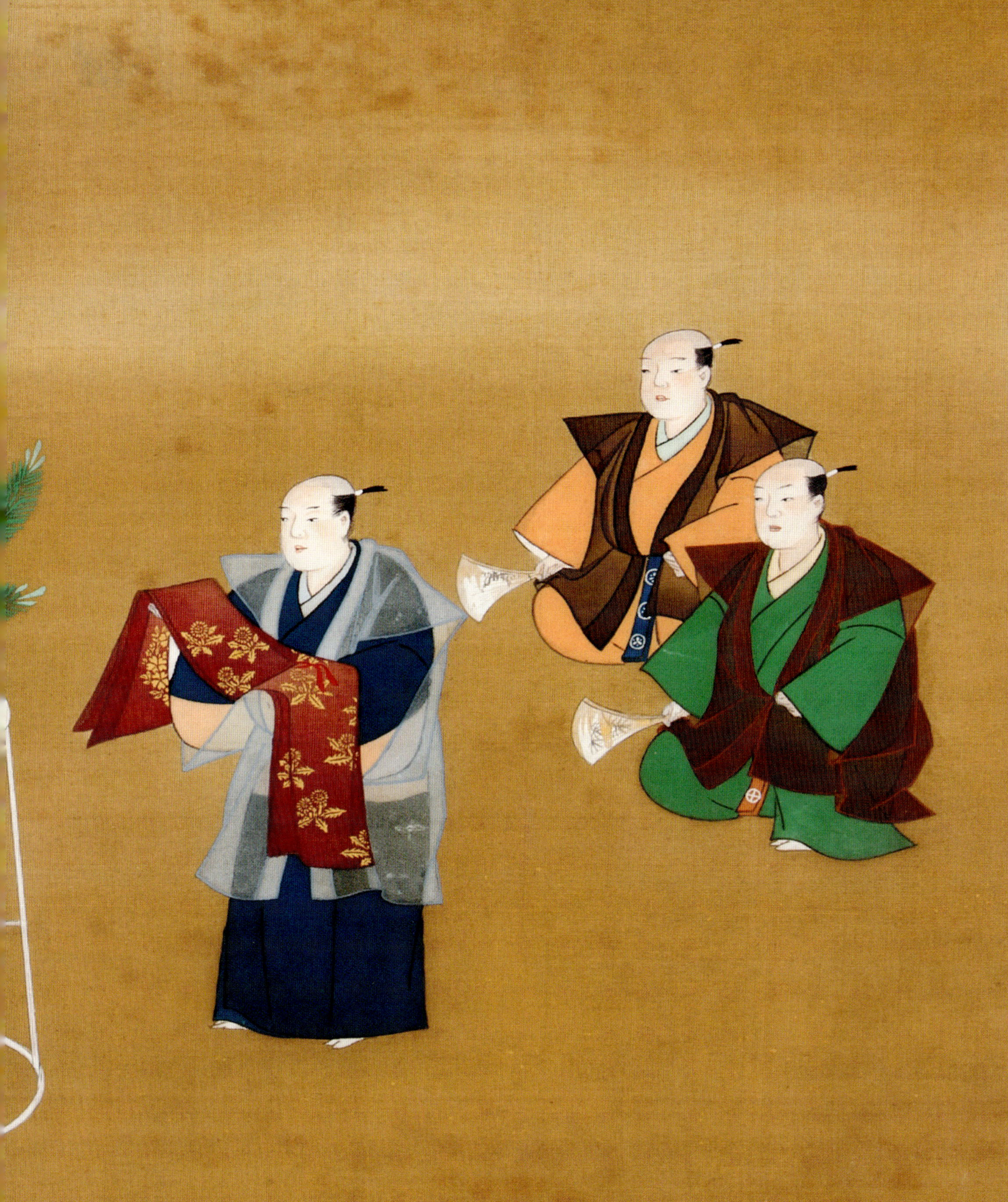

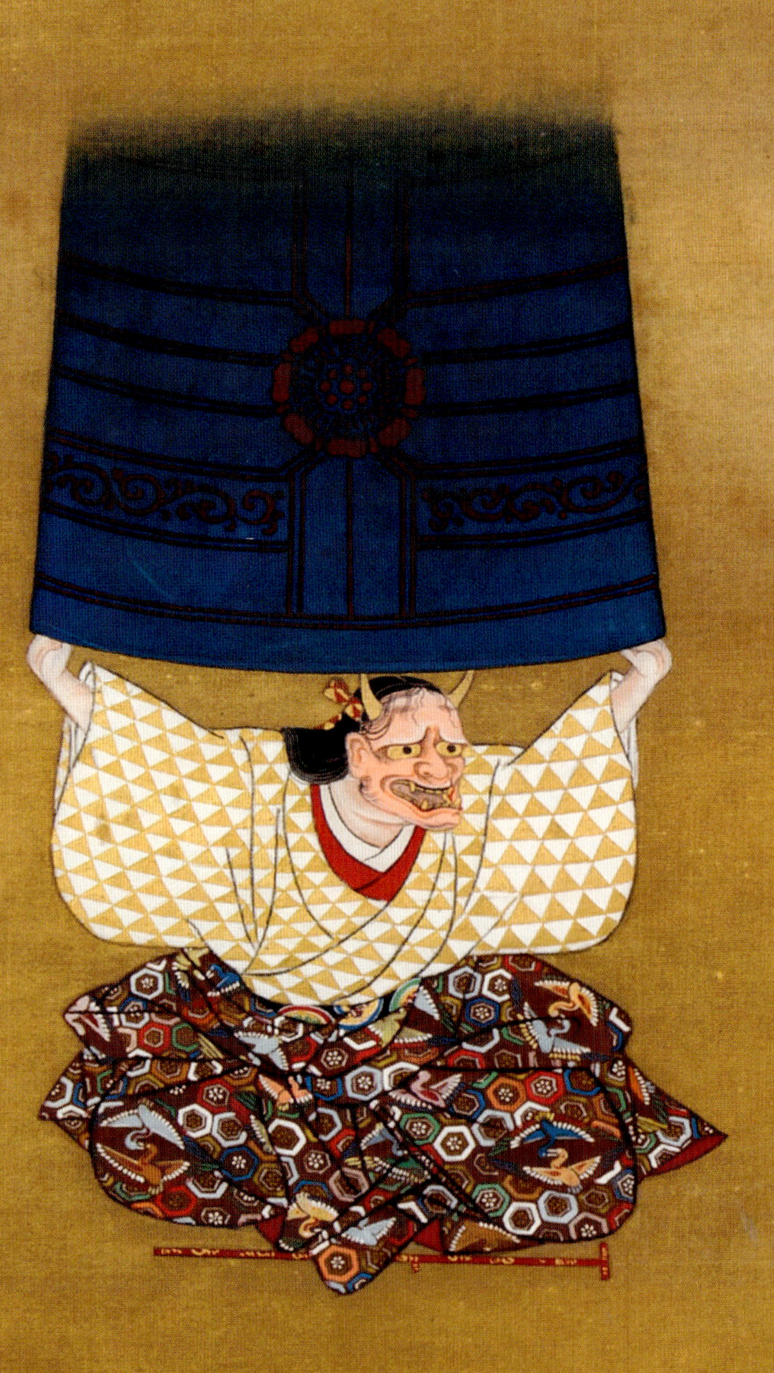
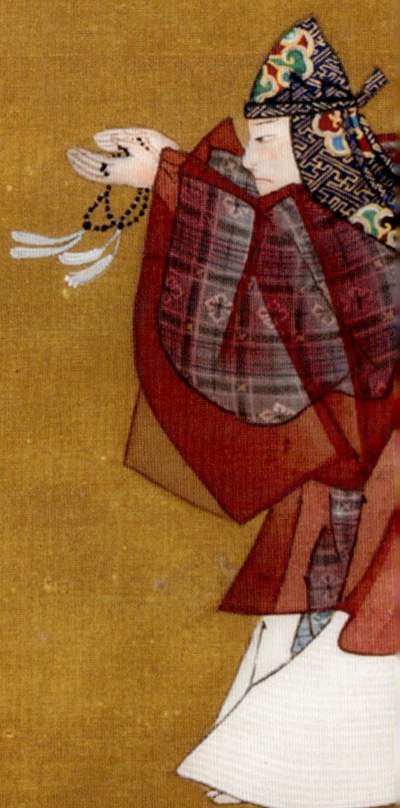

nō
& kyōgen in Japan

EDITED BY
Khanh Trinh

WITH ESSAYS BY
Monica Bethe
Eric C Rath
J Thomas Rimer
Takemoto Mikio
Khanh Trinh

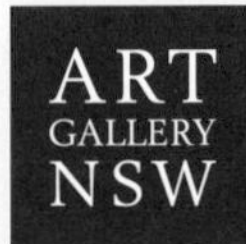

The Art Gallery of New South Wales is very fortunate to have the unique opportunity to present the exhibition *Theatre of dreams, theatre of play: nō and kyōgen in Japan* from the collections of the National Noh Theatre and the Agency for Cultural Affairs of Japan (Bunkachō). For the first time in Australia, a comprehensive exhibition of the outstanding masks, costumes, musical instruments, paintings and songbooks from the fifteenth to the early nineteenth century will highlight the sophisticated culture of *nōgaku (nohgaku)*.

We are indebted to the Japan Arts Council and the National Noh Theatre, in particular director Mogi Shichizaemon, for his generosity in lending such superb pieces, and to Kadowaki Yukie for sharing her time and expertise on the collection. I extend our gratitude to the Agency for Cultural Affairs of Japan, with special thanks to commissioner Aoyagi Masanori, whose assistance was invaluable in allowing this exhibition to travel outside Japan, and to Kobayashi Ayako for her enthusiasm and support.

I acknowledge the contributions of experts and scholars Takemoto Mikio, J Thomas Rimer, Eric C Rath and Monica Bethe, and thank them for their thoughtful research and essays in this publication accompanying the exhibition. I also acknowledge the contribution of specialist editor Amy Reigle Newland for her advice, translations and editing for the book.

I thank Qantas, the Gallery's official airline, for bringing this exhibition to Australia and extend the Gallery's appreciation to VisAsia, for its long support of Asian art, and for its financial contribution to this exhibition.

Above all, the exhibition and publication would not have been realised without the efforts and expertise of the Gallery's curator of Japanese art, Khanh Trinh, who has worked on this project for the past three years to ensure it came to fruition in Australia. My special thanks also go to the many other Gallery staff members who have contributed to the success of this project.

Michael Brand
Director
Art Gallery of New South Wales

The Japan Arts Council takes great pleasure in presenting the exhibition *Theatre of dreams, theatre of play: nō and kyōgen in Japan* in collaboration with the Agency for Cultural Affairs of Japan (Bunkachō) and the Art Gallery of New South Wales.

The Japan Arts Council was established in 1966 as the National Theatre for the purpose of preserving and promoting traditional Japanese performing arts. This work is carried out primarily through performance and education programs at our theatre facilities in Japan. The National Noh Theatre in Tokyo, established in 1983 under the auspices of the Japan Arts Council, disseminates knowledge of *nohgaku* (noh [nō] and kyōgen) through research, performance and the education and training of younger actors. The National Noh Theatre also boasts a considerable collection of cultural objects relating to *nohgaku*, which are regularly exhibited to the public.

Noh has been continuously performed for over 600 years and the Japanese are proud of its rich cultural heritage. The performance and production styles of noh have been constantly refined to the highest levels over its long history, and even today they still influence a wide range of arts beyond Japan's borders. Many of the robes and masks used onstage by performers are heirloom objects, and they represent great technical and aesthetic achievements in their own right.

Theatre of dreams, theatre of play presents a striking selection of works from the National Noh Theatre and other collections, including important masks, costumes, historical documents and paintings. It is my sincere hope that this exhibition will offer viewers an opportunity to deepen their understanding of this time-honoured Japanese performing art.

I would like to express my heartfelt thanks to the Art Gallery of New South Wales and all those in Japan and Australia who worked tirelessly to bring this exhibition to fruition.

Mogi Shichizaemon
President
Japan Arts Council

It is my great honour to be involved with *Theatre of dreams, theatre of play: nō and kyōgen in Japan*. Organised by the Agency for Cultural Affairs of Japan (Bunkachō) and the Japan Arts Council in cooperation with the Art Gallery of New South Wales, this special exhibition showcases a diverse selection of artworks related to nō and kyōgen theatre.

The Agency for Cultural Affairs of Japan has held annual exhibitions overseas since 1951, with the aim of promoting the understanding of Japanese culture and history, and mounted its first show in Oceania at the Art Gallery in 2003. Now a decade later, the Agency is proud to be associated with *Theatre of dreams, theatre of play*, which displays masterpieces from the collection of the Japan Arts Council's National Noh Theatre, as well as pieces from other collections in Japan.

Nō theatre is one of the most significant forms of traditional Japanese performance art. The fascination this unique theatre holds for audiences in both Japan and abroad has led to its inclusion, since 2008, on UNESCO's Representative List of the Intangible Cultural Heritage of Humanity. It is hoped that the current exhibition and publication will bring alive the beauty of this rich aesthetic and performative tradition through the display of sumptuous nō robes, finely carved masks, musical instruments and libretti, along with paintings, prints and albums illustrating scenes from celebrated nō plays.

I would like to express my heartfelt thanks to those who have collaborated with us to make this exhibition a resounding success.

Aoyagi Masanori
Commissioner
Agency for Cultural Affairs of Japan

Khanh Trinh

INTRODUCTION

Nō – the 'total theatre' combining elements of drama, music and dance – has a history spanning over 600 years. As such, it is not only Japan's oldest continuous performing art tradition but also one of the world's most ancient theatre forms. Throughout its long history, nō ('skill' or 'talent') experienced changes in patronage and audience as it underwent various stages of formal as well as stylistic development. Nonetheless, it could be said with a degree of certainty that a nō program (composed of dramatic nō plays and humorous kyōgen interludes) in the twenty-first century would still touch the hearts and challenge the intellect of its audience as it had done in the time of Kan'ami (1333–84) and his celebrated son Zeami Motokiyo (c1363–c1443), the acknowledged forefathers of nō theatre.

The enduring fascination of nō is due in no small part to the universal messages of its plays, which revolve around the many facets of human emotion, including jealousy, obsession, grief, vengeance, desire, loneliness, loyalty and deception. While such feelings and their conveyance in dramatic form are not unique to Japanese culture, it cannot be assumed that nō performance is easily comprehensible to everyone. Nō is governed by fixed rules: the minimalist architecture of the stage, the quasi non-existent scenery and the symbolic acting, all of which contribute to the dignified, ritual-like atmosphere of the performance. The challenge for nō (and kyōgen) actors is how to transmit a complex story replete with nuanced emotions employing rigorously prescribed gestures, movements and forms of recitation, one that is performed within highly abstracted stage settings, and with the use of a limited variety of masks and costumes. The challenge for the audience lies not only in the comprehension of the chanted lyrics and the sparse stage design, but also in the decoding of the stylised gestures and the meaning inherent in the ensemble of mask and costume. These aspects of nō are eloquently discussed in this publication in the essays by J Thomas Rimer, Eric C Rath and Monica Bethe. Takemoto Mikio's overview of the historical development and this author's observations on the hitherto less examined topic of the representation of nō and kyōgen in paintings and woodblock prints complete the picture of this unique dramatic art.

Nō (and kyōgen) are undoubtedly most appreciated in performance onstage, when the mesmerising sound of the orchestra's drums and flutes, the melodic chant of the chorus, the polished movements of the actors, the timeless beauty of the masks and the dazzling splendour of the costumes coalesce to embody the aesthetic concept of yūgen. In the absence of firsthand experience of the sound and movement of nō performance, then, a closer look at the masks, costumes, instruments, paintings, prints and other visual documents that constitute the rich material culture of the nō and kyōgen theatre in this publication offers us a visual alternative in appreciating this time-honoured performative art form.

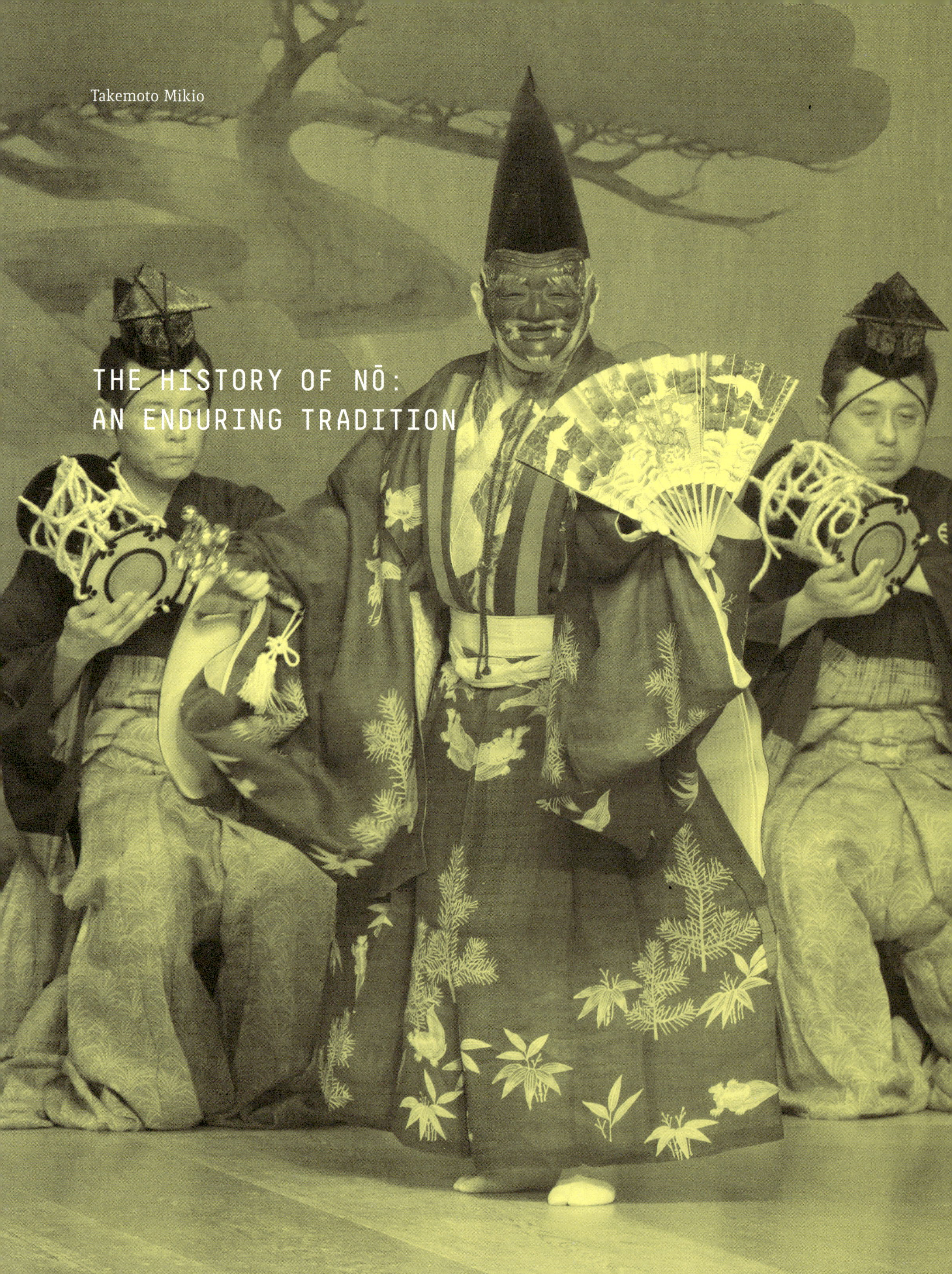

THE HISTORY OF NŌ: AN ENDURING TRADITION

The origins of nō theatre date back to *sangaku*, a performance tradition from Tang-dynasty (618–907) China known as *baixi* ('one hundred entertainment arts'). *Sangaku*, together with *bugaku* (court dance and music), was the only form of court entertainment in Japan before the Nara period (710–94). It comprised acrobats, magic tricks, song and dance staged to the accompaniment of music.[1] In 782, most likely due to economic reasons, the Nara court dismissed *sangaku* entertainers. From the late eighth to the thirteenth century, *sarugaku* – a performance style emerging from *sangaku* – became hugely popular, so much so that lower-ranking court officials would stage *sarugaku* ('monkey entertainment') as party tricks at official ceremonies. In the twelfth century, *sarugaku* performers and *shushi* participated in ritual ceremonies at important Buddhist temples. *Shushi* were originally Buddhist priests who conducted esoteric religious incantations and the gestures they used during these services developed into a form of entertainment. *Sarugaku* integrated such elements of ritualistic performance from the *shushi*, as confirmed in the treatise *A new account of sarugaku* (*Shin sarugakuki*) attributed to Fujiwara no Akihira (986–1066).

Such presentations by *shushi* eventually became the ritual performance known as *Okina sarugaku*, which was the predecessor to the *Okina* (also referred to as *Shiki sanban*, or 'Three rituals') that is still performed today. A record from 1349 states that *Okina sarugaku* was staged together with a dramatic form of *sarugaku*, the latter beginning around 1300 and eventually evolving into the mainstream *sarugaku* that was henceforth variously called *Okina*, nō or kyōgen depending on its performance style. Other troupes of entertainers, such as those practising *dengaku* ('field music'), also called their art *sarugaku*.[2] It can be assumed that this branch of *sarugaku* developed into Japan's oldest staged dramas, which later became nō. (Kyōgen, the comical drama usually performed as interludes to nō pieces, has its roots in the humorous mimicry of *sarugaku*). Over 500 years later, in 1881, *sarugaku* would be renamed '*nōgaku*', a term subsuming both nō and kyōgen.

THE ARRIVAL OF KAN'AMI AND ZEAMI

Kan'ami (1333–84) was the third son of Yamada Sarugaku, a *sarugaku* troupe (*za*) performer from Yamato province (present-day Nara prefecture). Kan'ami's stage name was Kanze, and before the age of 30 he had already performed in Kyoto with the *Okina sarugaku* troupe Yūzaki. He was an exceptionally talented musician, studying *kusemai*, a type of narrative singing with dance then fashionable, which he incorporated into the *sarugaku* song repertoire. His *sarugaku* songs, known as *Yamato ongyoku* or 'Yamato-style songs' – so called after his roots in the Yamato region – were enormously popular.

In around 1374, Kan'ami performed *sarugaku* at the Imagumano shrine in Kyoto before the shogun Ashikaga Yoshimitsu (1358–1408) and the excellence of his staging so impressed the shogun that he was favoured with shogunal patronage. Yoshimitsu similarly supported the skills of Inuō (Dōami, d1417), a well-known master of the Hie *sarugaku* troupe from Ōmi province (*Ōmi sarugaku*) and the renowned nō chanter Kiami of the *Shinza dengaku*

('New troupe' *dengaku*). Together these three troupes enjoyed the fame and prestige associated with patronage from the Ashikaga shoguns until the fifteenth century.

Kan'ami's legitimate son was Saburō Motokiyo (c1363–c1443) – later (and better) known as Zeami. When he was 12, he and his father performed before Ashikaga Yoshimitsu. This resulted in shogunal patronage and thus from a very young age Zeami received the highest level of education in the arts. His training included the study of *waka* (31-syllable Japanese-style poem) and *renga* (linked verse), which later enabled him to produce *sarugaku* masterpieces that satisfied the critical tastes of the nobility. It should be noted, however, that Zeami always remained the second favourite of the Ashikaga shoguns: in his youth he was overshadowed by Inuō of the *Ōmi sarugaku* troupe, and later by Zōami of the *Shinza dengaku*. It would not be an exaggeration to say that Zeami's lifetime obsession was to overcome this hurdle and that this was the primary motivation for the creation of many of his nō masterworks and theories.

Inuō's song and dance was unrivalled in its popularity. Zeami studied his style and sought to incorporate Inuō's song and dance elements into his own *Yamato sarugaku*, the main elements of which were the characters of devils, gods and the use of realistic movement. Zeami began with making dance movements the climax of a piece and finally by integrating Inuō's favourite performance element – the 'dance of a heavenly maiden' (*apsara*) – into his work. This represented a fundamental transformation of the troupe's performance style since Kan'ami's time. Zeami enacted these changes with indomitable resolve and on occasion maintained they were his father's deathbed wish. Born from this struggle to innovate was Zeami's *yūgen nō*, characterised by the actors' often dance-like gestures and pure dance. Zeami worked in three main categories – *monogurui nō, saidō nō* and *kami nō* – and he reworked plays in these groups into *yūgen nō* by showcasing dance movements. *Monogurui nō* connotes the 'possession by an evil spirit' or a 'maddening desire'. The latter involves a protagonist who becomes 'deranged' following the separation from a lover, parent or child, travelling as an entertainer in search of their beloved who is eventually found. Zeami fine-tuned this idea of 'maddening desire' in *yūgen nō*. He divided *saidō nō*, or the 'evil spirit' nō, into two groups: a guardian of hell who displays mercy towards the condemned and a human spirit in hell. He claimed that only the second group could be used in his *yūgen nō* and he successfully assimilated tales of spirits unable to find peace due to unrequited love into elegant performances. *Kami* (god or deity) *nō* comprised the third category. While plays about gods predate even Kan'ami, they tend to focus on the intense movements of violent deities. By contrast, Zeami believed that a song-dance style performance was most appropriate for gods and he perfected a new form in which they dance to bless the imperial reign or to rejoice in peace and stability.

Zeami's invention using these three categories was *mugen nō* ('dream and vision'), one of the two types of nō (the other being *genzai nō*, or 'realistic nō').[3] In *mugen nō* the spirit tells its story: as the secondary supporting actor (*waki*) dreams, the main actor (*shite*) appears first in an assumed form, then in his true form stages the lead dance. These pieces included dancing to chants and instrumental music, at the centre of which was Inuō's 'dance of a heavenly maiden'. Eventually, *Yamato sarugaku* integrated this dance into much of its repertoire, later establishing the style of *maigoto* (nō dancing accompanied by instrumentalists) that is performed today.

Another of Zeami's significant accomplishments was his treatises on nō and they stand as the oldest theatre treatises in the world written by an actor. The approach to learning nō is at the core of Zeami's 21 surviving treatises, which include discourses on training and performance such as *Teachings on style and the flower* (*Fūshi kaden*, 1400), on playwriting such as *The three paths* (*Sandō*, 1423), on chanting such as *Oral instructions on singing* (*Ongyoku kuden*, 1419) and on the levels of excellence in performance such as *Nine levels* (*Kyūi*, 1420s) and *An account of Zeami's reflections on art* (*Sarugaku dangi*, 1430). Zeami's theories (and philosophies) would subsequently determine the direction of nō. While his rivals, the *Ōmi sarugaku* and *Shinza dengaku* troupes, were unable to find worthy heirs and would eventually die out, *nō* prospered under Zeami's successors. This is a clear indication of the enduring significance of his treatises for future generations.

Zeami initially intended to appoint his nephew Motoshige (later On'ami, 1398–1467) as his successor and bestow upon him his 'Saburō' name, but ultimately Zeami chose his eldest son Jūrō Motomasa (d1432) to continue his legacy. Motomasa excelled in playwriting and produced masterpieces such as *The river Sumida* (*Sumidagawa*), but it was Motoshige who enjoyed patronage by Ashikaga Yoshinori (1394–1441) before he became shogun. When Yoshinori became the sixth Ashikaga shogun in 1428, Motoshige was placed in charge of *sarugaku*, and this resulted in Zeami's and Motomasa's fall from favour. In 1434, two years after Motomasa's unexpected death, Zeami was exiled to the remote island of Sado. There are no further records of Zeami's life following his last work, *The book of the golden island* (*Kintōsho*, 1436), a collection of chanting verses describing his life in exile. Motoshige eventually swept aside all rival *sarugaku* and *dengaku* troupes, his new Kanze troupe achieving the highest status.

AFTER ZEAMI: SARUGAKU AND NŌGAKU IN THE LATER MUROMACHI AND MOMOYAMA PERIODS (1392-1615)

After the demise of the Kanze house following Zeami's death, Motoshige and Konparu Ujinobu (Zenchiku, 1405–70?), Zeami's son-in-law, became the leaders in the world of nō. As the rightful successor to Zeami's theories, Zenchiku perfected the elder master's theories of *yūgen nō*, as well as producing a number of plays. Works of this era are characterised by new subjects based on Chinese legends and the bold dramatisation of narratives taken from well-known Japanese epics such as the fourteenth-century *The story of Yoshitsune* (*Gikeiki*) and *Tale of the Soga brothers* (*Soga monogatari*). Zenchiku also created new interpretations of song-dance nō performance (*kabu nō*) drawing upon the style of *kabu nō* established by Zeami. In kyōgen, too, specific titles, some of which are still staged today, first appear in records at this time.

The main nō playwrights active during On'ami's and Zenchiku's later years and until the 1480s were On'ami's youngest son, the actor Kanze Nobumitsu (1450–1516?), Nobumitsu's son Nagatoshi (1488–1541) of the Kanze troupe and Motoyasu *tayū* (Zenpō, 1454–c1532) of the Konparu troupe. During this period, which corresponded in part with the Ōnin civil war of 1467–77, plays with demons, dragons and vengeful spirits proliferated, as did pieces about military battles that required numerous actors and special techniques. The techniques in music for *nō* were consolidated and the 'classics' from the Zeami era dominated performances. There was a specialisation and refinement of each role, which provided the basis for the preservation of nō as a classic theatre art. It was also then that magnificent costumes and refined masks appeared.

Scene from the nō play *The wind in the pines* (*Matsukaze*)

In 1593, Toyotomi Hideyoshi (1536/1537–1598), who successfully unified Japan after the years of civil war, issued an edict ordering Tokugawa Ieyasu and other daimyo to provide funds to maintain four *sarugaku* troupes, and to establish a rice stipend system (*sarugaku haitōmai*) for them. Before then some performers received land from their daimyo patrons, but this was the first time that nō actors were paid fixed salaries. The stipend system was a demonstration of the ruler's move to monopolise the four *sarugaku* troupes: Kanze, Hōshō, Konparu and Kongō. Other troupes denied of such stipends were fated to disappear.

SARUGAKU AND NŌGAKU OF THE EDO PERIOD (1615-1868)

The rice stipend system was re-introduced in 1618 under the new Tokugawa shogunate founded by Tokugawa Ieyasu (1543–1616), who situated his capital city in Edo (now Tokyo) in the country's east. Depending on their status and/or their history, performers could also receive additional rice for various reasons, including services in an administrative role or as salary. Each of the four troupes were originally organised with a *tayū* as its head. Originally, *tayū* (or *dayū* when inflected) was a pseudo-official title given to promising actors by the samurai affiliated with major temples. The receipt of this title was extremely prestigious and in the sixteenth century, troupe leaders adopted the title for themselves. *Tayū* would oversee the *shite* and the 'three roles': *waki* and kyōgen actors, and musicians called *hayashi*. All of these members were now recognised as the shogunate's *sarugaku* performers.

The second Tokugawa shogun Hidetada (1579–1632) patronised Kita Shichidayū (d1653) and granted his son permission to establish the fifth troupe, the Kita, which supplied performers to a number of domain lords. The fifth shogun Tsunayoshi (1646–1709) was enthusiastic about nō and declared nō a mandatory part of the costly reception ceremonies required when one daimyo visited another. His successor Ienobu (1662–1712) was equally fond of nō, even though this fondness for the theatre did not lead to the same

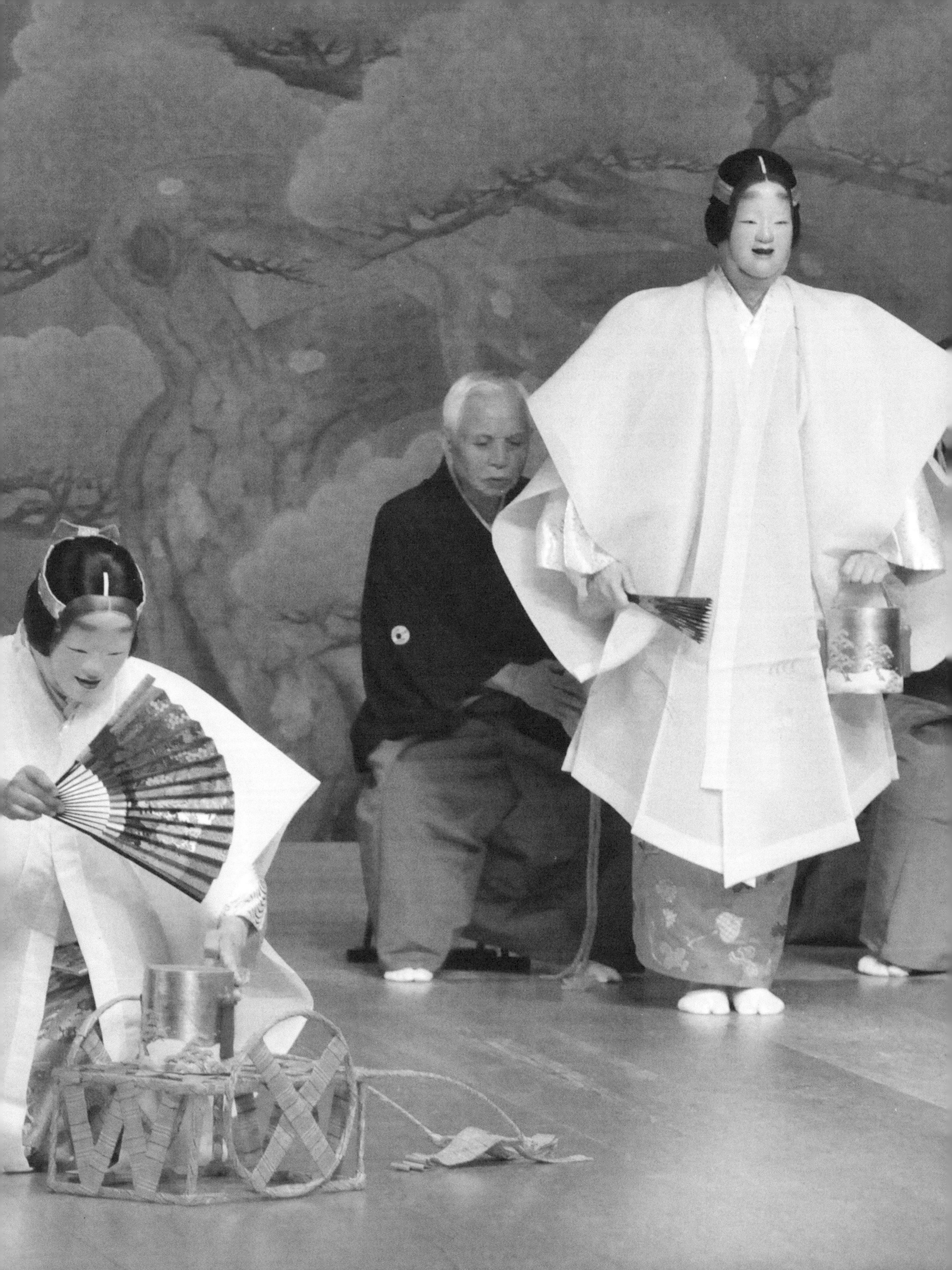

excesses as his predecessor. A major review of the *sarugaku* system took place during the rule of the eighth shogun Yoshimune (1684–1751), when the solemn style of nō theatre known today was largely established.

Throughout the Edo period, nō and kyōgen were also popular with commoners. Nō songs – *utai* or *yōkyoku* – were compiled in books with songs and musical notation that were used for training. The production of these songbooks, or *utaibon*, became a popular market for publishers and they were disseminated widely. From the shogun and daimyo down to the commoners, many people learned *utai*, and the number of students who trained as nō performers or musicians (*hayashi*) was remarkable. However, such a large demand for instruction in nō could not be supported solely by the official *sarugaku* troupes, which served the shogun's immediate circle in the study and appreciation of nō. As a result, daimyo granted students of the official troupes the right to lead their own school as nō *tayū* and ordered all amateur actors living in their respective domains to become members of these schools. In major cities like Kyoto and Osaka, students of the main troupes who were granted teaching licences became town actors and teachers for urban commoners.

NŌGAKU IN THE MEIJI PERIOD (1868-1912)

With the dissolution of the Tokugawa shogunate and its system of feudal domains following the Meiji Restoration in 1868, salaried nō performers lost their livelihoods and a considerable number of actors from the official troupes abandoned their art. The situation began to improve for nō theatre in around 1877 when the elder statesmen of the Meiji Restoration re-evaluated nō, recasting it as 'national theatre'. Nō enthusiasts from among the former daimyo and aristocracy now had opportunities to stage performances again, and this development contributed to the resurgence of *nō*. In 1881, the same year *sarugaku* was renamed *nōgaku*, members of the aristocracy and the government, together with leading nō actors, established the Nōgaku Society (Nōgakusha). They were instrumental in the construction of the commercial, independent nō theatre venue, the Nō Hall (Nōgakudō), in the Shiba district of Tokyo. The venue represented a fresh start for nō. Sadly the Nō Hall went bankrupt in 1902, nevertheless nō performance schools had regained their footing and were once again prosperous.

NŌGAKU IN THE TAISHŌ AND SHŌWA ERAS (1912-89) AND INTO THE PRESENT

The catastrophic loss of the wood and stone printing blocks following the Great Kantō earthquake of 1 September 1923 prompted *utaibon* publishers to revise and issue these books in new formats. The result were modern *utaibon* for each of the nō schools, and it was also at this time that the authority of school heads established in the Edo period vastly increased.

In 1909, the historian Yoshida Tōgo (1864–1918) publicised Zeami's *nōgaku* treatises, leading to further in-depth scholarly studies on Zeami and nō. As the historical significance of Zeami as a nō playwright was being acknowledged, so was the literary value of nō plays. This resulted in ground-breaking research, including *The encyclopaedia of nō plays* (*Yōkyoku taikan*, 1930–31) by Sanari Kentarō, *Study of the origin of nō and kyōgen* (*Nōgaku genryū kō*, 1938) by Nose Asaji, as well as the unearthing of a group of old Konparu family documents housed at the Hōzan temple in Nara by Kawase Kazuma.

The work of the celebrated performer Kanze Hisao (1925–78) defined the world of post-World War II nō and the enormous strides made in the study of nō are due to his efforts. Kanze criticised the stagnation of the nō theatre in the modern era and advocated a deeper understanding of the plays and the need for ongoing interpretation.[4] Two of his contemporaries, Yokomichi Mario (1916–2012) and Omote Akira (1927–2010), were also pioneers in nō scholarship. Yokomichi focused on the study of nō styles, pushing the theories of nō to a new level, while Omote concentrated on researching the history of nō, revising Zeami's theories and tackling numerous questions surrounding this performance art form. In 1983, construction began on the National Noh Theatre. A symbol of the official sanctioning of *nōgaku*, it was the first modern public nō theatre and its opening was a landmark event in the history of nō in the postwar period.

As a drama art, nō evolved under official patronage. This distinguishes nō from kabuki, a younger theatre form that grew out of commoner urban culture. Nō did not follow a commercial path – unlike its populist kabuki counterpart – because the conditions that would have fostered the development of a large-scale commercial performance tradition did not eventuate during the medieval period. From roughly the mid nineteenth century onwards the system of public tuition fees supplanted private patronage and became the economic base for nō and kyōgen. This placed certain constraints on the freedom with which performers could pursue their art. Another threat to the survival of this ancient art form (and to its practitioners) is the rapidly dwindling number of students. The future of *nōgaku* thus hinges on its ability to maintain excellence in performance, while remaining a vital and enduring theatre art in contemporary society.

Translated by Chiaki Ajioka

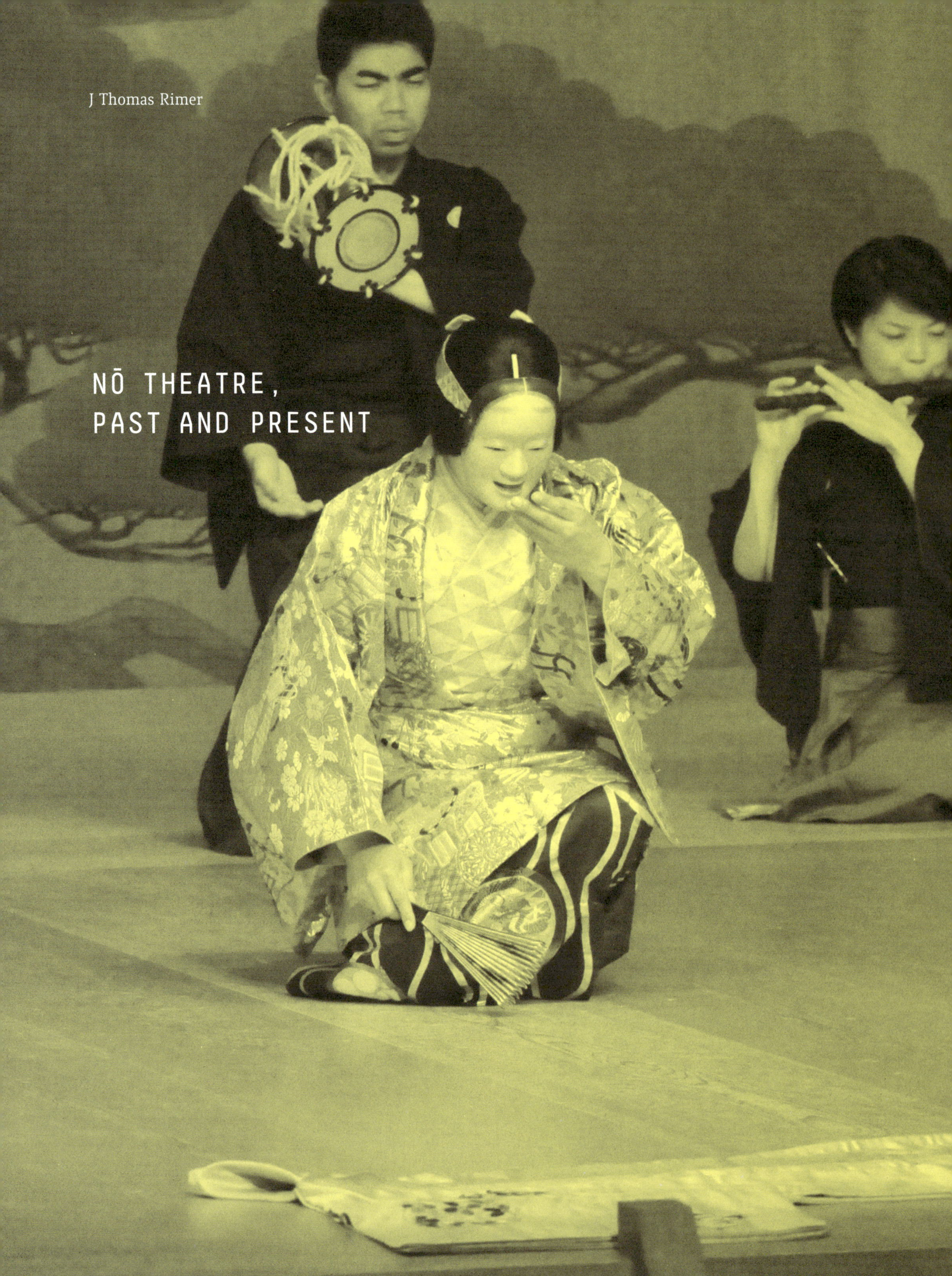

J Thomas Rimer
NŌ THEATRE,
PAST AND PRESENT

As with other forms of theatre, the true beauty and power of nō can only be experienced in performance. Perhaps some of the unique properties and remarkable insights into this ancient theatrical art can be suggested by moving through the successive scenes of an individual play, in order to reveal something of both its structure and larger purpose.

Lady Aoi (*Aoi no ue*), a fourth-category 'miscellaneous' play, one of the masterpieces of the repertoire, can serve as an example of nō at its most elevating. The text is based on a celebrated incident described in the eleventh-century classic *Tale of Genji* (*Genji monogatari*) by Murasaki Shikibu. The play is often attributed to Zeami Motokiyo (c1363–c1443), arguably the greatest playwright and theoretician in the history of the form. The name of the genre itself – 'nō' – is written with the Sino-Japanese character that means 'talent' or 'skill', a term that seeks to define what we in the twenty-first century might refer to as 'total theatre', in which dance, poetry, song, music, text, costumes and masks all contribute towards the totality of a single integrated performance. What would the experience of *Lady Aoi* bring to the spectator?

The performance begins on an open stage (fig 1.1). There is no curtain or barrier between the performers and the audience. Three musicians sit to the rear on the polished wooden floor, in front of a wooden wall on which is painted a ceremonial pine tree. A chorus of singers sits on the side of the stage, to their right. The characters in the play, all performed by male actors, enter from a bridge that runs from stage left to an offstage area where actors prepare for their entrances known as the 'mirror room' (*kagami no ma*) (fig 1.2). Stage attendants may enter from elsewhere. There is no scenery as such, although the costumes worn by major characters are frequently elegant and colourful, and props can sometimes be quite elaborate. As the performance begins, an attendant places a beautiful folded kimono on the stage floor. This kimono represents Lady Aoi, for whom the text is named; she herself does not appear as a character on stage. Immediately the symbolic nature of nō is made clear to the audience.

A courtier enters the stage from the roofed bridge (*hashigakari*) and announces that, in order to cure Lady Aoi, Genji's chief or 'official' wife, of what seems to be her possession by an evil spirit, the emperor, Genji's older brother, has invited a famous sorceress, Teruhi. He wishes her to ascertain, using her birch-bow, if the haunting spirit is that of a dead or a living person. The language in which he speaks reveals at once that the recited text, in medieval Japanese, is closer to chant than spoken dialogue and will sometimes be underscored with music (flute and drum) from the onstage musicians.

Teruhi chants an incantation and the phantom appears on the bridge and makes her way to the stage. She is the living ghost or spirit of Lady Rokujō, the main actor (*shite*) of the play who therefore wears a mask. She performs a lengthy monologue, reminiscent in structural terms, of an opera aria, interspersed by comments from the chorus. She fears the power of her feelings for Genji:

Scene from the nō play
Lady Aoi (Aoi no Ue)

Rokujō then puzzles over the sound of the birch-bow, while the sorceress sees a woman 'riding in a ragged coach'. She demands to know her name. Rokujō answers:

Why did I leave the way of truth?
Attracted by the birch-bow's sound,
Here I now appear. Am I unknown to you yet?
I am the ghost of Princess Rokujō.[2]

She remembers her happy days in court by confessing that:

Fallen in life, I am today no more
Than a morning-glory that withers with the rising of the sun.
My heart knows no rest from pain;
Bitter thoughts grow like fern shoots
Bursting forth in fields.
To vent my vengeance, here have I appeared.[3]

Rokujō now walks to the kimono on the ground and prepares to strike Lady Aoi, telling her that 'present vengeance is the retribution/of past wrongs you did to me' (fig 1.3).

The 'wrongs' that Rokujō feels are only hinted at in the play text itself: Genji had formerly been her lover but lost interest in her and is now joined with Lady Aoi through an officially arranged marriage. In the incident that has brought about Rokujō's distress, her carriage is jostled out of the way by that belonging to Lady Aoi when both ladies attended an outdoor festival in Kyoto, shaming Rokujō terribly. The playwright and the performers assume that the audience is familiar with these events. As the first section of the play comes to a conclusion, the chorus, speaking in the first person as Lady Rokujō, express the pain and bitterness she feels towards the hapless Aoi. Rokujō throws a fan and covers herself with a kimono.

The second part of the play begins when a messenger comes to seek another who might assist Lady Aoi, a mountain priest named Kōjiri from Yokawa who practices Buddhist *shugendō*, a mystical religious tradition developed in ancient Japan. The priest enters and agrees to examine the sick woman. He begins to perform his exorcism, calling forth the living ghost of Lady Rokujō, now wearing the horned *hannya* mask appropriate for a jealous demon (fig 1.4). 'Return at once, good monk, return at once/else will you be burdened with regret', she tells him, but he and the chorus reply with incantations and a reminder that:

Who hears my teaching
Shall gain profundity of wisdom;
Who knows my mind
Shall gain the purity of Buddhahood.[4]

The spell is successful. At the final climax of the play, Rokujō renounces her desire
for vengeance:

Rokujō: *How fearful is the chanting of the sutra!*
My end at last has come.

Chorus: *Hearing the voice of incantation,*
Hearing the voice of incantation,
Gentle grows the demon's heart.
Forbearance and mercy incarnate,
The Bodhisattva comes to meet her.
She enters nirvana
Out of life and death – Buddha be praised!
Out of life and death – Buddha be praised![5]

As the performance ends with this mystical moment, the actors disappear onto the
bridge and out of sight of the audience. The tempo of the play has moved from slow to
fast, with an ever-increasing intensity. Somewhere between an hour and a half to two
hours have passed.

Lady Aoi is one of the most admired pieces in the classical nō canon, which includes
upwards of 200 plays, most of them written beginning during the time of Zeami and
his father Kan'ami (1333–84) and well into the Edo period (1615–1868). In his treatises
on nō, Zeami insisted that for real success, a text should be based on a source that the
audience can recognise. It is therefore no surprise then that so many of the major plays
involve characters or incidents in works central to the Japanese cultural tradition, such
as *Genji*, the medieval warrior epic *Tale of the Heike* (*Heike monogatari*), Buddhist or Shinto
legends, or incidents in the lives of such great poets as Saigyō (1118–90) or Fujiwara no
Teika (1162–1241). Such a dramaturgy connects a particular nō text to the larger world
of its source. Such a strategy is familiar in classical Western theatre as well; most of
the dramas by Shakespeare draw on a variety of borrowed sources. The practice is less
familiar in our times, however, where originality of plot is most frequently seen as
paramount for success.

Then too, nō texts are composed in a style of elegant and suggestive poetry that sets
them at a considerable distance from the kind of down-to-earth realism required of most
of our contemporary drama. In a nō drama, time and space are stretched, and real and
imagined characters mix freely together. In Zeami's view, as explained in his treatises,

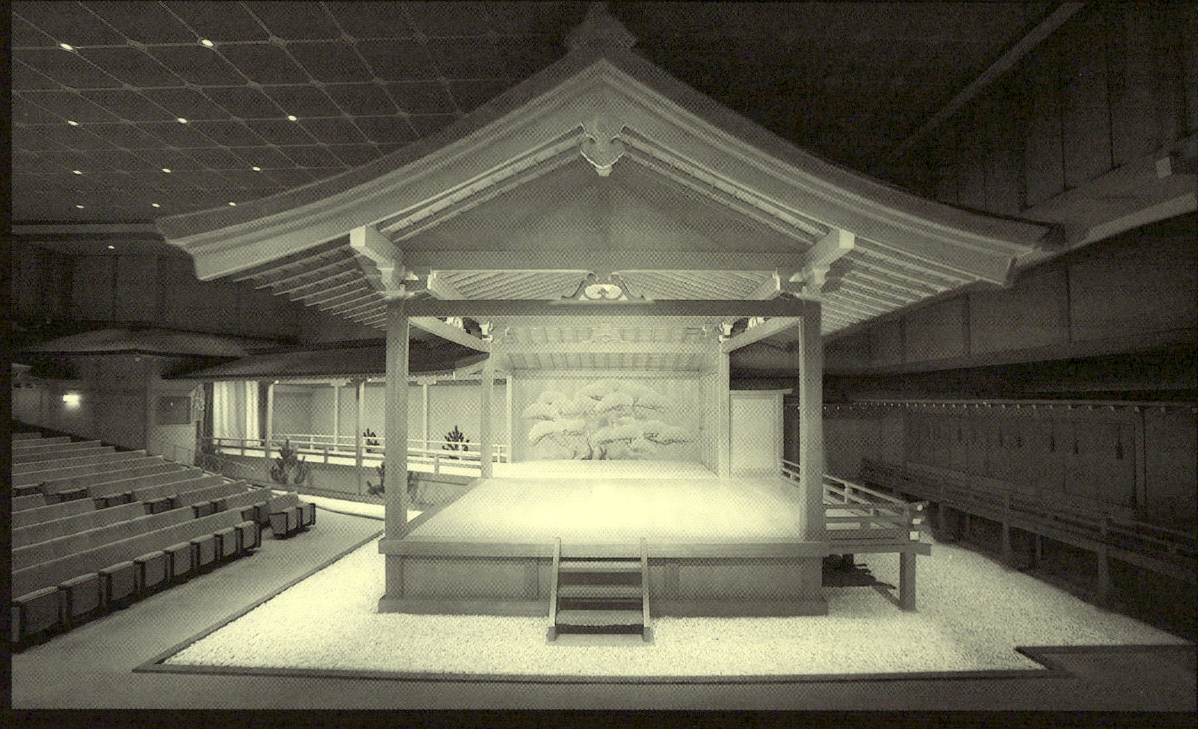

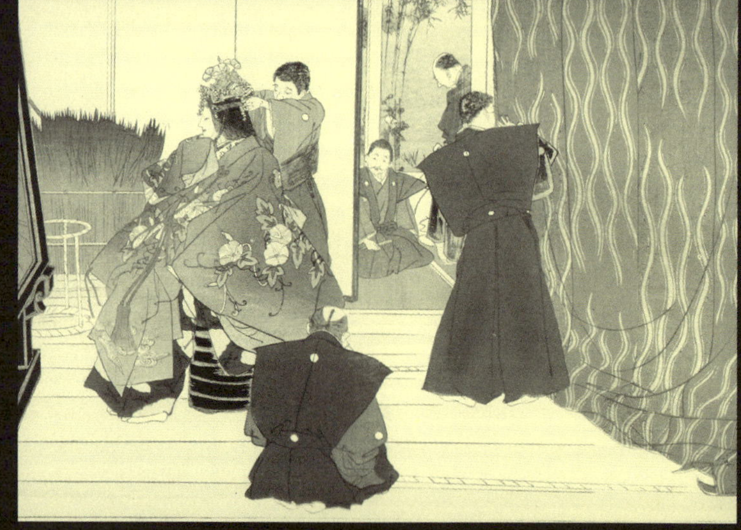

fig 1.1
Nō stage
National Noh Theatre

fig 1.2
Tsukioka Kōgyo
'*Asagao*', from the series
Pictures of nō plays (Nōgaku zue)
1897–1902
colour woodblock print, 24.2 x 35.8 cm
National Noh Theatre

fig 1.3
Scene from Act I of the nō play
Lady Aoi (*Aoi no ue*)
National Noh Theatre

fig 1.4
Tsukioka Kōgyo
'Lady Aoi', from the series
One hundred nō plays (*Nōgaku hyakuban*)
1922–26
colour woodblock print, 42.3 x 29.8 cm
National Noh Theatre

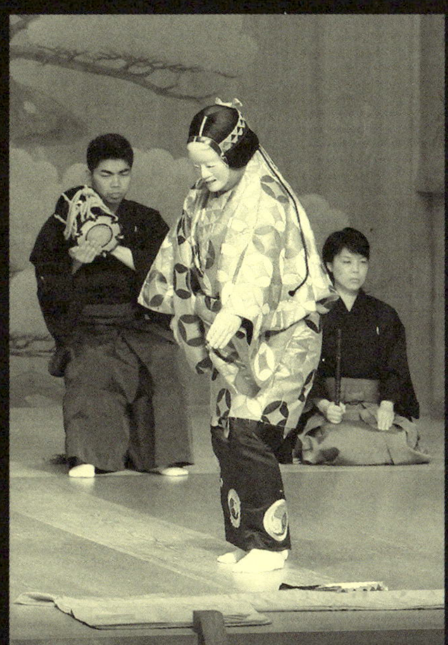

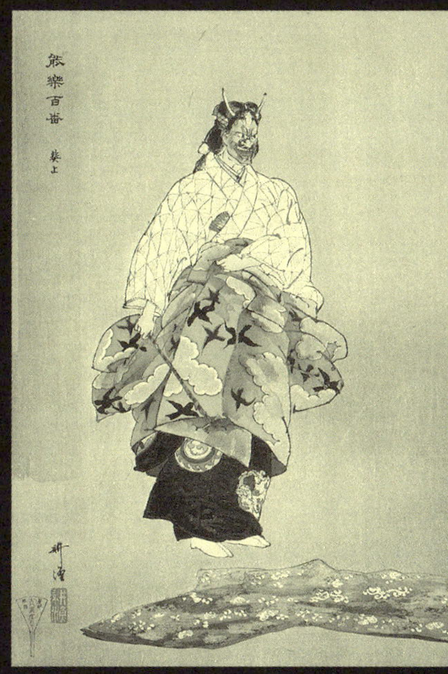

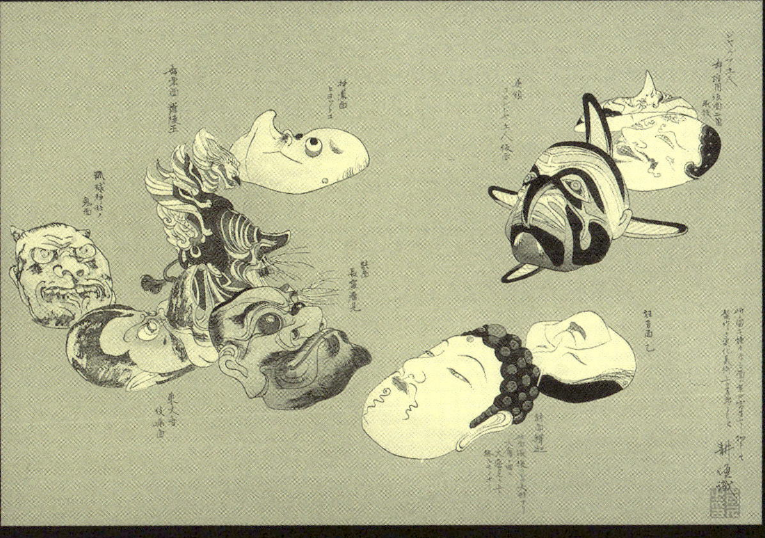

fig 1.5
Tsukioka Kōgyo
'Nō masks', from the series
Pictures of nō plays (*Nōgaku zue*)
1897–1902
colour woodblock print, 24.2 x 35.8 cm
National Noh Theatre

the emotional state he hopes to evoke in his audiences is that of *yūgen*, a term notoriously difficult to explain. The word has sometimes been defined as a sense of mystery and depth, calling on a gentle, saddened understanding of the mystery of human existence. Some see the development of this aesthetic from Buddhist roots, but whatever its basis, the texts of these nō plays, even in translation, wield a universal theatrical power.

Given this fact, it is perhaps surprising that nō had its beginnings as a popular theatre.[6] Early performances were often staged in connection with Shinto shrine and Buddhist temple festivals, and troupes moved from place to place, seeing themselves as little more than wandering beggars, raising money as best they could from their presentations. This situation was suddenly altered when the shogun, Ashikaga Yoshimitsu (1358–1408), witnessed stagings by Kan'ami's troupe. Convinced of the genius of the boy actor Zeami, he arranged for him to receive a classical education, transforming Zeami into a poet and intellectual. Yoshimitsu served as patron of the troupe, a pattern that continued in later periods. The five major troupes or 'schools' still performing today – Konparu, Hōshō, Kanze (Zeami's original troupe), Kongō and Kita – all received some kind of aristocratic patronage at one point or another in their history.

Despite the elevation of Kan'ami's troupe, and so of nō as an art form in itself, Zeami and his successors never forsook their popular roots, and nō continued as a widely appreciated form of theatre until the 1600s. Some of the plays were elliptical and difficult, of course, even at the time they were written, but ordinary, even illiterate spectators relished these performances, learning of their own literary and artistic heritage through their contact with them. In many ways, at least during Zeami's time until the Edo period, nō served as a means to convey the central cultural values of Japanese society at that time.

During the Edo period, however, nō troupes were basically patronised by the daimyo. The troupes generally performed only for their patrons and nō began to lose its popular audience base. While whole nō plays, or sections of them, were adapted for kabuki and *bunraku* puppet troupes, nō presentations themselves were usually seen only by the political and intellectual elite. This situation is reminiscent of eighteenth-century Europe, where, for example, a great composer such as Joseph Haydn spent much of his career preparing concerts for his Austrian patrons, the Esterhazy family. Thus, nō gradually lost its centrality in the Japanese theatrical culture of its time.

With the coming of the Meiji period, in 1868, the former political structures were dissolved and nō companies lost their old sources of patronage. Traditional values were sometimes set aside as new Western ideas flooded in, a trend as important in the theatrical arts as in all other aspects of Japanese society. There was soon a real danger that this long theatrical tradition, one of the oldest in the world, would now die out. The story of how fresh patronage was created through performances sponsored for the general public is a remarkable one of renaissance and rebirth. It is of particular interest that some of this more general growing fascination with nō, at least among the Japanese intelligentsia, was sometimes spurred on by Western enthusiasts. Nō was eventually to achieve again its role as an art form central to the traditions of high Japanese culture. That status endures today.

Because of the efforts of several generations of translators, the texts of many nō plays in the canon have come to be widely read outside Japan and are now accepted as masterpieces of world dramatic literature. In fact, translations into English, French and other European languages beginning with those made by such noted writers and scholars as Ernest Fenollosa, Ezra Pound, Arthur Waley, Noël Peri and many others came to make nō a presence in European theatre. WB Yeats, Bertolt Brecht, Paul Claudel and any number of contemporary playwrights have used elements in nō dramaturgy in the composition of their own plays. The same is true for several twentieth-century Japanese playwrights writing in contemporary language, among them Mishima Yukio (1925–70) and Kinoshita Junji (1914–2006).

Nō has been a signal influence on composers as well, both in and outside Japan. One of Benjamin Britten's most eloquent achievements is his one-act opera *Curlew river*, which had its debut in 1964. Britten's work is based on the nō play *The river Sumida* (*Sumidagawa*), which the composer saw performed during his visit to Japan in 1956. Britten and his librettist, William Plomer, reworked the original into a medieval Christian setting. The distinguished postwar Japanese Western-style composer Ikuma Dan created at least two operas based on nō themes, and as recently as 2011, the Japanese composer Hosokawa Toshio adapted the nō play *The wind in the pines* (*Matsukaze*) for an opera, which premiered to considerable acclaim at La Monnaie in Brussels. Further productions met with great success in two American venues in 2013, the Spoleto Festival in Charleston, South Carolina, and the Lincoln Center Festival in New York.

These Western adaptations have come about through an admiration by writers, actors and musicians for the texts, and to some extent, the dramaturgy of the Japanese originals. Nevertheless, in terms of the traditional aesthetics of nō, the text of a given work, no matter how eloquent or powerful, is understood as only one element in a successful performance. For many Japanese spectators during this long tradition, the skill of the main actor has always remained supreme in the larger aesthetic structure. And 'actor' is the proper word, as all performers are male, a situation paralleling that in Shakespeare's England. (It should be mentioned that there are now quite a number of very gifted female nō actors in Japan, but they are normally seen only in exceptional stagings.)

Actors in nō are divided into several categories. The divisions are based on the type of role undertaken. The major roles fall into the *shite* category (*shite* literally means 'the one who does'). In the case of *Lady Aoi*, the *shite* is the unhappy Lady Rokujō. In most cases, only the *shite* wear the remarkable masks, often old and considered great works of art in themselves (fig 1.5). Important secondary characters are termed *waki* ('to the side'), in this case the Buddhist priest Kōjiri, and subsidiary characters are termed *tsure* ('to accompany'). In *Lady Aoi*, the sorceress Teruhi fulfils that latter function. Smaller parts are performed by actors designated as kyōgen (literally 'wild words'). These actors also perform comic plays staged between nō presentations in a full program, which traditionally included several nō. Each of these role types has their own separate training and performing traditions.

The *shite* are considered great artists and are regarded by nō enthusiasts in somewhat the same fashion that opera lovers may single out a favourite soprano or tenor. In the modern period, many have achieved considerable fame among the general public. The great nō actor Kanze Hisao (1925–78), for example, worked with the eminent French actor and director Jean-Louis Barrault and performed in a number of modern plays altogether outside the field of nō. Nevertheless, honing physical, vocal and musical skills necessary for the roles assigned to the *shite* requires a lifetime of dedication. These roles, spread over five generally accepted categories, range from slow and solemn plays, based on Shinto and Buddhist legends, through plays dealing with historical figures, fictional characters, such as Lady Aoi, who express their thwarted love, to plays of quick action in the fifth category (see p 226). Just as the categories of nō texts move from slow to fast, so does the pacing in each individual play. Both musically and dramatically, a play goes through three stages, referred to in Japanese terminology as *jo*, *ha* and *kyū*. These terms might be rendered as 'introduction', 'development' and 'fast finale'. As the performance moves forward, the musical and dramatic tempos grow ever more intense and rapidly to a powerful conclusion. The *shite* is in charge of setting the pace.

Despite the fact that there are a variety of musical and vocal textures used in the course of a performance, which include the chanting of the chorus, there is no conductor. A rough analogy might be made with a jazz band (although certainly not in sound!) where everyone involved listens to each other and works together. In every sense, nō is an ensemble effort.

To a casual spectator nō may seem a venerable art form, frozen in time. But as Zeami wrote in one of his treatises, '… as our art is based on the desires of our audiences, successful performances depend on the changing tastes of each generation'.[7] Shifting audiences and patrons over the centuries have made just such changes inevitable. And, although the plays in the established canon have always remained central, new plays were regularly introduced, some retaining their appeal, down to the Meiji Restoration in 1868. Even in the modern period, these newly created nō have occasionally been staged, often with success. Actors in one generation after another bring their own special skills to what Zeami has called the 'flower' of a great performance. In the twentieth century a comparison of filmed presentations of different *shite* in the same nō can now make it possible to observe a considerable diversity in gesture and movement among various top *shite* actors. In that sense, one of the oldest performing traditions in the world continues to sprout fresh shoots and is reborn in every generation.

At the beginning of the long tradition of nō performance, Zeami quoted a poem, which suggested to him that the art of nō can be capable of an endless flowering:

> *Break open the cherry tree*
> *And look at it:*
> *There are no flowers,*
> *For they themselves have bloomed*
> *In the spring sky.*[8]

The skill and dedication of the actor brings renewal and rebirth. Zeami would surely have been pleased to know that such has been the history of this remarkable art form.

Eric C Rath

NŌ, THE MASKED DRAMA

Nō is a theatre of masks. In the late fifteenth century – 100 years after the invention of nō as a performing art – nō actors physically attacked and brought legal claims against performers from other traditions who dared to use masks on stage.[1] Today, the masked nō actor is quickly distinguishable from the kabuki performer in heavy make-up. Kabuki, which developed from the early seventeenth century in Kyoto, was from the beginning a theatrical form that spotlighted the star-value of the actor. Accordingly, kabuki performers decided not to hide their faces with masks so that their own personas could shine through just as they frequently broke character on stage to play up to their fans or even promote their merchandise. The nō actor's own personality is not as much on display as that of the kabuki performer, but neither is the audience ever completely allowed to forget the actor beneath the mask. Thus, nō is different from other genres of traditional Japanese performing arts that employ masks to hide the performer's identity. For example, *gigaku*, a dance enacted as part of religious processionals at Buddhist temples from the seventh to the late twelfth century, has left behind a number of evocative masks of creatures and holy men, even though the specifics of the pageants in which these masks were utilised are now lost (fig 2.1). Another performance genre with masks is *kagura*, a broad designation for folk performing arts that range from costumed dramas enacted on Shinto shrine stages to the familiar dancing lions that prance their way in festival parades. In contrast to *gigaku* and *kagura* masks, which typically conceal the entire face of the performer, nō masks are worn high on the face so that the performer's chin is visible. The glimpse of the nō actor's face reminds audiences that nō masks are a means of representation rather than a disguise – a point made especially clear when a rotund actor with a double chin puts on the mask of a young girl (fig 2.2).

Wearing the mask high on the face means that the actor usually looks out of the mask's mouth or nostrils instead of the eyeholes. As a consequence, an actor has only a limited field of vision. Indoor nō stages maintain the pillars supporting the roof of the main stage despite the fact that these block the sight lines for some parts of the audience. Mask-wearing actors need these pillars as guides to know their location because a wrong turn on stage could result in falling off. One mid eighteenth-century nō treatise, *Rinchū's collection of secrets* (*Rinchū hishō*), includes an anecdote about the leader of the Konparu nō troupe who would practice using a mask that rendered him unable to see so that he learned his place on the stage by his feet rather than trust his vision.[2]

Not all plays use masks and only the most important characters in nō drama wear them. In plays with masks, the main actor, or *shite* (literally 'the one who does'), will have one. Sometimes the *shite* might have a *tsure* ('companion') who may also be masked. The mask helps set the identity of the *shite*, so a change in masks indicates that the main actor has undergone a transformation. In the play *Yashima*, for instance, a humble fisherman in a *jō* mask of an old man later reveals himself to be the ghost of a warrior by appearing in the second half of the play in a *heida* mask [23] depicting a noted samurai. In the play *Takasago*, an elderly couple prove to be deities of matrimony in disguise: in the first part

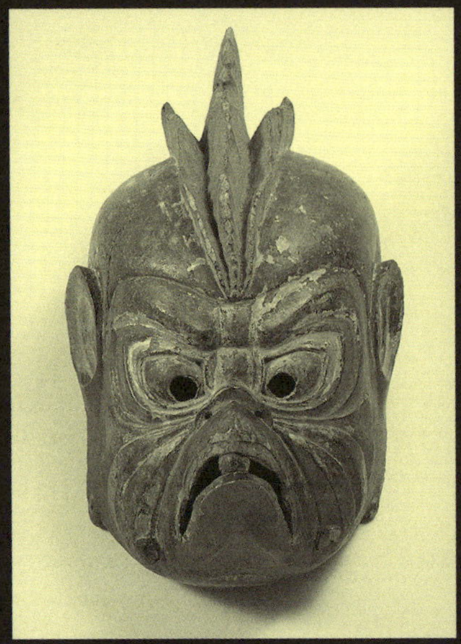

fig 2.1
Garuda gigaku mask
8th century
wood copy, 37.6 x 23.2 cm
Kyoto National Museum

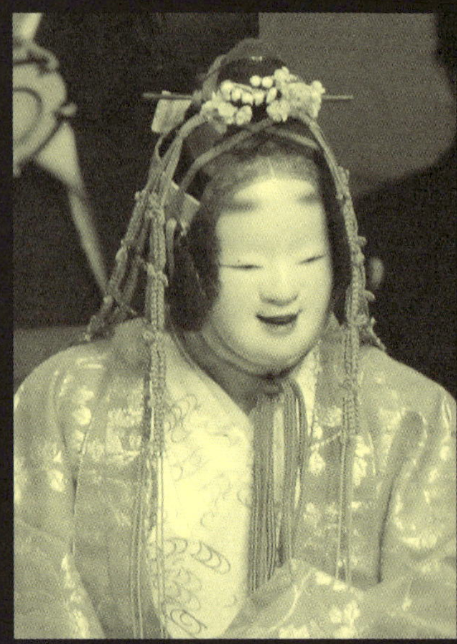

fig 2.2
Actor Nomura Shirō in the nō play
The iris (*Kakitsubata*)
National Noh Theatre

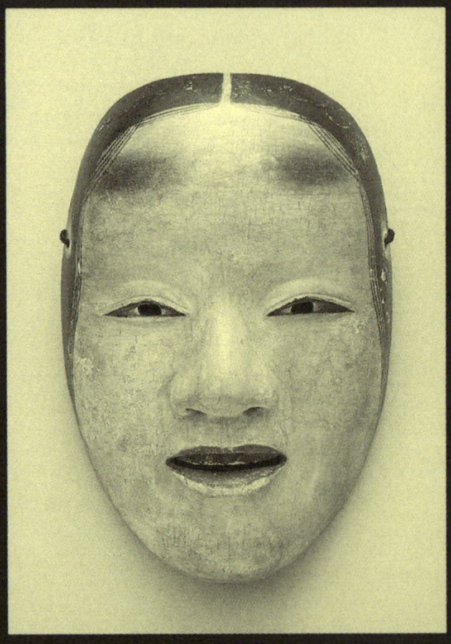

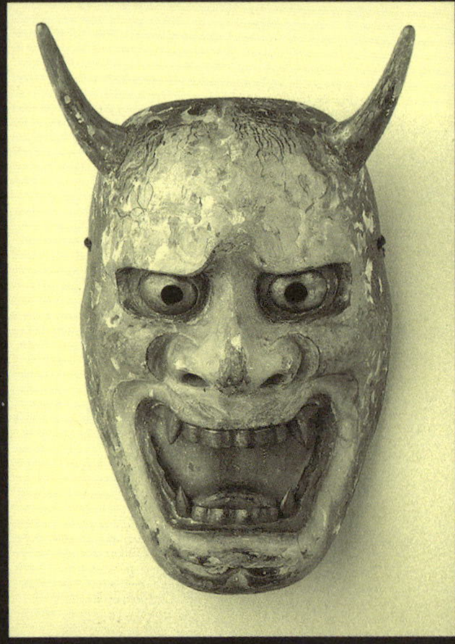

fig 2.3
Fukai mask
17th century
pigment on wood, 7.3 x 20.8 x 13.6 cm
National Noh Theatre

fig 2.4
Shinja mask
16th century
pigment on wood, 9.3 x 21.3 x 14.7 cm
Agency for Cultural Affairs of Japan

of the play the *shite* portraying the old man is in a *kojō* mask [4] and in the second half the actor switches to a *kantan otoko* mask [21], representing a younger character, to express the deity's eternal youth.

One of the most frightening transformations signalled by a change in masks occurs in the play *Dōjōji*. A beautiful female entertainer enters the temple and requests to dance in celebration of the inauguration of a new bell (suspended over the main stage). The *shite* appears in a young woman (*waka onna*) mask, a fleshier version of the *ko-omote* [24]. At the end of the first half, the youthful performer, whose dance gradually reveals her troubled state of mind, leaps into the temple bell as it falls to the main stage. When the bell is lifted, the woman has transformed into a snake-demon signified by the terrifying *hannya* mask [32], a horned manifestation of jealousy, caused in this case by a monk from the temple who spurned her love.

The play determines the types of masks worn, but a common saying among nō performers is 'a nō play begins with a mask'. In other words, although nō is a codified drama with rules governing every aspect of performance including the masks acceptable for certain plays, actors have some leeway in mask selection to affect the interpretation of a drama.[3] For instance, the actor portraying the *shite* in *Dōjōji* could choose the *waka onna* mask or employ instead the *fukai* mask depicting a middle-aged woman (fig 2.3). Moreover, an especially esteemed or old mask imparts a greater level of dignity to a play than a newer carving of the same mask. The connection between specific masks and plays became codified by the late sixteenth century, as seen in the most widely disseminated collection of technical writings about nō performance in early modern Japan, the *Treatise on the transmission of the flower in eight chapters* (*Hachijō kadensho*), compiled in the late sixteenth century and published numerous times subsequently. The text provides a list of plays and the masks the main actors could use depending on their interpretation of the performance.[4]

One might think that putting on a mask is a hindrance to acting because the static features of a mask might be believed to inhibit the expression of emotion, but there are two reasons why this is not the case for nō. First, nō is a symbolic rather than a realistic theatre. When an actor cries, he does not tear up and wail as he might in real life. In nō, crying is usually signified by an actor simply raising a hand in front of his face, indicating that they are sobbing into their sleeves in the manner of an aristocrat from a Heian-period (794–1185) romantic novel. Realism has run counter to the spirit of nō acting since at least the time of the theatre's greatest playwright and theoretician, Zeami Motokiyo (c1363–c1443), who sought to move his art away from imitation (*monomane*) towards the quality of mysterious grace (*yūgen*). Zeami stated that even demonic and plebeian roles have to embody grace. One never sees a blood-dripping demon or a dirty peasant on the nō stage: both have to be elegantly attired and demonstrate poise rather than ferocity or vulgarity. Nō masks contribute to the promotion of grace by conveying a sense of eternity to characters by imparting a remote beauty that remains untouched by circumstance.

Second, nō masks themselves are not static, facilitating acting rather than detracting from it. Nō actors refer to masks as 'faces' (*omote*) to acknowledge that the masks have the capacity to show emotion due to their physical features. Mask carvers, who create works out of a single block of Japanese cypress (*hinoki*), make sure that the eyes of the mask are carved such that the sight line of each pupil is different. A nō mask does not simply stare straight ahead. The eyes gaze in alternate directions, allowing an actor to change the expression of the mask by a turn of the head. At times, performers tilt their heads downwards to cloud the features of the mask to suggest sadness or brooding. Tilting the mask upwards to catch more light renders a more cheerful demeanour. While nō masks can certainly be appreciated for their beauty in an exhibit, their features evolved in accordance with the theatricality of the nō drama and thus it is within the setting of a nō play that masks come alive.

The power of masks to represent the divine allowed them on occasion to become objects of worship and magic. Shinto shrines typically have a deity enshrined and venerated in a mirror or some other talismanic object, which can include masks. One sacred mask in the Renge temple in Fukui prefecture is said to cause rain if washed on a sunny day.[5] The nō critic Miyake Noboru (1897–1965) wrote that a noted example of a *ja* mask (compare fig 2.4) – a more fearsome version of the *hannya* mask [32–34]) – was said to cause rain when worn in performances of *Dōjōji*. Apparently, that particular *ja* mask was so terrifying that the warlord Toyotomi Hideyoshi (1536/1537–98) – a figure well accustomed to violence in his campaign to unify Japan and his two invasions of the Korean peninsula – prevented any carver from copying it.[6] It was also believed that when used inappropriately masks might cause harm. In 1471, one actor spurned the chance to hear a sermon by a famous theologian and a mask of an old man adhered to his face.[7] Another actor coveted a statue of a Buddhist guardian in a temple, cut off its head and had a mask made from it. He could only remove the mask with difficulty and when he finally did he found, to his horror, that he had also pulled off part of his face. This earned him the nickname 'The nose' (Hana) in honour of his lost features.[8] The 1964 horror film *Onibaba*, written and directed by Shindō Kaneto (1912–2012), relates the tale of a mother and daughter who ambush and kill wounded samurai to steal their possessions. The mother obtains a *hannya* mask from a dead warrior, wears it to frighten her daughter, and suffers when she discovers that she cannot remove it. The film assisted in popularising the notion in modern times that a nō mask could punish a wearer for their misdeeds.

Like nō actors, who endeavour to replicate exactly the motions and vocalisations learned from their teachers, mask carvers have the task to take old masks as models and copy rather than innovate to the point that they reproduce every blemish and abrasion when replicating older masks. On the one hand, the long-standing concern with copying masks, which began after nō masks assumed their final form some 400 years ago, ensures the fidelity and preservation of the different types of nō masks.

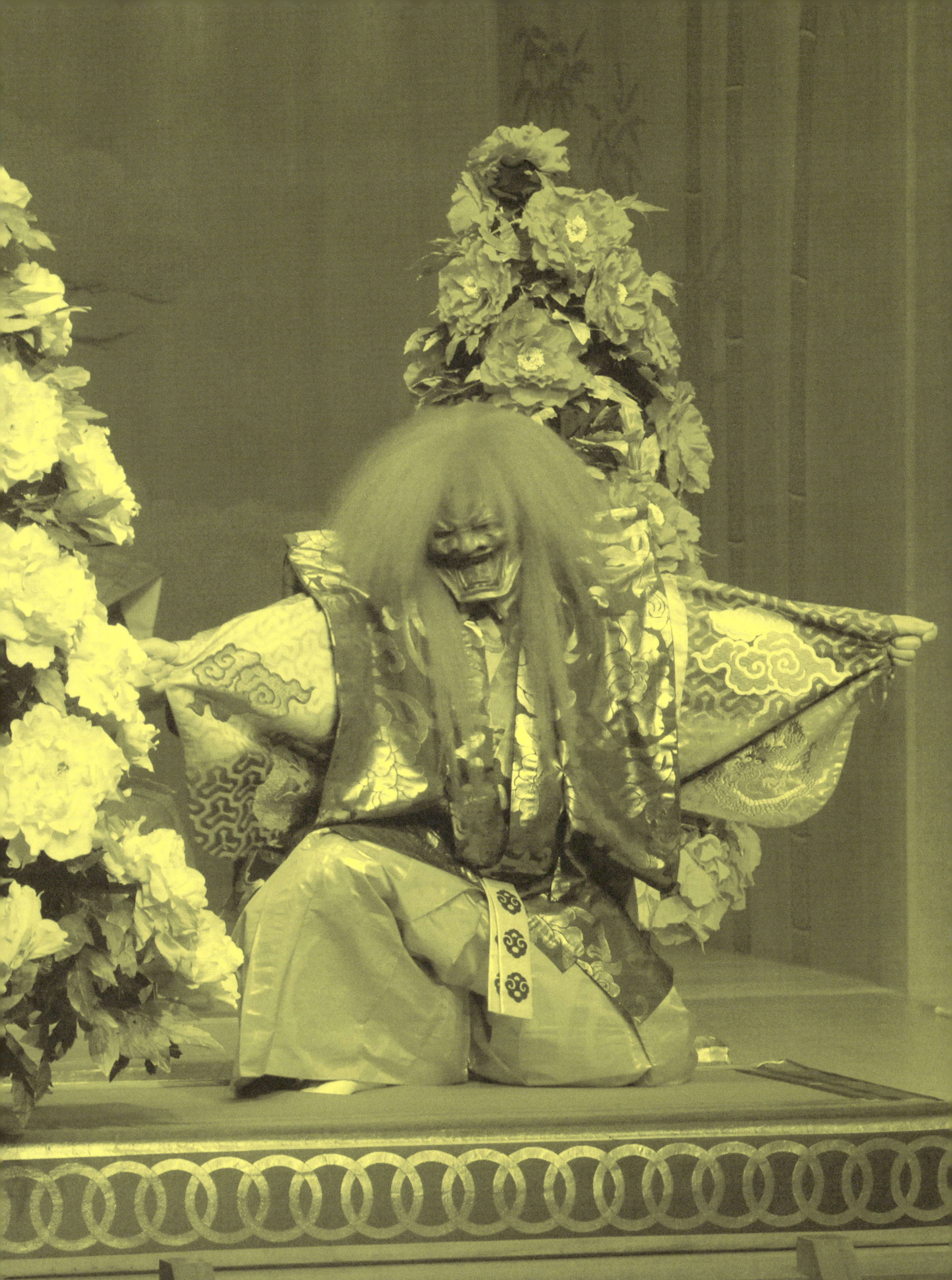

CATEGORIES OF MASKS [Numbers refer to catalogue number]

NŌ MASKS		KYŌGEN MASKS

NŌ MASKS

Okina
Hakushikijō (okina) [see 1]
Kokushikijō (Sanbasō) [see 2]
Chichinojō [see 3]

Old man
Kojō [see 4]
Higeakobujō [see 5]
Washibana akujō [see 6]
Amazakuro akujō [see 7]
Higebeshimi [see 8]

Demon
Ōbeshimi [see 9]
Kobeshimi [see 10]
Deikotobide [see 11]
Ōtobide [see 12]
Kotenjin [see 13]
Kurohige [see 14]
Shintai [see 15]
Shishiguchi [see 16]

Male
Kasshiki (kokasshiki) [see 17]
Ōkasshiki [see 18]
Shōjō [see 19]
Atsumori [see 20]
Kantan otoko [see 21]
Chūjō [see 22]
Heida [see 23]

Female
Ko-omote [see 24]
Manbi [see 25]
Nakizō [see 26]
Shakumi [see 27]
Rōjo [see 28]
Deigan [see 29]
Hashihime [see 30]
Yamanba [see 31]
Hannya [see 32]
Aka (red) hannya [see 33]
Shiro (white) hannya [see 34]

KYŌGEN MASKS

Deities
Noborihige [see 85]
Buaku [see 86]
Bishamon [see 87]

Spirits
Tsūen [see 88]
Hanahiki [see 89]
Kentoku [see 90]
Usofuki [see 91]

Humans
Ōji (kaijakushi) [see 92]
Oto [see 93]
Fukure [see 94]
Ama [see 95]

Animals
Saru (monkey) [see 96]
Hakuzōsu [see 97]
Kitsune (fox) [see 98]

On the other hand, the duplication of purportedly ancient nō masks makes the dating and authentication of masks and the ability to distinguish between later copies and older examples notoriously difficult.

Okina is the oldest type of nō mask [1]. Also known as *hakushikijō*, the *okina* mask is only used in the performance of the 'Three rituals' (*Shiki sanban*) (see [144]). The lack of a discernable plot and special pre-performance backstage ceremonies mean that the 'Three rituals' are not considered a play. Rather than represent a character on stage – according to tradition (and contrary to conventional nō drama) – the actor in the role of *Okina* is said actually to become temporarily the wizened, yet ageless, deity onstage. Masks for the 'Three rituals' predate the creation of nō and the earliest extant examples are from the Kamakura period (1185–1333). However, nō actors have claimed that their *okina* masks

NŌ COSTUMES

Since the fourteenth century, nō costumes had
been influenced by the everyday garments of the
samurai classes. Inspiration came directly from
actual garments: during the early Muromachi period
(1392–1573) members of the audience would throw
their own sumptuous and expensive garments –
many embroidered or stencilled in gold or silver
leaf – onto the stage in appreciation of a superior
performance. Donations of military wear and
imperial court attire were also made to the theatre.
Early on, the renowned actor-playwright Zeami
Motokiyo (c1363–c1443) began to make notations in
his treatises on the types of textiles, motifs, styles
and drapery to be utilised in nō costumes. Support
for nō came from the highest echelons during the
Edo period (1615–1868): by the middle of this era nō
costumes had evolved for distinct use onstage and by
the end of the Edo they developed into the stylised
robes that we today associate with the nō theatre.

Developments in garment decorations occurred
at different eras. For example, in the Momoyama
period, *nuihaku* and *karaori* had patterns of flowers
(eg cherry blossoms, chrysanthemums, paulownia),
animals (eg butterflies, birds) and geometrical
motifs (eg lozenges, hexagons, circles). With time,
nō costumes underwent further changes, with
the decoration including motifs possessing greater
literary meaning. By the mid Edo period they
became more elaborate, integrating designs of shells,
carriages, fans and rafts. Motifs could, moreover,
have seasonal references, such as chrysanthemums
with autumn, and in some cases they allude to
poetic imagery derived from Japanese classic
literature. Colour and gender also played a role in
determining the types of robes worn by characters
and in their interpretation. For instance, a robe
signifying a young woman would be red, this
colour appearing either in the background or in
the pattern. (NS)

Scene from the nō play *Eguchi*

NŌ MASKS
AND COSTUMES

NŌ MASKS

The mask is the most important 'tool' of the nō
actor. Principally worn by the main actor, or *shite*,
the nō mask strongly evokes the presence of the
character being portrayed and hence commands the
attention of the audience. By the Momoyama period
(1573–1615), approximately 60 types of nō masks had
been recorded, most of which are still in use today.

Nō masks can be divided into five types. The oldest
is the *okina*, with the earliest examples of this
kind dating from the early fourteenth century.
The distinctive feature of the *okina* mask is its hinged
jaw. Other masks in the *okina* category consist of
the *kokushikijō* and the *chichinojō*. In the past they
were also utilised in rituals and were on occasion
worshipped. The second type, the old man mask,
is typified by the inclusion of hair and a beard.
Old man masks personify a variety of facial
expressions: they can be evil or compassionate
and can represent a living figure or a ghost.

The third type, the demon mask, is separated into
those with open or closed mouths and with eyes
painted in gold. Some demon masks show animal
spirits such as foxes, others goblins or supernatural
lions. Male masks form the fourth type; distinct
from the old man mask they illustrate young
men and are sometimes made for a specific role.
The final type, female masks, includes both younger
and older women and they are categorised according
to the age of the character. Like male masks, there
are a large number of female masks in the nō mask
repertoire. Male and female masks do not have
many individual features and thus can be employed
for a wide range of characters. (NS)

were far more ancient and of divine origin, with particular *okina* masks associated with the miraculous founding of their theatrical traditions. A story in *Rinchū's collection of secrets* describes how an actor dreamed of seven masks on a rock in the middle of a pond, but upon checking discovered only one *okina* mask. Nevertheless, this mask brought good health to everyone who wore it in performances.[9] The 'snow-raked *okina*' (*yukikaki no okina*) mask belonging to Uji shrine, in Uji, south of Kyoto, is said to have drifted down from the heavens in a snowfall.[10] There are numerous similar legends of *okina* masks that add to their eminence and contribute to the authority of those who own and wear them in performance.[11]

Masks other than *okina*, which are also used in the ceremony of the 'Three rituals', include *sanbasō* (also called *kokushikijō*, [2]) and *chichinojō* [3], although the latter is rarely worn today. These three masks are the only examples with hinged jaws and collectively they comprise the first of five main categories of nō masks, a rough grouping of some 450 different types. The other four categories are old man, demon, male and female – all represented by exemplary works in this publication (see categories opposite).[12]

Mask carvers also adhere to tradition in replicating kyōgen masks, of which there are four main types: deities, spirits, humans and animals. Since kyōgen is a drama based on everyday life actors do not usually wear masks – even when male actors perform female roles. Consequently, kyōgen masks of humans depict especially comical or haggard faces as the examples in this volume well demonstrate (especially 92 & 94). Apart from *sanbasō*, which is worn by a kyōgen actor, the most revered kyōgen mask is the *kitsune* (*fox*) mask [98] employed in *Fox hunter* (*Tsurigitsune*), a play that, like *Dōjōji*, is known for its difficulty and the successful performance of which marks the pinnacle of an actor's career. Young kyōgen actors make their first significant stage debut in the role of the monkey in the play *Monkey-quiver* (*Utsubozaru*), using the *saru* (*monkey*) mask [96]. Thus, it is often said that kyōgen performers begin their careers as monkeys and reach the height of their professions as foxes.

Using masks is central to the artistic and career development of nō and kyōgen actors, because masks are the faces of nō and kyōgen dramas. Masks give life to the characters of aristocratic women, suffering warrior ghosts, malevolent demons and lost youths in nō plays. Kyōgen masks allow for the addition of supernatural and other non-human elements to plays in a theatrical mode that parodies everyday life. The adherence by mask carvers to ancient models exemplifies the significance of maintaining tradition in nō. Yet, the knowing looks and timeless smiles of nō masks embody the ways in which this art expresses the eternal and the universal.

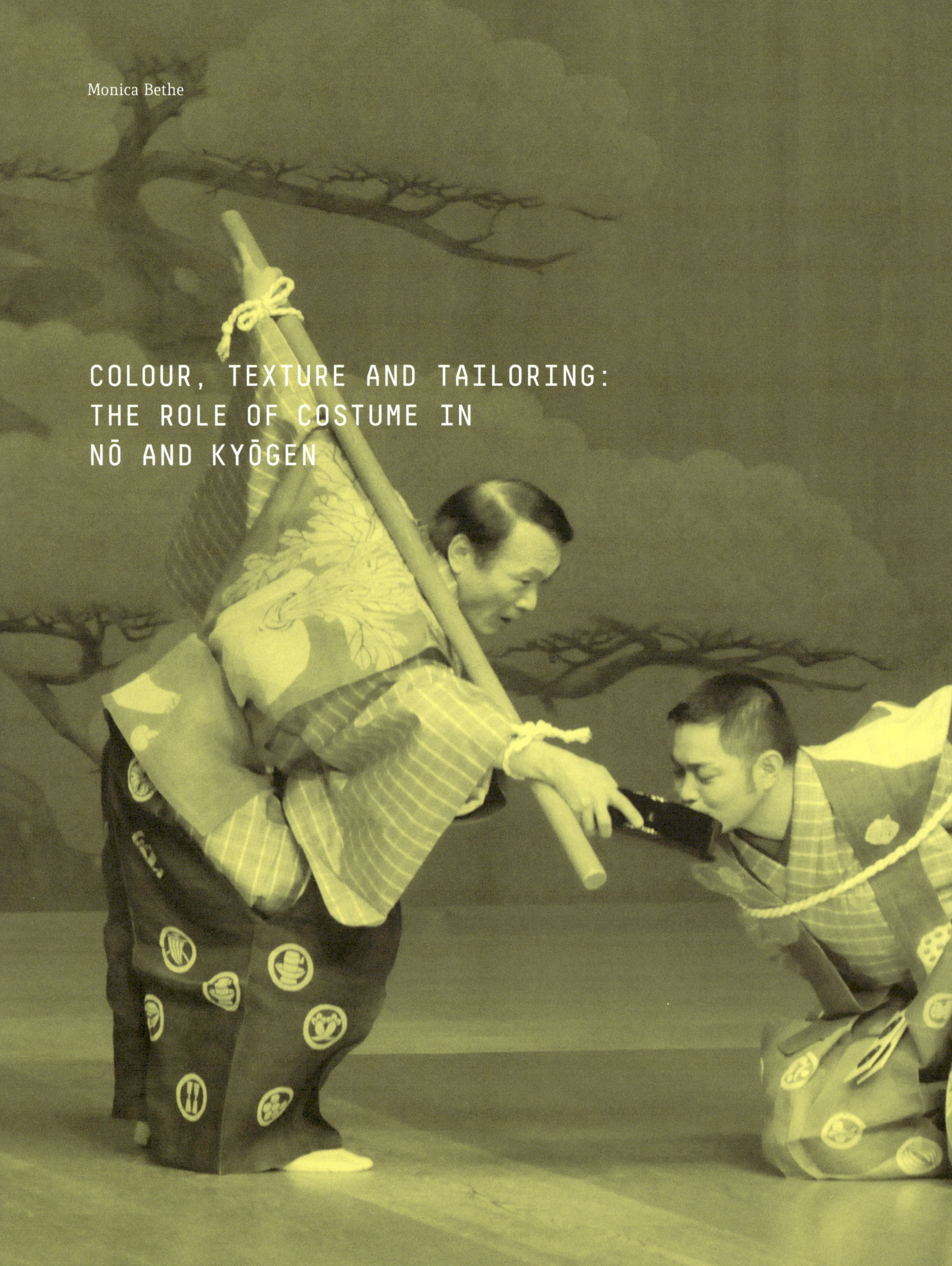

Monica Bethe
COLOUR, TEXTURE AND TAILORING:
THE ROLE OF COSTUME IN
NŌ AND KYŌGEN

Bold gold emblems on a voluminous dark ground, delicate flower tendrils scrolling over diaphanous sleeves, sober blues and browns in plain, simple tailoring: this is the vocabulary of nō costumes. The garments are combined, layered and juxtaposed so as to create a wide spread of stage figures, and to evoke the atmosphere of scene and season on the bare stage.

Though the types of robes worn for a specific role are designated by tradition, the actor chooses the colour and pattern according to the image he wishes to portray in a specific performance. Already in the fifteenth century, the prominent actor-playwright, Zeami Motokiyo (c1363–c1443) recognised the critical impact made by costuming. He cautioned that to enact a noblewoman one must pay utmost attention to the rules prescribed for court robes, suggested that gaudier clothing might be appropriate for a madwoman role and stated that Chinese figures should be dressed colourfully.[1] He also notes times when the costume could be adjusted on stage, or when manipulation of the sleeve can underscore a gesture. Always observant of the costume choices of others, Zeami appraises them objectively, finding some effective, but not within the tradition of his own troupe.[2]

Perhaps one of the most outstanding costuming differences Zeami mentions is that for the *Okina*. When staged in a shrine as the 'Three rituals' (*Shiki sanban*), the actors dress in the white robes of a Shinto priest. This practice is still followed today in the annual spring performance of *Okina* at Kasuga shrine in Nara. When, however, *Okina* was produced on stage as a formal opening to a long program, Zeami stipulates that 'He should be dressed unobtrusively, generally not in gold-patterned cloth. The colours should be pure (prime) colours'.[3]

The triptych *Okina, Sanbasō and Senzai* (fig 3.1 & [144]) by Kano Naganobu gives a clear picture of how the main roles in the play are costumed. The middle figure shows the god-like old man Okina dressed like a courtier in a round-collared, broad-sleeved *kariginu*, ballooning pleated trousers bound at the ankles (*sashinuki*) and a black-lacquered courtier's cap (*eboshi*). The pattern on the *kariginu* of octagons linked with small squares known as *shokkō nishiki* has a formal, Chinese flavour in its dense geometrical symmetry. The design comes in many subtle variations, but the colours tend towards blues and greens.

Before Okina's dance, Senzai (fig 3.1, right figure) purifies the stage. Both he, and the dark-faced old man Sanbasō (fig 3.1, left figure) who follows Okina, wear matched suits known as *hitatare* (in shape and material similar to the *suō kamishimo* shown in [102]). Senzai's suit sports large irregular blue lines set against a solid white ground. Sanbasō's has cranes and long-tailed tortoises resist-dyed on the sleeves and on the loose pleated trousers. These designs reference imagery of longevity and prosperity that pervades the text and gives meaning to the performance.

The role of Okina is played by a nō actor, who generally wears silk, often with woven patterns, while the role of Sanbasō is danced by a kyōgen actor, whose garments are frequently made of commoner's fabrics woven from bast fibres, like hemp, and are dyed with paste-resist patterns. In this way, rank and role are maintained even in the ritual ceremonial piece *Okina*.

Social rank can be read in the material, the tailoring and to some extent the motifs used in nō and kyōgen costumes (see opposite). For instance, in the Heian period (794–1185), the nobility wore brocaded silk robes with broad sleeves and open cuffs, more formal garments sporting an overlapping round collar.[4] Reflecting these costumes, ministers and courtiers in nō dress in round-collared *kariginu* with woven patterns incorporating court motifs (*yūsoku monyō*), like the undulating vertical lines seen in [37]. Strong deities, however, would don a *kariginu* with large, bold designs. Unlined *kariginu* have an open weave giving a gossamer translucency.[5] The unlined *kariginu* in [38] is woven with gold and silver patterning wefts forming scattered plums and mist that evoke the promise of early spring.

Similar to the *kariginu*, the *happi* has broad, open sleeves and gold or silver patterning on a solid ground, however, the front panels are tailored to fall straight with no overlap and are attached to the back panels with a strap at the hem. Goblins, demons, bandits and victorious warriors dress in *happi* girdled at the waist over broad pleated trousers (*hangiri*, 83 & 84), often combining two strong geometric patterns, like linked circles, hexagons, lightning or waves on a dark ground. Warrior-courtiers, such as the heroes in the *Tale of the Heike* (*Heike monogatari*) who combine poetic or musical sensitivity with the arts of bow and sword, form the core of warrior nō plays and might be garbed in a gossamer unlined *happi* in open weave with gentler designs like the floral scrolls seen in [39]. For warrior roles the *happi* sleeves are frequently tied up at the shoulders to free the arms for vigorous action. Sometimes a sleeveless variant of the *happi*, the *sobatsugi*, is used instead. These vest-like garments can also be worn for Chinese roles, as would probably be appropriate for the two *sobatsugi* with dragon motifs illustrated in [41] and [42].

Decorative broad-sleeved outer garments for women are woven in an open weave. There are two styles. The first, the *chōken* [43–48], has open front panels, long cords attached with bows at chest level and tassels attached to the bottom outer corners of the sleeves. It is donned in the second half of nō plays featuring women who perform a long instrumental dance, like the celestial maiden in *Naniwa* dancing centre stage in the screen *Nō performance* [135] or Lady Rokujō in *Nonomiya* (fig 3.2). The lightweight sleeves catch the breeze and at designated moments in the dance the sleeves are gently twirled around the arm or one cast upwards to shroud the head. No wonder the poetry speaks of 'dancing sleeves'.

The second style of woman's gossamer cloak is a 'dancing cloak' (*maiginu*). It is worn belted at the waist so the sewn-together front and back panels lie snug against the body.

NŌ AND KYŌGEN COSTUME TYPES

TAILORING TYPE	COSTUMES WITH WOVEN PATTERNS	SURFACE PATTERN
'broad sleeves' (*ōsode*) outer garments, distinguished by tailoring (Only the most common decorative methods are mentioned)	***kariginu***: (male) round collar. Gold or silver weft patterning on a satin or twill ground (lined): on an open weave (unlined). ***happi***: (male) straight collar, side straps. Gold or silver weft patterning on a satin or twill ground (lined); on an open weave (unlined). ***sobatsugi***: sleeveless *happi* ***chōken***: (female, child, [warrior]) free panels, cords and tassels. Gold, silver and coloured weft patterning on an open weave. ***maiginu***: (female) front and back panels attached. Weave similar to *chōken*.	***suō kamishimo***: matched suit in hemp or other bast-fibre plain weave with stencilled paste-resist designs. ***naga-kamishimo***: similar to *suō* but with sleeveless vest instead of jacket. ***kataginu***: kyōgen hempen vest with paste-resist designs.
'small sleeve' (*kosode*) undergarments (male) and outer garments (female), distinguished by patterning technique	***karaori***: (female) supplementary weft patterning in many colours on a twill ground. Seasonal flowers, 'Japanese' court imagery. ***atsuita***: (male) twill checks or twill ground with supplementary weft patterning in many colours. Bold, geometrical, 'Chinese' patterns.	***surihaku***: (female) stencilled gold or silver foil repeat patterns on satin or other glossy silk. ***nuihaku***: (nō and kyōgen female, child, courtier-warrior) embroidery over stencilled gold or silver foil pattern on satin or glossy silk.
'trousers' (*hakama*)	***hangiri***: broad pleated pants with extra bulge at the rear. Gold or silver weft patterning on a satin or twill ground. ***sashinuki***: pleated pantaloons bound at the ankles. Medallion patterns on a twill ground.	***hanbakama***: hempen short trousers often bound at the calf. ***nagabakama***: long pleated trousers; the bottom half of a *naga-kamishimo* matched suit.

The large 'dancing cloaks' that have straps between front and back panels [51 & 52] are a rare variation.[6] *Maiginu* have no cords or tassels. Worn by shamans and female deities performing a Shinto dance (*kagura*), *maiginu* are very similar to *chōken* in weave, patterning techniques and use of sleeves. Typically, however, the design distribution for *chōken* has large discrete motifs spanning the seams at the shoulder, like the overlapping fans in [45] or the weeping cherries in [47], and sparser, smaller motifs scattered along the hem and bottom of the sleeves. In contrast, *maiginu* tend to have evenly distributed patterns like the flower bouquets on ocean waves in [49], though there are exceptions for both types of robes, as exemplified by some of the garments illustrated in this publication [50–52].

Not all women performing a dance don broad-sleeved, open-weave cloaks. Court ladies might put on a brocaded 'small-sleeved' *karaori* tucked up (*tsuboori*) over wide pleated trousers (*ōkuchi*), as seen in fig 3.3 showing Yang Guifei (Jp: Yōkihi), the courtesan to Emperor Xuanzong in the nō play *Yōkihi*. A *karaori* with lavish gold ground, like that seen in [54] could be worn for this role.

Depending on the way it is draped, the brocaded *karaori* can represent a variety of roles. Drawn snuggly around the thighs and crossed loosely on top (*kinagashi*), it is a standard garb of a woman appearing in the first act of a nō play. For manual labour like rowing a boat, or if the woman is disturbed, one sleeve of the *karaori* is slipped off (*nugisage*), exposing the undergarment (*surihaku*). The entertainer in the nō play *Dōjōji*, discussed below, wears a *karaori* tucked up over another kimono (fig 3.4).

Karaori often appear to be embroidered, because the thick, glossy patterning threads of a dozen or so colours add weight and texture to the twill ground. The pattern is, however, woven in a repeat that generally spans the some 30 cm width of the cloth. The weaver freely changes where he uses which colours. Sometimes he places white against white, effacing the image and creating blank spaces, in others he juxtaposes bright colours in dense clusters.

The pattern is woven using small weft shuttles working in discrete areas while a draw boy perched above pulls up the required warp threads for each pattern weft shot.[7] Metallic thread – actually gold- or silver-leaf on thin strips of paper – is pulled through the shed with a long hooked stick. The draw boy might flip the pattern vertically (assuring the pattern runs upwards on both front and back) or horizontally to create a mirror image. Adjacent panels with different orientations were arranged variously (see [53], [54] and [56]). The chequerboard ground of [53] is achieved by resist dyeing the warp threads (*ikat*/*kasuri*) into large blocks of red and white, before threading the warp onto the loom. Playful variety within the limitations set by pattern and prescribed colours – shifts in emphasis that draw the eye across the garment – creates a world of expanding associations, a technique that lies at the core of nō texts as well.

Very similar in tailoring, but totally different in material and patterning technique, is the embroidered satin *nuihaku* ('embroidery and gold/silver foil') worn by women and children. The soft, glossy cloth drapes easily around the body, unlike the stiff, sculptural draping of the brocaded *karaori*. Greater freedom of expression is possible, since the designs are added after, rather than during, the weaving process. *Nuihaku* employ two decorative techniques: *haku*, or gold- or silver-leaf stencilled designs that form a background, and *nui*, or embroidery. Garments that only have metallic stencilled patterning and no embroidery are called *surihaku* and are generally worn as an undergarment in combination with *nuihaku*. Examples include [79] and [80].

The embroidered figures added to *nuihaku* may cover the entire garment in dense patterning [74] or evoke an overall scenic picture, like the herons rising from tall reeds at the hem to soar through clouds at the shoulders [76]. This imagery recalls the devotion and free spirit expressed in the nō play *The heron* (*Sagi*). Great care is given to creating realistic detail through embroidery, but without resorting to heavy, three-dimensional techniques like padding and couching.

Many *nuihaku* incorporate empty spaces. Sixteenth-century *nuihaku* were often decorated only at the shoulders and hem [71] (*katasuso*). Asymmetric, scattered designs [73] incorporating blank areas followed seventeenth-century street fashions, while *nuihaku* with no embroidery at the midriff, as in [75] where mythical *kirin* and buckets are caught in huge eddies, were particularly suited to the 'waist-wrap' draping style (*koshimaki*). For this, the upper part of the *nuihaku* is folded down so the sleeves hang over the hips and the *surihaku* undergarment is exposed above.

For most plays, the actor's choice of colours and design constitutes one vehicle of interpretation, but for some plays tradition is stricter. An example is the aforementioned *Dōjōji*, a nō play based on the story of a girl whose misplaced love expectations towards a mendicant priest forces him to hide from her in a temple bell. Transformed into a spitting-fire snake, she coils herself around the bell and melts it.[8] The nō play begins years later at the re-installation of the bell. The girl appears first as an entertainer, with a brocaded *karaori* tucked up over a 'waist-wrap' outfit, a tall dancer's hat and carrying a red fan with a single large peony flower on it (fig 3.4).[9] The *karaori* differs in each nō school. Facing cranes forming rows of diamonds [59] belong to the Konparu and Kongō traditions, while Hōshō school actors use a *karaori* with snow-covered camellias on a red ground [55].

Quite unexpectedly in the middle of her mesmerising dance, the entertainer jumps up into the bell, which promptly falls down and envelopes her. When she re-emerges, drawn by the prayers of the priests, she is crouching under the *karaori*. As she stands, she reveals her upper *surihaku* with stencilled gold or silver triangles suggesting the serpent scales that indicate her jealous state [81 & 82] and her dark 'skirts' (*nuihaku* folded down at the waist) with scattered embroidered roundels [77 & 78]. Wrapping her *karaori* around her midriff, she attacks the priests with a wand. In the ensuing battle, she finally drops the useless robe, like a snake shedding its skin (fig 3.5).

Daimyo lords in both nō and kyōgen wear matched hempen suits (*suō kamishimo*, 99–104) with broad-sleeved upper jackets and pleated trousers that are often so long that one has

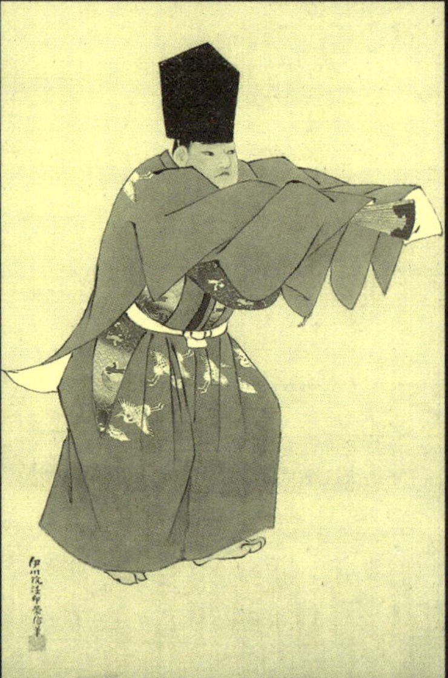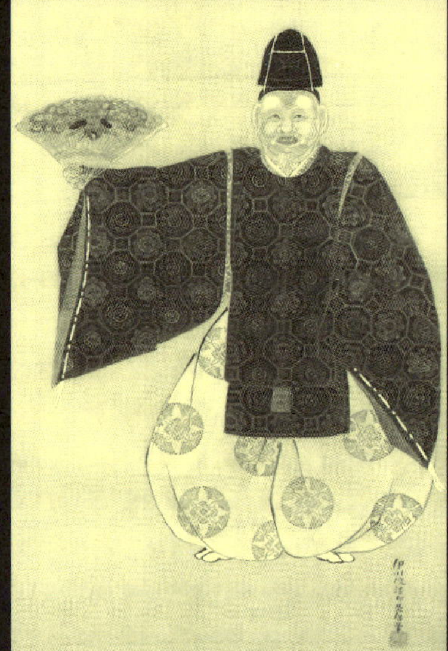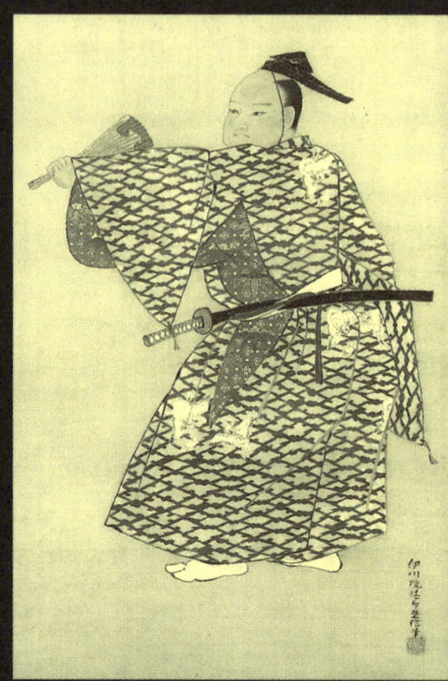

fig 3.1
Kano Naganobu
Okina, Sanbasō and Senzai
(see [144] pp 181 & 221)

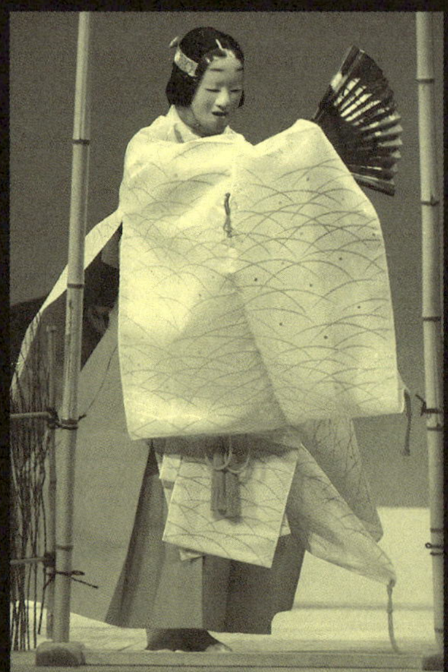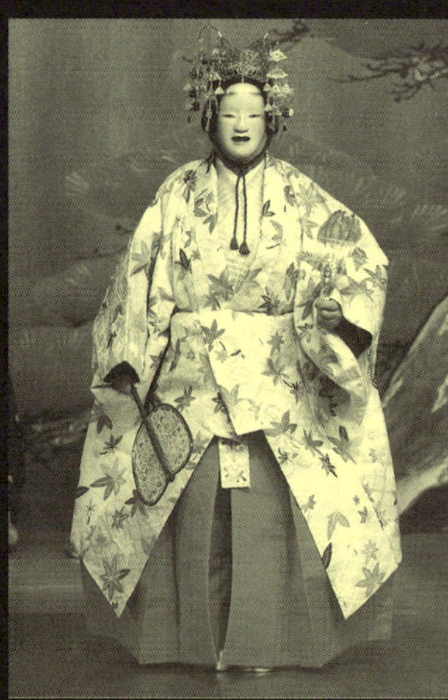

fig 3.2
Yoshio Izumi in the nō play
Nonomiya
Photo: courtesy of Yoshio Izumi

fig 3.3
Yoshio Izumi in the nō play *Yōkihi*
Photo: courtesy of Yoshio Izumi

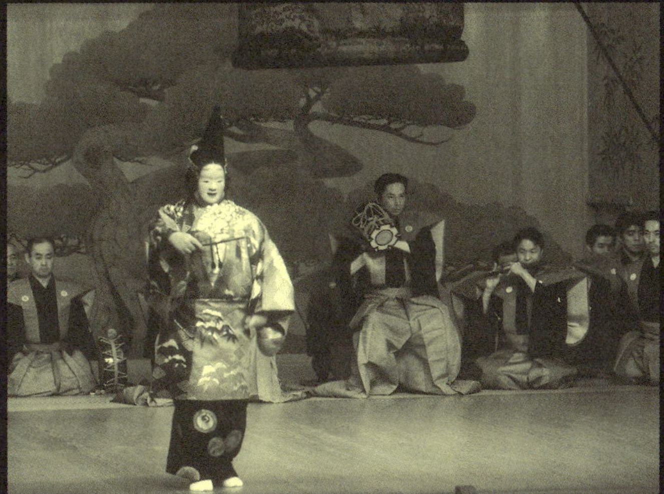

fig 3.4
Scene from Act I of the
nō play *Dōjōji*
National Noh Theatre

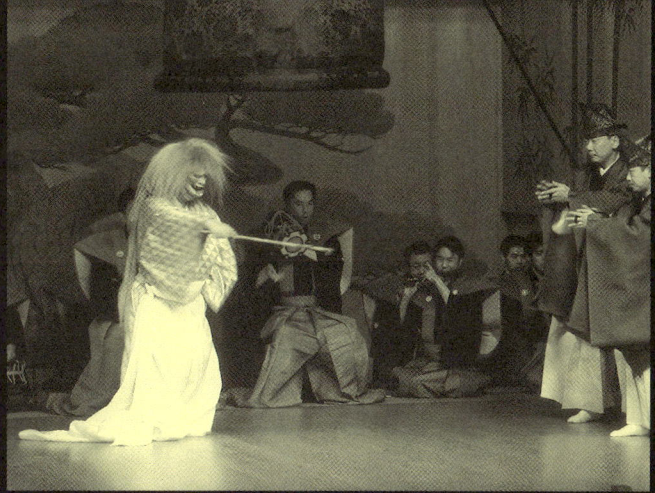

fig 3.5
Scene from Act II of the
nō play *Dōjōji*
National Noh Theatre

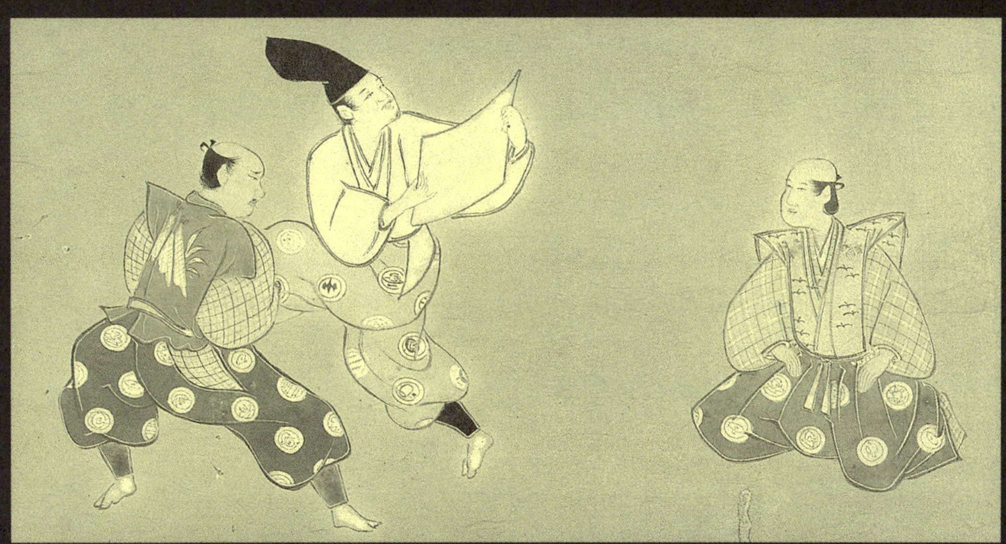

fig 3.6
'Letter wrestling', from
Album of old paintings of kyōgen
17th century
(see [143] pp 180 & 221)

to tread on them. The small, dense patterns are made by pressing paste through a stencil laid on the cloth and then immersing the cloth in a dye bath of indigo or black or brown. When the paste is removed, the design appears in white. Family crests span the seams of these suits: at the chest, in the centre back and frequently on the sides of the trousers. More elaborate suits might combine two contrasting colour zones [99].

An abbreviated form of the matched hempen suit eliminates the large sleeves and substitutes a vest with flared pleats at the shoulder. Chorus members and drummers also wore such *naga-kamishimo* suits [105 & 106] on very formal occasions. The upper part of these abbreviated suits probably inspired the kyōgen *kataginu* vest worn by servants and other less exalted characters. Although early patterning was similar to the designs on matched suits, later in the Edo period bold freehand patterns came to lend a homely, often humorous, touch to the *kataginu*: turning his back on the audience, the servant may reveal a huge snail that is seen crawling over a broken banana leaf [109]. The round-bodied, stick-legged herons in [107] have a comic simplicity sharply contrasting with the herons in [76].

The two actors illustrated in 'Letter wrestling' from the *Album of old paintings of kyōgen* (fig 3.6, see also [143]) shows them in *kataginu* vests: one facing towards the front with the vest tucked into the trousers, the other exposing the picture on the back and the vest belted over the pleated trousers. These short leggings (*hanbakama* or *kukuribakama*, [115–120]) are bound at the calf. Their paste-resist designs incorporate scattered crest-like rounds of various types.

Both actors portrayed in 'Letter wrestling' have chequered garments under their vests. These are *atsuita*, one of the basic undergarments (*kitsuke*) worn by men in both nō and kyōgen.[10] The *atsuita* in [63–70] appear very similar to the brocaded *karaori* in shape and technique, and are primarily distinguished by their bold geometric patterns.[11] The subdued colours and discrete design of alternating blocks of lattices and ivy [70] would be suitable for an old man, but the strong colour contrasts and large gongs and paulownia scattered over multi-coloured, nested linked hexagons [68] would be worn by a deity, demon or vigorous warrior. The impact of the *atsuita*, visible mostly at the sleeves, is strengthened or subdued by combining it with an outer cloak and pleated trousers that have large gold patterns against a dark ground or ones that have smaller patterns and subtler colours.

Historically, both the *atsuita* and the *karaori* were first woven in Japan long after Zeami's death – in the later half of the sixteenth century – and their design elements, like the chequerboard ground, reflect fashions of the period. By the early seventeenth century, however, sumptuary laws restricted the use of clothing with woven patterns as everyday wear to members of the imperial court, and the nō robe evolved into purely theatrical costumes. Over time, the patterns became larger and denser, exhibiting greater technical finesse, like outlining flower petals or holding down the weft pattern floats to add textural play. Garments sporting gold patterning on solid grounds, like *kariginu, happi* and *hangiri* trousers, also developed a more theatrical expression. The embroidered *nuihaku* enjoyed a longer overlap with everyday dress, while the matched hempen suits continued to be among the apparel presented to the actors from the wardrobes of the audience in appreciation of a fine performance.[12]

The selection of the mask and costume is often the initial step in an actor's preparation of a role, for it provides a visual image that he then brings to life through song and movement, poetry and rhythm. As he steps out onto the stage, beckoned perhaps by the calls of the drummers and flute, costume also provides the first impact on the audience, from which they read his vision of the play. As the imagery evoked by the text and actualised by the movement builds layer upon layer, the costume also gains new meaning. A cloak turns out to be a lover's keepsake, which when donned, grafts his spirit onto hers so they dance as one and the swirling sleeves bring back the past, fulfil her yearning and engulf the identity, drawing the audience into the whirl. A hat serves first to identify a dead hunter, is then set up on an altar and prayers offered, but when his ghost returns, the same hat becomes a nest of baby birds. As he descends into hell and it no longer serves to protect him against the blood tears of parent birds, he sends the hat twirling in a vortex across the stage. In this way, the world of recurring imagery, reshaped in each new context, lies at the centre of the nō experience. So also the enjoyment of the costumes, onstage and off, invites the eye to travel across the patterns, to focus on textural details, to zoom out to envisage the extension of the design in space, and to enjoy what is both hidden and revealed by the shifting light and shadow.

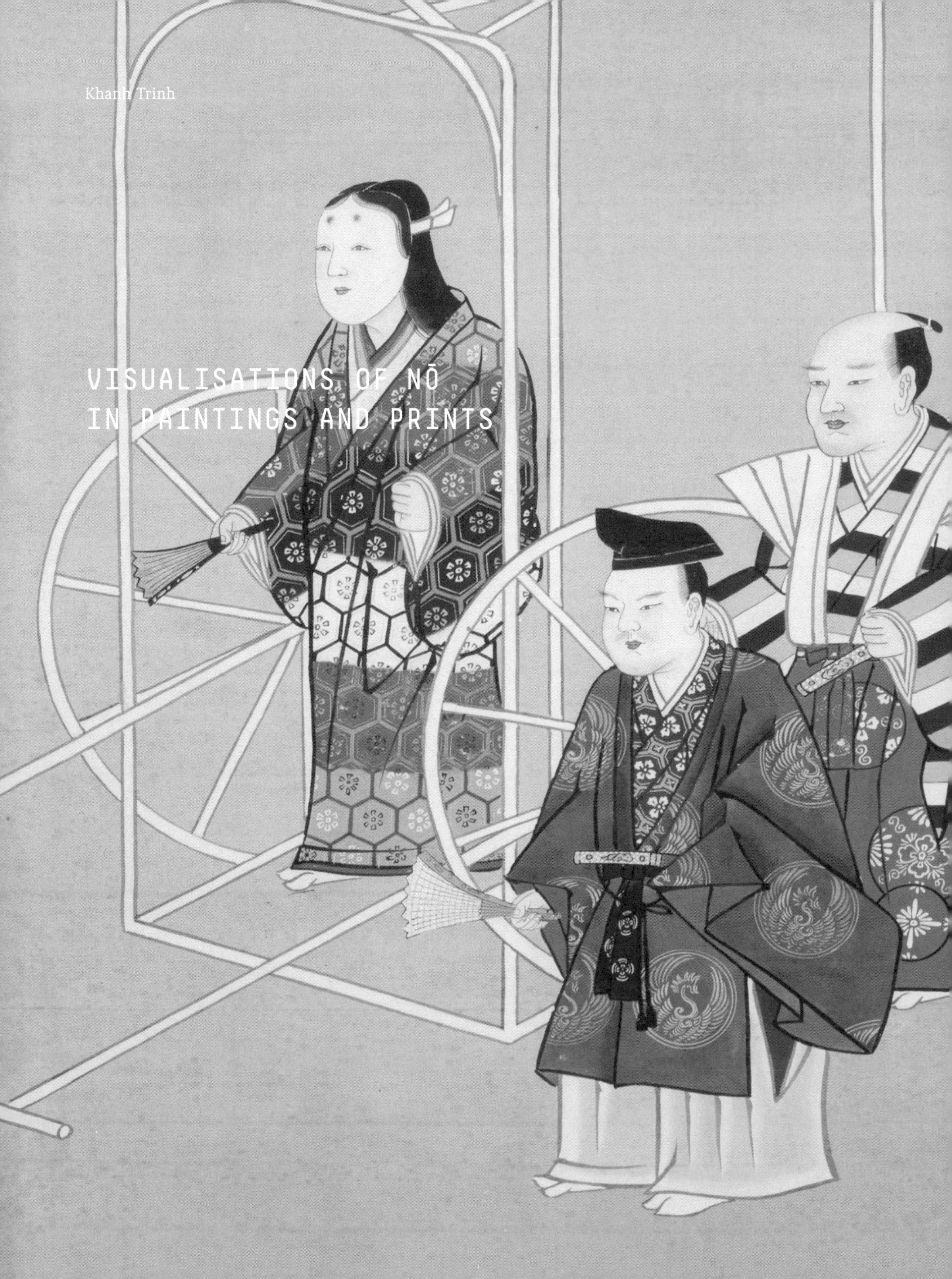

VISUALISATIONS OF NŌ
IN PAINTINGS AND PRINTS

The richly textured painted and printed illustrations of the kabuki theatre and its actors have been the topic of much in-depth research, but comparatively little is known about the imagery of the older nō (and kyōgen) theatre. The paucity of surviving 'nō pictures' (*nōga* or *nō-e*) has contributed to this situation as has, and perhaps more importantly, the fact that *nōga* are primarily enjoyed and studied as invaluable historical records of an ancient performance tradition. As a result, the artistic and aesthetic significance of these works has been little discussed. Examining *nōga* from an art historical perspective, this brief overview thus touches upon the various stylistic and compositional modes surrounding nō paintings and prints, as well as the socio-historical context of their production and consumption.

Visualisations of nō (and kyōgen) actors onstage have existed since the time of the celebrated actor-playwright Zeami Motokiyo (c1363–c1443), however, these early images took the form of instructional sketches that illustrated Zeami's treatises on dance movements, and they were not intended for aesthetic appreciation.[1] The first depictions of nō and kyōgen as staged performances are seen in genre paintings (*fūzokuga*) on folding screens from the beginning of the sixteenth century. These intricate compositions portray the noted 'scenes in and around the capital (Kyoto)' (*rakuchū rakugaizu*) or the bustling atmosphere of festivals at temples and shrines (*saireizu*). The military ruling class of this era favoured these two genres and commissioned lavish large-scale paintings of them to show off their political and cultural prowess following the restoration of prosperity and peace in Japan after a protracted era of civil war. As exemplified in the vignette 'Kanze nō performance at Tōfuku temple' on the pair of six-panel folding screens *Scenes in and around the capital* that are today housed in the National Museum of Japanese History (fig 4.1), nō stages included in cityscape and festival screens like this are usually located within temple or shrine precincts. Such illustrations underline the historical roots of nō as a performance within a religious context. The standard mode of representation prescribes a bird's-eye view of the stage, offering an all-encompassing outlook onto the stage and the audience, which up to the early seventeenth century comprised commoners from a broad spectrum of society.

From the early Edo period (1615–1868) onwards, the staging and the enjoyment of nō became a privilege reserved for the court and military aristocracy. Works from this era reflect this exclusivity with their inclusion within a painting genre showing leisure activities hosted at aristocratic mansions referred to as *teinai yūrakuzu*. The three panels in the collection of the National Noh Theatre (NNT) [131] dating to the Keichō era (1596–1615) are not only treasured early nō paintings, but are also valuable resources for the study of nō theatre history. They reveal that performances during this period were conducted within domestic settings in which spectators were seated in a room adjacent to the 'stage'. The orchestra is separated from the actors by a folding screen or curtain [131, right panel]. However, the visualisations of indoor spectacles like this were the exception rather than the rule. More common are compositions of a purpose-built stage in the gardens of palaces or other aristocratic residences. One of the most remarkable and oldest examples of this type is the c1607 eight-panel screen *Watching nō* in the collection of the Kobe City Museum (fig 5.2).

Findings regarding the date of production, authorship and historical background of the Kobe screen remain inconclusive, nevertheless it is generally accepted that the work depicts a nō program at a nobleman's mansion held in honour of an illustrious personage.[2] On a roofed stage open on all four sides (concealed in the composition by decorative bands of clouds), actors perform the felicitous piece *Okina* before the emperor seated in the main palace building behind the drawn bamboo blinds. His female entourage, the famed warlord Toyotomi Hideyoshi (1536/37–98), a considerable number of courtiers and other high-ranking military leaders are seen outside on the veranda. An intriguing detail is the representation of European emissaries, who mingle with other courtiers in the garden. The screen is neither signed nor dated, but considering the political and historical significance of the event and its participants, it can be surmised that the work was commissioned and executed by a master painter specialising in the native Japanese painting style known as *Yamato-e*.

While this screen and other later examples illustrating nō performances in aristocratic mansions, such as the NNT's six-panel folding screen by an unknown artist [135] and Kano Naganobu's hanging scroll *Nō performance at the Imperial palace* [134], possess great visual appeal and are of high artistic quality, their true value are as records of the evolution of the nō stage. Notable changes, for example in the structure of the stage, are visible between the early seventeenth-century Kobe screen and the mid Edo-period screen and hanging scroll in the NNT collection. In the Kobe screen the stage appears to be a plain raised square platform, erected quickly for a special performance. The roofed bridge (*hashigakari*) that links the main and backstage areas is not yet present, with only a low screen or curtain separating the 'mirror room' (*kagami no ma*), where actors prepare for their entrance, from the actual stage. A folding screen decorated with a design of white herons and reeds on a gold ground forms the backdrop of the rear stage. By contrast, the NNT screen and hanging scroll show the complete stage with a roofed bridge, the 'mirror board' (*kagami ita*) with a painted pine tree as back wall and the chorus area (*jiutaiza*) to stage left. The features in the NNT pieces evolved in the later part of the sixteenth century and are still in use today.

The second major group of *nōga* comprise those with much simpler compositions that omit the surrounding landscape, the stage architecture and at times even the orchestra and chorus. As a result, the viewer's focus is on the main actor (*shite*) who is captured interacting with the supporting characters (*waki/tsure*) in a key moment. Occasionally, stage properties characteristic of a scene or play are also included. These highly abstracted, mostly small-scale, scenes were frequently collected into concertina albums or mounted as handscrolls that are conducive to intimate viewing [132, 133, 139, 141–43].

A survey of these albums and handscrolls reveals that artists might have relied on manuals that prescribed the scene to be illustrated, together with the compositional and stylistic modes. Artists of these paintings or compendiums might have been members of specialised workshops based in the Kyoto area,[3] or established practitioners of the orthodox schools of official painters for the court and military aristocracy such as the Kano, Tosa or Sumiyoshi.[4] The representations are largely standardised and show the actors (and stage props) as abstracted patterns set against a blank ground. The portrayal of the performers is schematised, displaying no individual physiognomic traits, and this is due in part to the fact that masks often cover their faces. What matters is not the actor's stage presence, rather an accurate rendition of the pose, costume and mask ensemble displayed by the character during a key scene. This contrasts with the kabuki actor, whose persona was considered as important as his acting skills, thus leading to the highly developed production and consumption of paintings and woodblock prints of kabuki actors on and offstage. No such cultish adoration of the individual 'star' existed for nō and kyōgen performers at this time, and consequently the visualisation of the highlights of a specific nō play was not done to promote the 'star-status' of actors or of their affiliated theatres or troupes. Further, these images were not avidly collected by aficionados and fans who wished to emulate the fashions and even the lifestyles of these stars, as was the case with kabuki actors.

With the exception of plays featuring fearsome demon masks, which are worn to heighten a sense of dramatic tension, the solemn, restrained beauty characteristic of nō pervades the majority of the images in these albums and handscrolls. It should be noted that a kyōgen picture is generally more lively and dynamic, and an apt reflection of the humorous, exuberant nature of this comical drama. To the uninitiated *nōga* are striking for the meticulous brushwork, the vibrant colour and the attention to detail employed in the depiction of diverse textile designs. The recognition (and understanding) of the subtle differences in the costumes and masks between the various schools, however, remains the reserve of nō theatre connoisseurs.

Extant albums and handscrolls delineating nō scenes were privately commissioned works for coteries of nō connoisseurs, with the more sumptuously produced deluxe anthologies [139 & 141] known to have been handed down in daimyo households. Daimyo were not only the principal patrons of the various nō schools during the Edo period, but were themselves devoted students of the theatre. In general, such works might have served as resources for the selection of plays for one-day programs or visual reference works in the identification of some 200 plays in the repertoire at that time. But equally as important, they were appreciated for their aesthetic value.

With the codification of nō in the Edo period, each of the five official schools – Kanze, Kita, Hōshō, Konparu and Kongō – began to document their performance styles in painted and printed handbooks that were handed down within the family of a school's head.

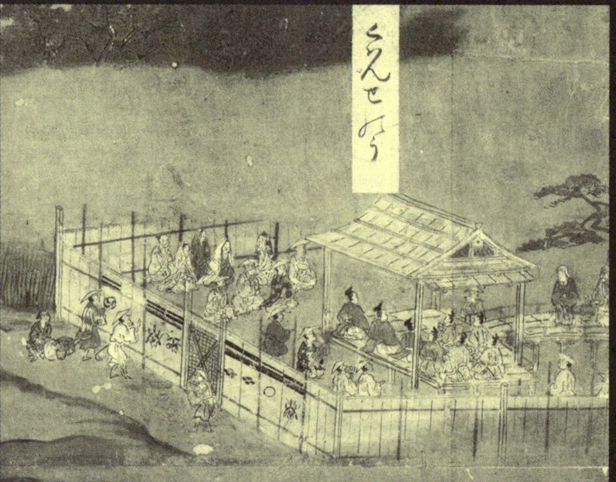

fig 4.1
Artist unknown
'Kanze nō performance at Tōfuku temple',
detail from right screen of *Scenes in and
around the capital* (*Rakuchū rakugaizu*)
c1525
pair of six-panel folding screens: ink, colour and
gold on paper, 138 x 58.7 cm each
National Museum of Japanese History, Sakura

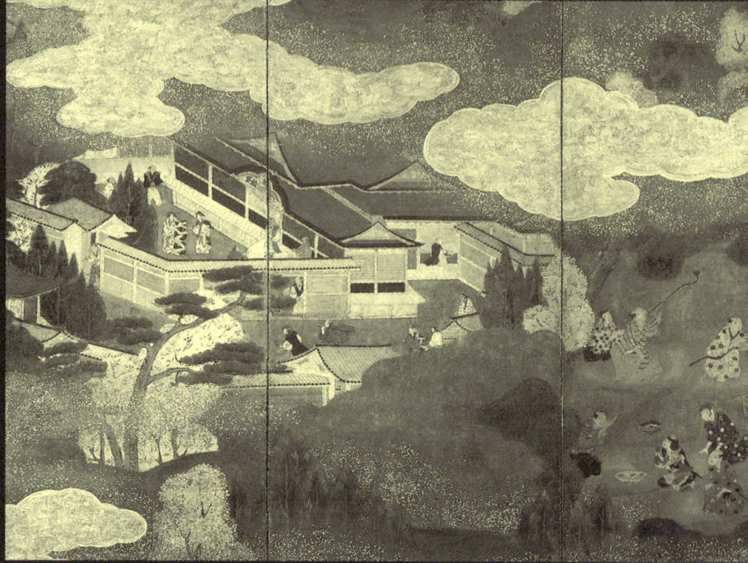

fig 4.2
Artist unknown
Watching nō
c1607
eight-panel folding screen: ink, colour
and gold on paper, 106.5 x 425.8 cm
Kobe City Museum

fig 4.3
Ogata Kōrin
Red and white plum blossoms
1710s
pair of two-panel folding screens:
ink and colour on gold ground
156 x 172.2 cm each
MOA Museum of Art, Atami

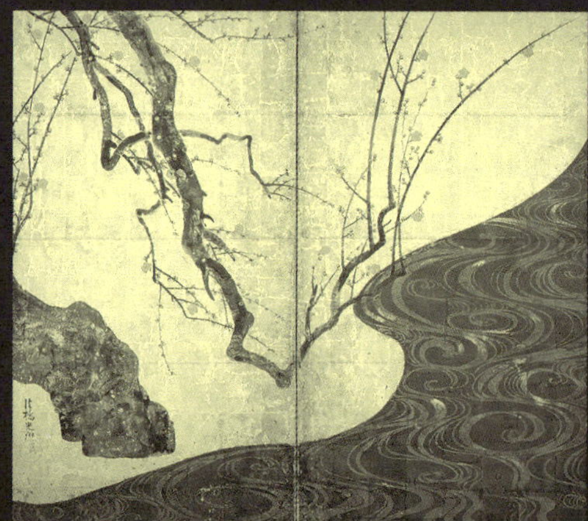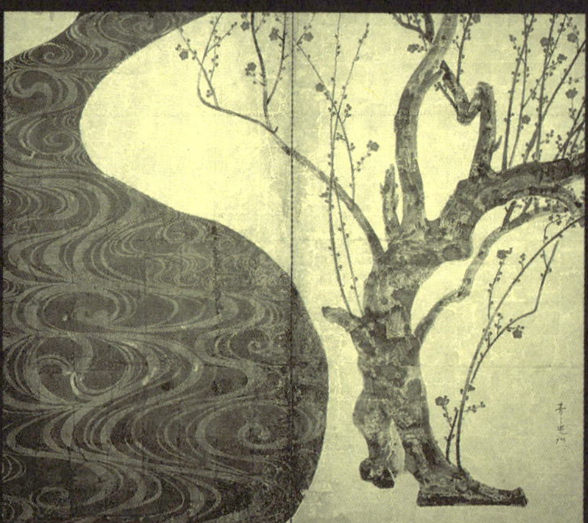

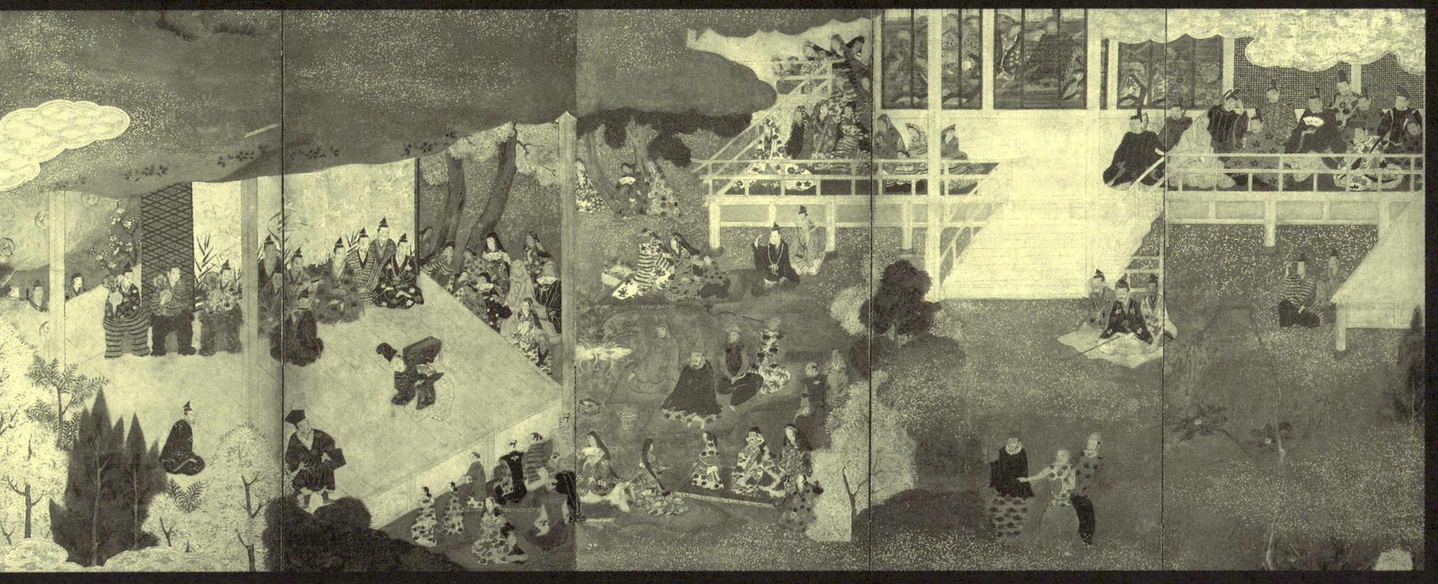

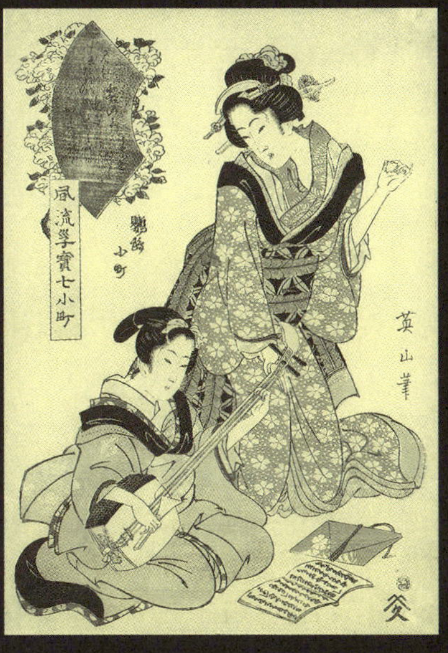

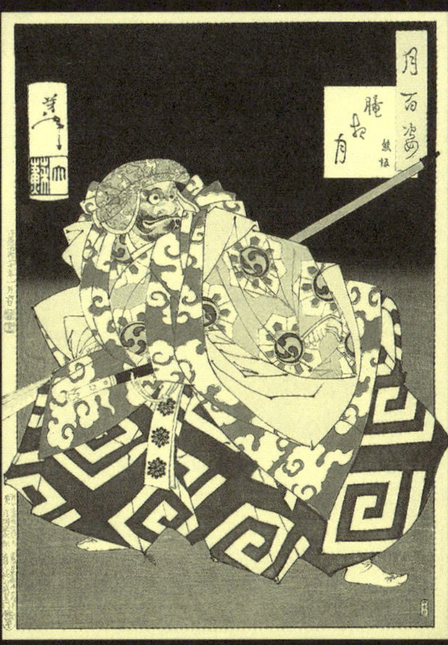

fig 4.4
Kikugawa Eizan,
'Parrot Komachi', from the series
*Treasure children: parody of the
Seven Komachi (Fūryū kodakara
nana Komachi: Ōmu Komachi)*
c1815–42
colour woodblock print, 37.2 x 25.5 cm
Art Gallery of New South Wales,
purchased 1930

fig 4.5
Tsukioka Yoshitoshi
'Hazy-night moon – Kumasaka',
from the series *One hundred aspects
of the moon (Tsuki hyakushi:
Oboroyo no tsuki Kumasaka)*
1885–92
colour woodblock print, 39 x 26 cm
Art Gallery of New South Wales,
Yasuko Myer Bequest Fund 2012

Works [152] to [155] in this publication are excellent examples of such teaching materials, which demonstrate the use of costumes and masks for specific roles, as well as the spatial relationship between the main and supporting actors in certain scenes or characteristic stage properties (and sometimes their construction).

The third major group of nō imagery includes designs for folding screens and hanging scrolls, lacquerware, ceramics and book illustrations. They depict select nō characters (eg the historical or legendary figures portrayed in a play) or the landscape setting of a nō play. As the direct link to nō in these works can be obscure, they should perhaps be seen as 'nō-related paintings' rather than as purely 'nō paintings'. One of the best representatives of this category is probably the pair of two-panel folding screens by Ogata Kōrin (1658–1716) in the collection of the MOA Museum of Art (fig 5.3). On one level, these screens can be appreciated as a magnificent decorative composition of two plum trees – the older with white flowers, the younger with red blossoms – separated by a meandering stream with stylised waves. However, it has also been suggested that the work can be read as a visualisation of the nō play *Tōboku*, in which the blossoming plum tree at the Tōboku temple embodies the spirit of the tenth-century court lady and poet Izumi Shikibu.[5]

Kōrin is generally acknowledged today as the best-known practitioner of the decorative painting school known as Rinpa, an artistic tradition whose members were not bound by hereditary lineage or a close master-pupil relationship, rather by a shared dedication to a particular style. Beginning with Hon'ami Kōetsu (1558–1637) and Tawaraya Sōtatsu (active c1600–43), the recognised founders of the tradition, Rinpa artists were closely affiliated with the class of affluent, cultivated merchants who, despite their low ranking in the strict Tokugawa social hierarchy, were the most financially influential art patrons. Among the various cultural pursuits favoured by these wealthy commoners, the study and performance of unaccompanied nō chanting (*su-utai*) was a popular pastime.[6] Kōetsu, Sōtatsu, Kōrin and their followers in the Rinpa tradition either hailed from families belonging to or had an intimate relationship with this class and thus would have had the opportunity to learn and practice nō chanting. The imagery and poetics of nō also offered them a rich source of inspiration for numerous ingenious designs that testify to their knowledge of this venerated art form and reflected the sophisticated tastes of their nouveau-riche patrons.[7]

Further evidence of the dissemination of nō among the broader population is the emergence of nō-related subjects in *ukiyo-e* woodblock prints, which surfaced early on in the works of masters such as Hishikawa Moronobu (1618–94), Torii Kiyomasu II (1706–63) and Suzuki Harunobu (1725–70). These and other *ukiyo-e* artists borrowed scenes from noted nō plays – some in fact adapted for the more popular theatre forms of kabuki or *bunraku* puppet theatre – for their prints of expressive kabuki actors (*yakusha-e*). Nō-related themes also appeared in *ukiyo-e* of languid, beautiful women (*bijinga*) and privately printed new year's greeting cards known as *saitan surimono* ('printed things' of the new year).[8] The general public may not have been able to identify or appreciate the nō play illustrated, and as such these 'parodied' compositions (*mitate*) were reserved for the pleasure of the more informed viewer. The coding and decoding of these hidden allusions was a means for the artist and a select audience to demonstrate their level of cultivation and taste. One of the most celebrated groups of nō plays that captured the imagination of *ukiyo-e* print artists was that of the seven plays recounting the various episodes surrounding the virtues and the loves of Ono no Komachi (c825–c900), a woman renown for her poetry, beauty, intelligence and capriciousness. An example by Kikugawa Eizan (1787–1867) is among one of the many woodblock prints that proves how the sophistication and femininity of Komachi's character easily lent itself to a subject in the *bijinga* genre (fig 5.4).

Nō risked becoming a passé art form in the wake of the Meiji Restoration in 1868 when the patronage for many traditional artistic expressions was threatened due to the abolition of the feudal system. However, its fortunes turned thanks to the efforts of the statesman Iwakura Tomomi (1825–83), who advocated the value of nō as a dignified art and one that could represent Japan's cultural achievements on the international stage (and on a standing similar to opera in the West). Nō experienced a revival and even gained prestigious imperial patronage from 1881 when Iwakura, members of the nobility and eminent nō performers founded the Nōgaku Society (Nōgakusha) and had an independent theatre, the Nō Hall (Nōgakudō), constructed in the Shiba district of Tokyo. This renewed interest in nō was equally echoed in the visual arts, most notably in the works of Kawanabe Kyōsai (1831–89), Tsukioka Yoshitoshi (1839–92) (fig 5.5), and Yoshitoshi's pupil and adopted son Tsukioka Kōgyo (1869–1927). Drawing upon their own experiences as amateur nō and kyōgen performers, Kyōsai and Yoshitoshi breathed new life into nō representations through the greater emphasis on the visualisation of the mood of the performance, the inclusion of glimpses backstage as if to create the illusion that the viewer possessed insider knowledge and the integration of Western-style expression to heighten the realism of the scenes.[9] Such innovations were essential for these traditionally produced woodblock prints to remain competitive in the face of modern reprographic media. It was against the background of these shifting cultural trends that Kōgyo produced his ambitious print series *Pictures of nō plays* (*Nōgaku zue*, 1897–1902) [147], *One hundred nō plays* (*Nōgaku hyakuban*, 1922–27) [148] and *A great mirror of nō pictures* (*Nōga taikan*, 1920–30) with Matsuki Heikichi of the Daikokuya, one of the leading publishing houses in Meiji-period Japan. While in essence relying on the conventional repertoire of nō imagery, Kōgyo modernised his images with numerous innovative compositional devices, some influenced by Western styles. Further, by making extensive use of soft colour washes, bold cropping and specialised printing techniques such as blind-printing or metallic pigments, Kōgyo and the Daikokuya produced high-calibre works that invite comparison with Edo-period painted anthologies.

Kōgyo's print series marked the final creative phase in the history of 'nō pictures'. As photography, and eventually film, gained greater currency in chronicling and portraying nō performances, the popularity of painted and printed imagery waned and was soon eclipsed altogether. For that reason, the scrolls, screens and albums illustrated in this publication stand today as valuable historical documents of the formal and stylistic changes that nō theatre experienced over the centuries. But more than that, they are also artworks whose accomplishment and charm enhance our pleasure and appreciation of them.

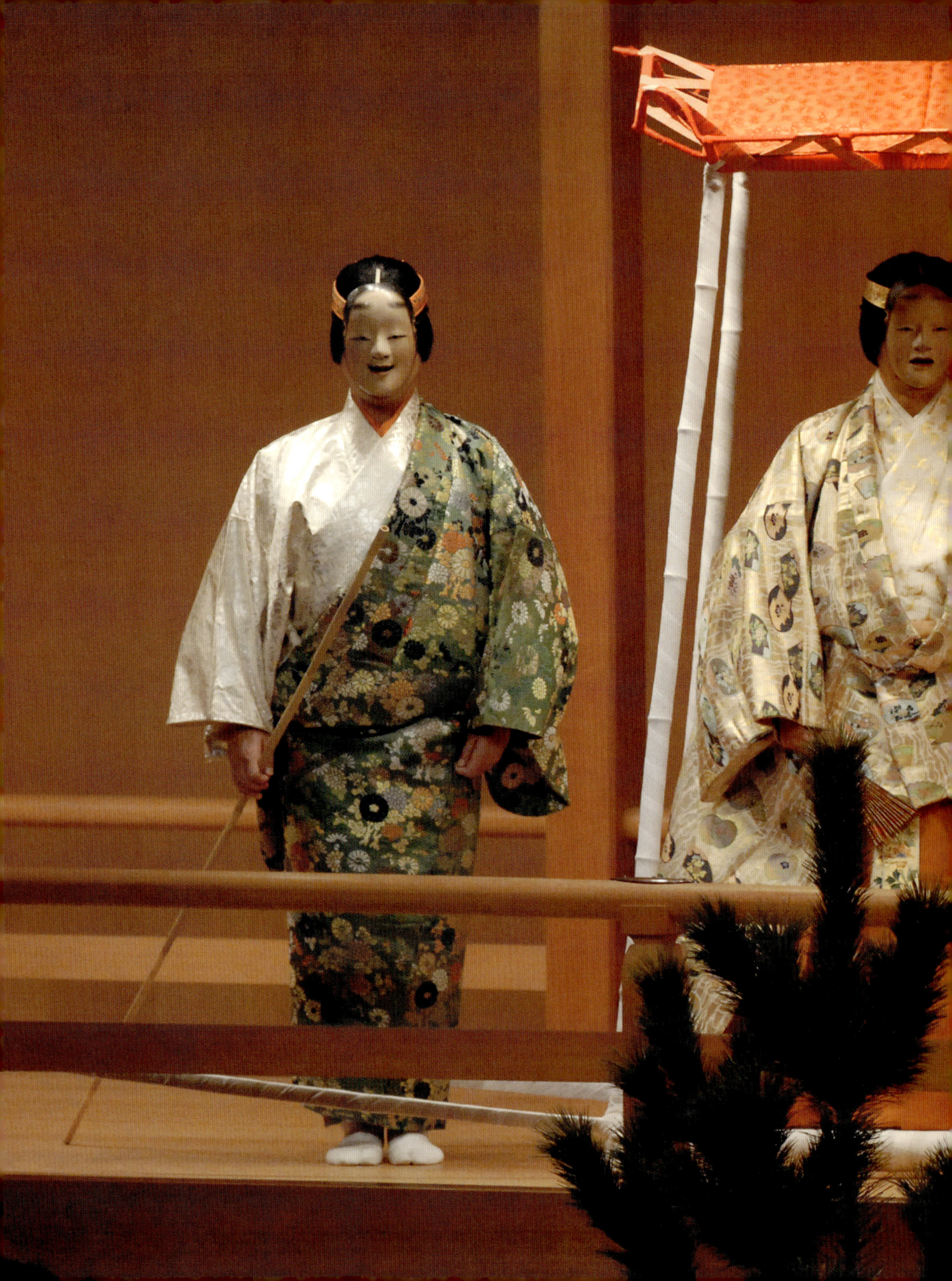

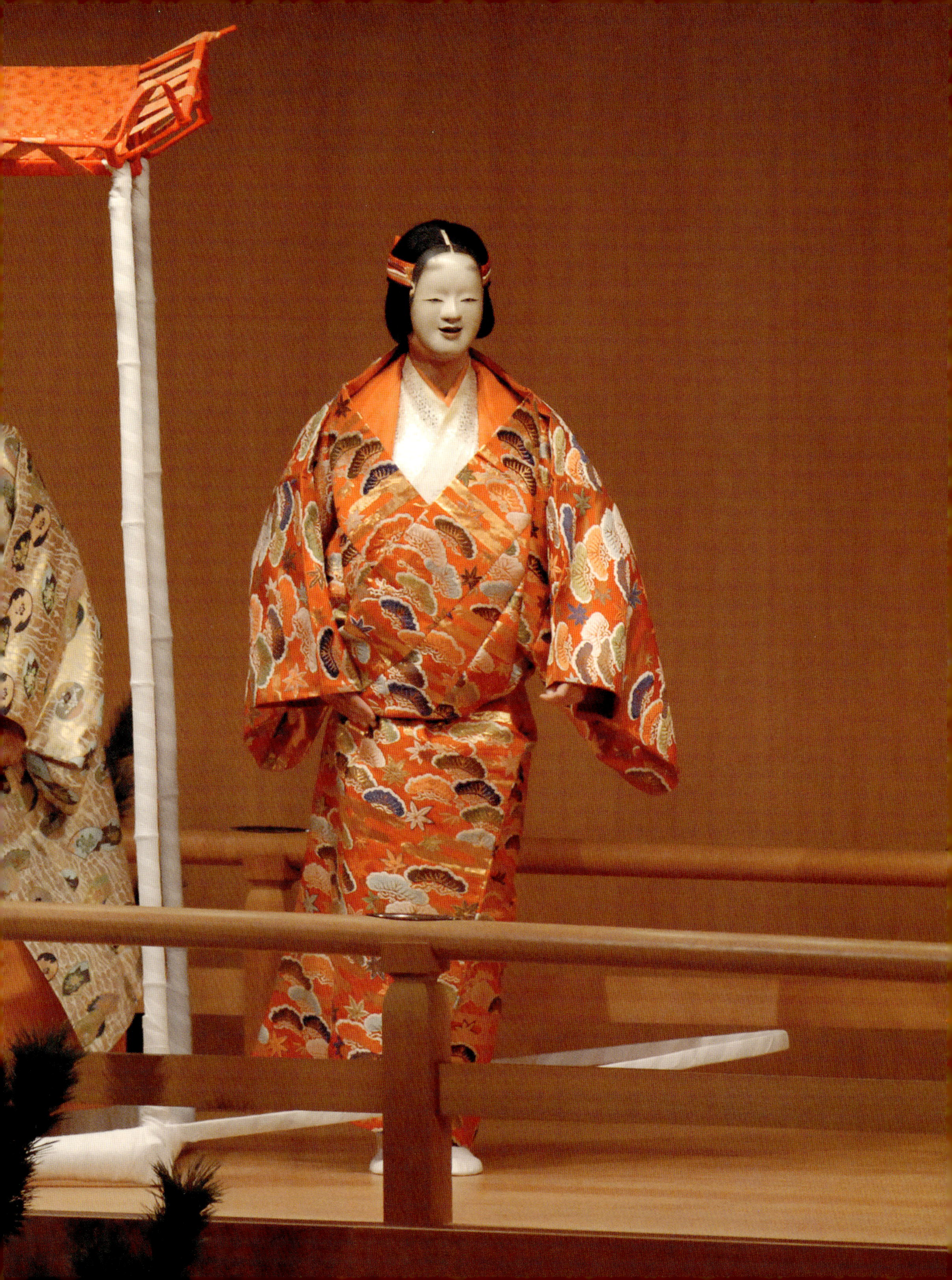

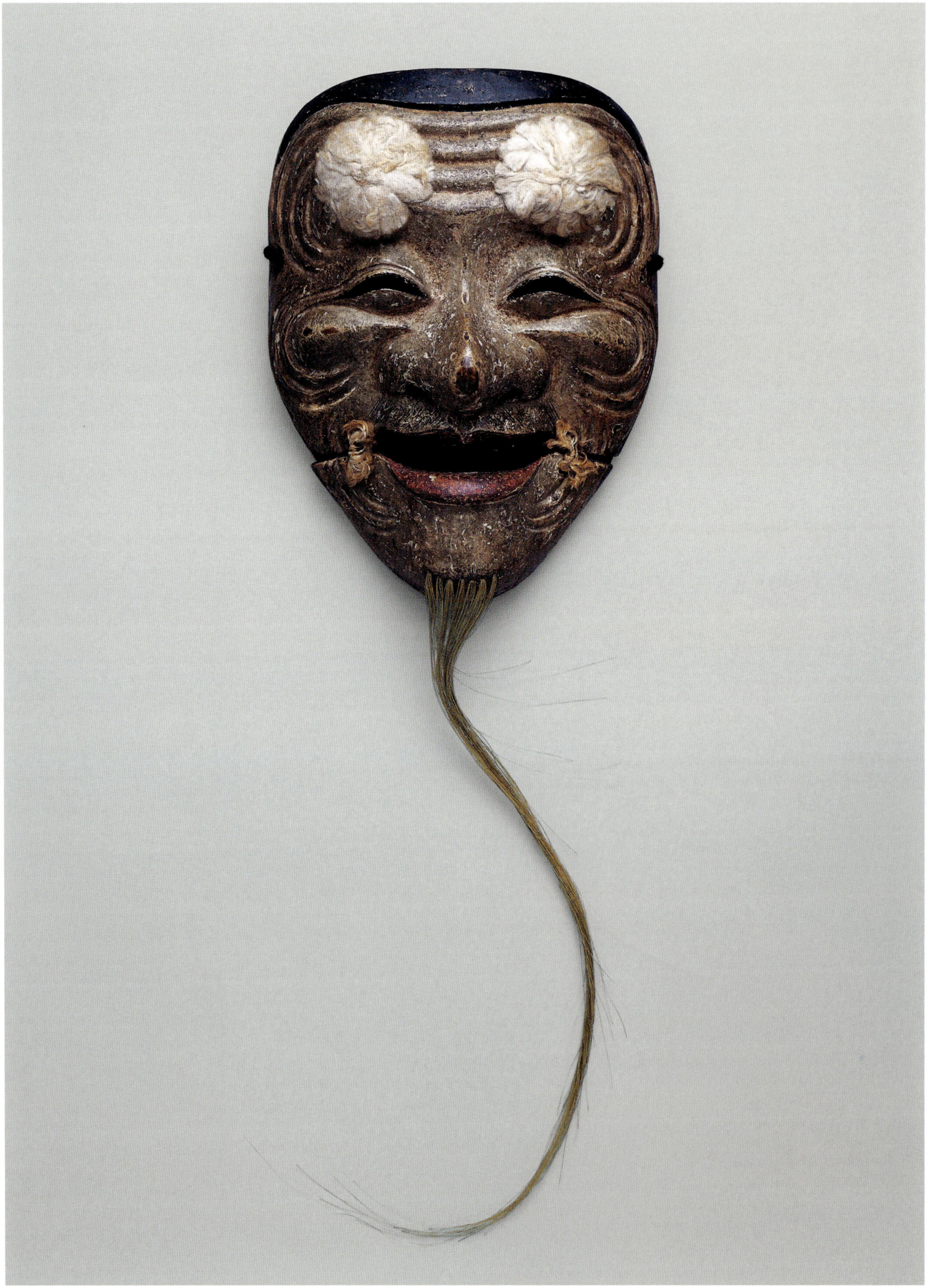

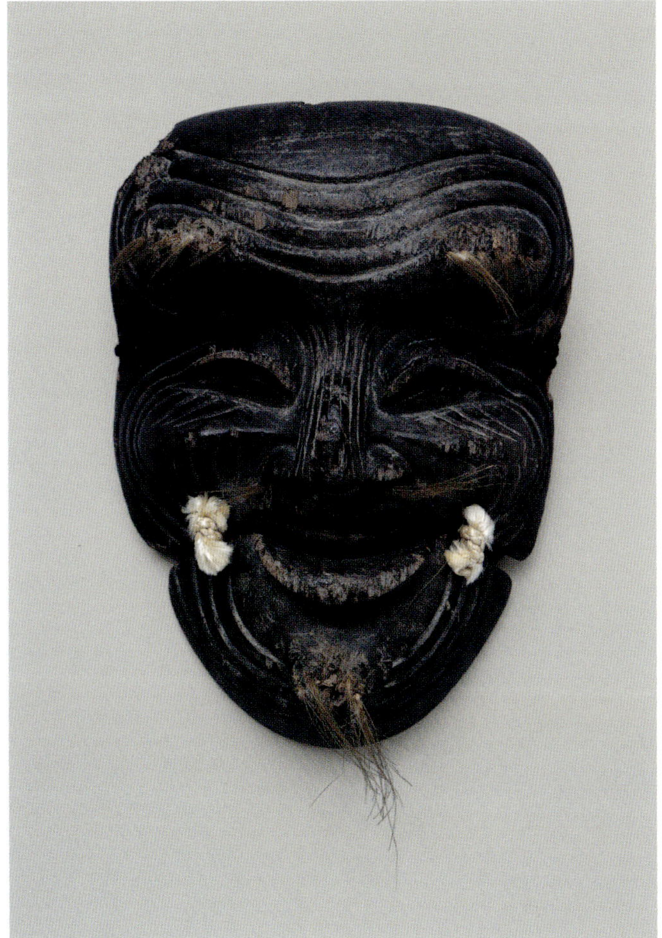

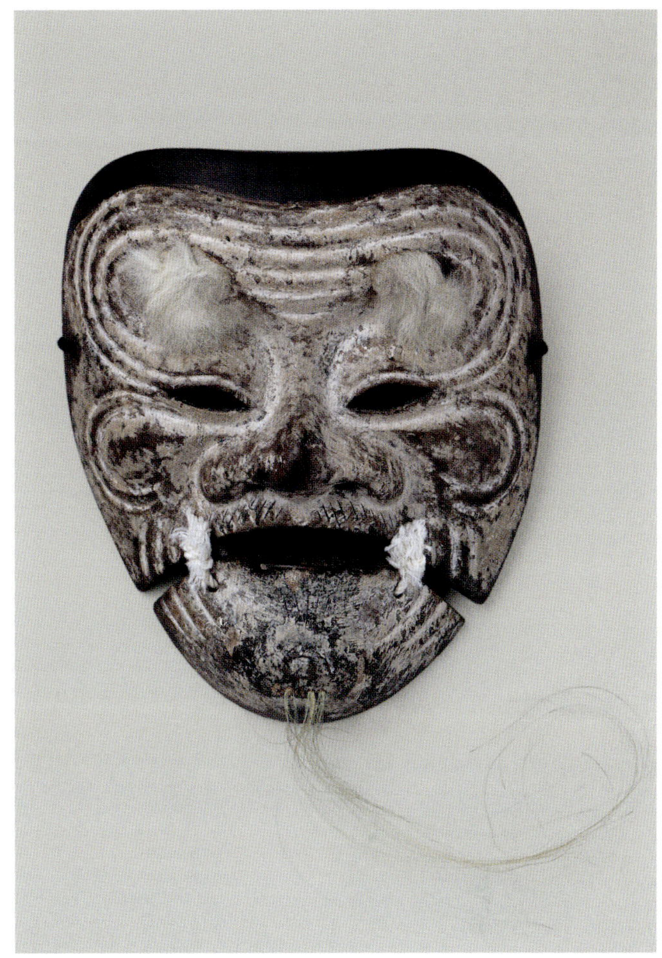

1 *Hakushikijō (okina)* mask
Momoyama–Edo period,
16th–17th century
National Noh Theatre

2 *Kokushikijō* mask
Momoyama–Edo period,
16th–17th century
National Noh Theatre

3 *Chichinojō* mask
Muromachi period,
15th–16th century
National Noh Theatre

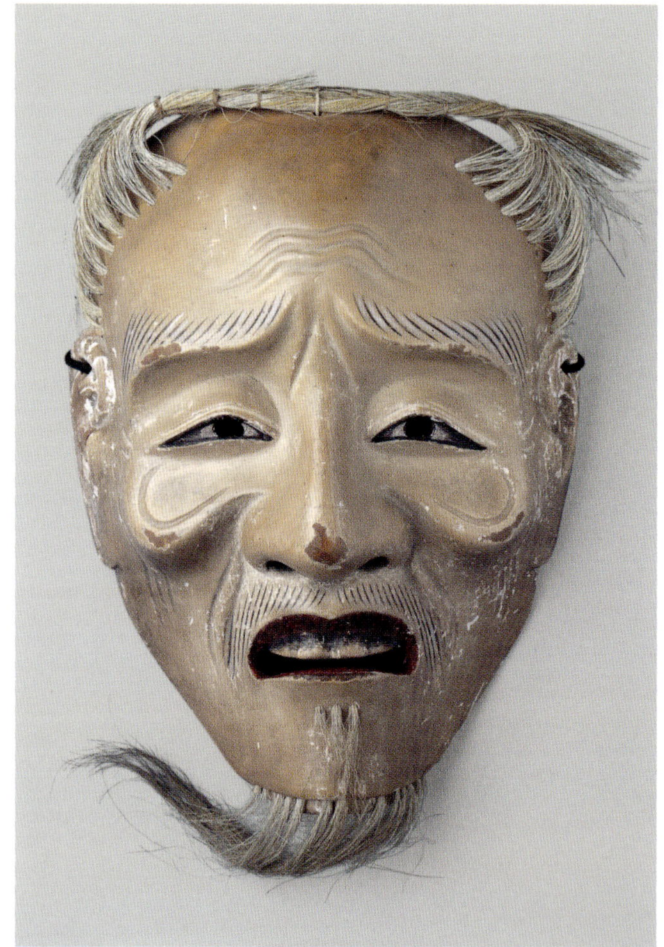

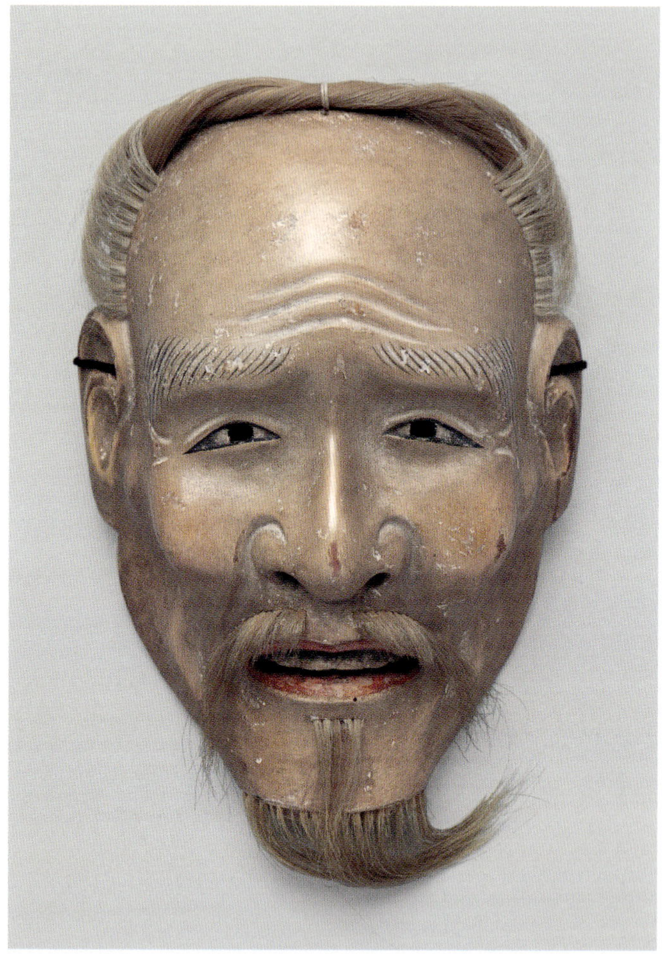

4 *Kojō* mask
Edo period, 17th century
National Noh Theatre

5 *Higeakobujō* mask
Edo period, 17th–18th century
National Noh Theatre

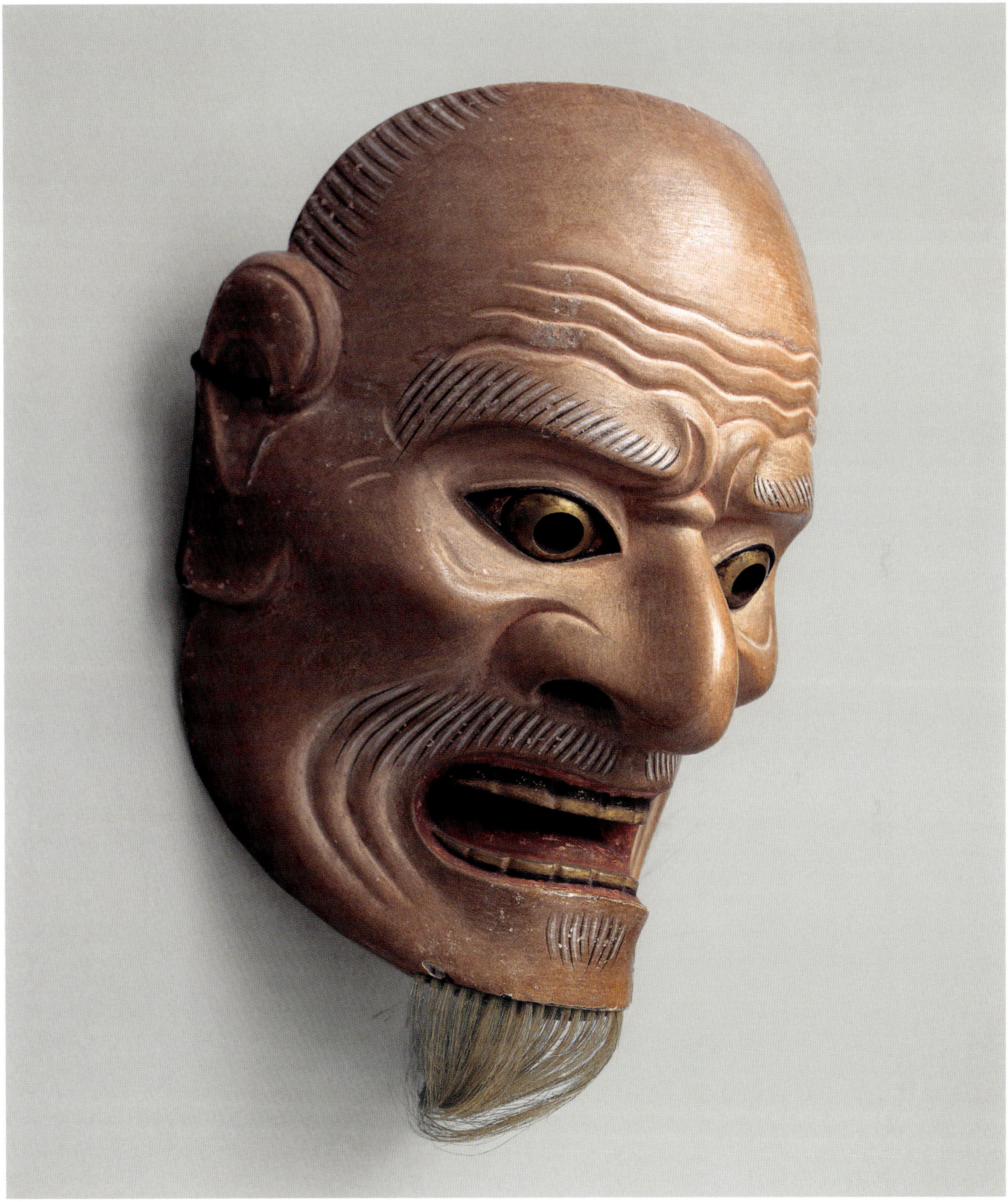

6 *Washibana akujō* mask

Edo period, 18th century
National Noh Theatre

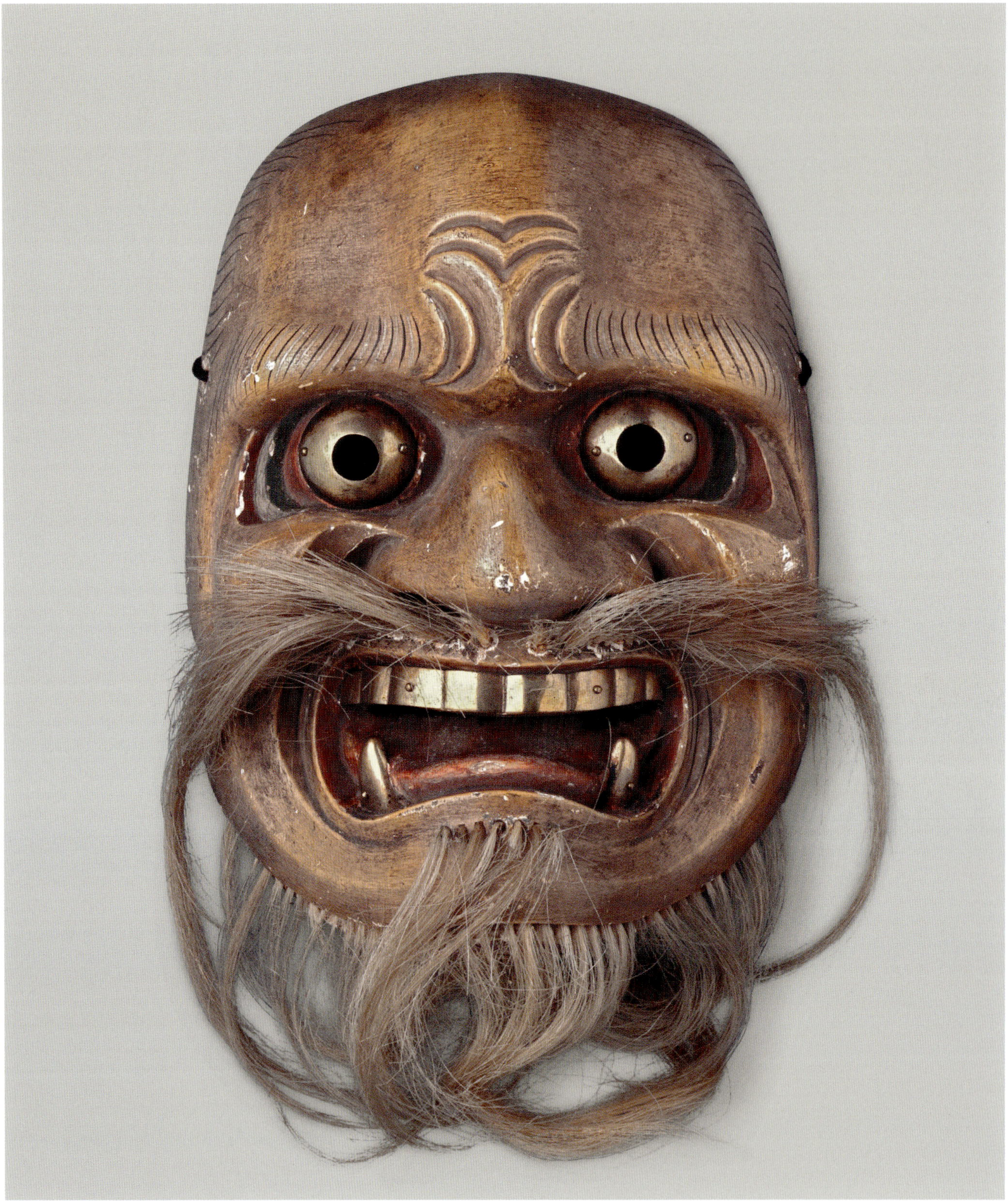

7 *Amazakuro akujō* mask
Muromachi period, 16th century
Agency for Cultural Affairs of Japan

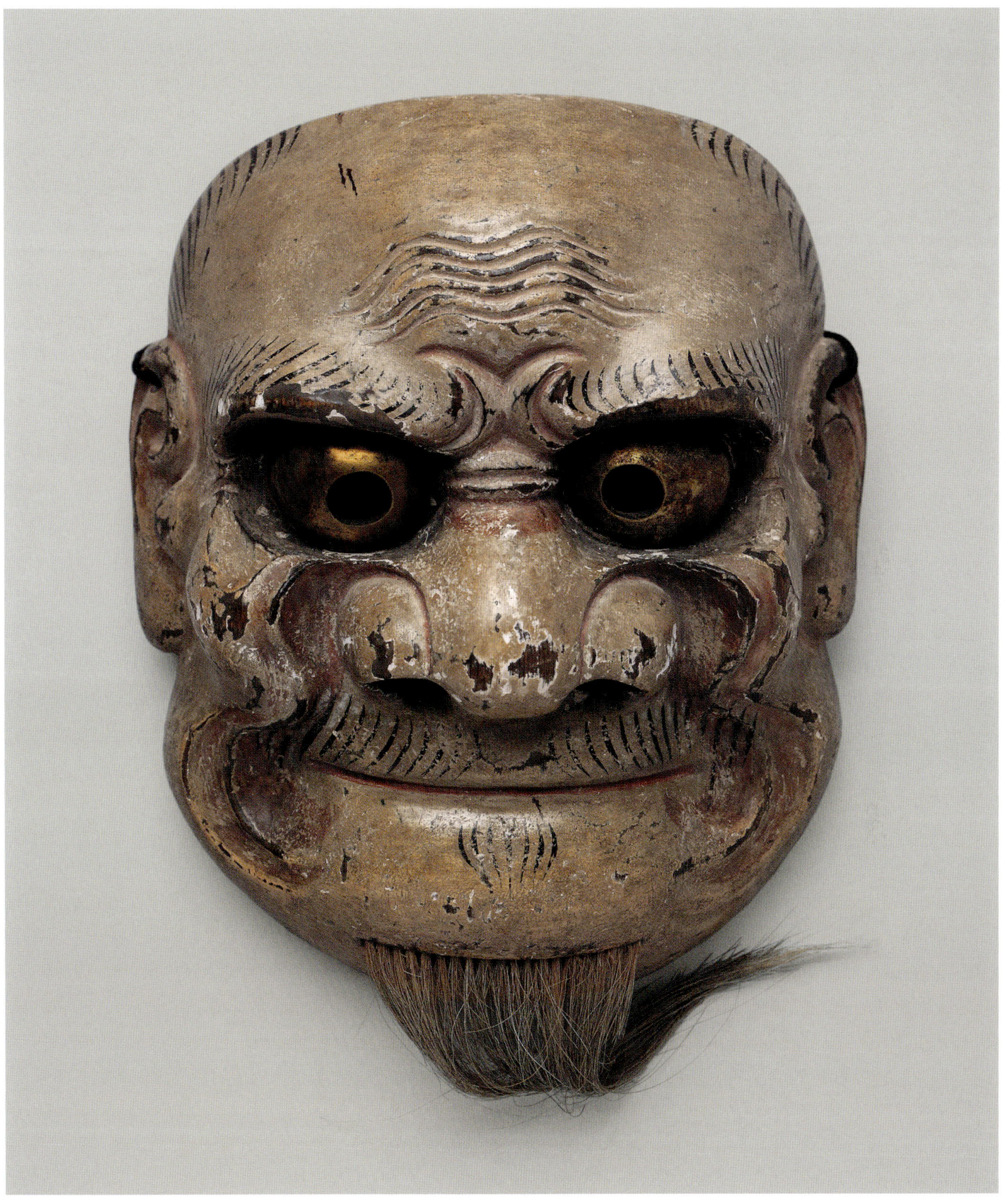

8 *Higebeshimi* mask

Muromachi–Momoyama period,
15th–16th century
National Noh Theatre

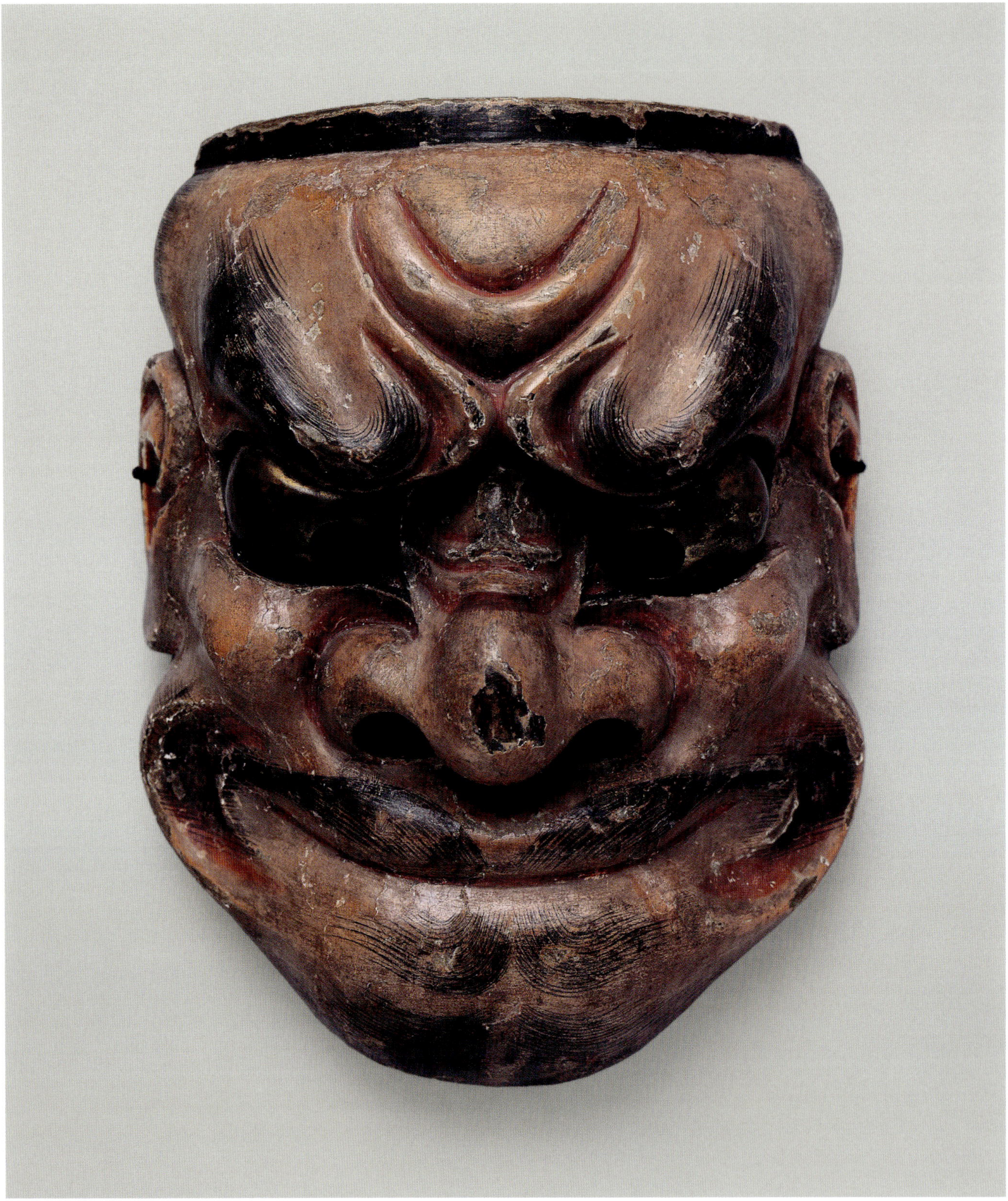

9 *Ōbeshimi* mask
Muromachi period, 15th–16th century
Agency for Cultural Affairs of Japan

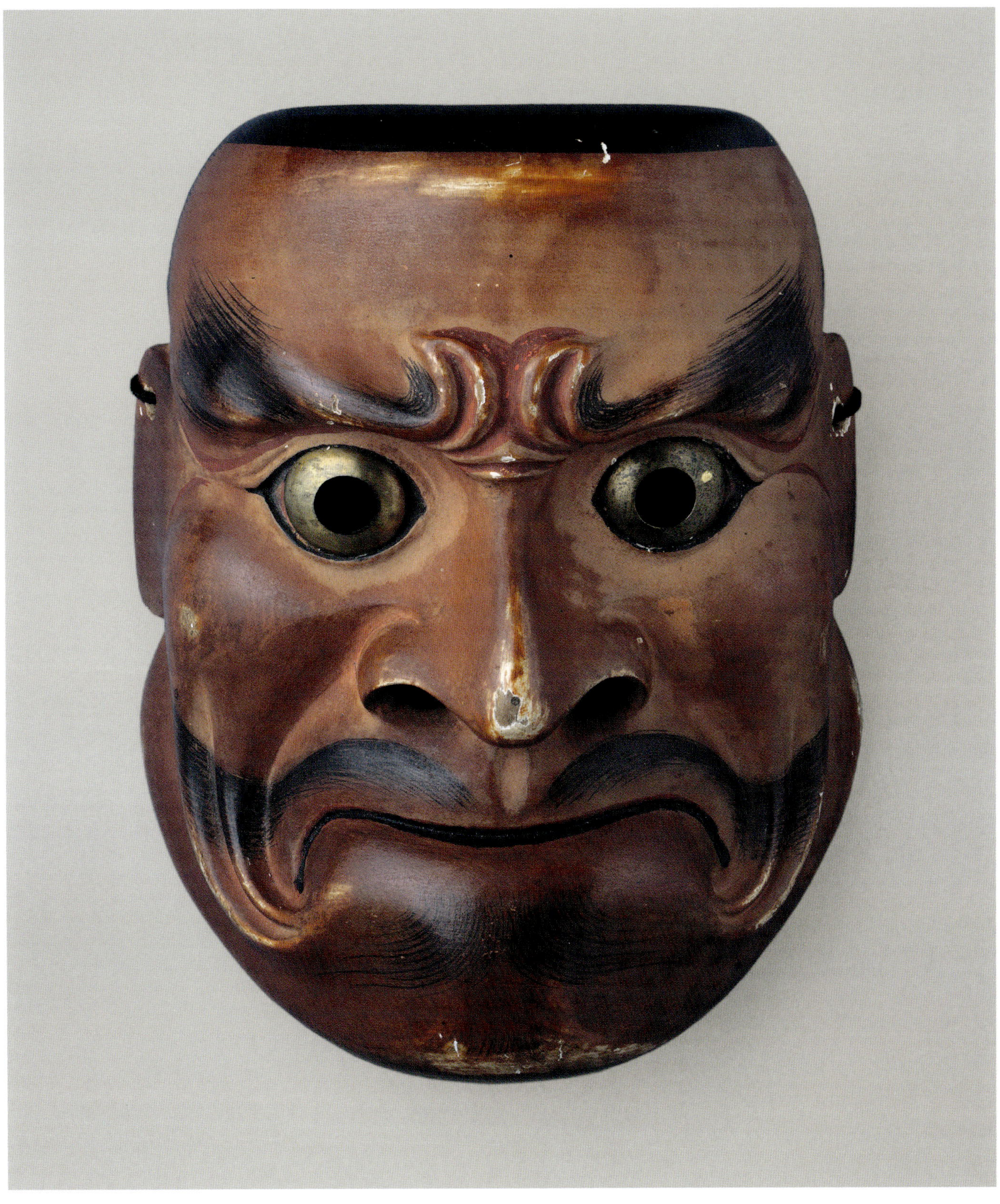

10 *Kobeshimi* mask

Edo period, 19th century
National Noh Theatre

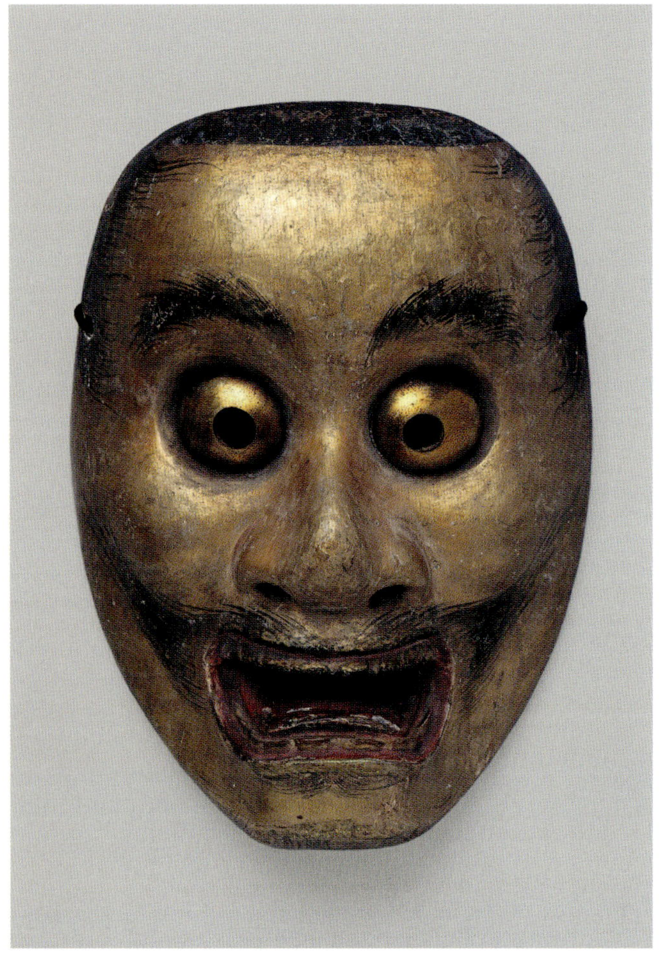

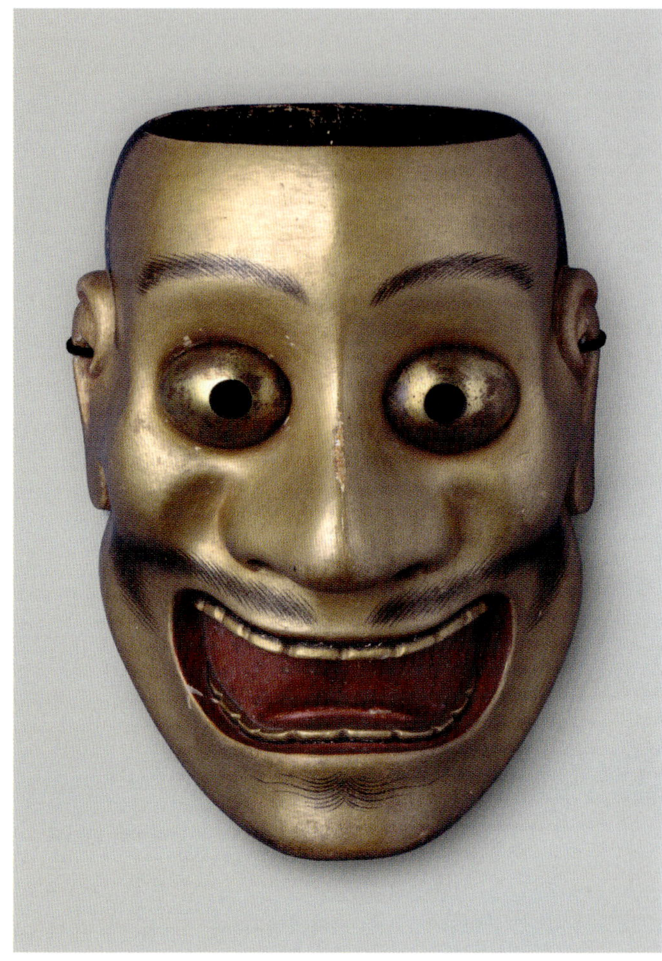

11 *Deikotobide* mask

Muromachi period, 15th–16th century
National Noh Theatre

12 *Ōtobide* mask

Edo period, 18th–19th century
Agency for Cultural Affairs of Japan

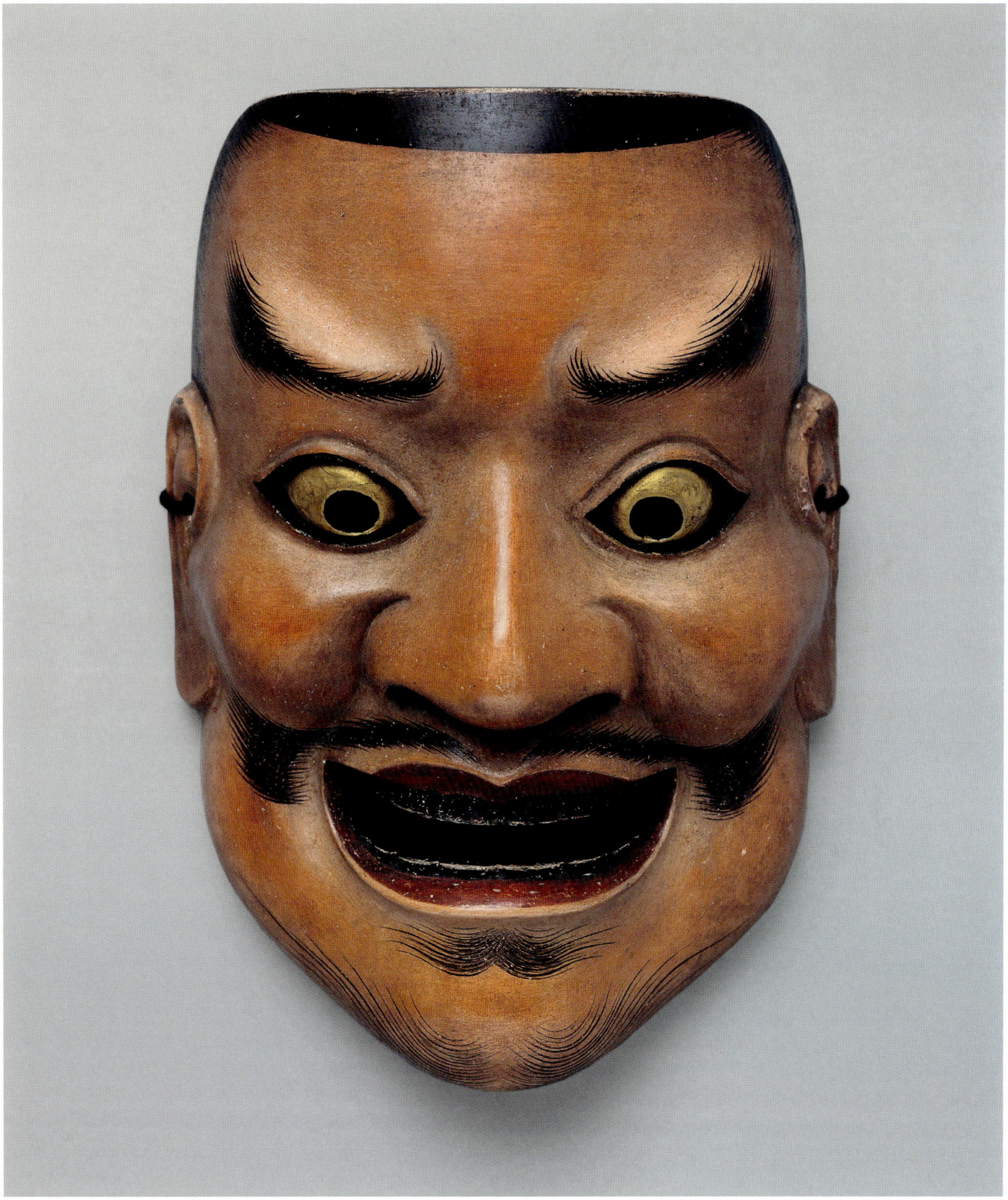

13 *Kotenjin* mask
Edo period, 18th century
National Noh Theatre

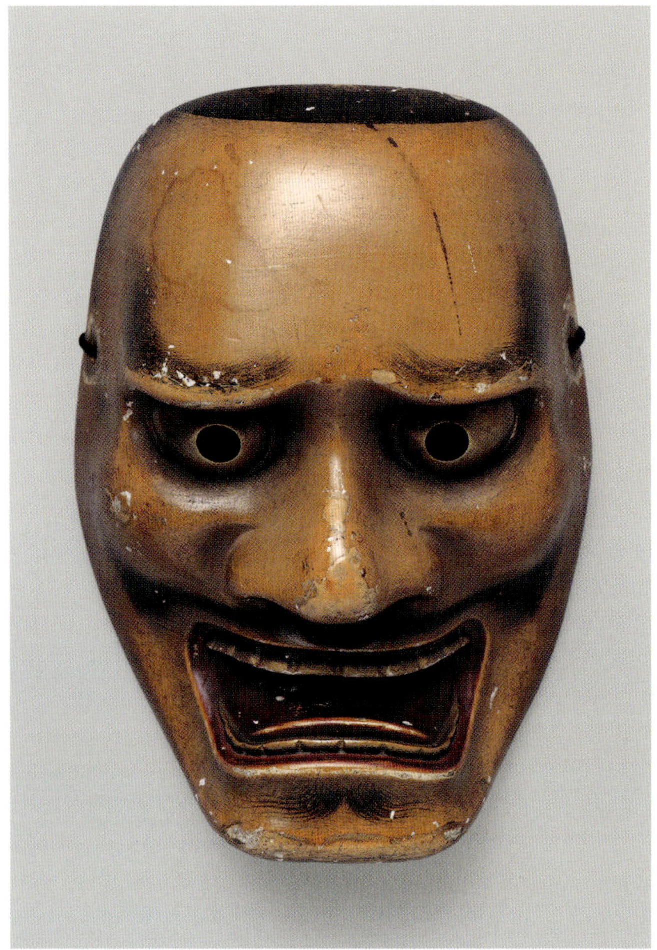

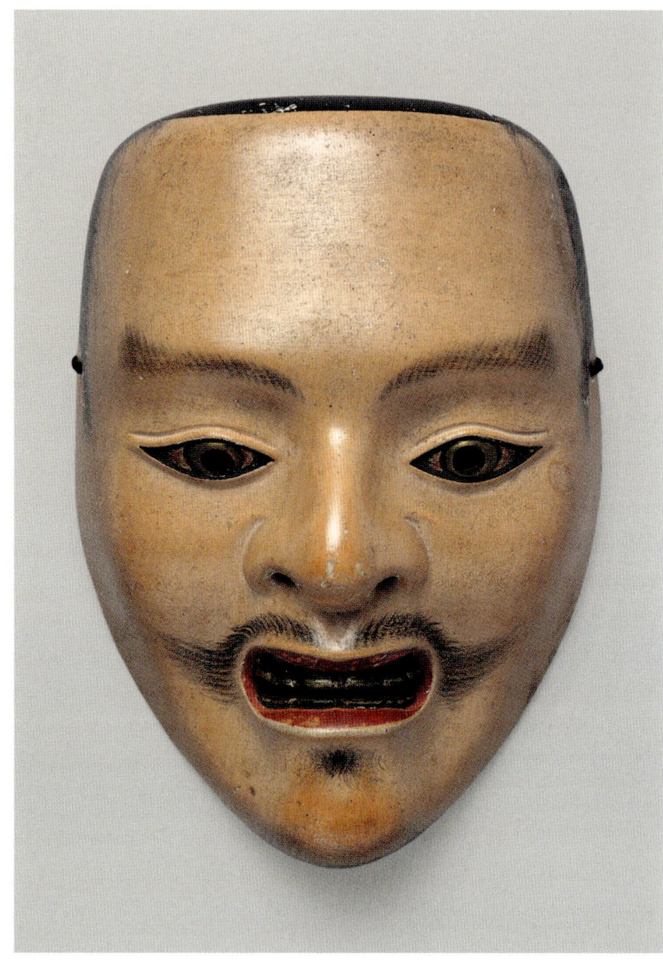

14 *Kurohige* mask
Edo period, 18th century
National Noh Theatre

15 *Shintai* mask
Edo period, 17th–18th century
National Noh Theatre

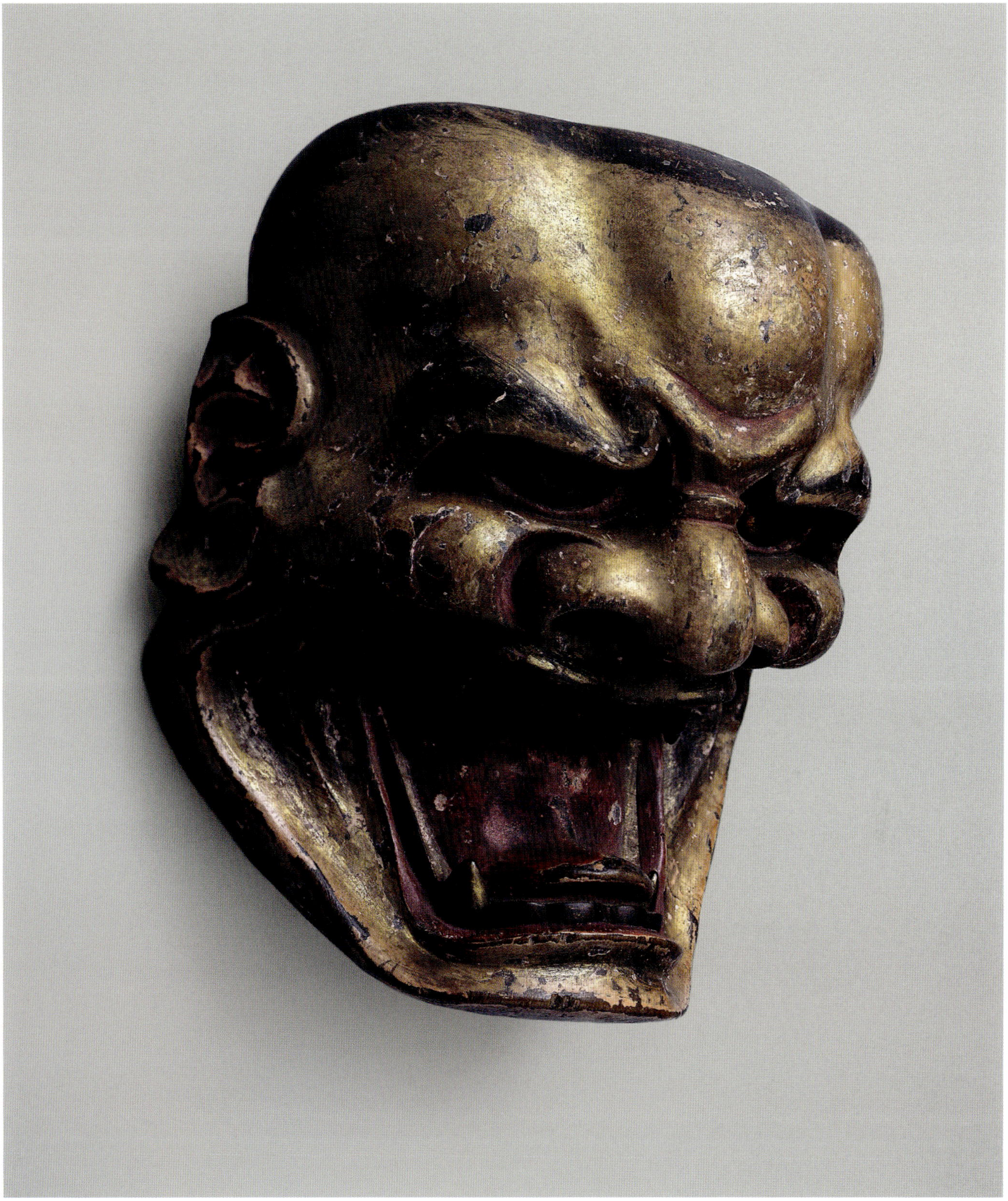

16 *Shishiguchi* mask
Muromachi period, 15th–16th century
National Noh Theatre

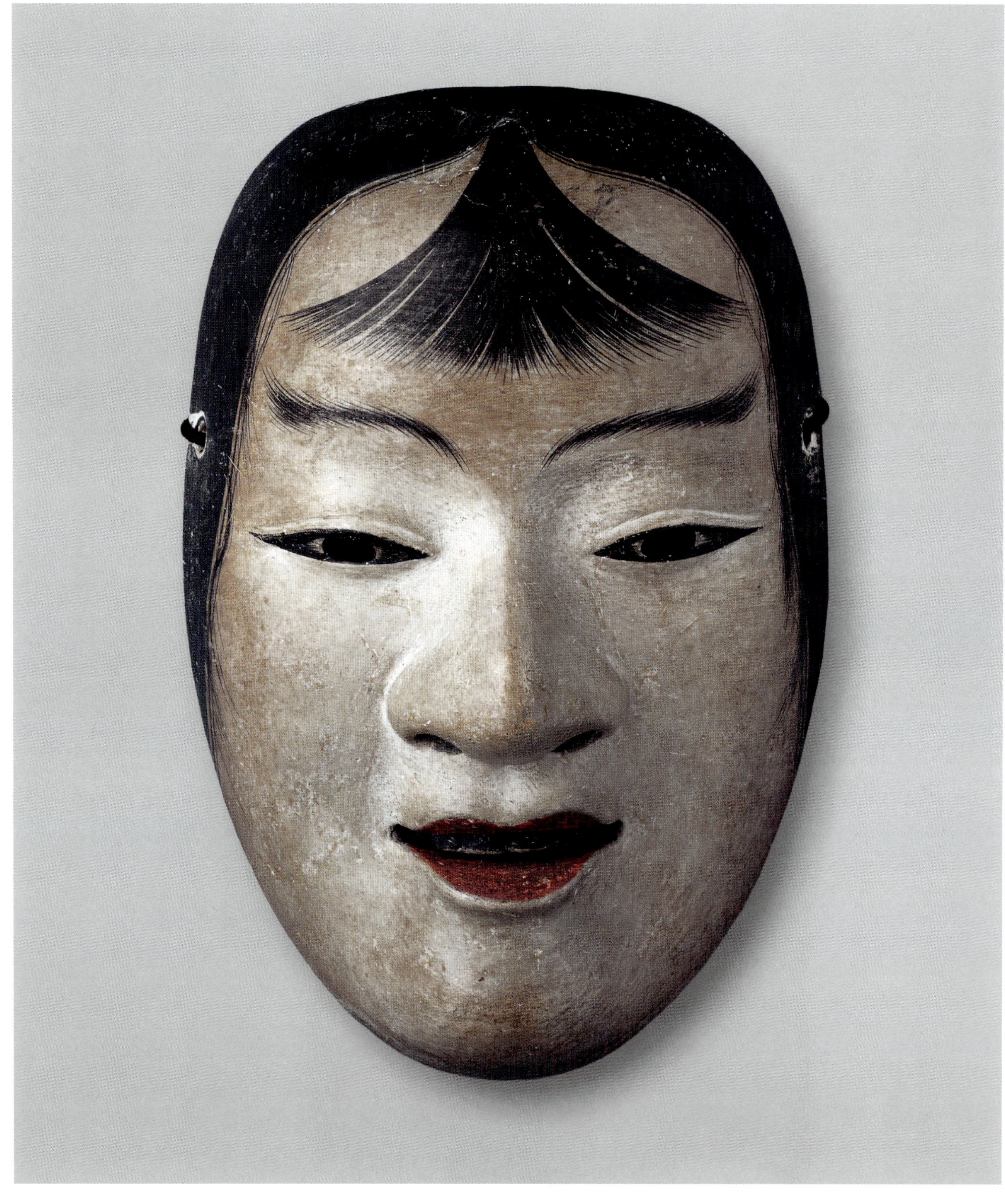

17 *Kasshiki (kokasshiki)* mask
Muromachi period, 16th century
Agency for Cultural Affairs of Japan

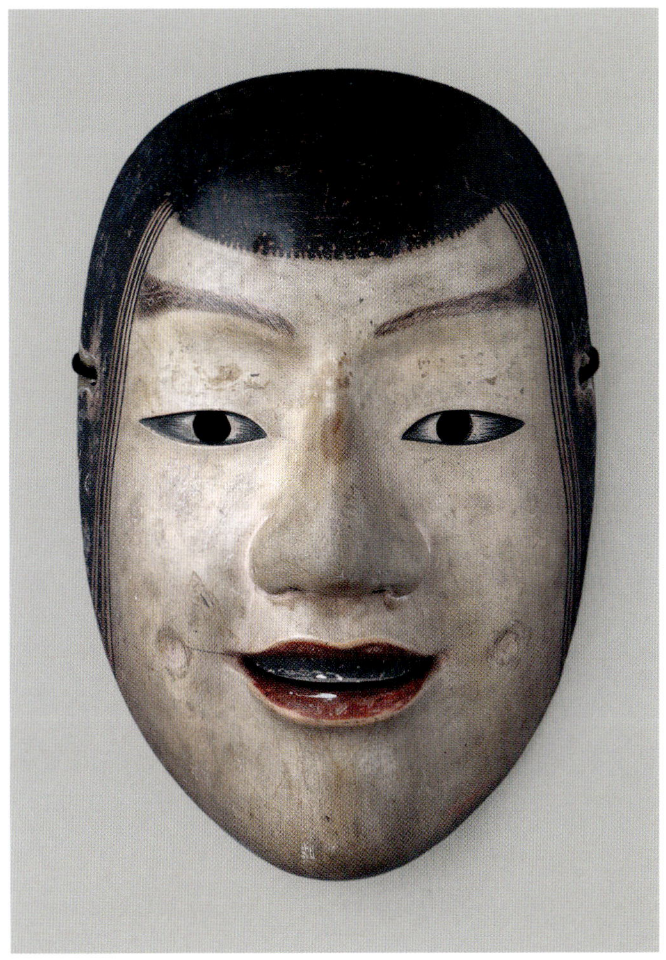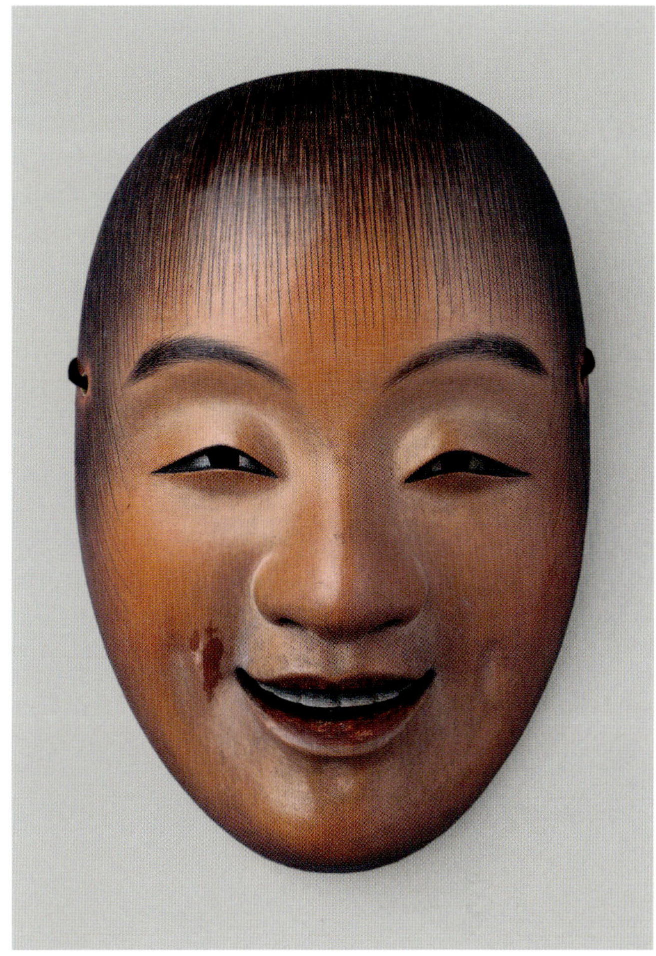

18 *Ōkasshiki* mask
Edo period, 19th century
Agency for Cultural Affairs of Japan

19 *Shōjō* mask
Edo period, 18th century
Agency for Cultural Affairs of Japan

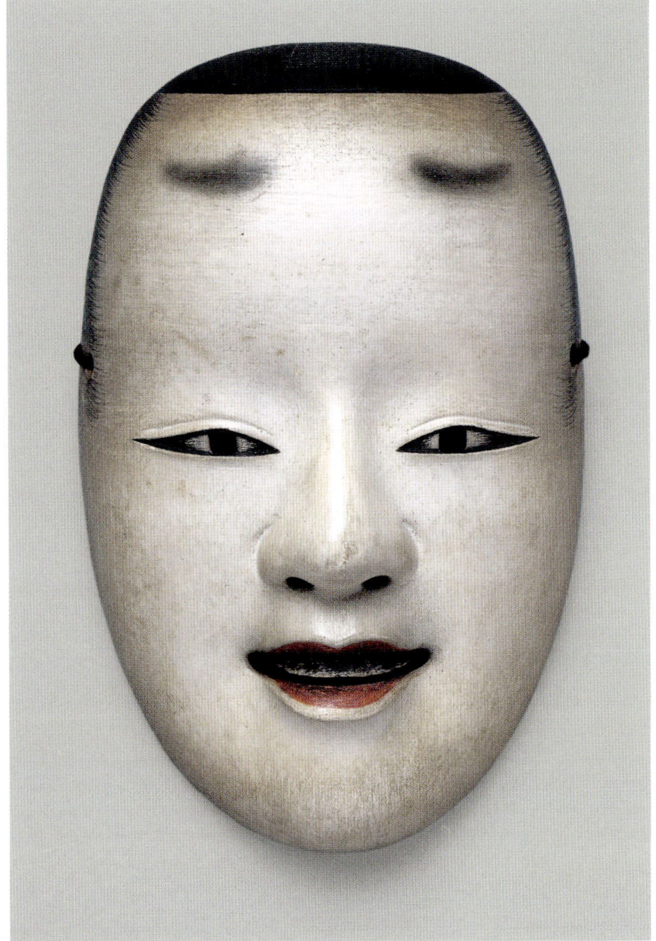

20 *Atsumori* mask
Edo period, 18th–19th century
National Noh Theatre

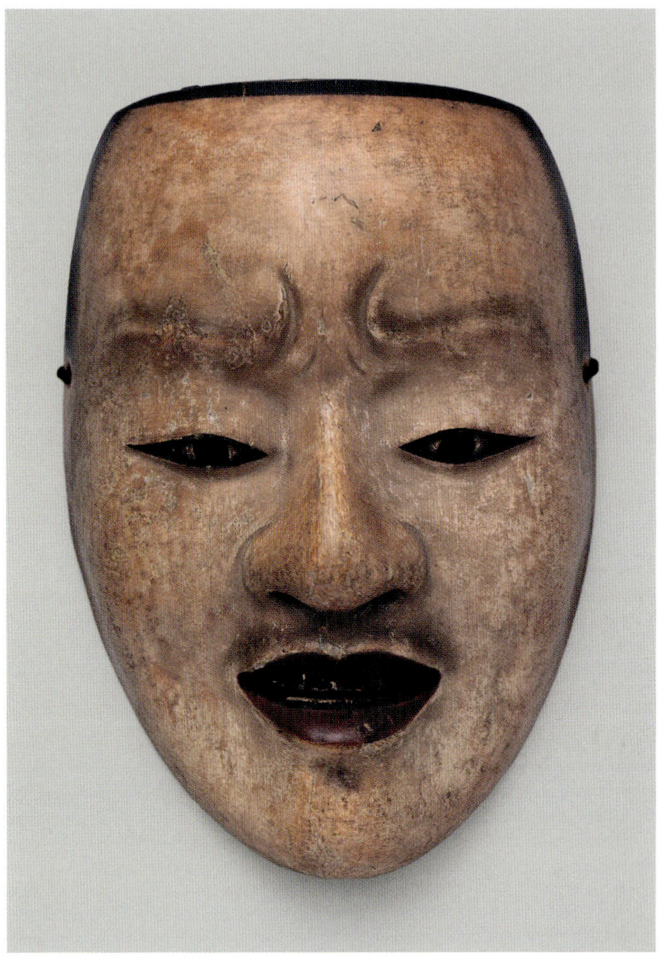

21 *Kantan otoko* mask
Edo period, 18th century
National Noh Theatre

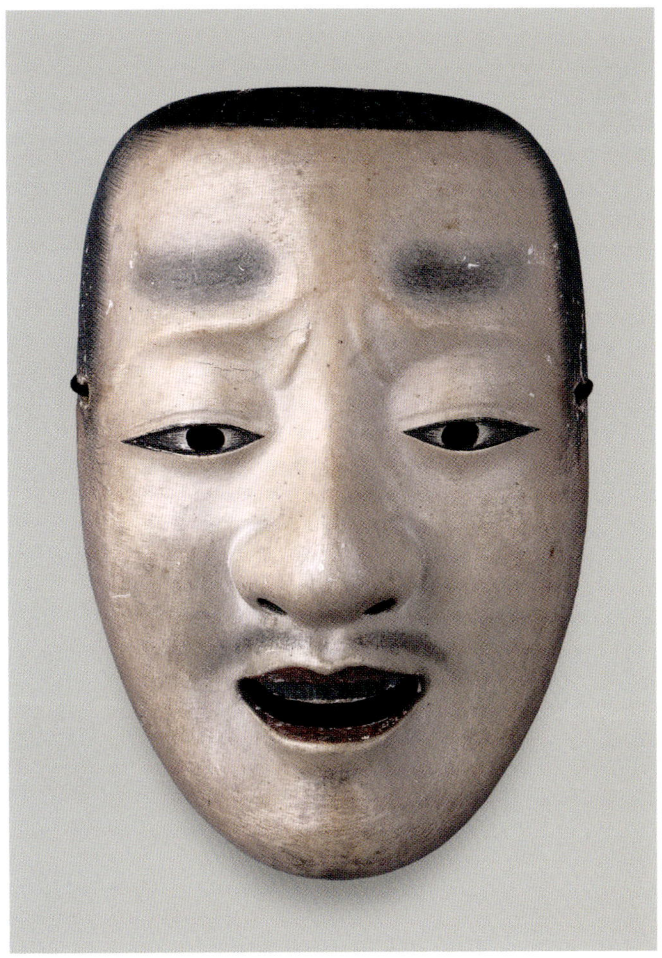

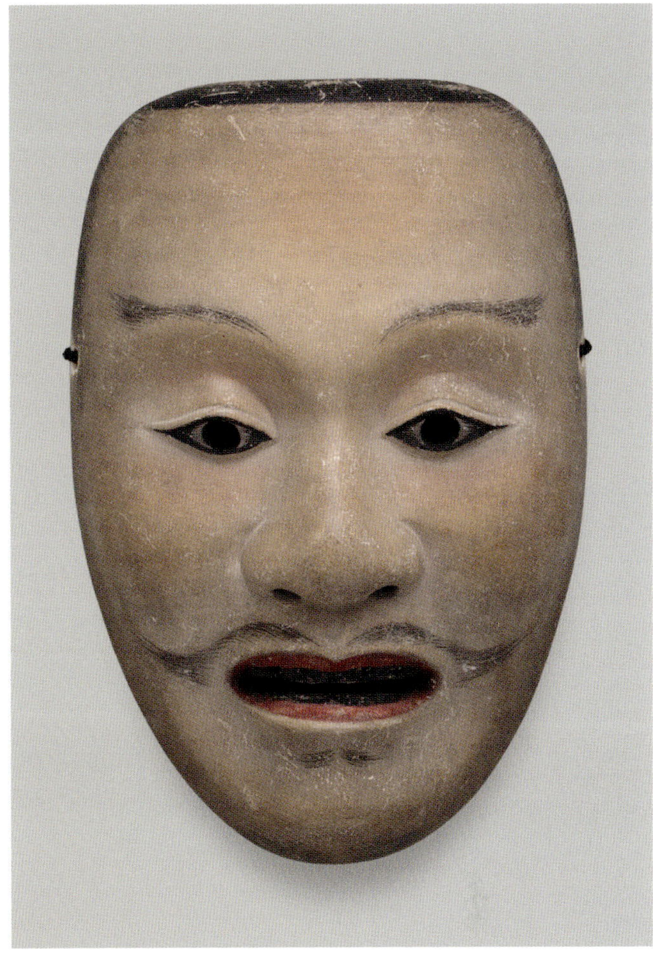

22 *Chūjō* mask
Edo period, 17th century
National Noh Theatre

23 *Heida* mask
Edo period, 17th–18th century
National Noh Theatre

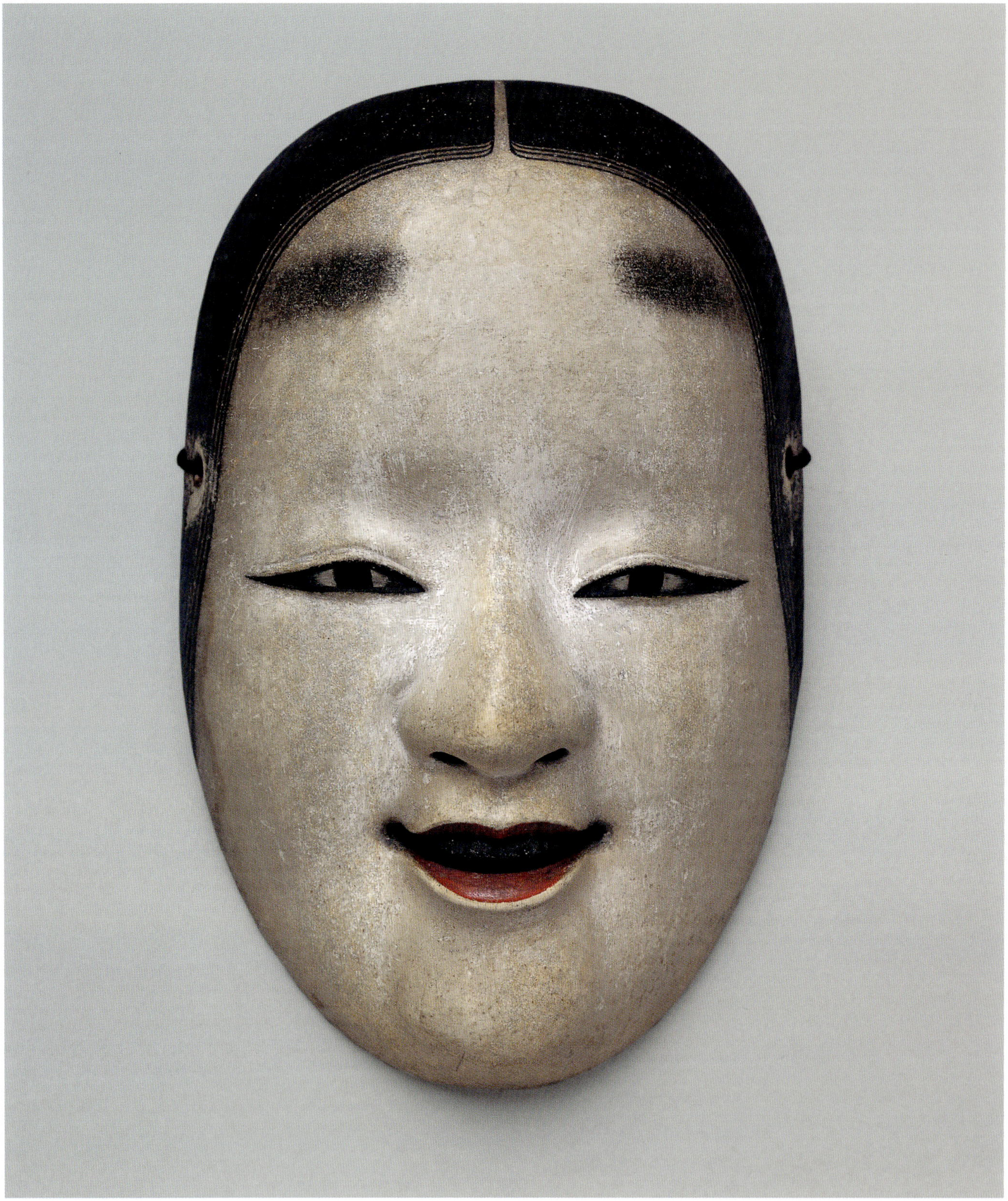

24 *Ko-omote* mask

Edo period, 17th century
National Noh Theatre

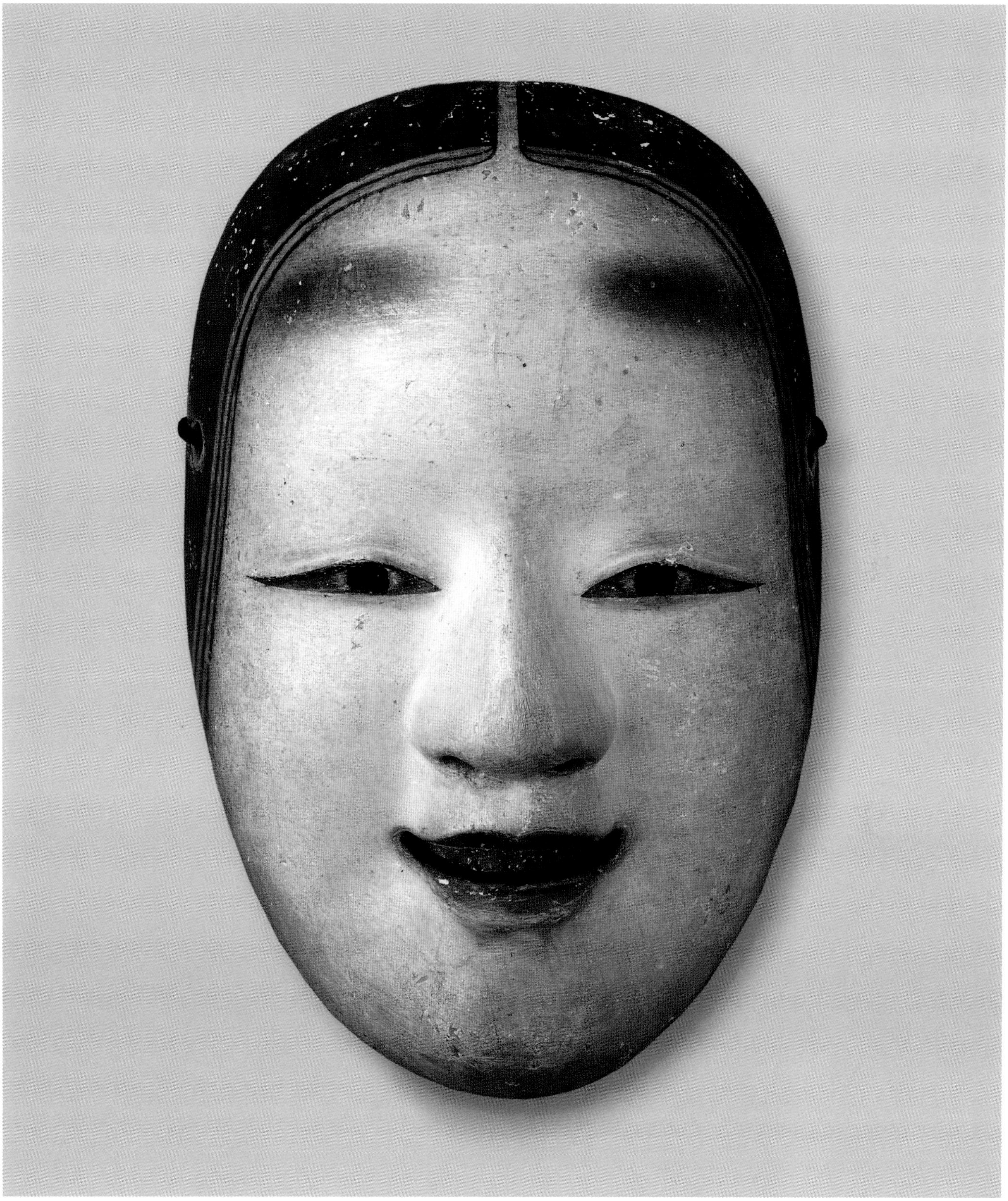

25 *Manbi* mask
Momoyama–Edo period, 16th–17th century
Agency for Cultural Affairs of Japan

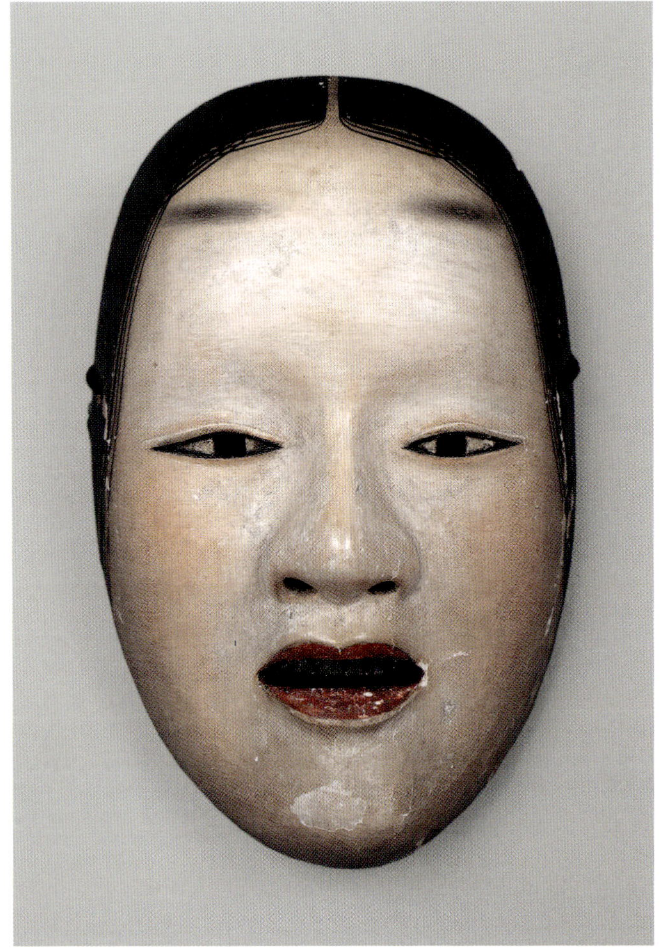

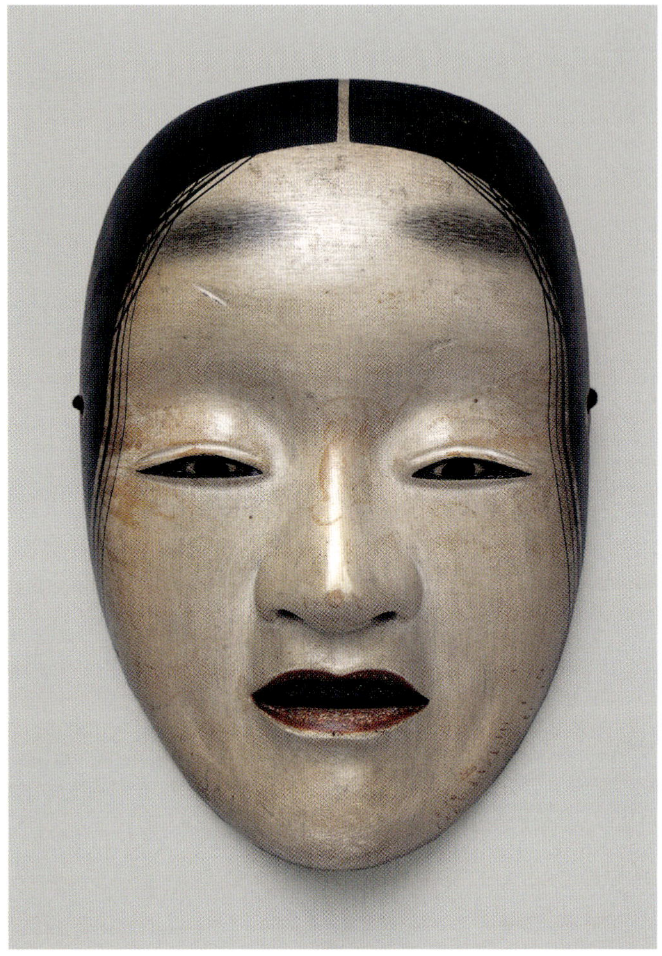

26 *Nakizō* mask
Edo period, 17th century
Agency for Cultural Affairs of Japan

27 *Shakumi* mask
Edo period, 17th–18th century
National Noh Theatre

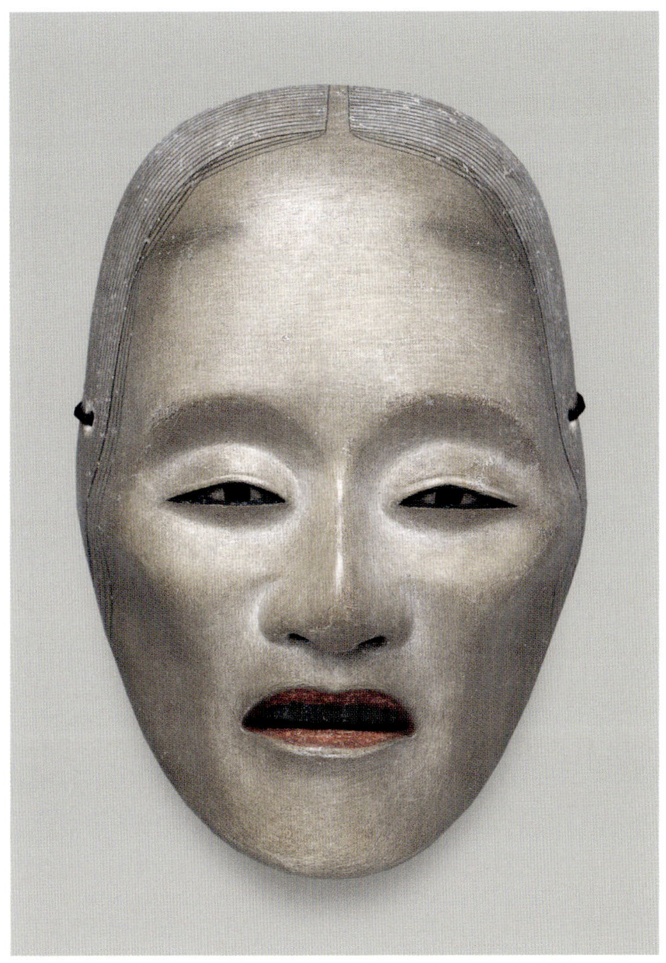

28 *Rōjo* mask
Edo period, 18th century
National Noh Theatre

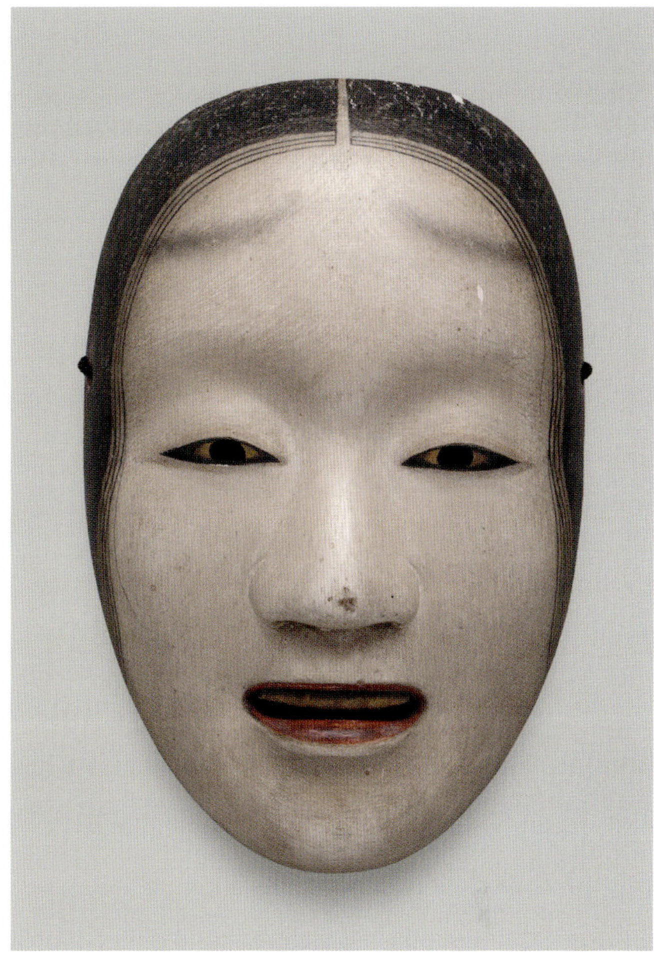

29 *Deigan* mask
Edo period, 17th century
National Noh Theatre

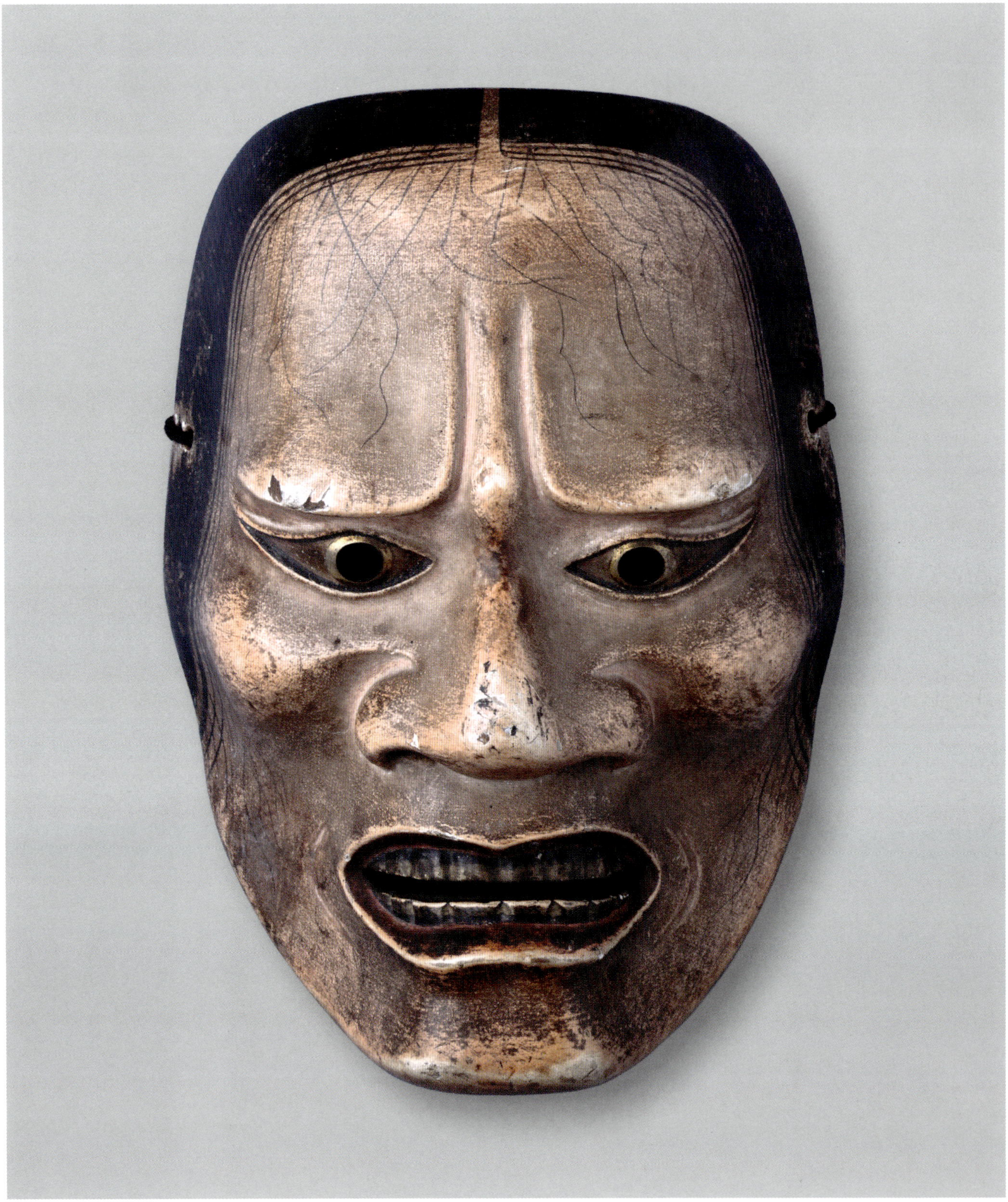

30 *Hashihime* mask
Edo period, 18th century
Agency for Cultural Affairs of Japan

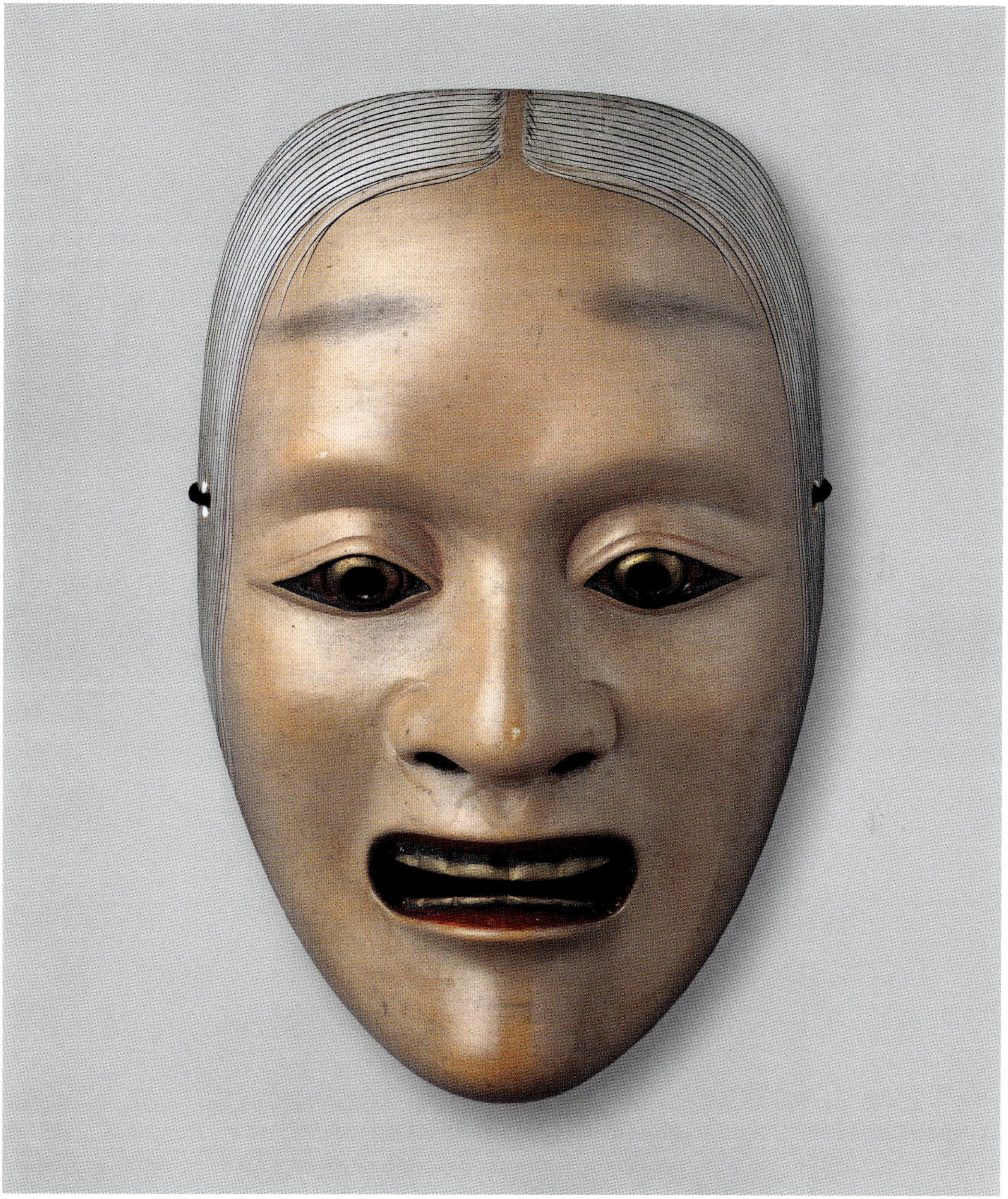

31 *Yamanba* mask

Edo period, 18th century
National Noh Theatre

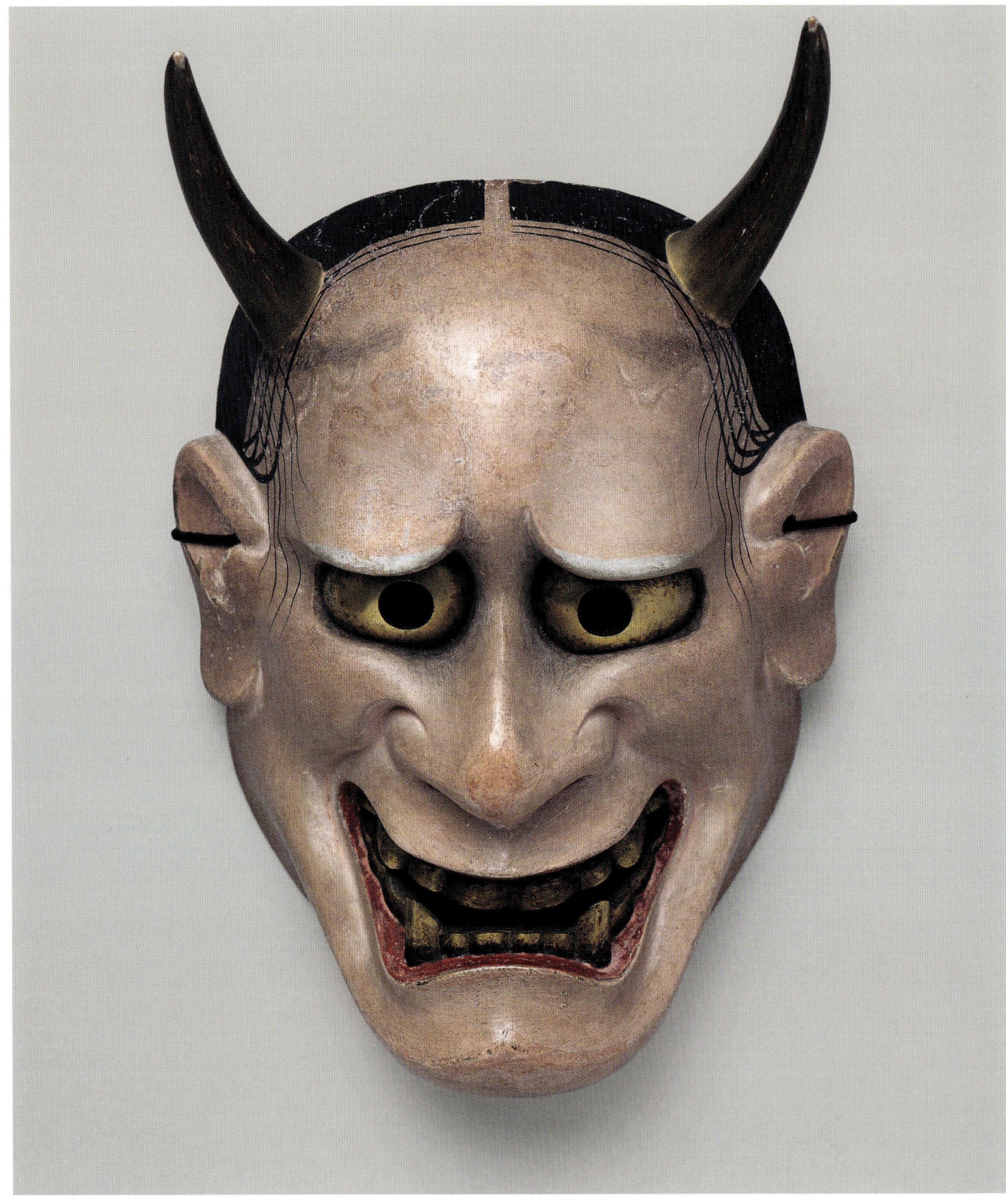

32 *Hannya* mask
Edo period, 18th century
National Noh Theatre

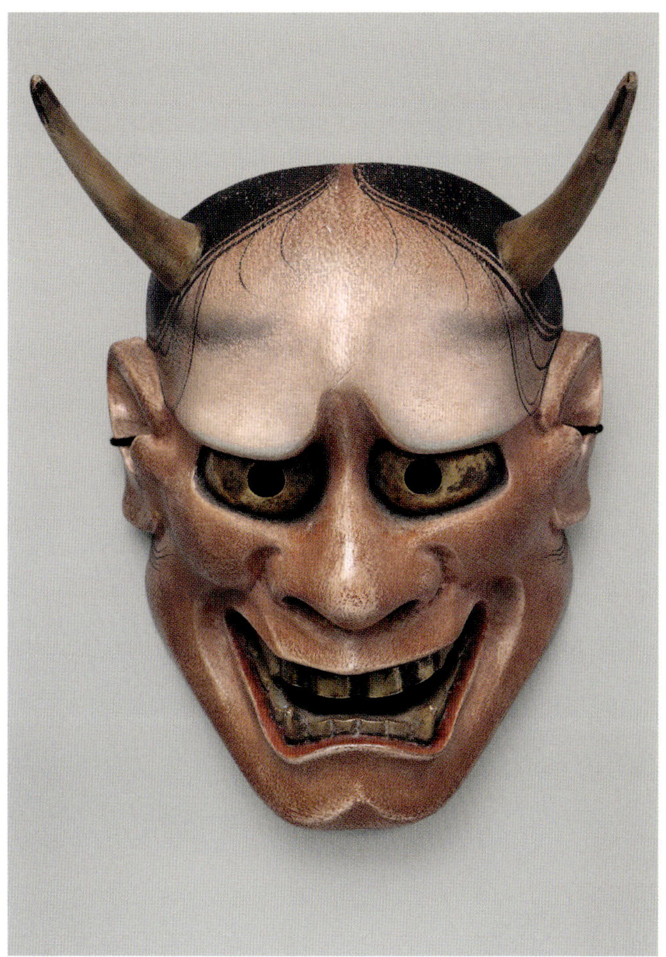

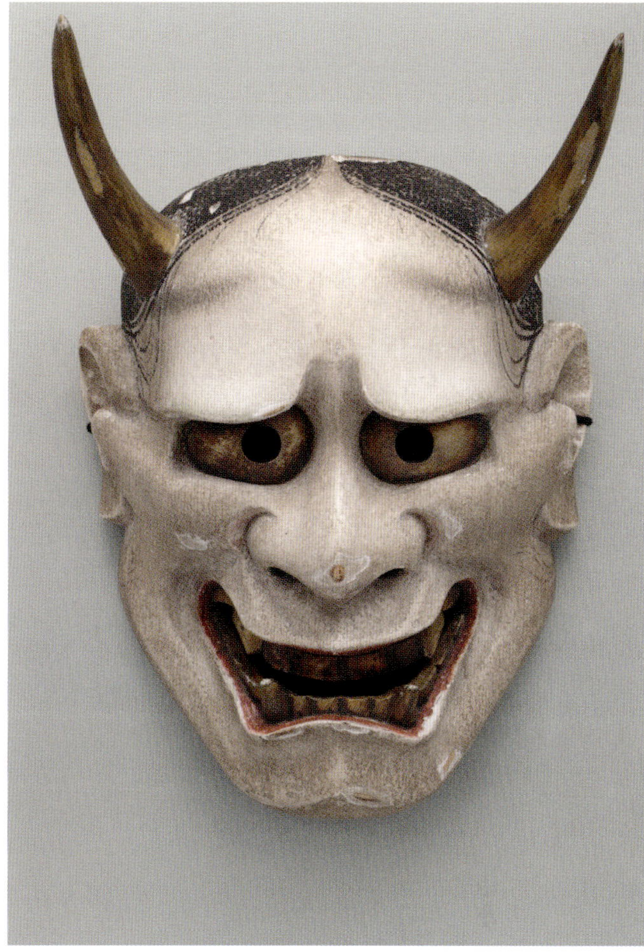

33 *Aka (red) hannya* mask
Edo period, 18th–19th century
National Noh Theatre

34 *Shiro (white) hannya* mask
Edo period, 18th–19th century
National Noh Theatre

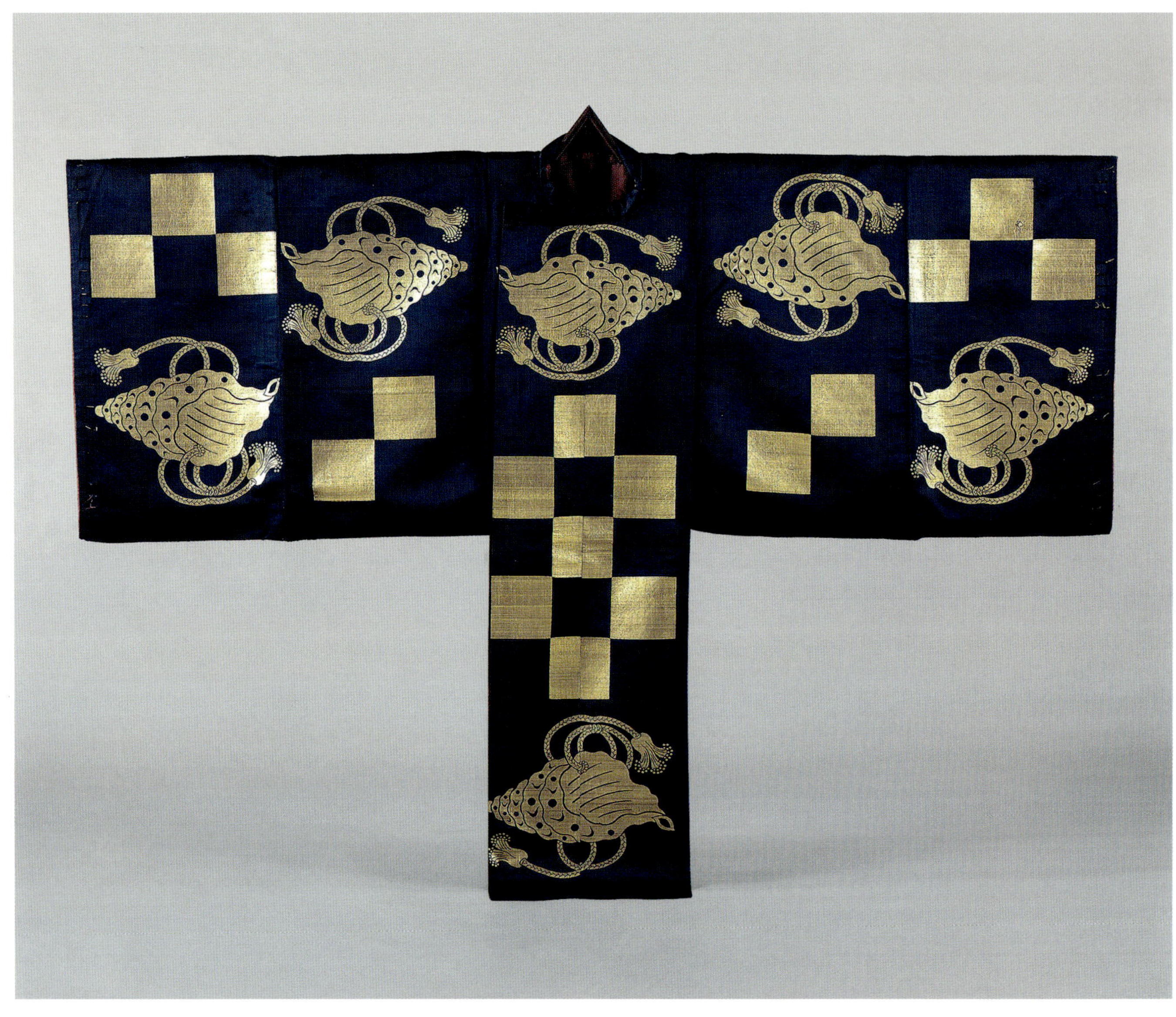

35 Lined *kariginu* with design of cobblestones
and conch shells on dark blue ground

Edo period, 19th century
Agency for Cultural Affairs of Japan

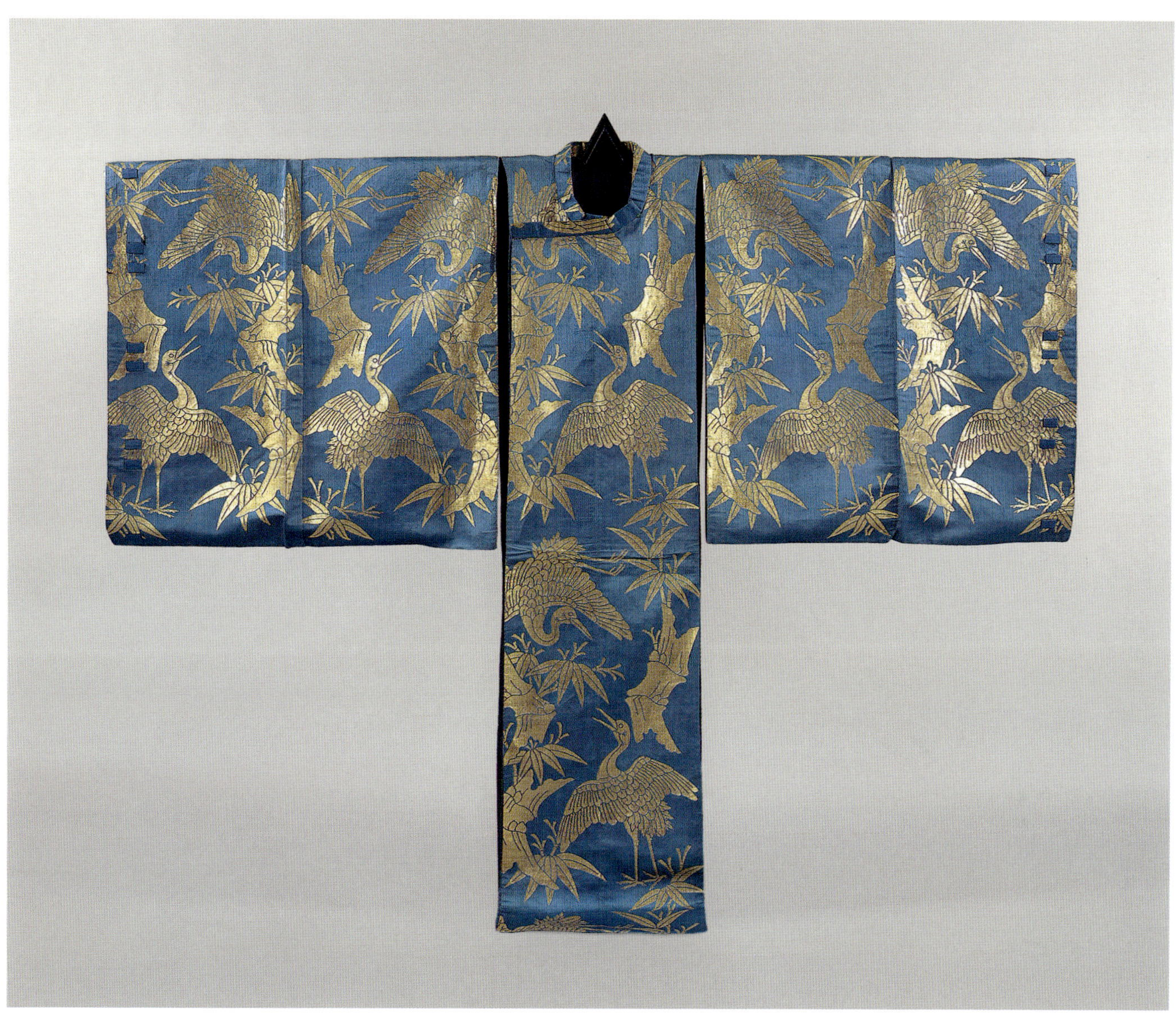

36 Lined *kariginu* with design of bamboo
    and cranes on light blue ground

Edo period, 19th century
Agency for Cultural Affairs of Japan

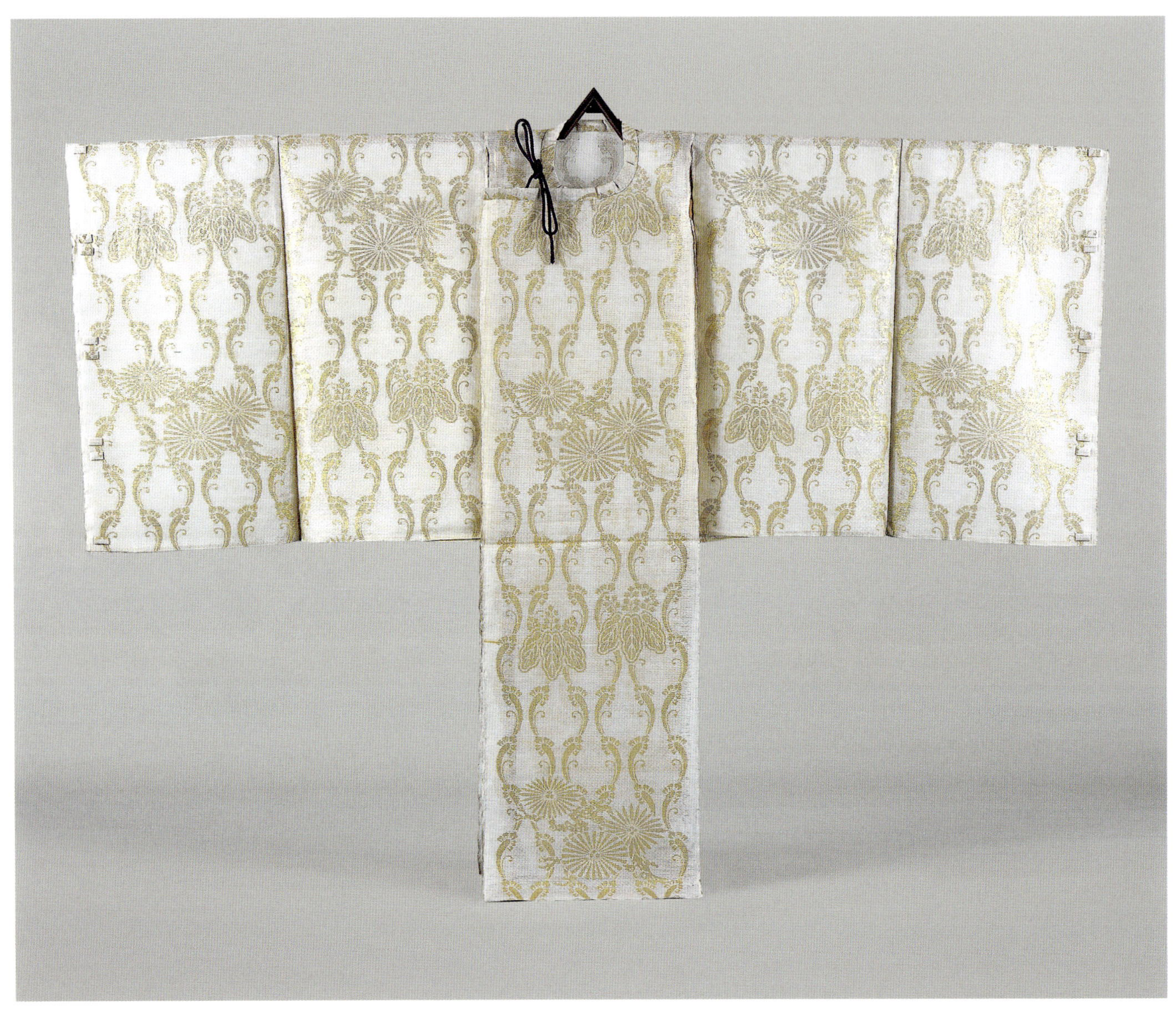

37 Unlined *kariginu* with design of undulating
vertical lines with clove-shaped crests,
paulownia and Chinese pine on white ground

Edo period, 18th–19th century
National Noh Theatre

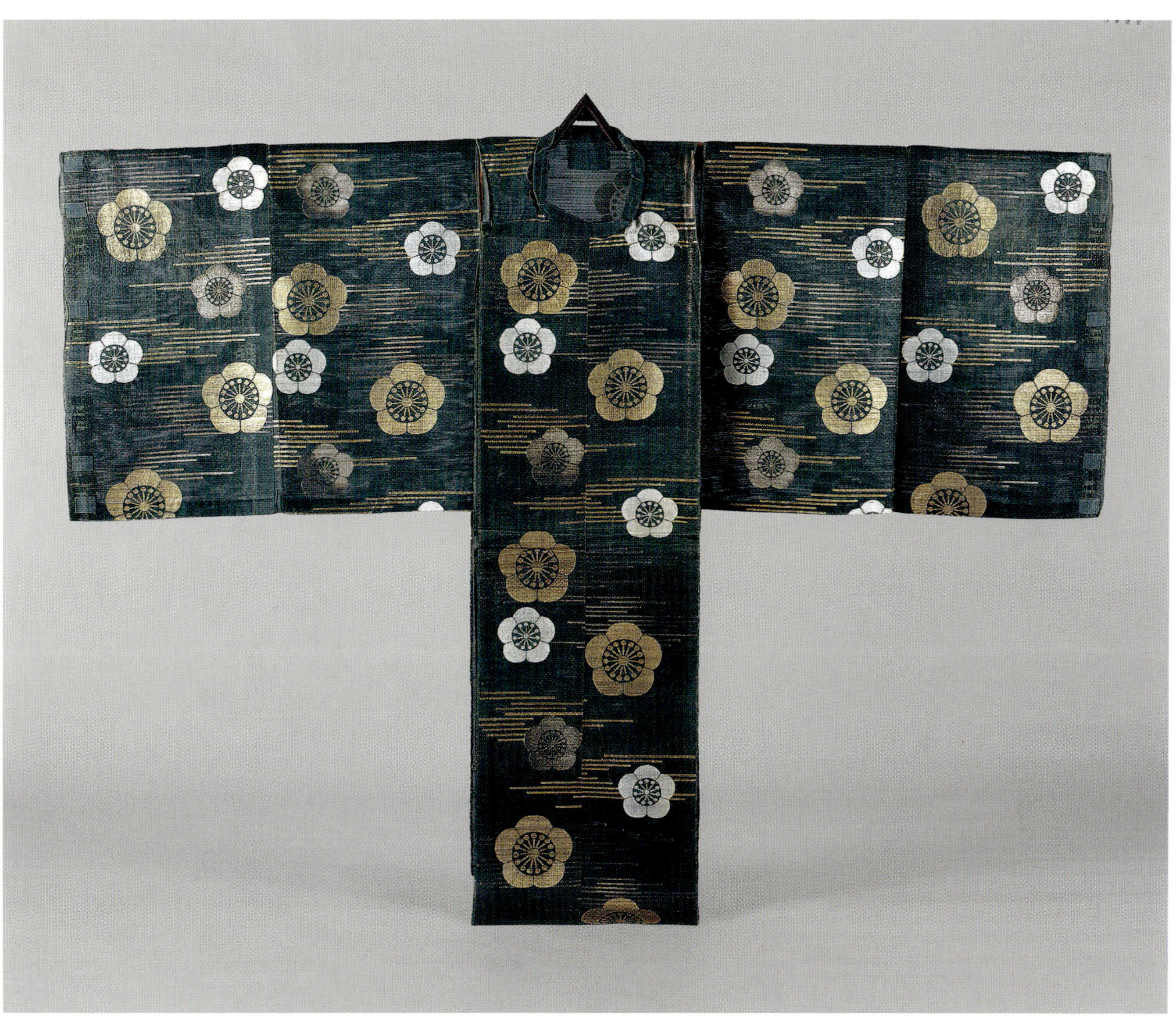

38 Unlined *kariginu* with design of plum blossoms
in mist on yellow-green ground

Edo period, 19th century
Agency for Cultural Affairs of Japan

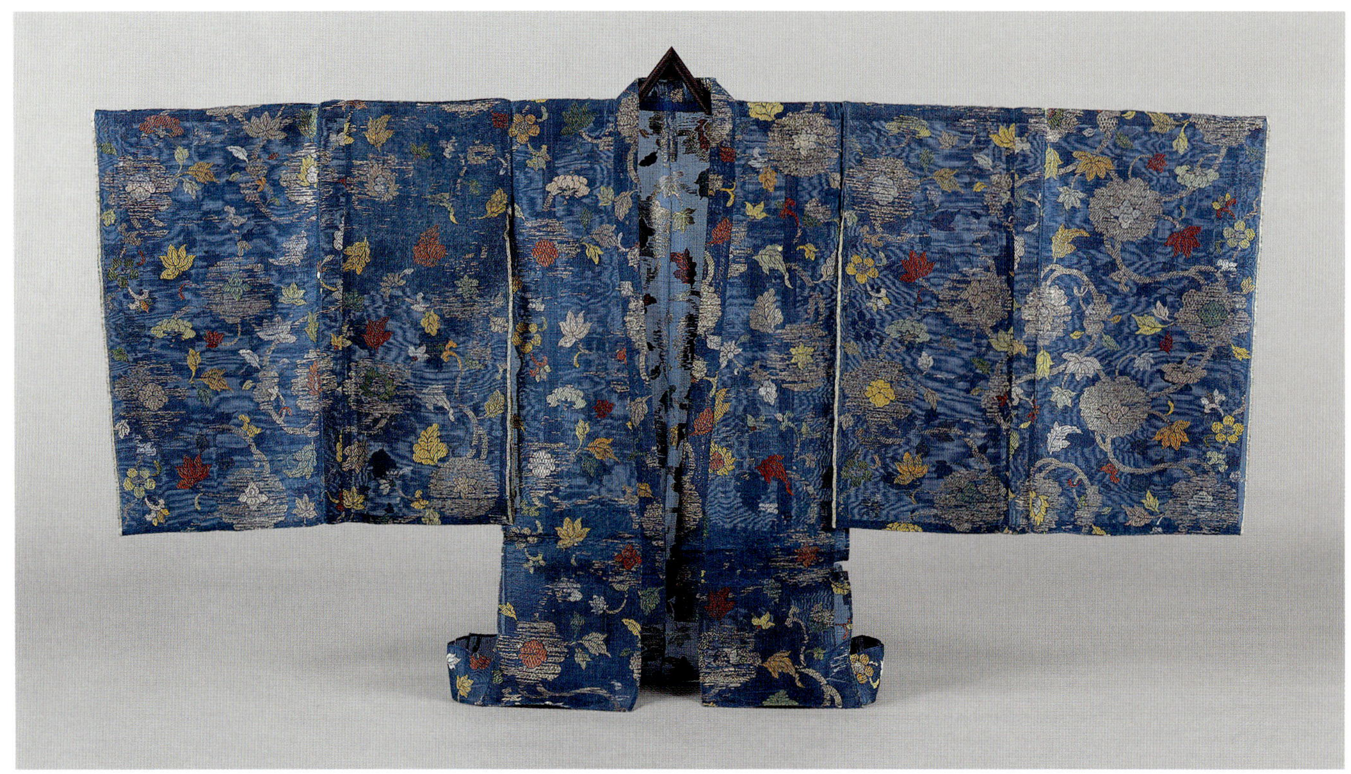

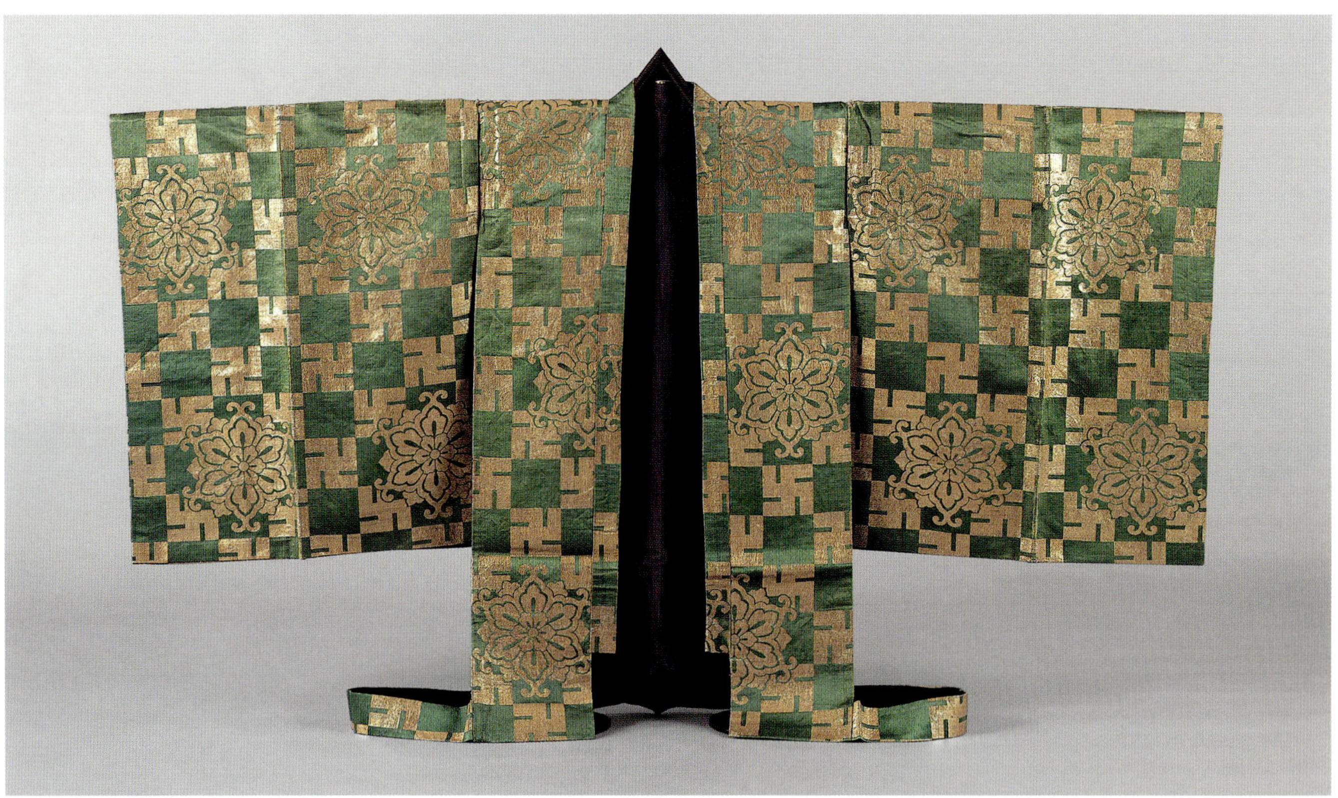

39 Unlined *happi* with design of
floral arabesques on blue ground

Edo period, 18th century
National Noh Theatre

40 Lined *happi* with design of Buddhist swastika
and arabesques on yellow-green ground

Edo period, 19th century
National Noh Theatre

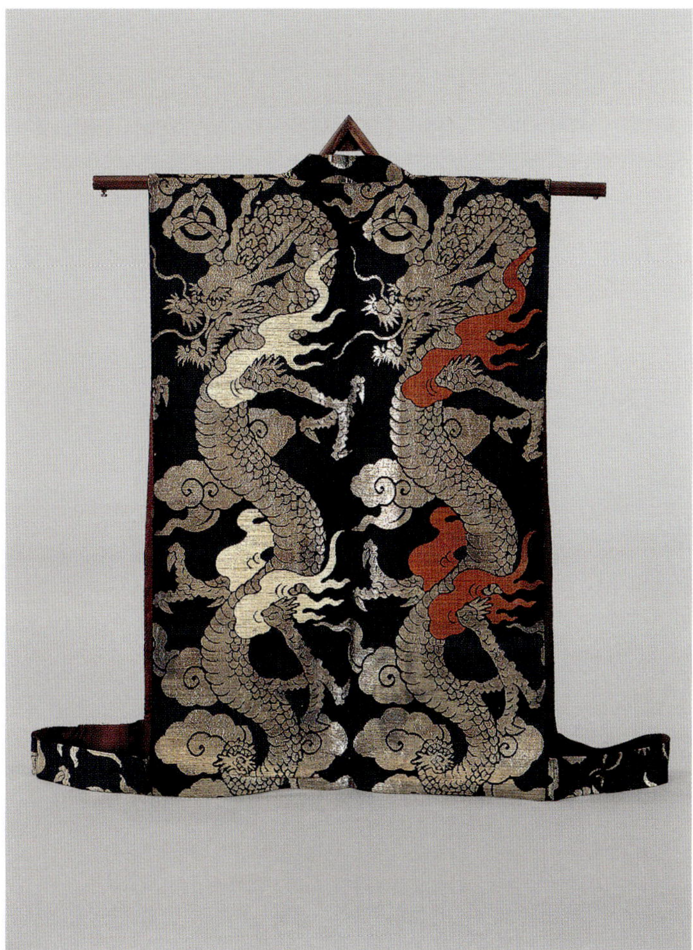

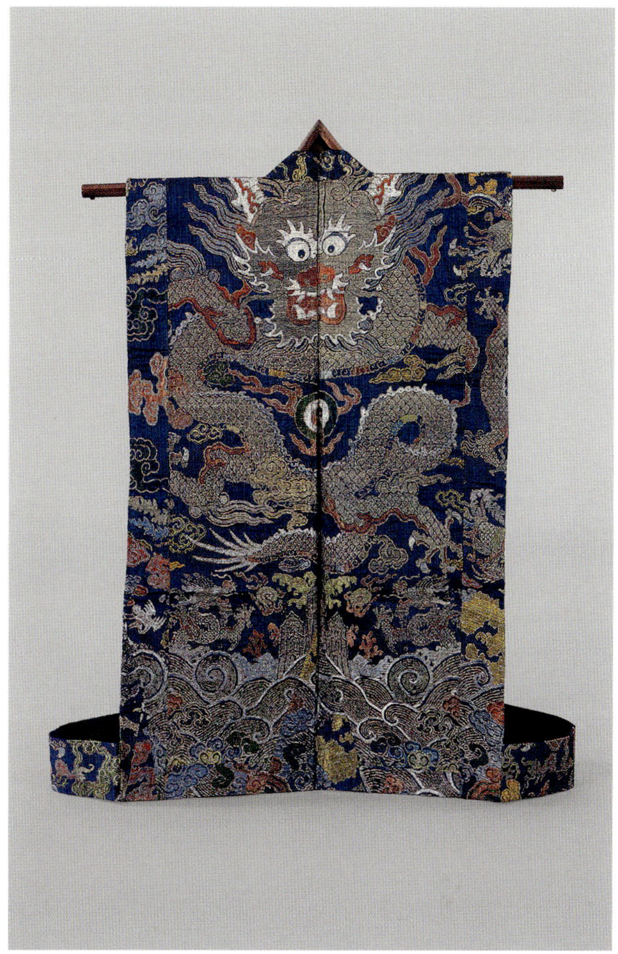

41 *Sobatsugi* with design of dragons
in clouds on dark blue ground

Edo period, 18th–19th century
Agency for Cultural Affairs of Japan

42 *Sobatsugi* with design of steep mountains
and dragon on dark blue ground

Edo period, 18th–19th century
Agency for Cultural Affairs of Japan

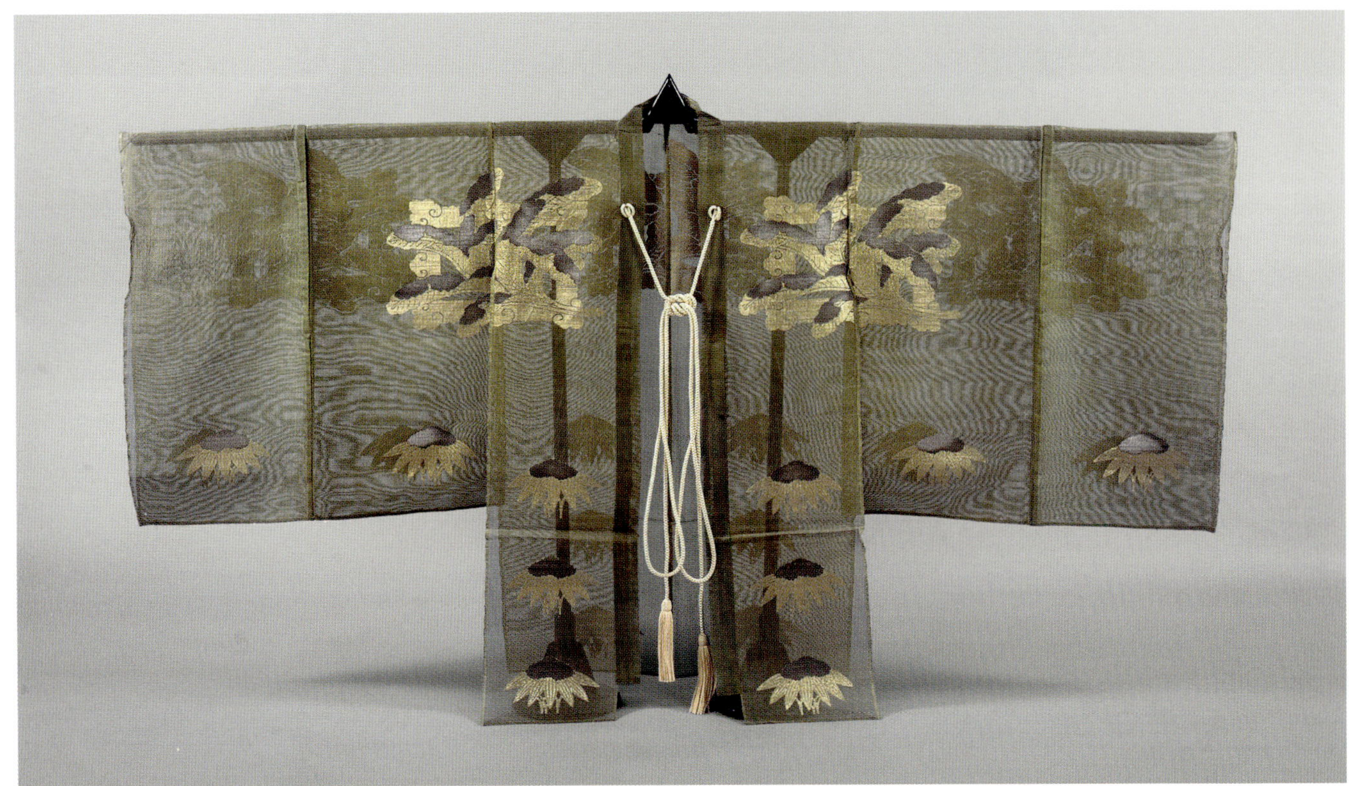

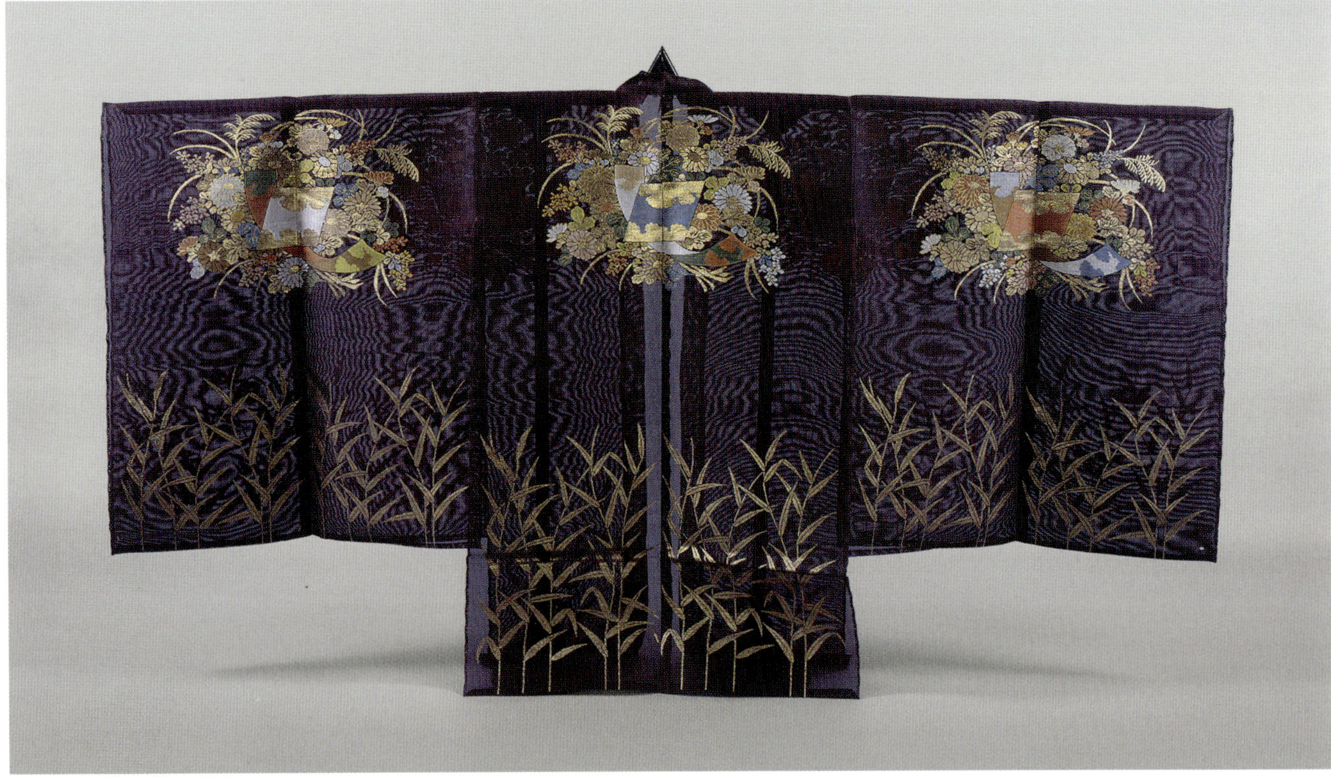

43 *Chōken* with design of Japanese banana
leaves on a trellis and snow-laden
bamboo leaves on light green ground

Edo period, 18th–19th century
Agency for Cultural Affairs of Japan

44 *Chōken* with design of decorative
poem cards, flower bouquets and
reeds on purple ground

Edo period, 18th–19th century
Agency for Cultural Affairs of Japan

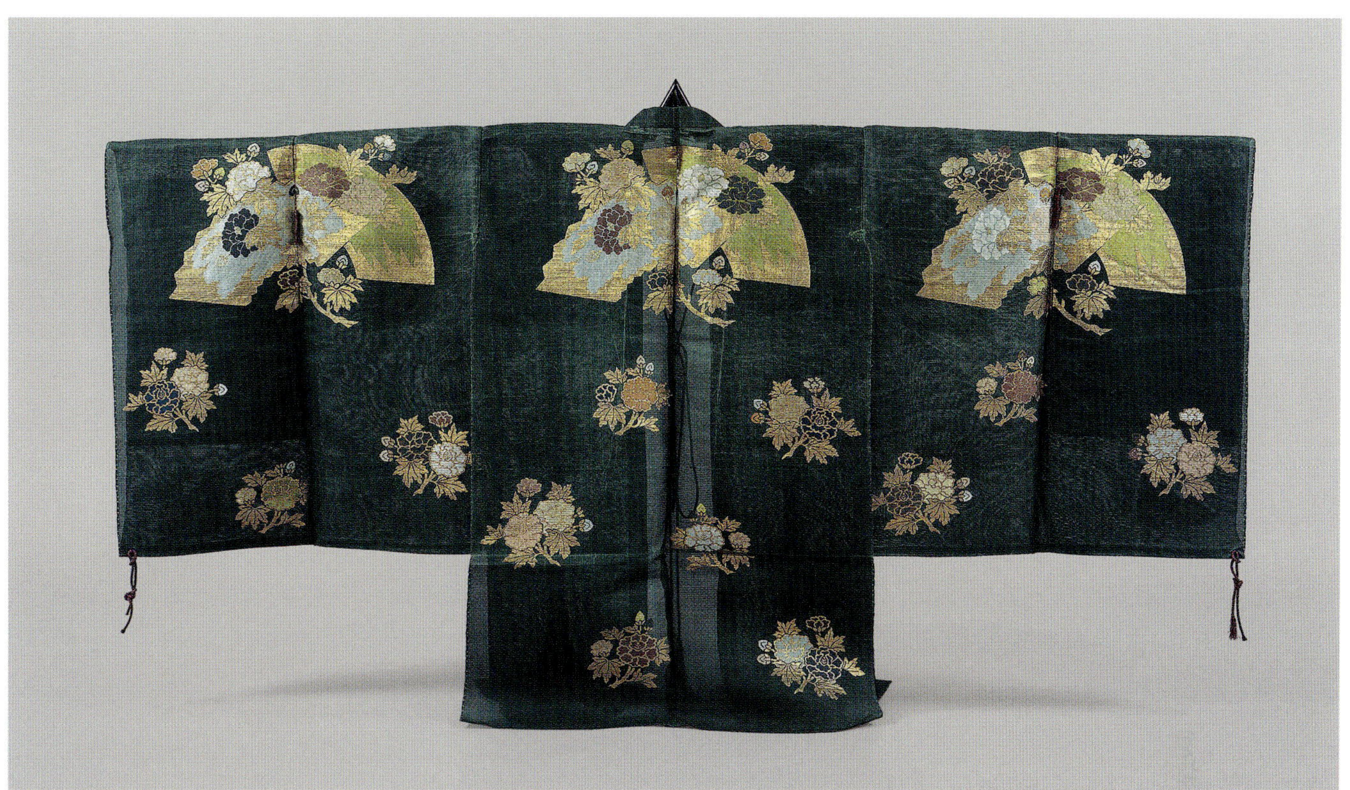

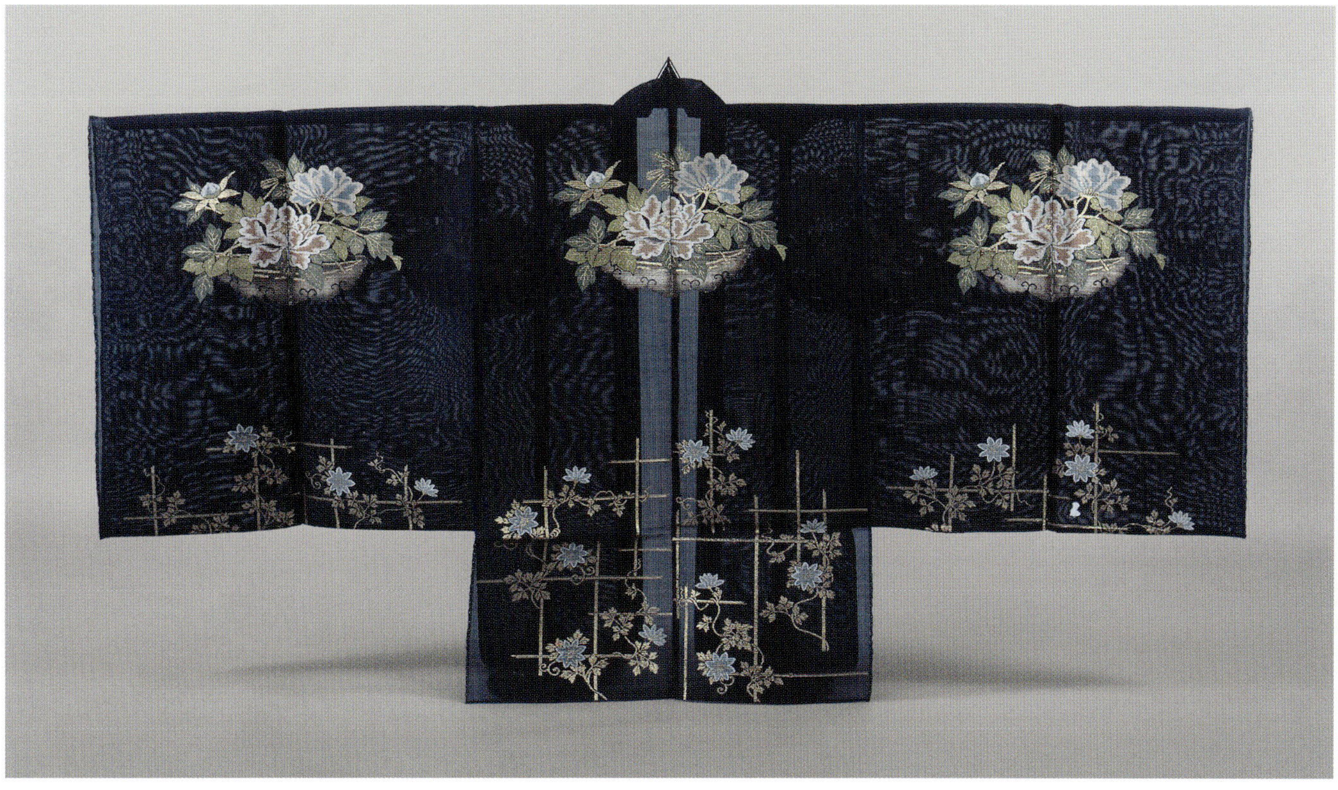

45 *Chōken* with design of fans and
peonies on yellow-green ground

Edo period, 18th–19th century
National Noh Theatre

46 *Chōken* with design of peony flowers
in vases and Chinese clematis
on a fence on blue ground

Edo period, 19th century
Agency for Cultural Affairs of Japan

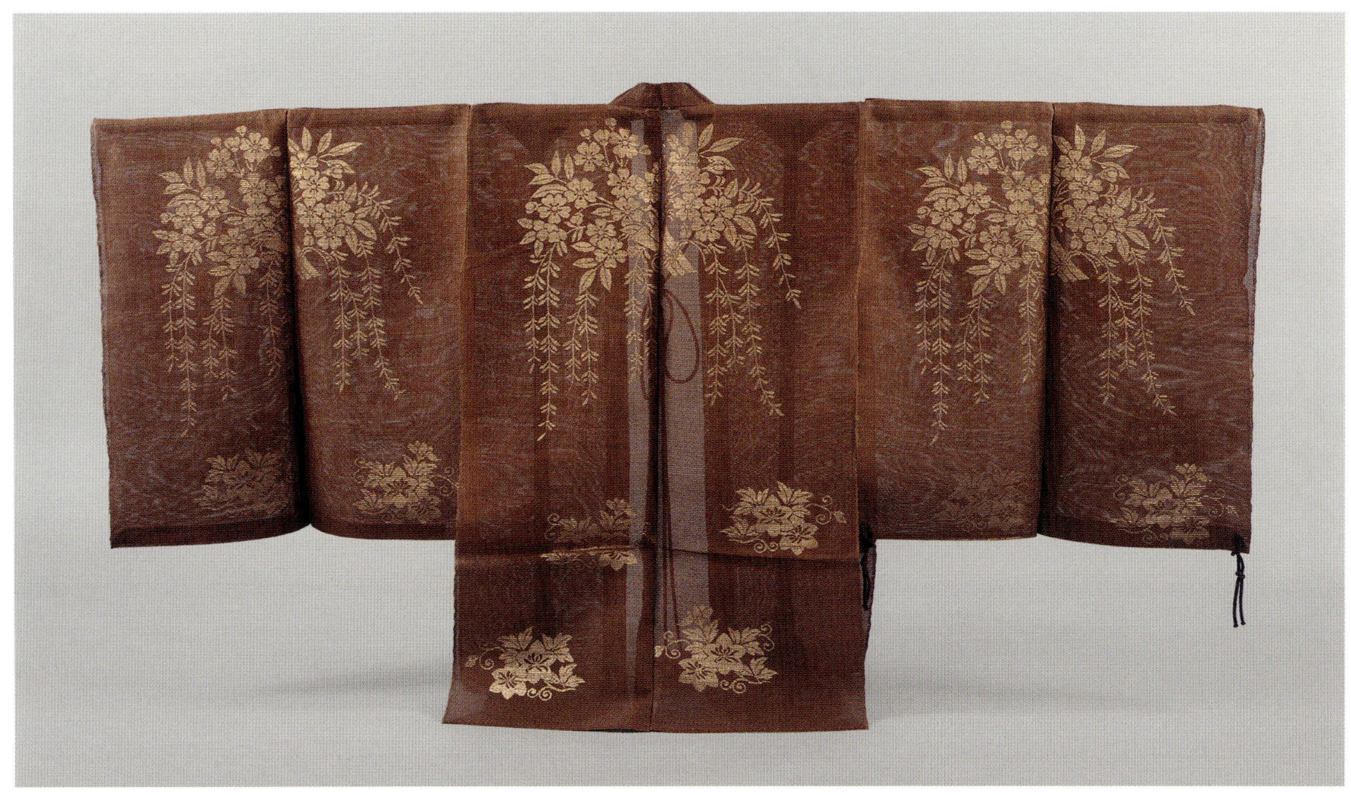

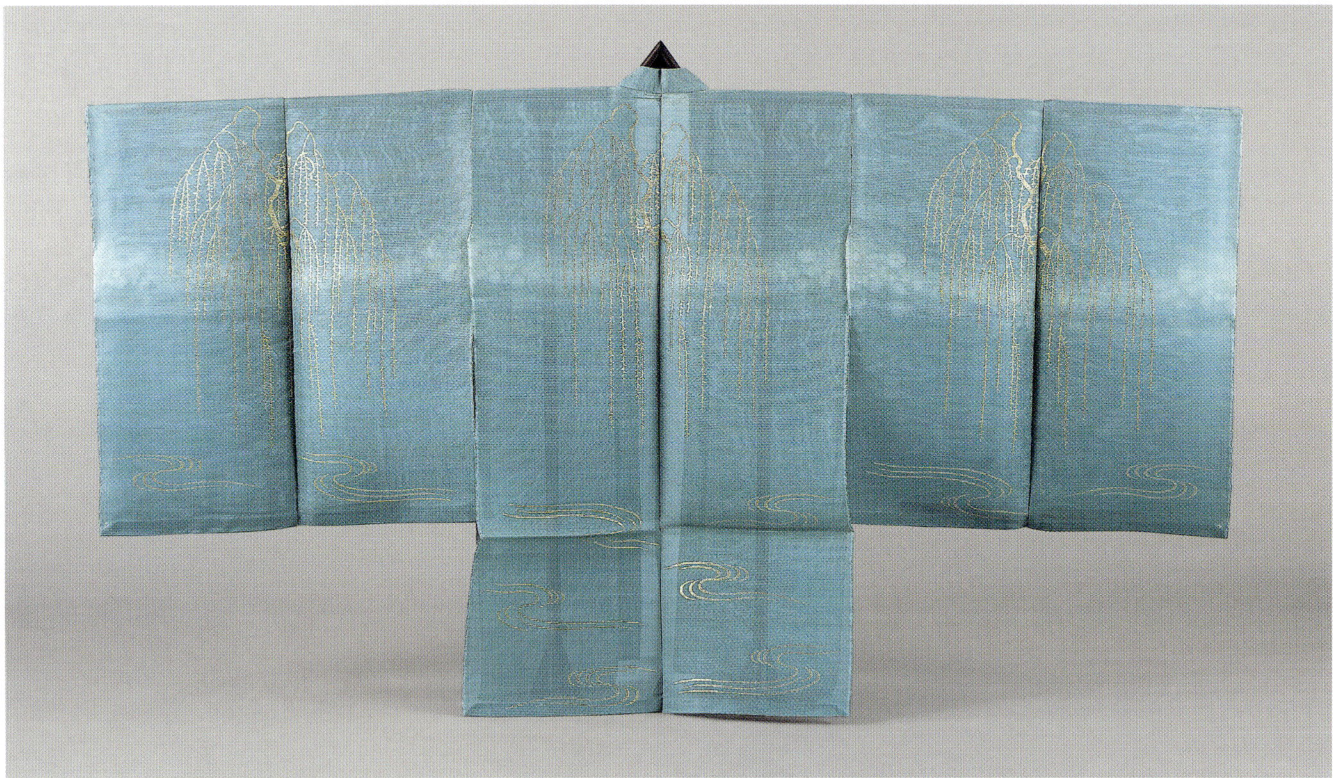

47 *Chōken* with design of weeping cherries and Chinese clematis on birch-coloured ground

Edo period, 18th–19th century
National Noh Theatre

48 *Chōken* with design of weeping willows and flowing water on light blue ground

Edo–Meiji period, 19th century
National Noh Theatre

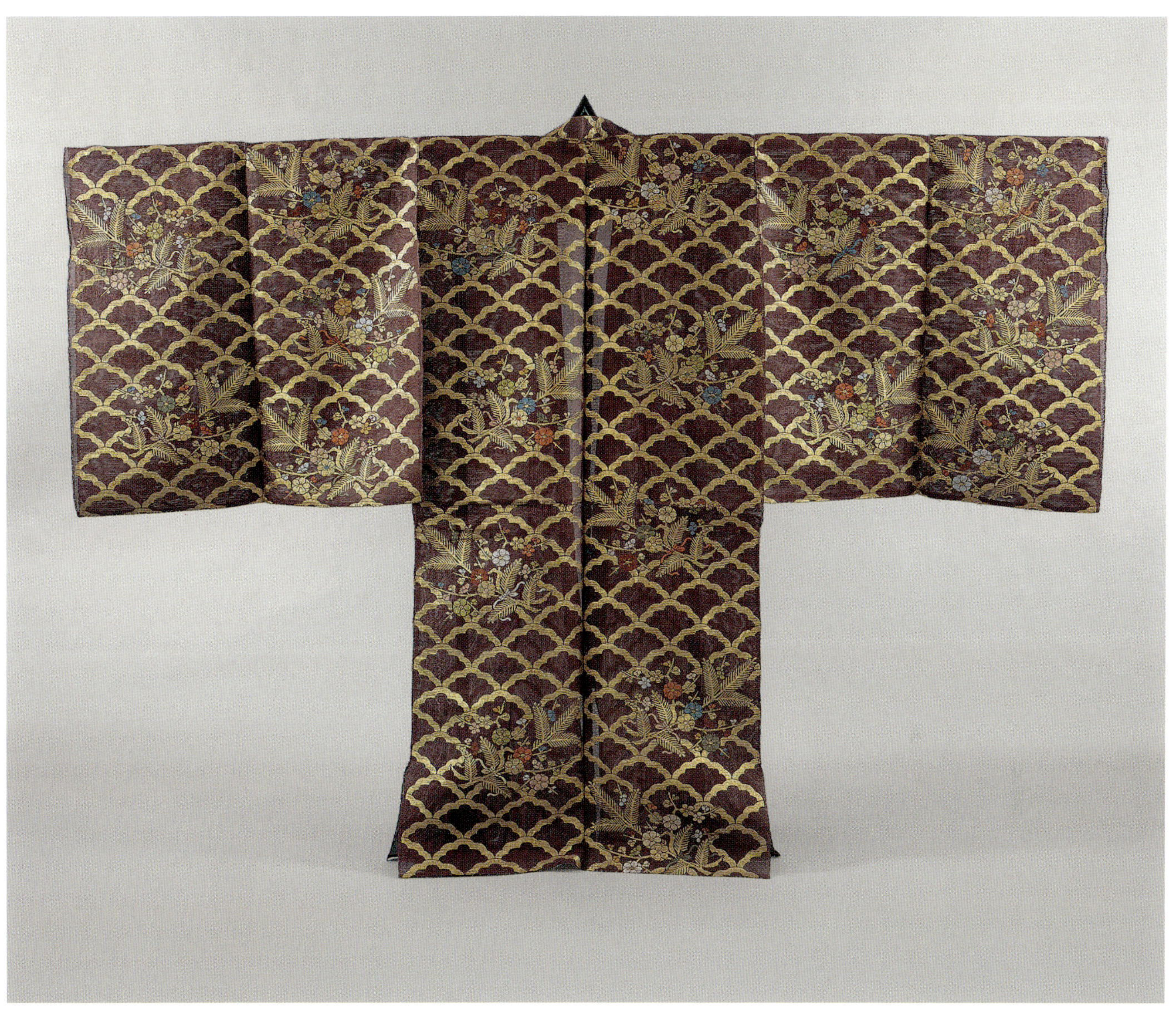

49 *Maiginu* with design of plum
and young pines on ocean waves
on purple ground

Edo period, 18th–19th century
Agency for Cultural Affairs of Japan

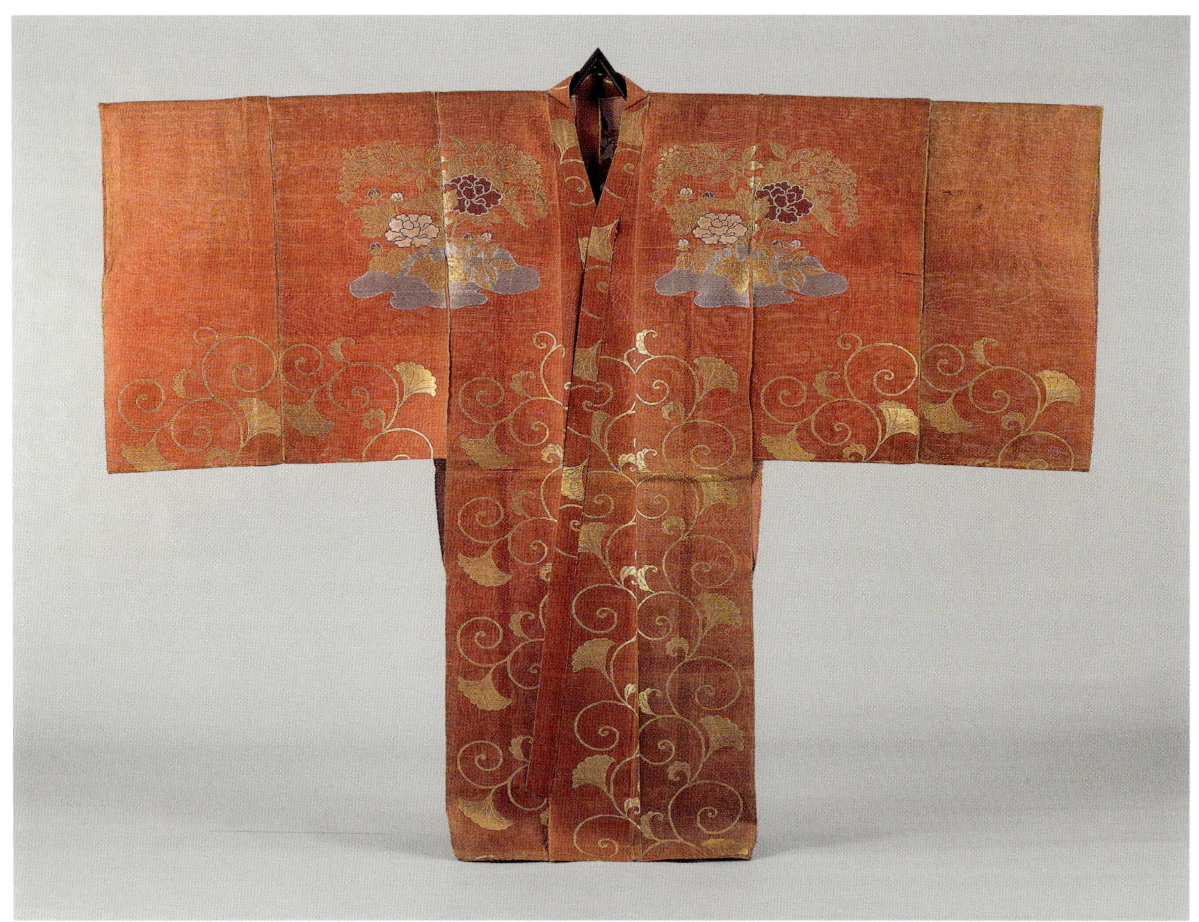

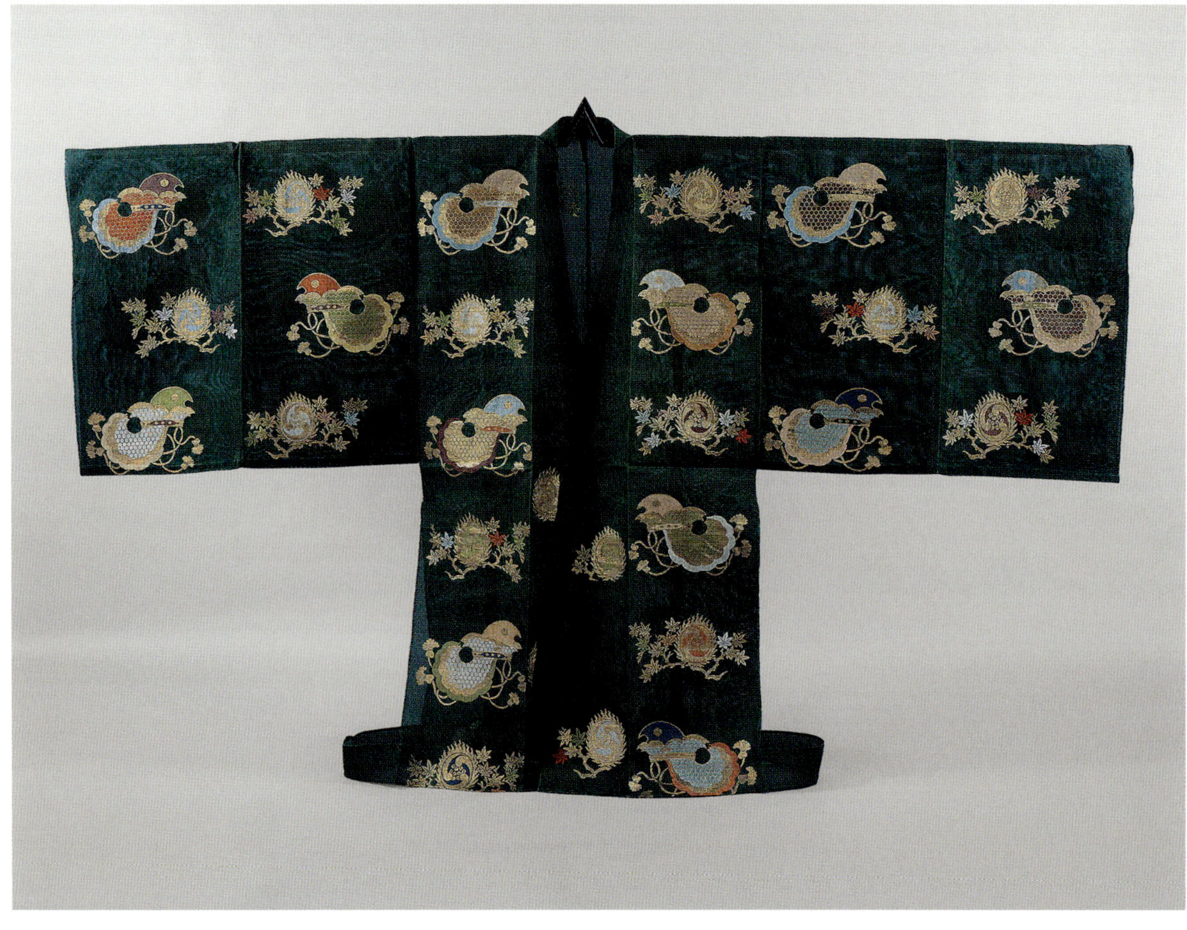

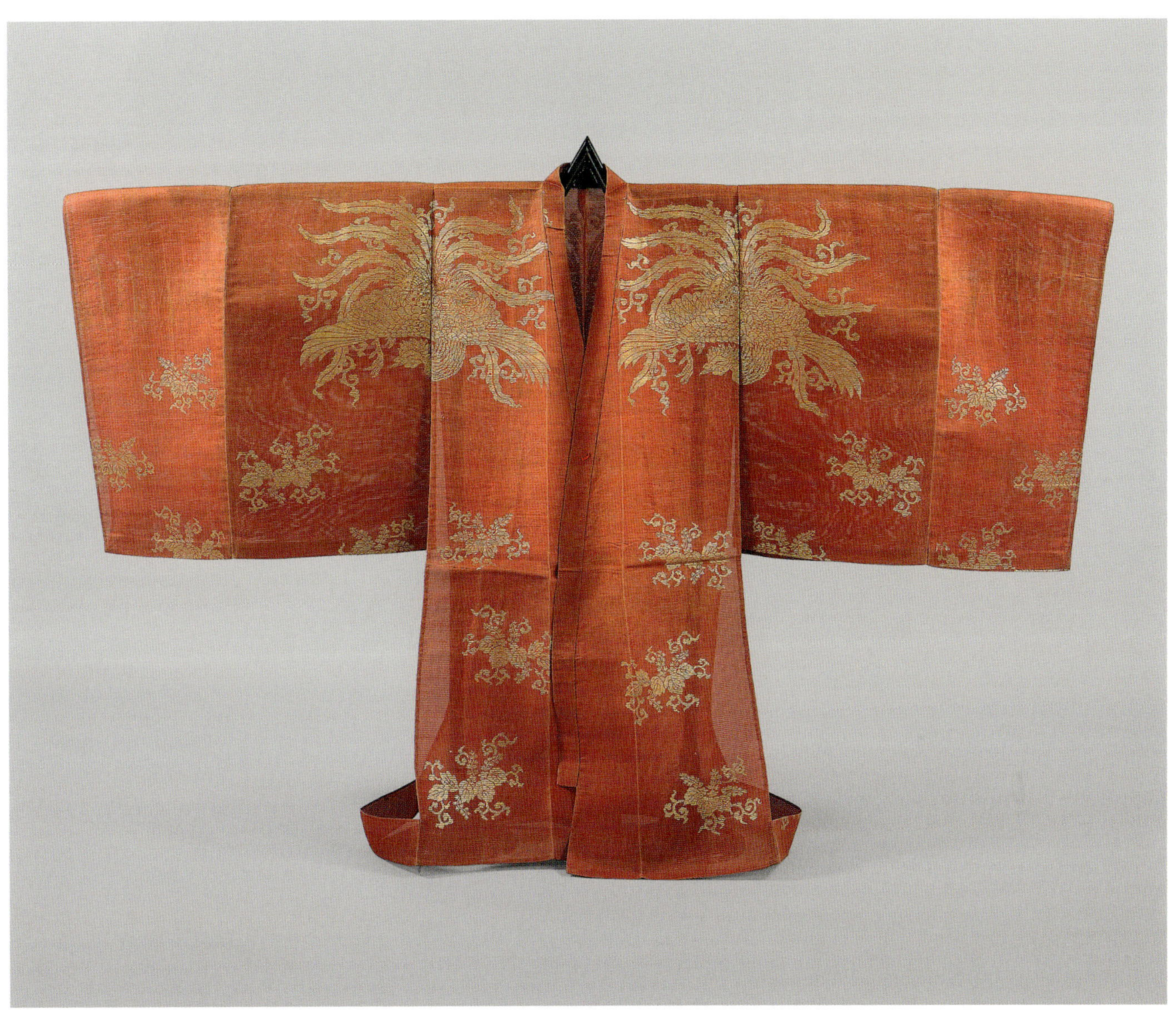

50 *Maiginu* with design of
    peonies and ginkgo arabesques
    on crimson ground

Edo period, 19th century
National Noh Theatre

51 *Maiginu* with design of the 'Autumn
    excursion' chapter from the *Tale of
    Genji* on dark yellow-green ground

Edo period, 18th–19th century
Agency for Cultural Affairs of Japan

52 *Maiginu* with design of phoenixes
    and paulownia on crimson ground

Edo period, 18th–19th century
Agency for Cultural Affairs of Japan

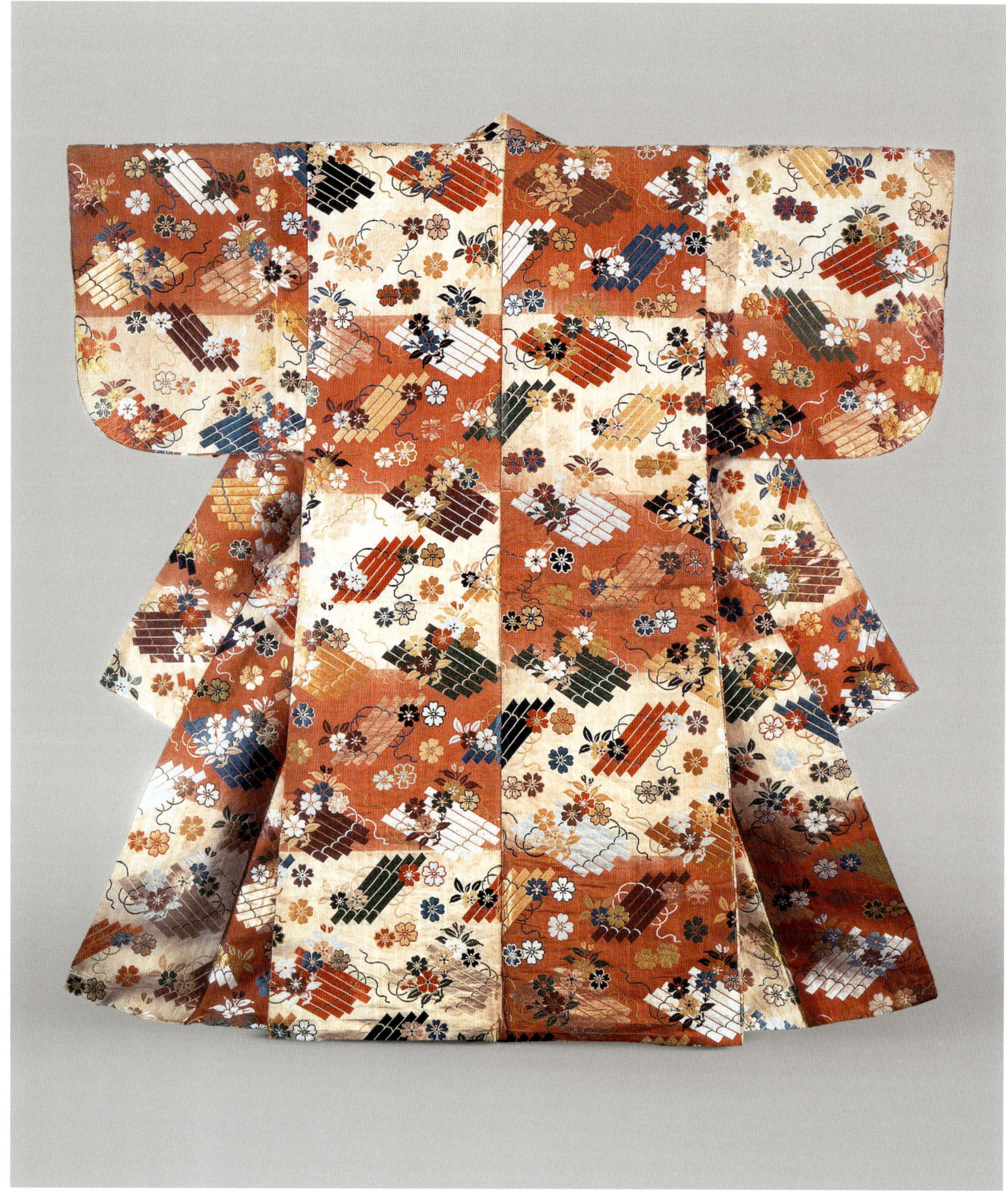

53 *Karaori* with design of flower rafts
on alternating blocks of crimson
and white ground

Edo period, 18th century
National Noh Theatre

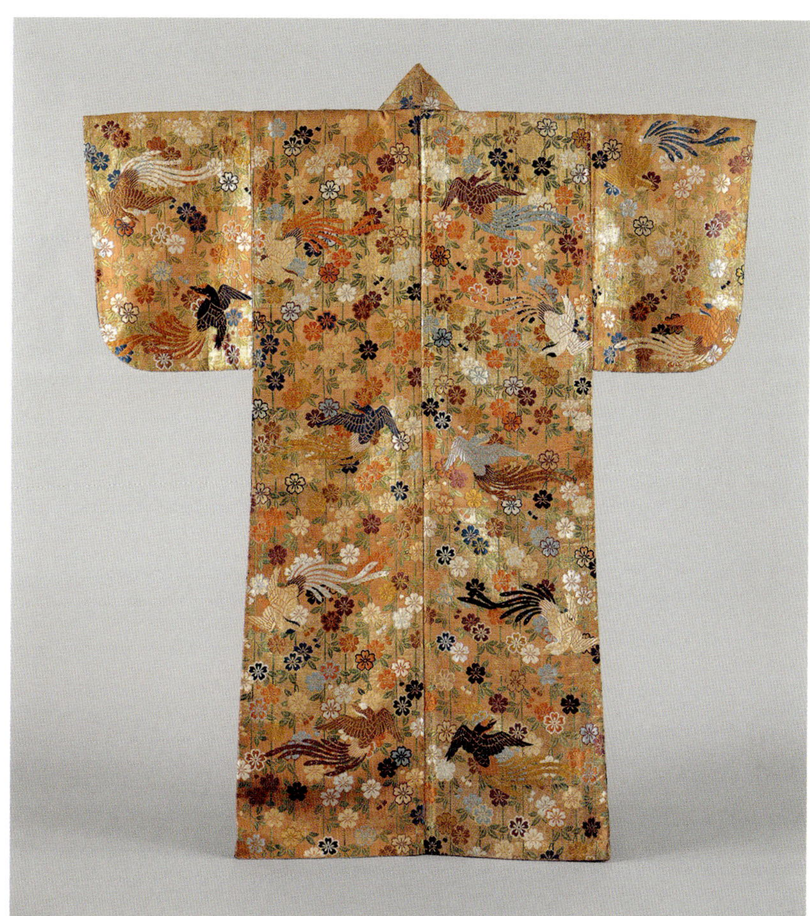

54 *Karaori* with design of
  weeping cherries and long-
  tailed birds on alternating
  gold and crimson ground
  Edo period, 18th century
  National Noh Theatre

55 *Karaori* with design of
  snow-laden camellias on
  crimson ground
  Edo period, 18th–19th century
  National Noh Theatre

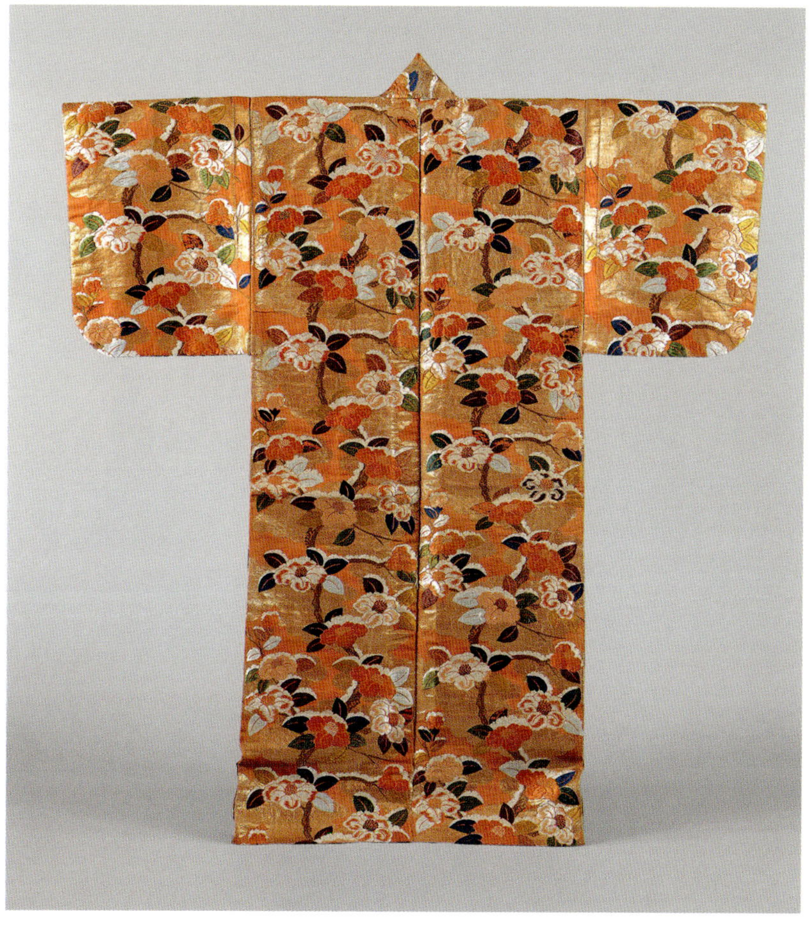

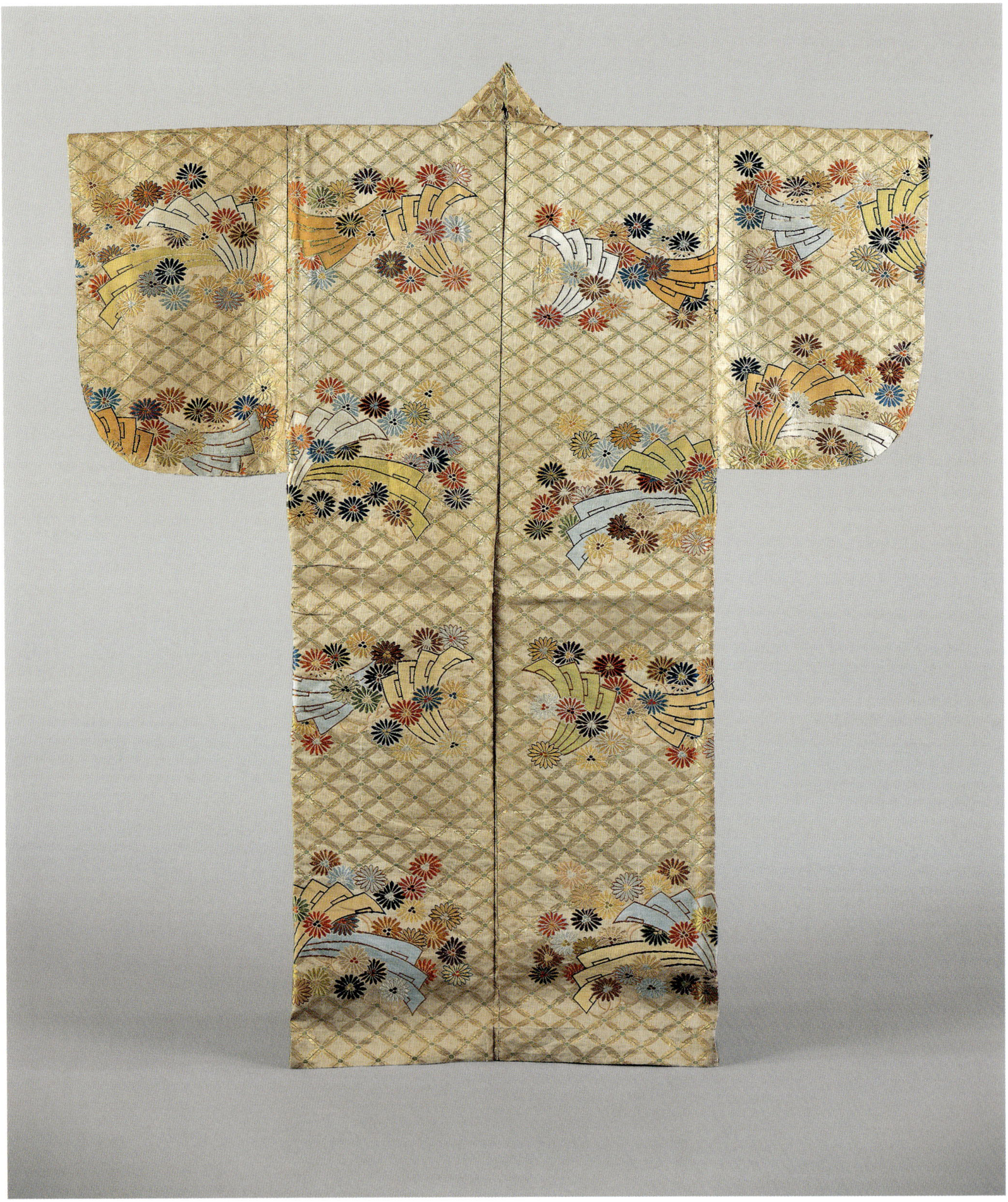

56 *Karaori* with design of interlocking
    seven jewels with fans and
    Chinese pine on white ground

Edo period, 18th–19th century
National Noh Theatre

57 *Karaori* with design of pine,
wisteria flowers, peonies
and bamboo baskets on
alternating blocks of white
and green ground
Edo period, 19th century
Agency for Cultural Affairs
of Japan

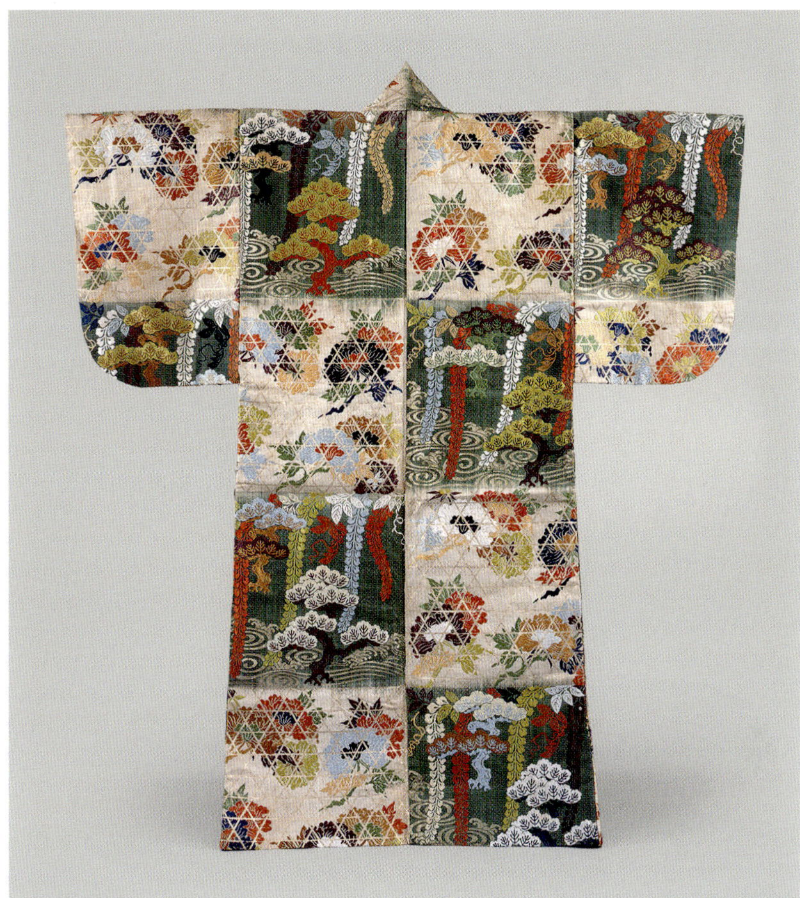

58 *Karaori* with design of flax
leaves, autumn plants and
maple leaves on alternating
blocks of dark brown and
pale blue-green ground
Edo period, 19th century
Agency for Cultural Affairs
of Japan

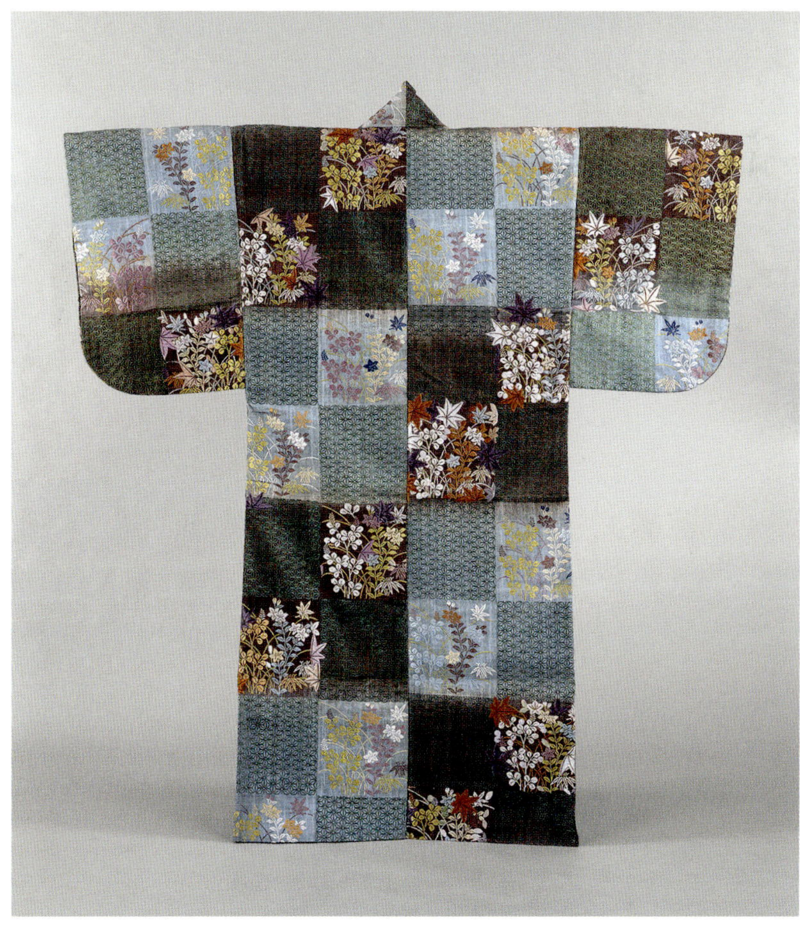

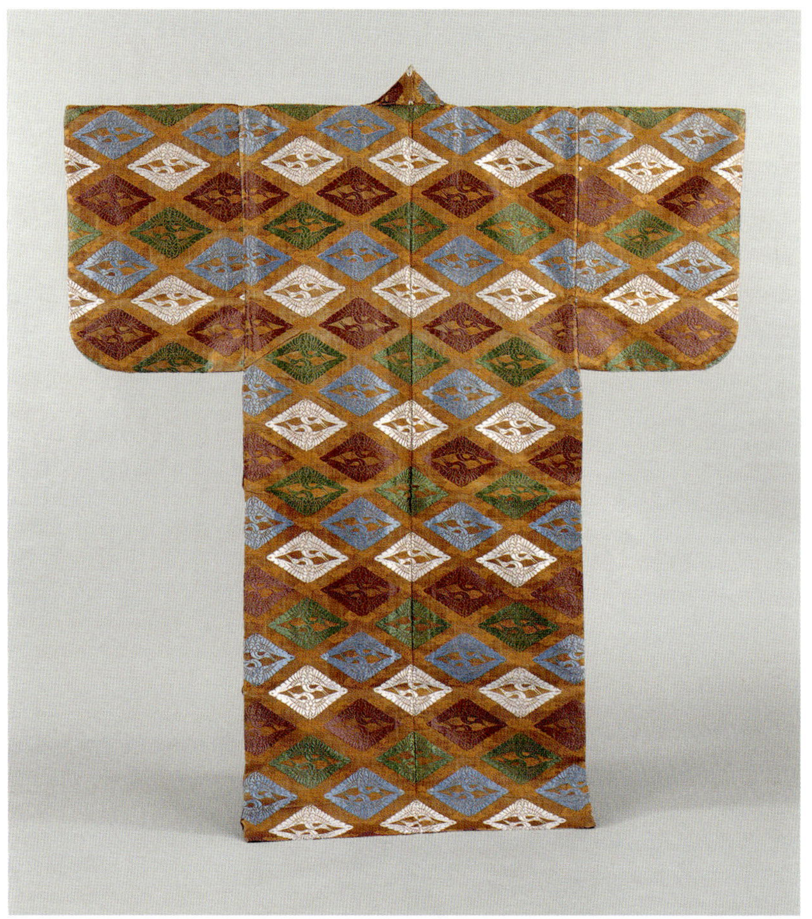

59 *Karaori* with design of
clouds and crane diamonds
on brown ground

Edo period, 19th century
Agency for Cultural Affairs
of Japan

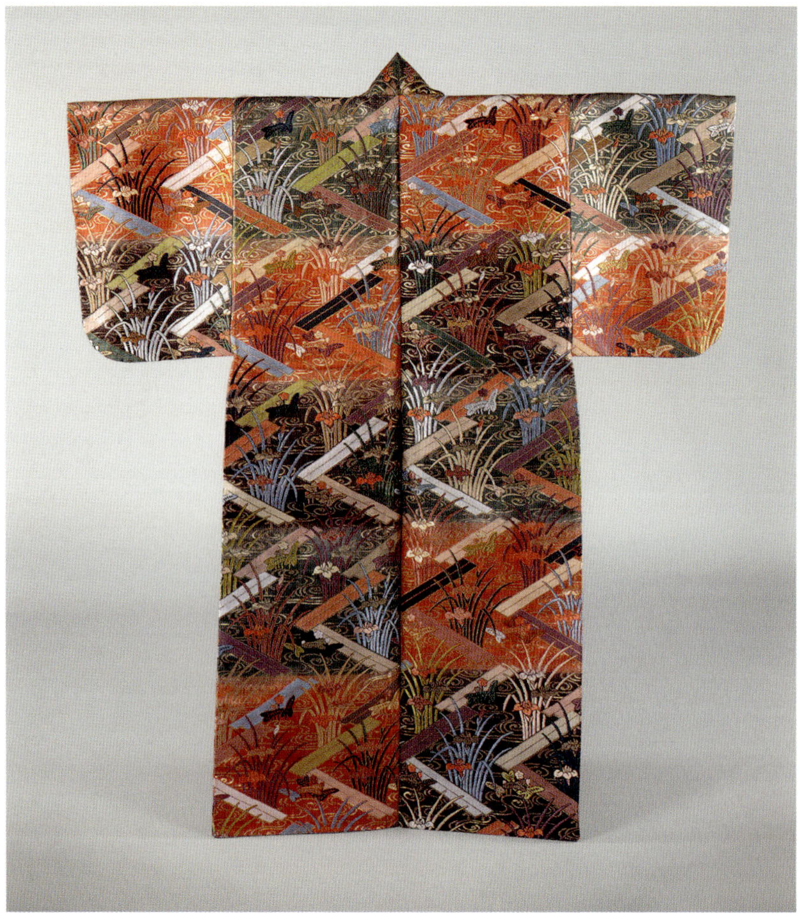

60 *Karaori* with design of
eight-plank bridge on
alternating blocks of
crimson, dark brown and
yellow-green ground

2nd month, Bunka 8 (1811)
National Noh Theatre

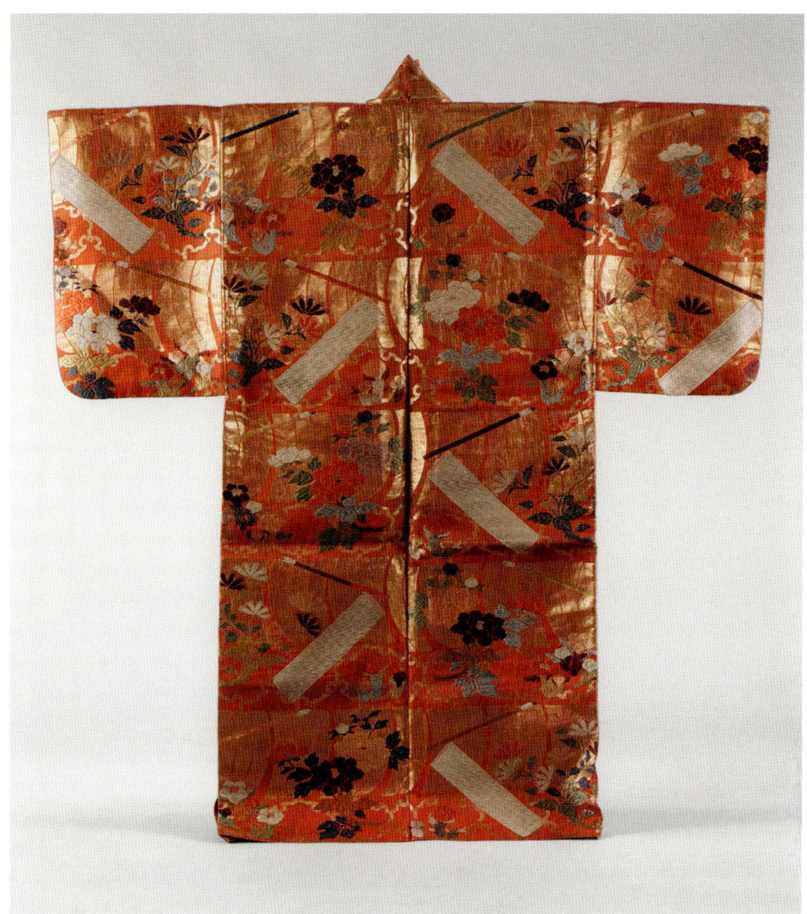

61 *Karaori* with design of sails,
snowflake rings, adonis,
thoroughworts, peonies,
letters and writing brushes
on crimson ground

5th month, Kōka 3 (1846)
National Noh Theatre

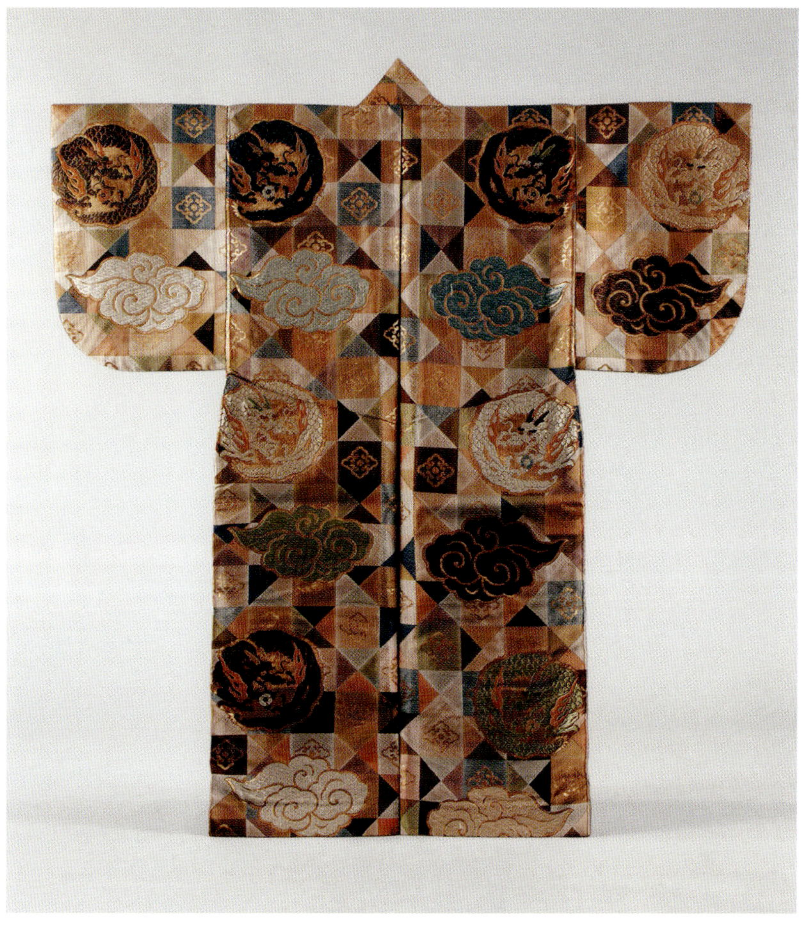

62 *Atsuita karaori* with
design of triangles, dragon
roundels and clouds on
light red ground

Bunka 5 (1808)
National Noh Theatre

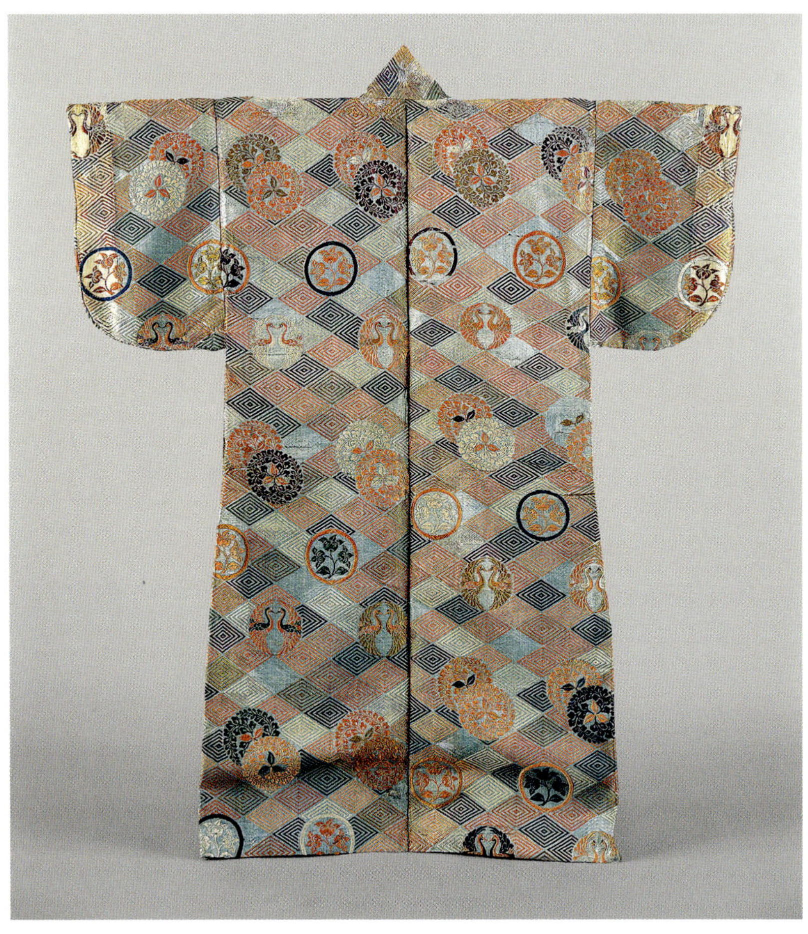

63 *Atsuita* with design of
nested diamonds and
scattered floral roundels
on pale blue ground

Momoyama period,
16th–17th century
National Noh Theatre

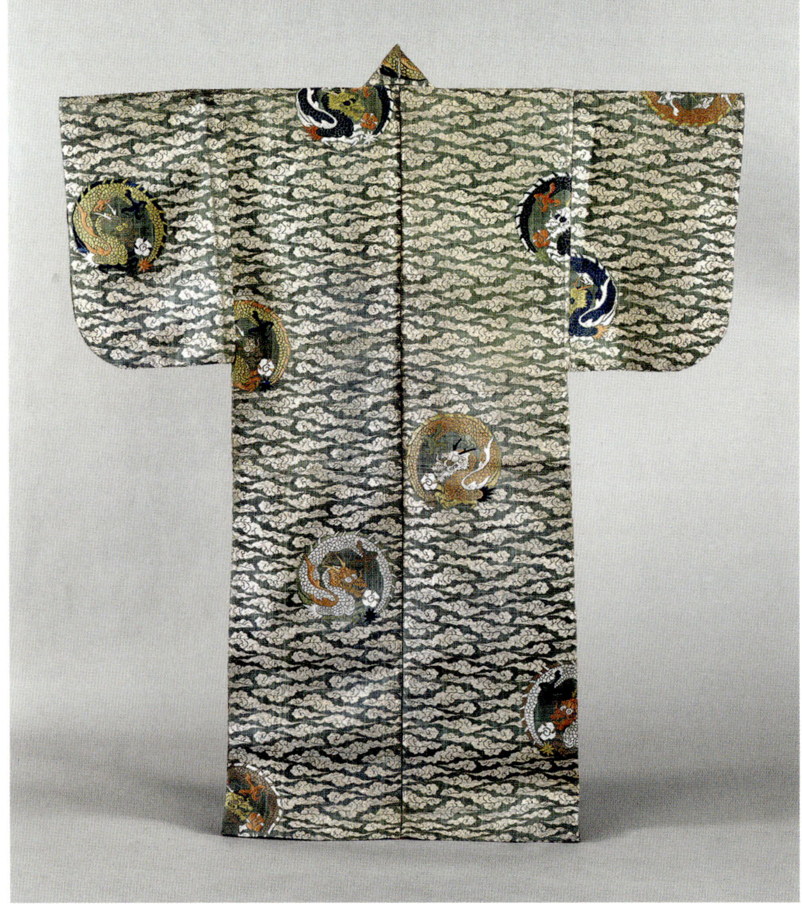

64 *Atsuita* with design of
dragon roundels and clouds
on yellow-green ground

Edo period, 17–18th century
Agency for Cultural Affairs
of Japan

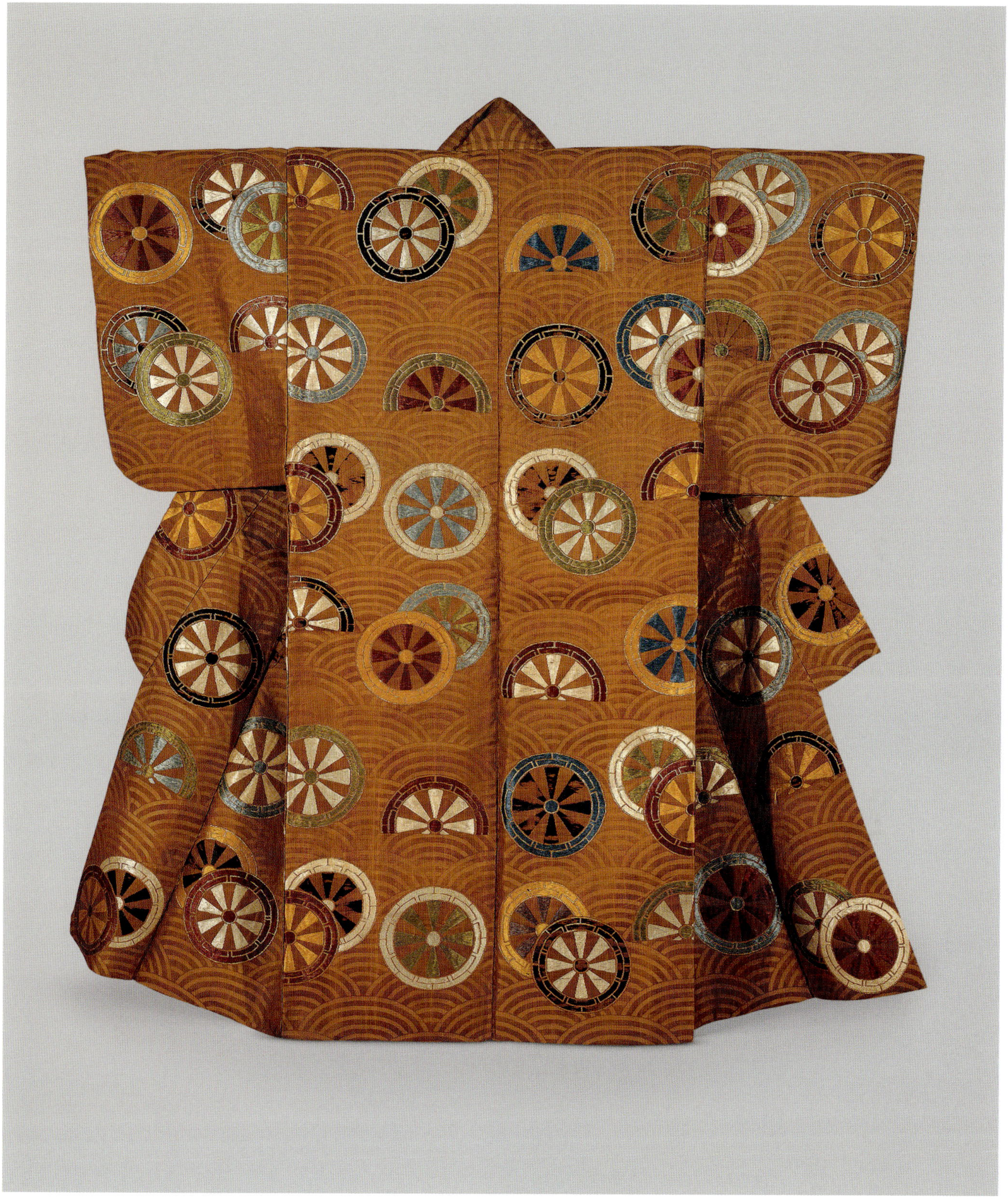

65 *Atsuita* with design of ocean waves
and Genji wheels on brown ground

Edo period, 18th century
National Noh Theatre

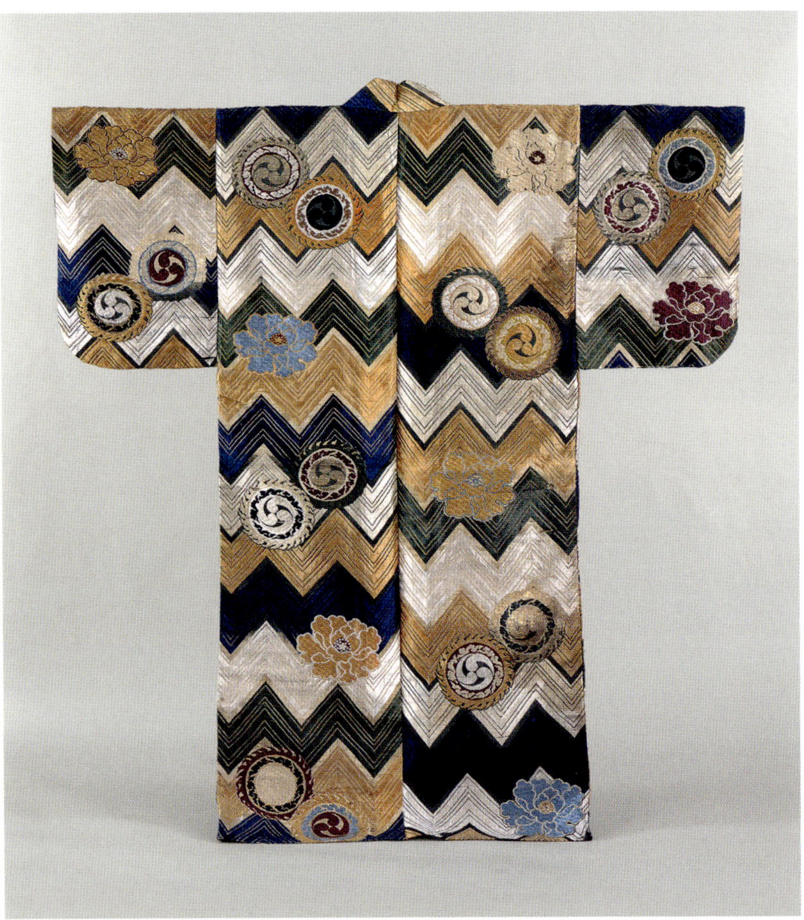

66 *Atsuita* with design of
'flame drums' and peonies
over cedar pattern on
dark green ground

Edo period, 18th century
Agency for Cultural Affairs
of Japan

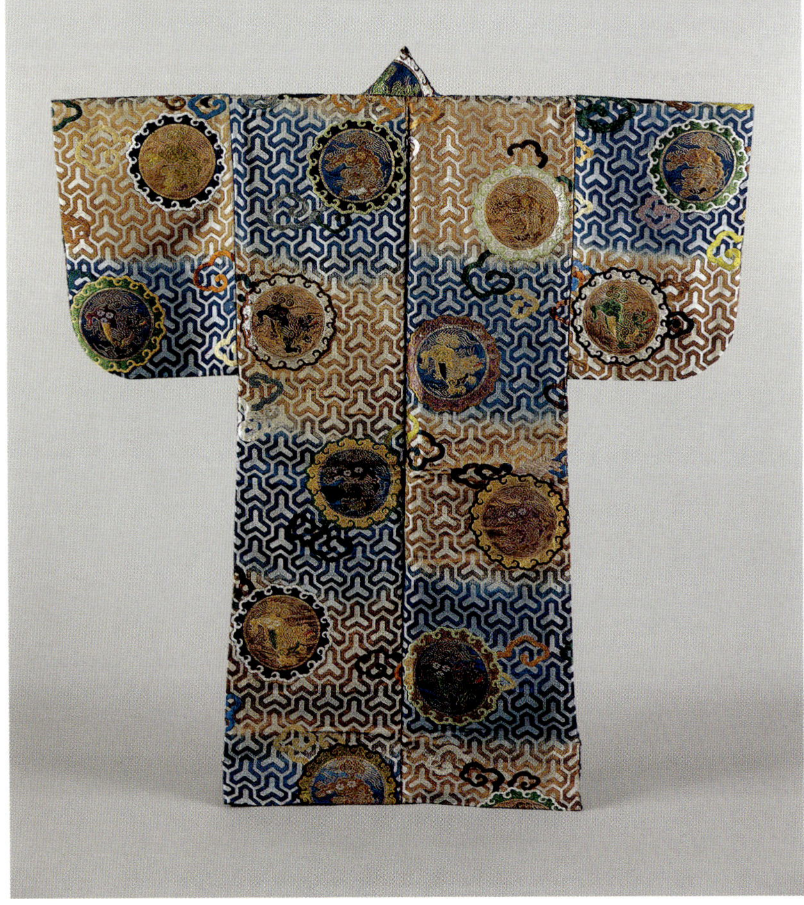

67 *Atsuita* with design of
Chinese lion roundels over
interlocking tortoiseshell
pattern on alternating
blocks of brown and greyish
blue ground

Edo period, 18th century
National Noh Theatre

68 *Atsuita* with design of
paulownia crests and
cloud-shaped gongs over
interlocking hexagonal
lozenges with flower motif
on alternating blocks of dark
blue and crimson ground

Edo period, 18th century
National Noh Theatre

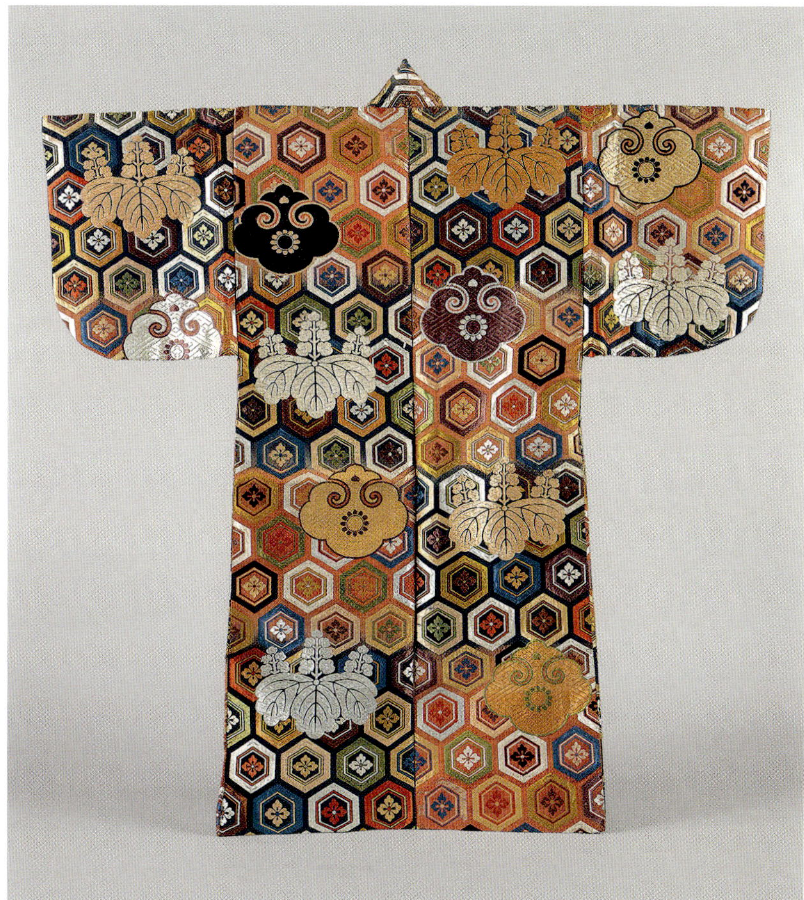

69 *Atsuita* with design of
paulownia crests and
comma–shaped motifs,
checks and cobblestones
on alternating blocks of
crimson and white ground

Edo period, 18th–19th century
National Noh Theatre

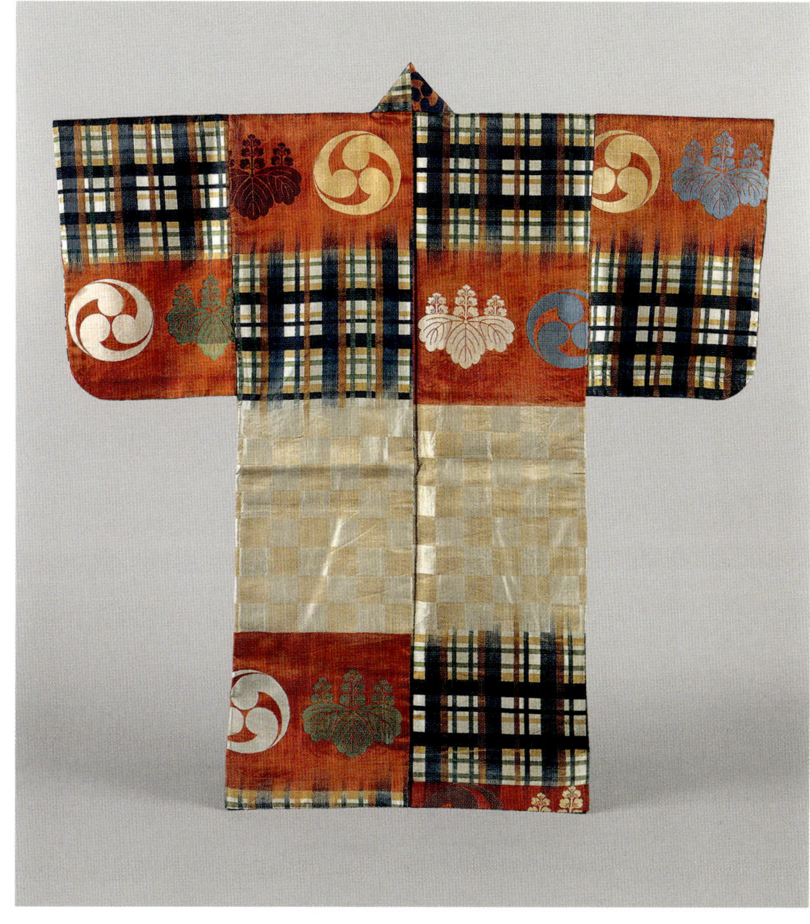

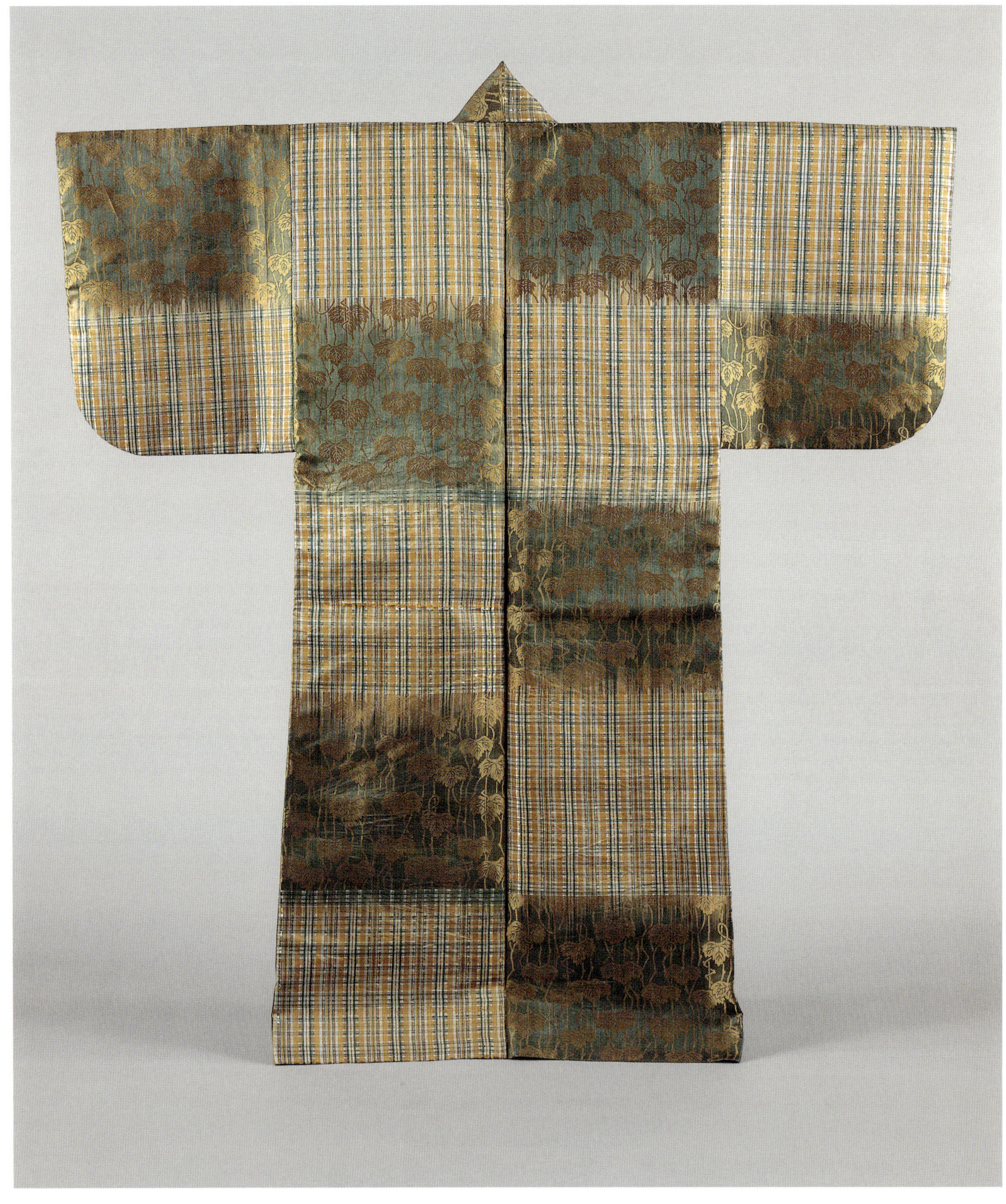

70 *Atsuita* with design of ivy and
lattices on alternating blocks of
white and green ground

Edo period, 19th century
National Noh Theatre

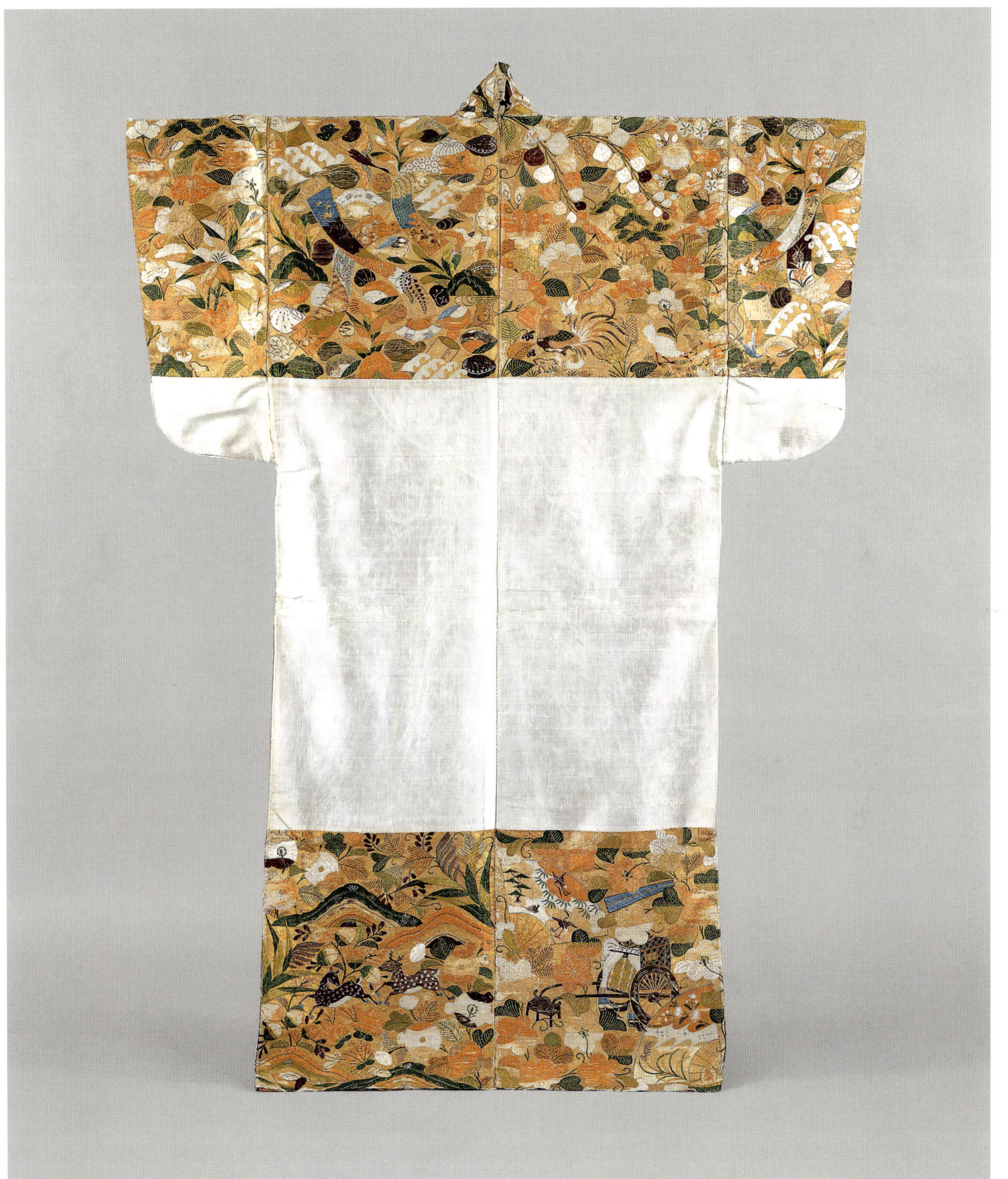

71 *Nuihaku* with design of plants
and animals on white ground

Momoyama period, 16th century
Agency for Cultural Affairs of Japan

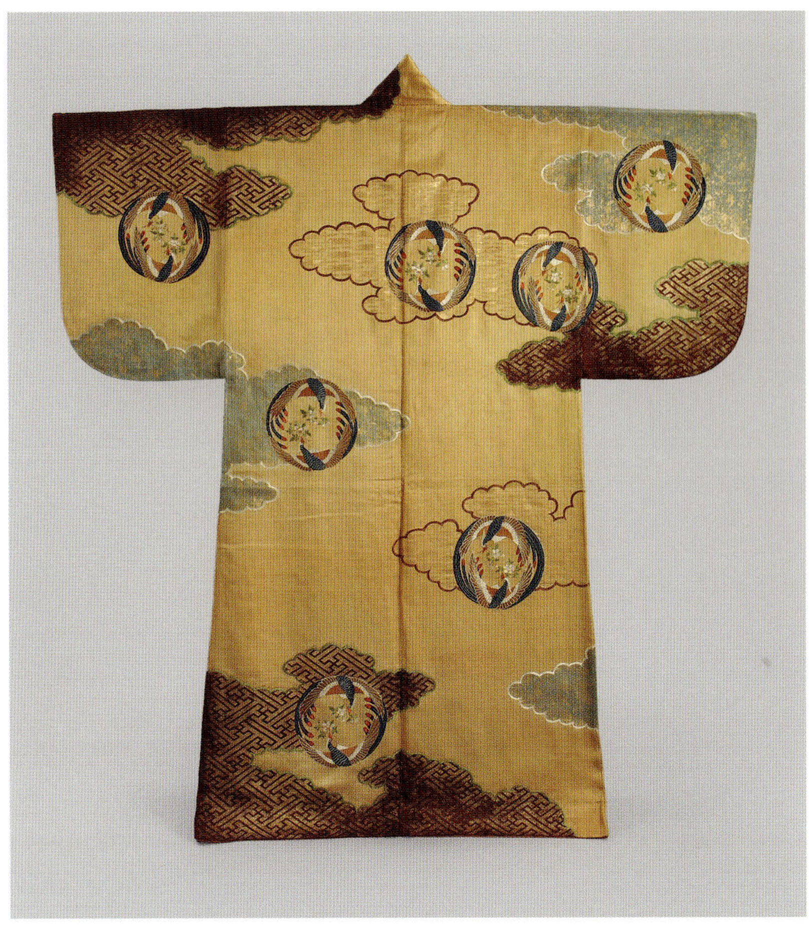

72 *Nuihaku* with design of
    clouds and long-tailed bird
    roundels on yellow ground
    Edo period, 18th century
    National Noh Theatre

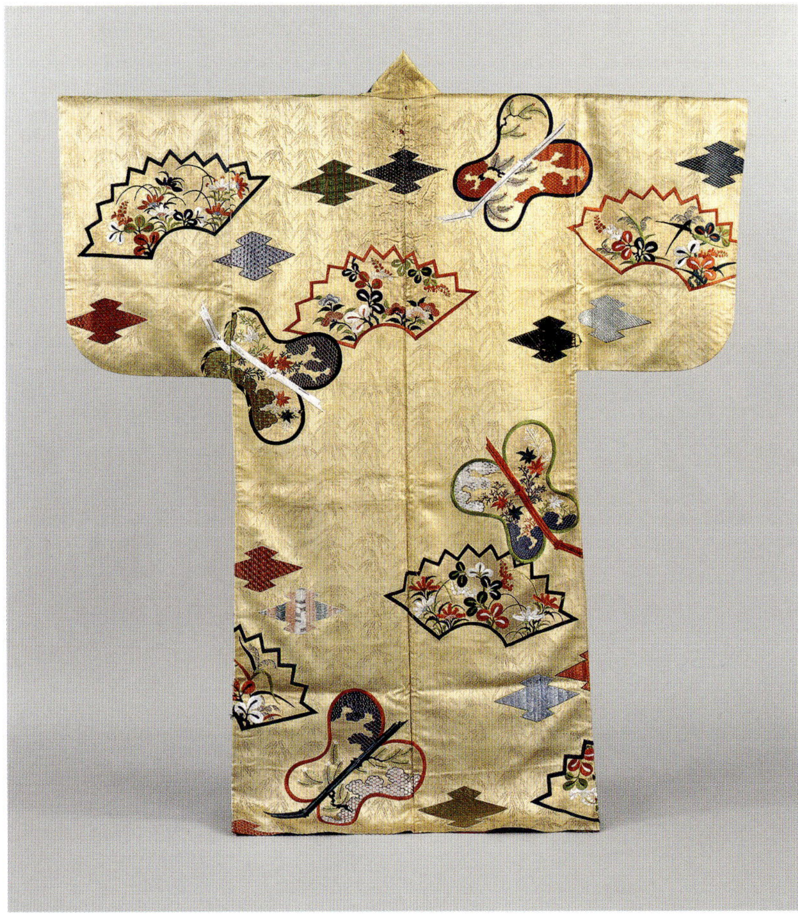

73 *Nuihaku* with design of
    fans and pine-bark
    lozenges over bamboo
    leaves on yellow ground
    Edo period, 18th century
    Agency for Cultural Affairs
    of Japan

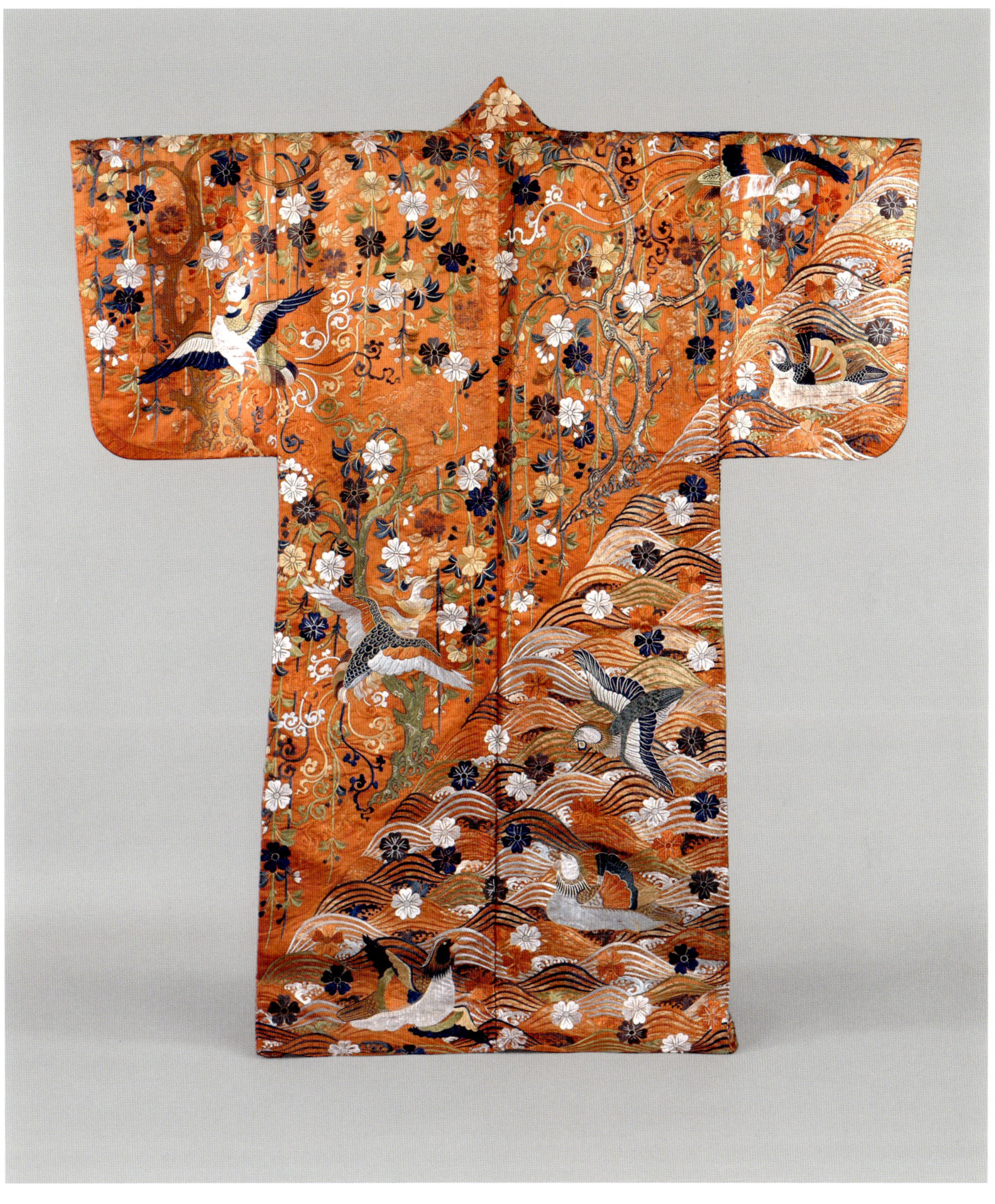

74 *Nuihaku* with design of weeping cherries,
phoenixes and mandarin ducks over waves
on crimson ground
Edo period, 18th–19th century
Agency for Cultural Affairs of Japan

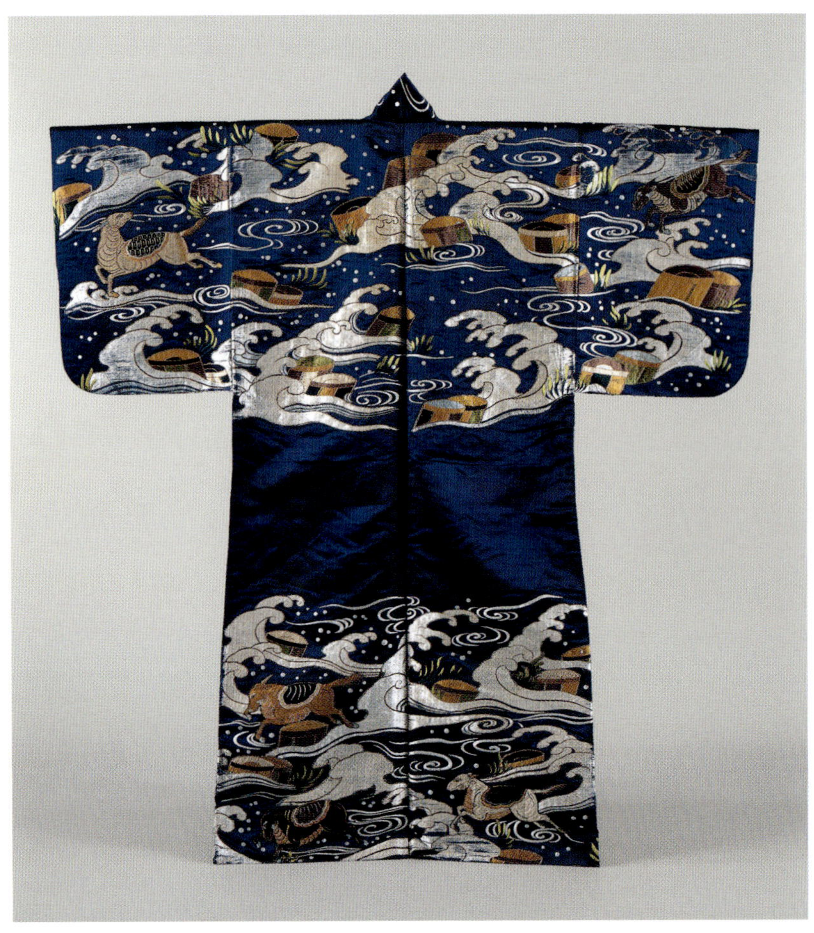

75 *Nuihaku* with design of
waves, *kirin* and buckets on
dark blue ground
Edo period, 19th century
National Noh Theatre

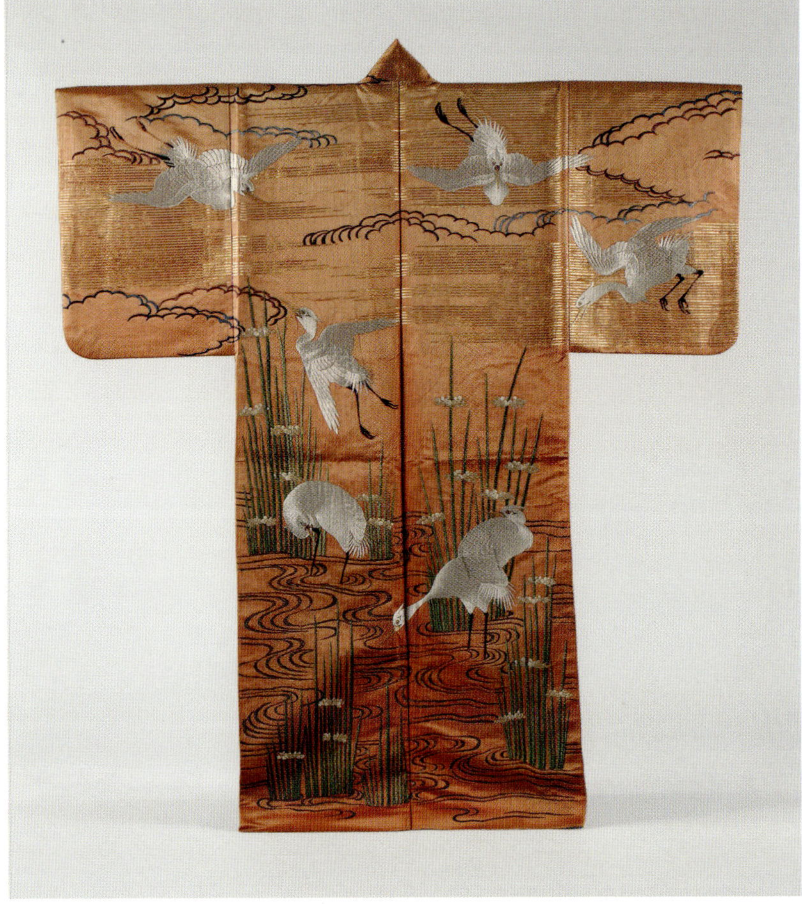

76 *Nuihaku* with design of
herons and bulrushes on
crimson ground
Ansei 5 (1858)
National Noh Theatre

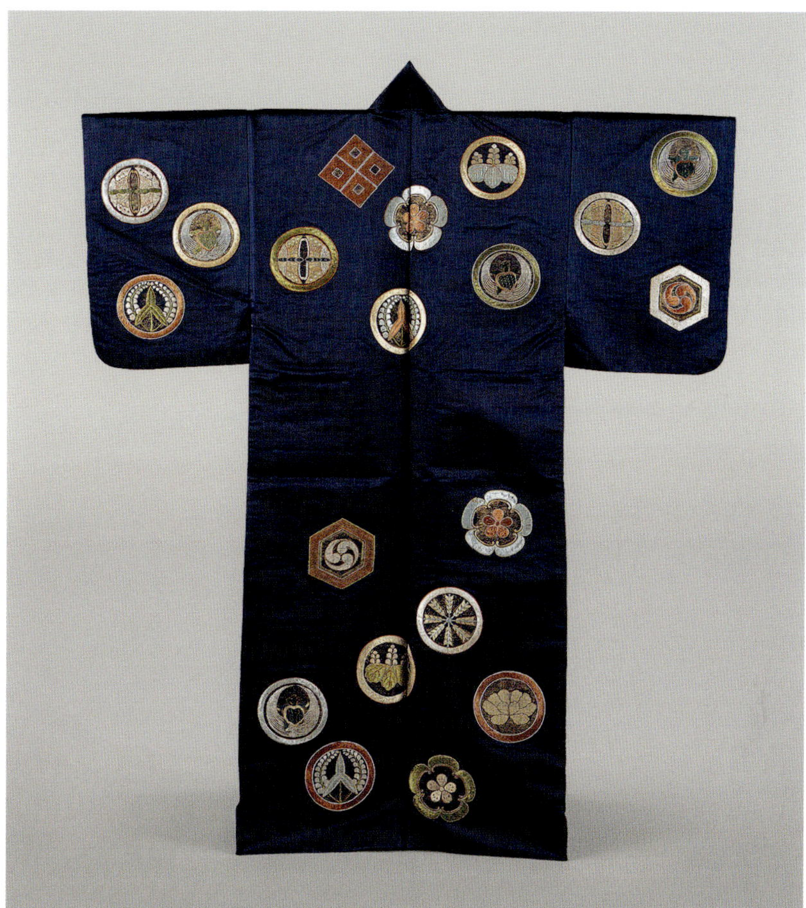

77 *Nuihaku* with design of
   scattered roundels on
   dark blue ground
   Edo period, 19th century
   National Noh Theatre

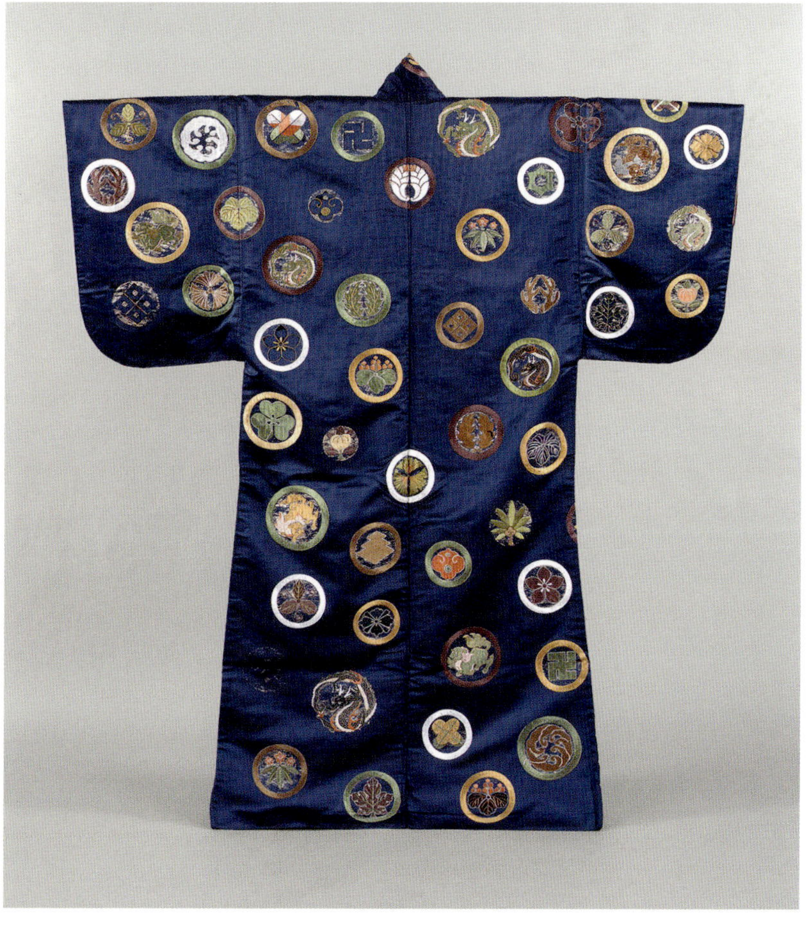

78 *Nuihaku* with design of
   scattered roundels on
   dark blue ground
   Edo period, 18th century
   Agency for Cultural Affairs
   of Japan

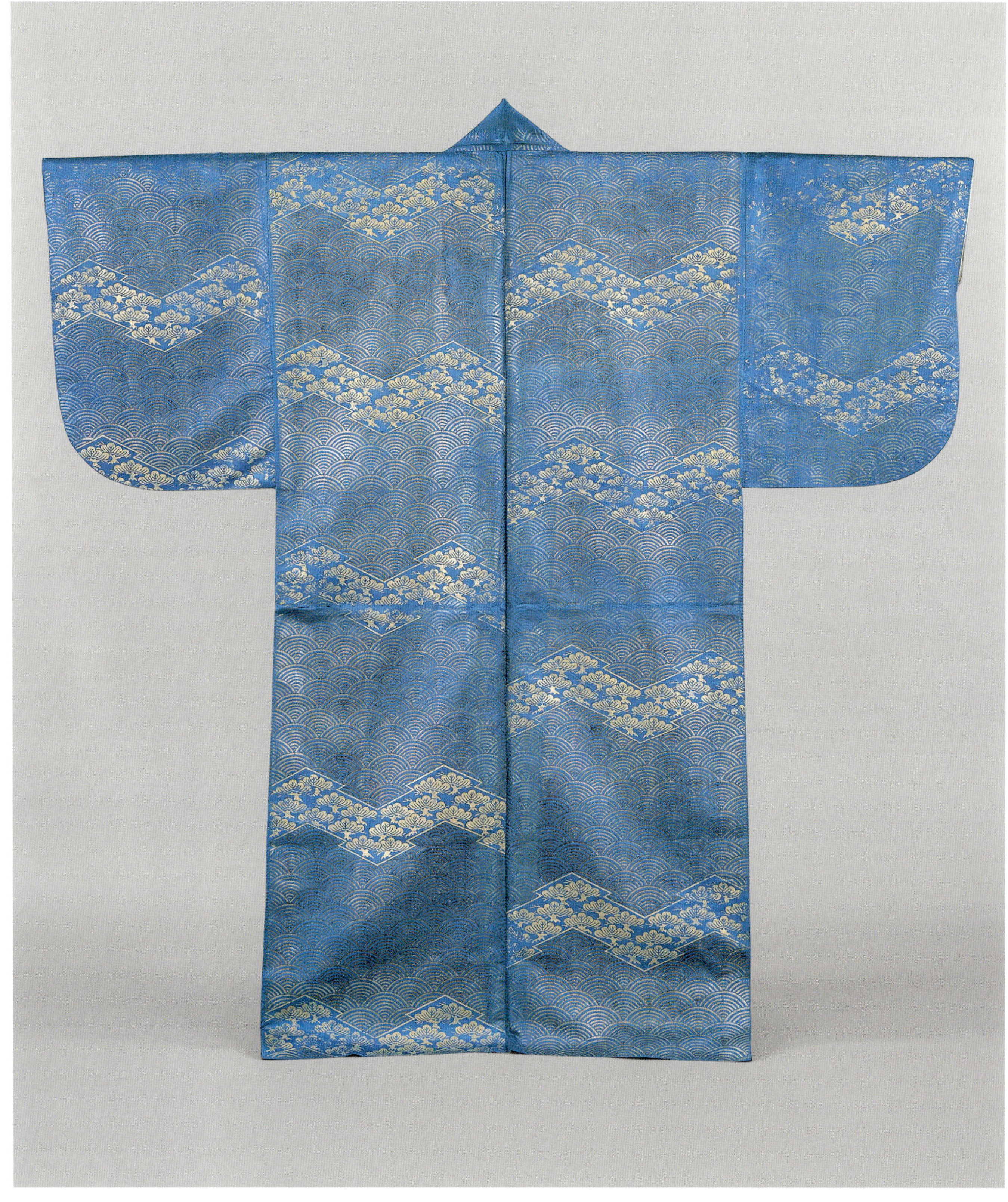

79 *Surihaku* with design of
ocean waves and pine-bark
lozenges on light blue ground

Edo period, 18th century
Agency for Cultural Affairs of Japan

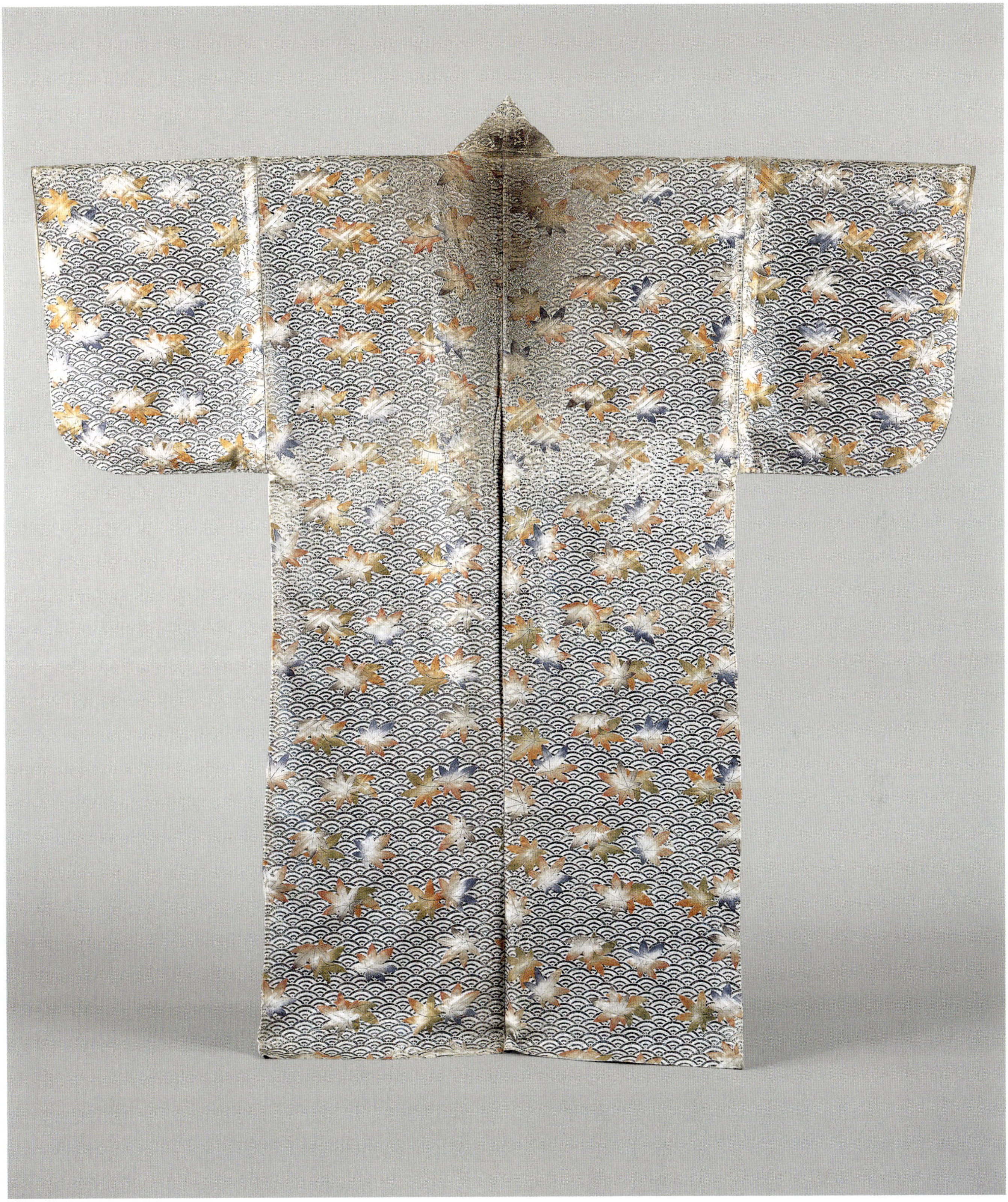

80 *Surihaku* with design of
ocean waves and autumn
leaves on white ground

Edo period, 18th century
National Noh Theatre

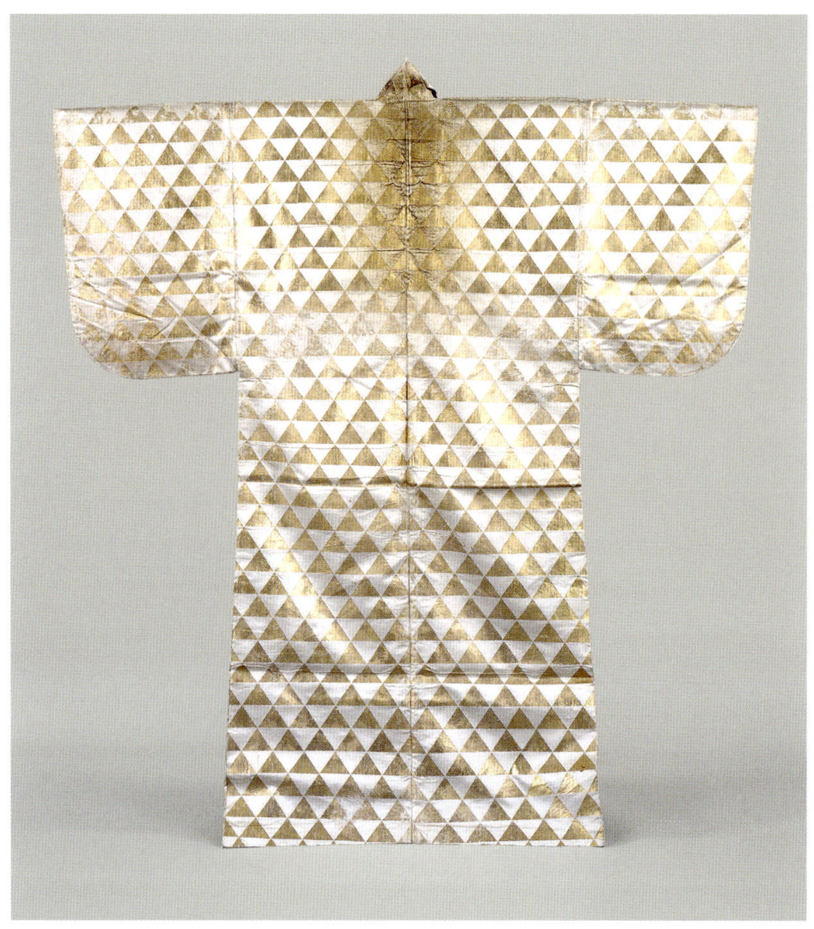

81 *Surihaku* with design
of triangular scales on
white ground

Edo period, 18th–19th century
Agency for Cultural Affairs
of Japan

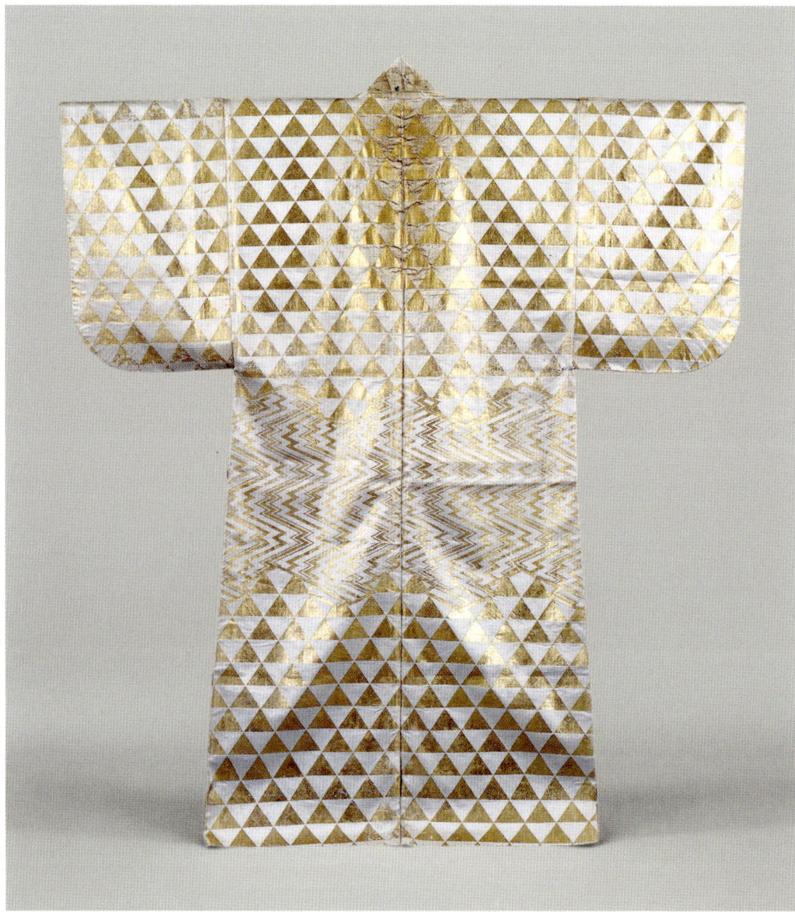

82 *Surihaku* with design
of triangular scales on
white ground

Edo period, 18th–19th century
Agency for Cultural Affairs
of Japan

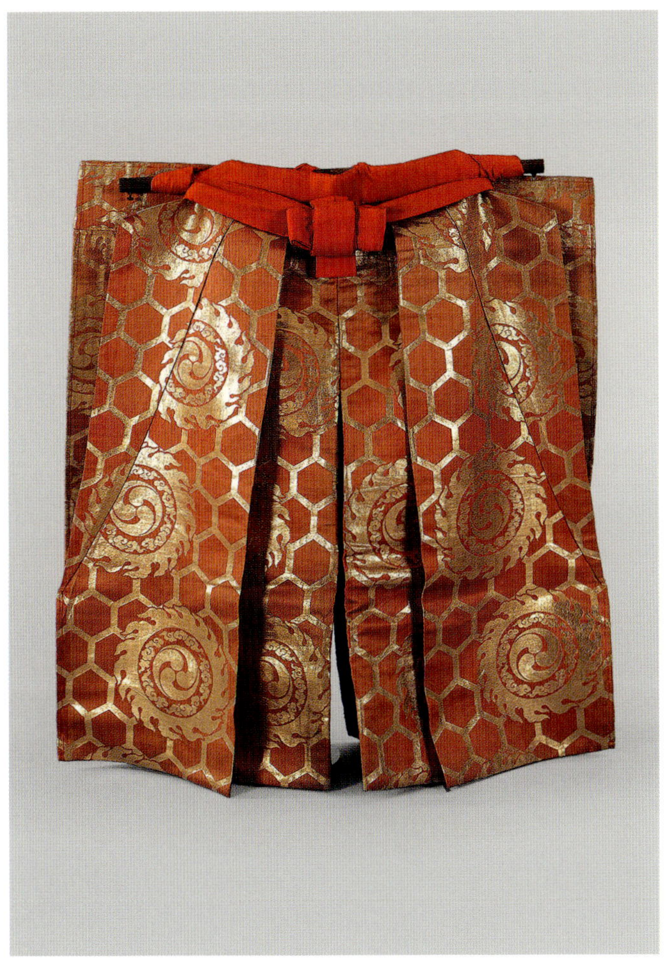

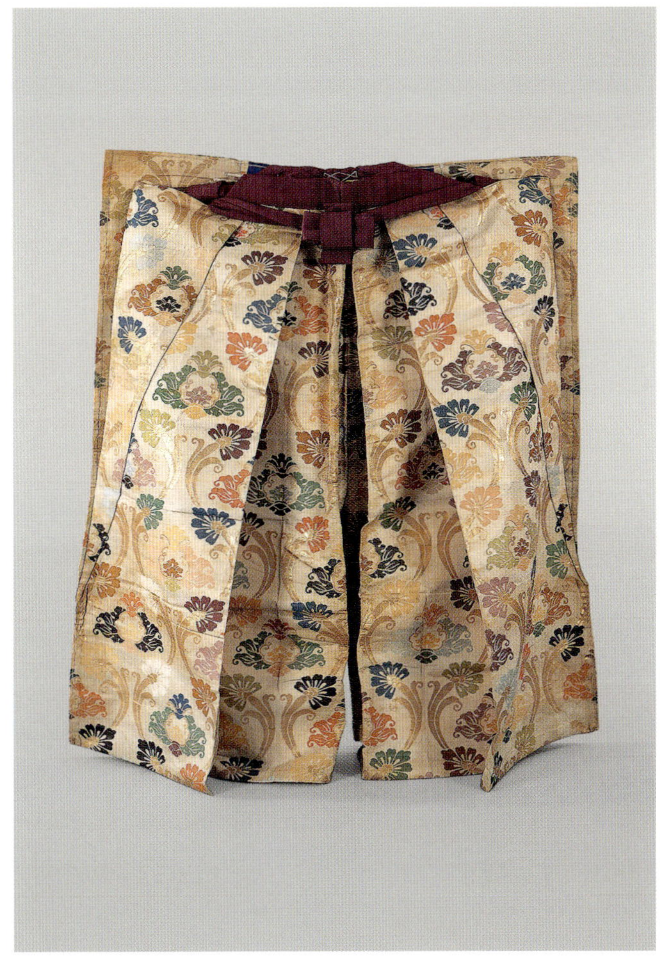

83 *Hangiri* with design of interlocking
hexagonal lozenges and 'flame drums'
on crimson ground

Edo period, 19th century
Agency for Cultural Affairs of Japan

84 *Hangiri* with design of undulating
vertical lines and clove-shaped crests
with flowers on white ground

Edo period, 19th century
Agency for Cultural Affairs of Japan

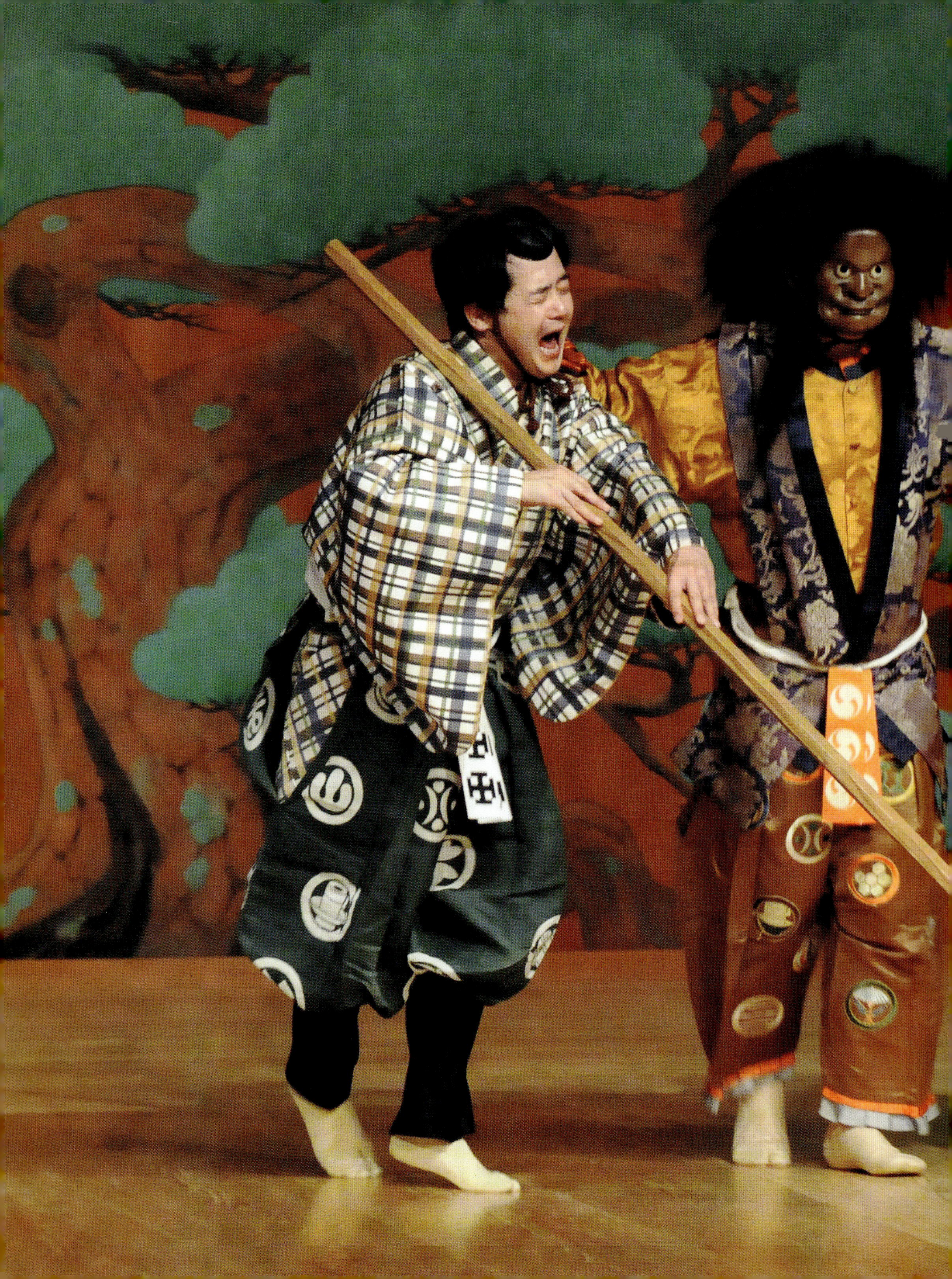

KYŌGEN MASKS AND COSTUMES

KYŌGEN MASKS

Masks are not utilised to the same extent in kyōgen plays as they are in nō. Kyōgen pieces are set in the present everyday world and thus kyōgen masks are intended as more realistic representations that create an immediate rapport between the audience and the character portrayed. There is some overlap between nō and kyōgen masks, with some nō masks also found in kyōgen. However, there are comparatively fewer examples for exclusive use in kyōgen: altogether there are approximately 20 kyōgen masks in the categories of deities, spirits, humans and animals. (NS)

KYŌGEN COSTUMES

The study of kyōgen costumes has not been as exhaustive as that of nō robes, and as a result it is more difficult to find kyōgen examples predating the Edo period. In essence, however, the design of the kyōgen costume is plainer than that in nō and was influenced by the everyday garments of ordinary people. In contrast to nō robes that entail intricate weaving techniques, the textiles for kyōgen costumes are noteworthy for the various dyeing techniques employed in their manufacture. They also comprise a greater number of plain silks and hemp, with more repetitive designs. Although similar costumes are on occasion seen in both in nō and kyōgen, there are differences in the types of characters wearing particular costumes. For example, a fallen warrior dons the *suō* costume in nō, whereas in kyōgen it indicates a person of status.

Approximately two-thirds of all kyōgen plays are about the master-servant relationship, involving types with which audiences could easily identify. One of the garments sported by such characters is the sleeveless *kataginu*. These robes usually have more complex motifs, including insects, ships, rivers or fish, some of which are more difficult to produce on textiles and which are rarely seen on other costumes.

Other kyōgen costumes include the *suō* and *naga-kamishimo*. The *suō* is an unlined vest, which is referred to as a *suō kamishimo* when matched with *hakama* (divided skirt). The patterns on the textiles often differentiated kyōgen characters. Striking, colourful designs produced by the repeat-stencil dyeing technique, mainly on hemp, are used for characters such as daimyo, wealthy commoners or bridegrooms. Smaller more muted patterns are found on garments for more stolid characters such as farmers or fathers-in-law. The *naga-kamishimo* is a combination of the *kataginu* and long *hakama*; characters whose status is above servant and below small landowner wear this robe. (NS)

Scene from the kyōgen play
Kaneyamabushi

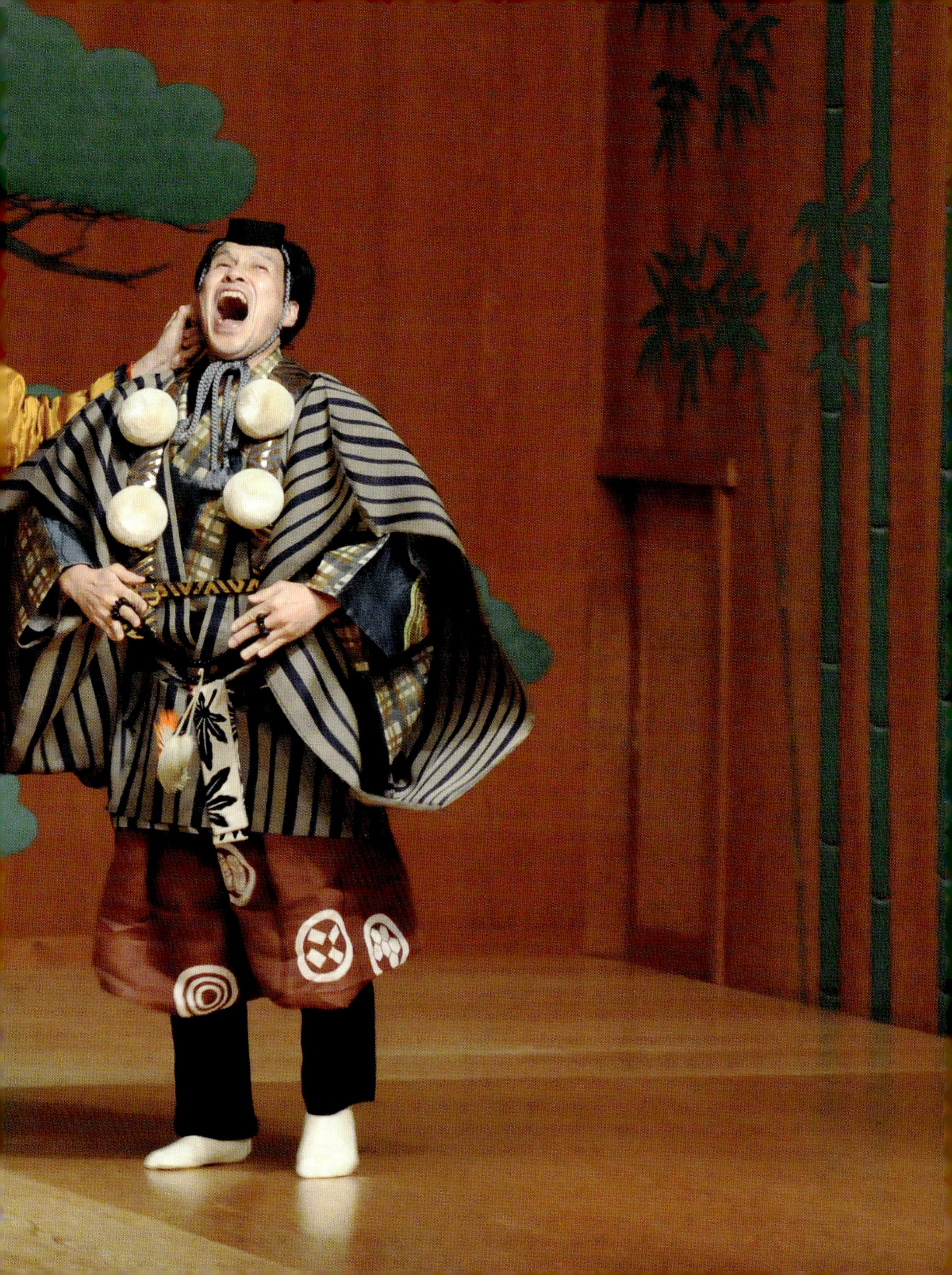

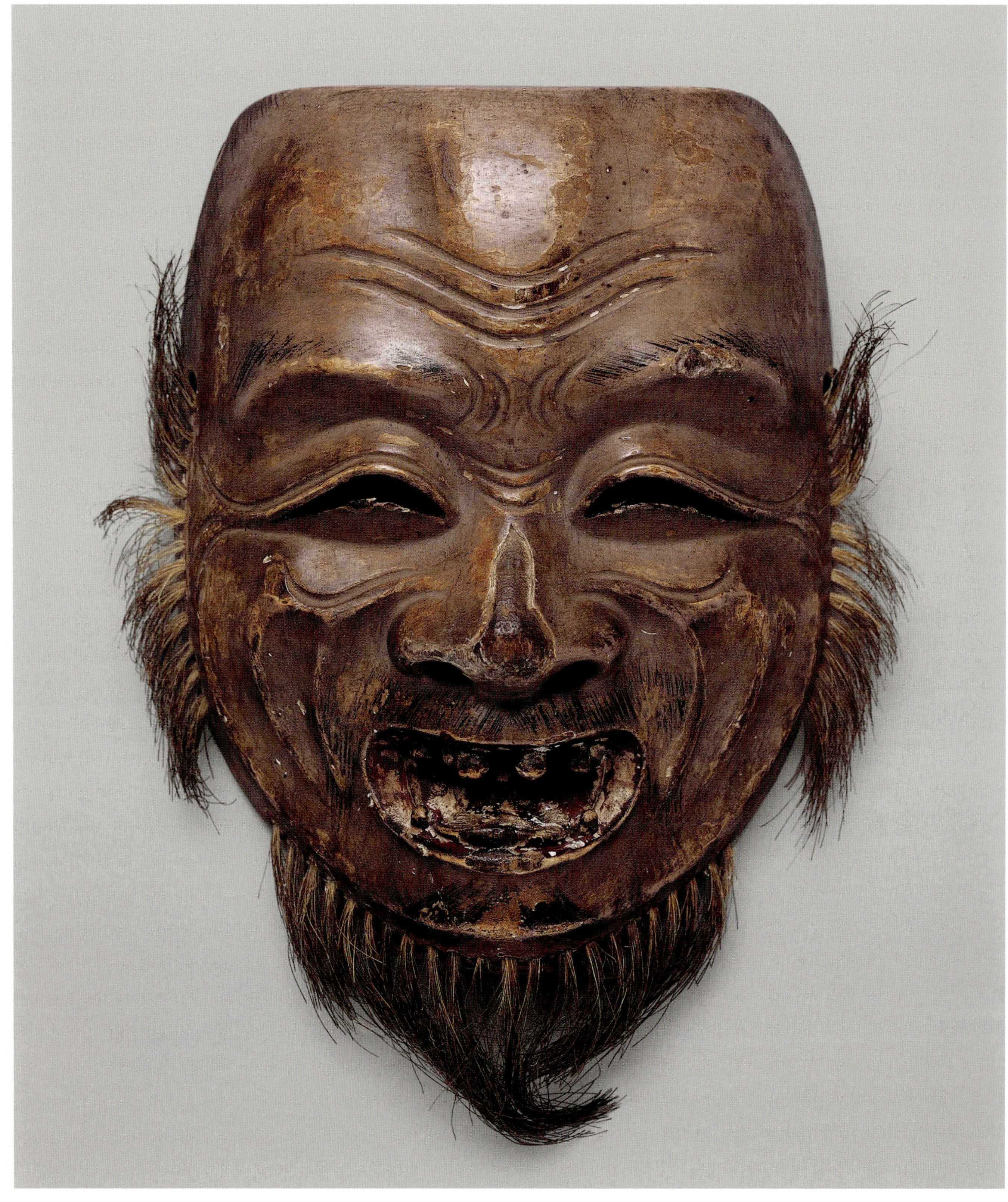

85 *Noborihige* mask
Edo period, 17th century
National Noh Theatre

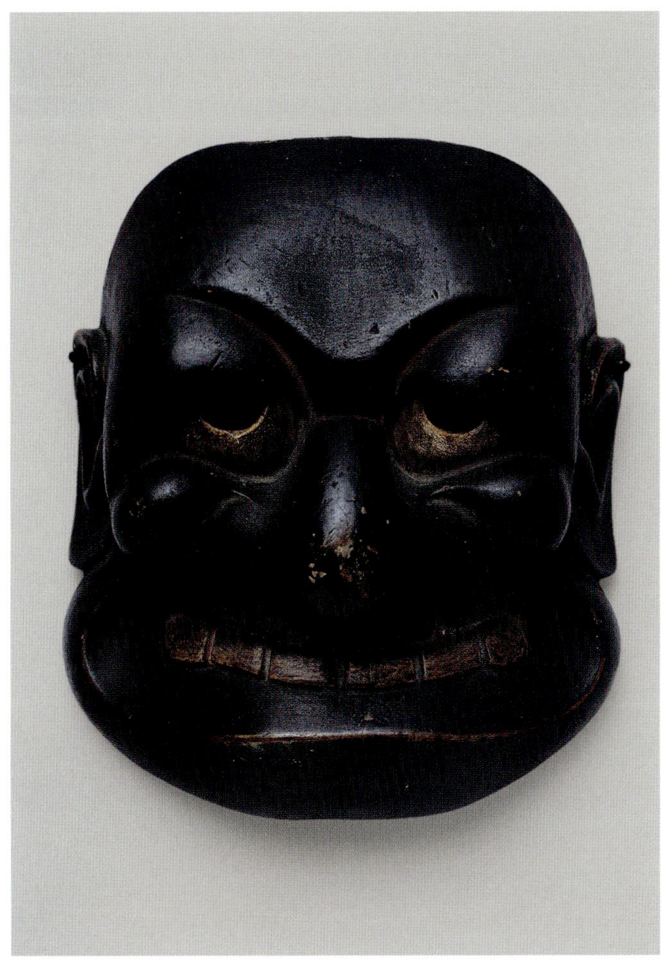

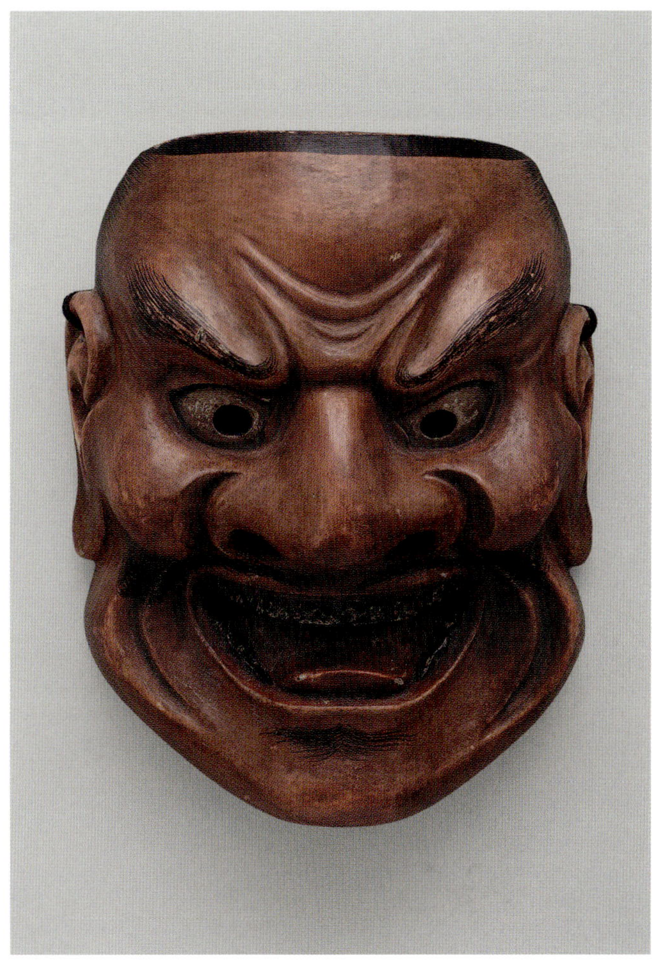

86 *Buaku* mask

Edo period, 18th century
National Noh Theatre

87 *Bishamon* mask

Edo period, 18th–19th century
National Noh Theatre

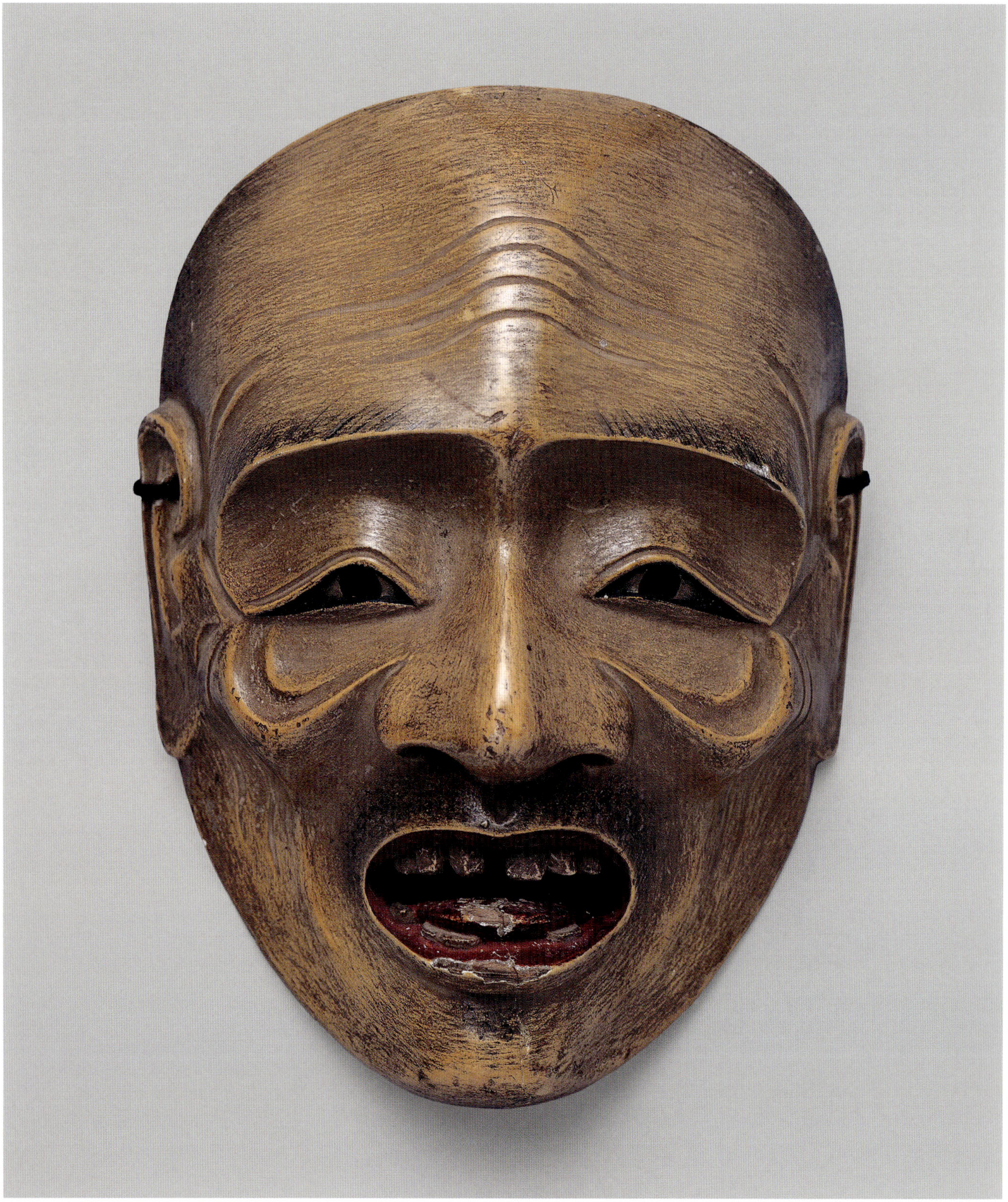

88 *Tsūen* mask

Edo period, 18th century
National Noh Theatre

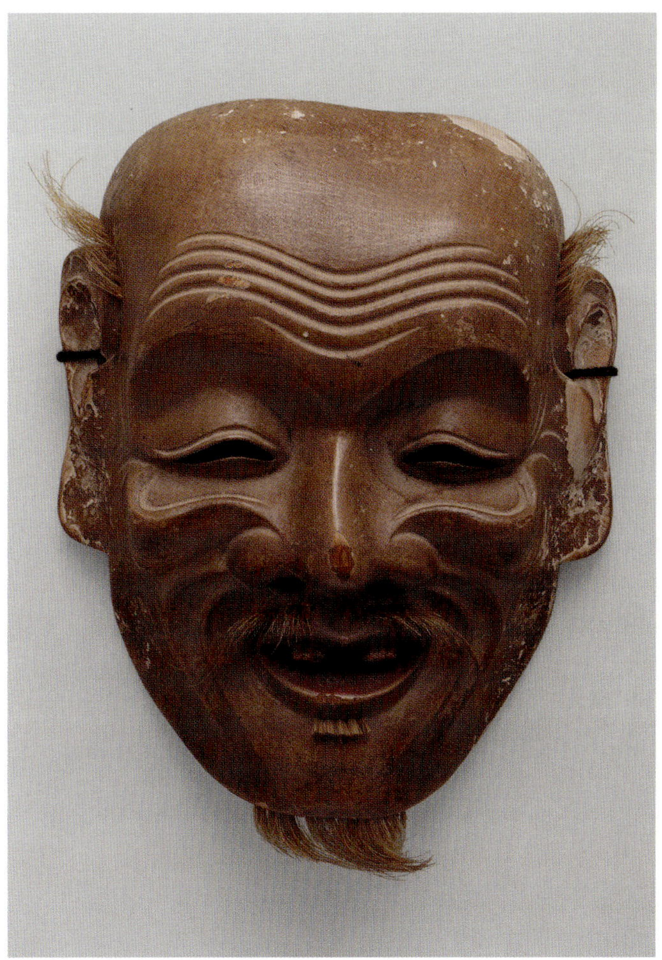

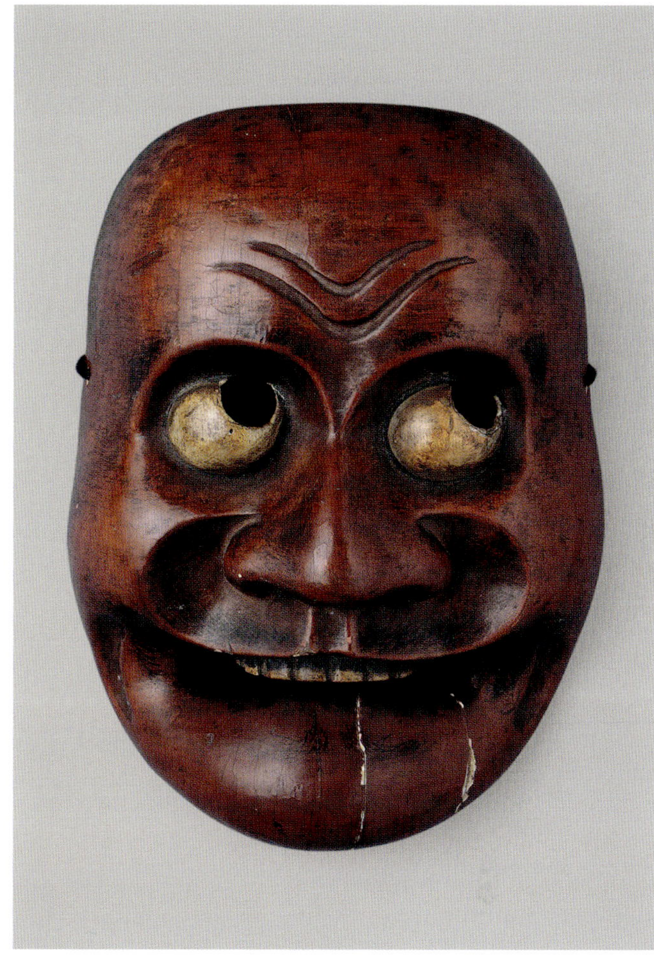

89 *Hanahiki* mask
Edo period, 18th–19th century
National Noh Theatre

90 *Kentoku* mask
Edo period, 18th century
Agency for Cultural Affairs of Japan

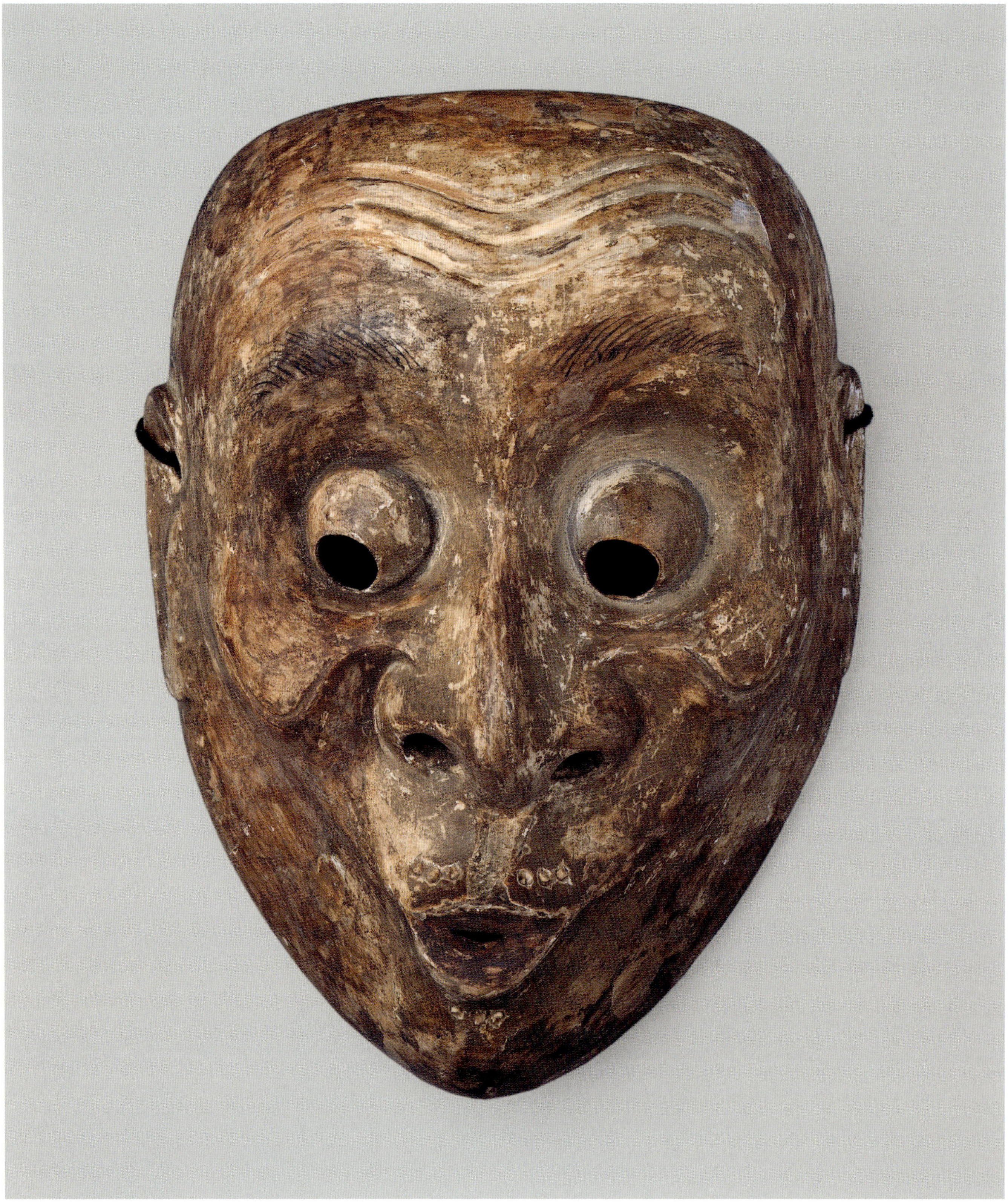

91 *Usofuki* mask
Edo period, 19th century
Agency for Cultural Affairs of Japan

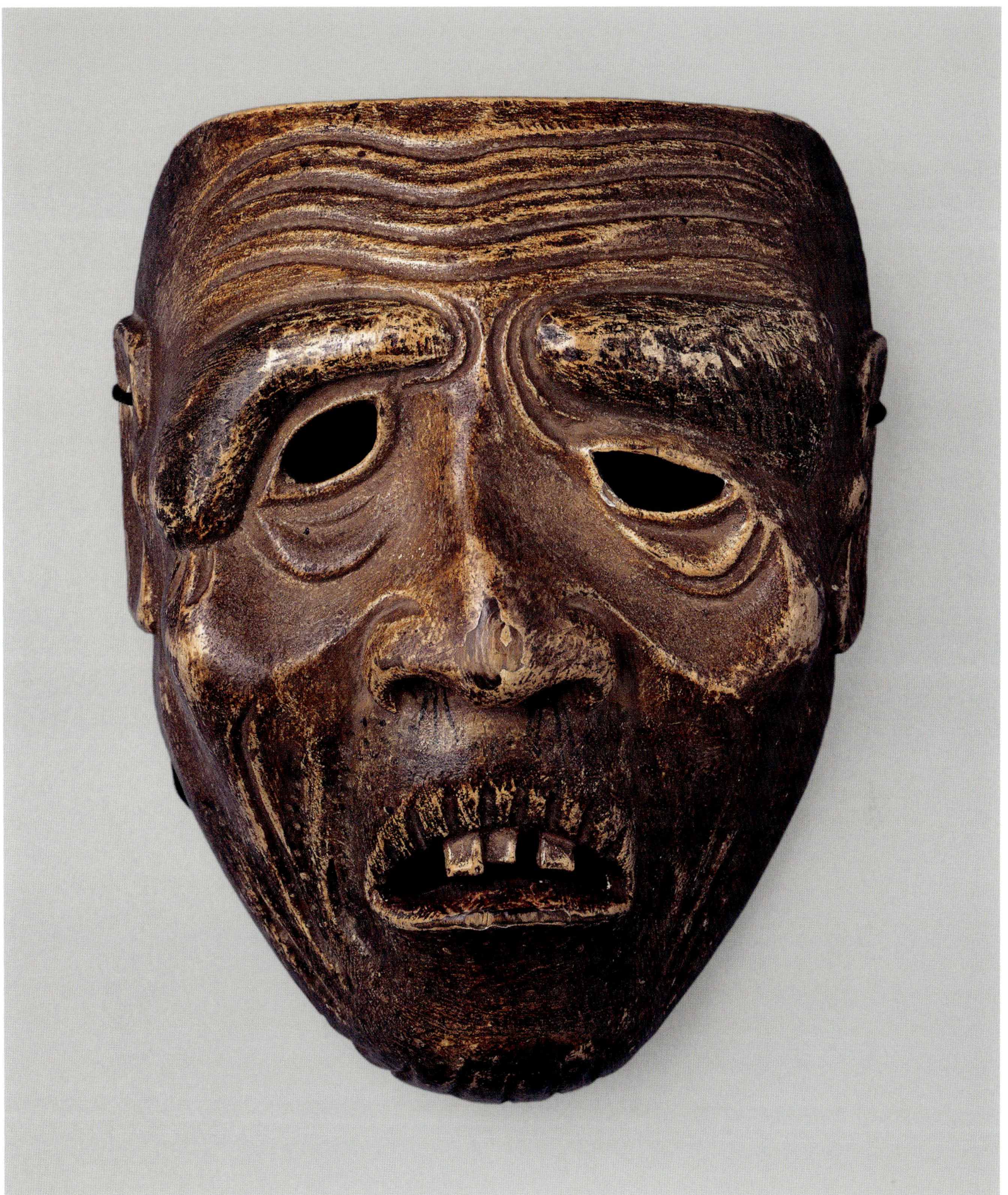

92 *Ōji* (*kaijakushi*) mask
Edo period, 18th century
Agency for Cultural Affairs of Japan

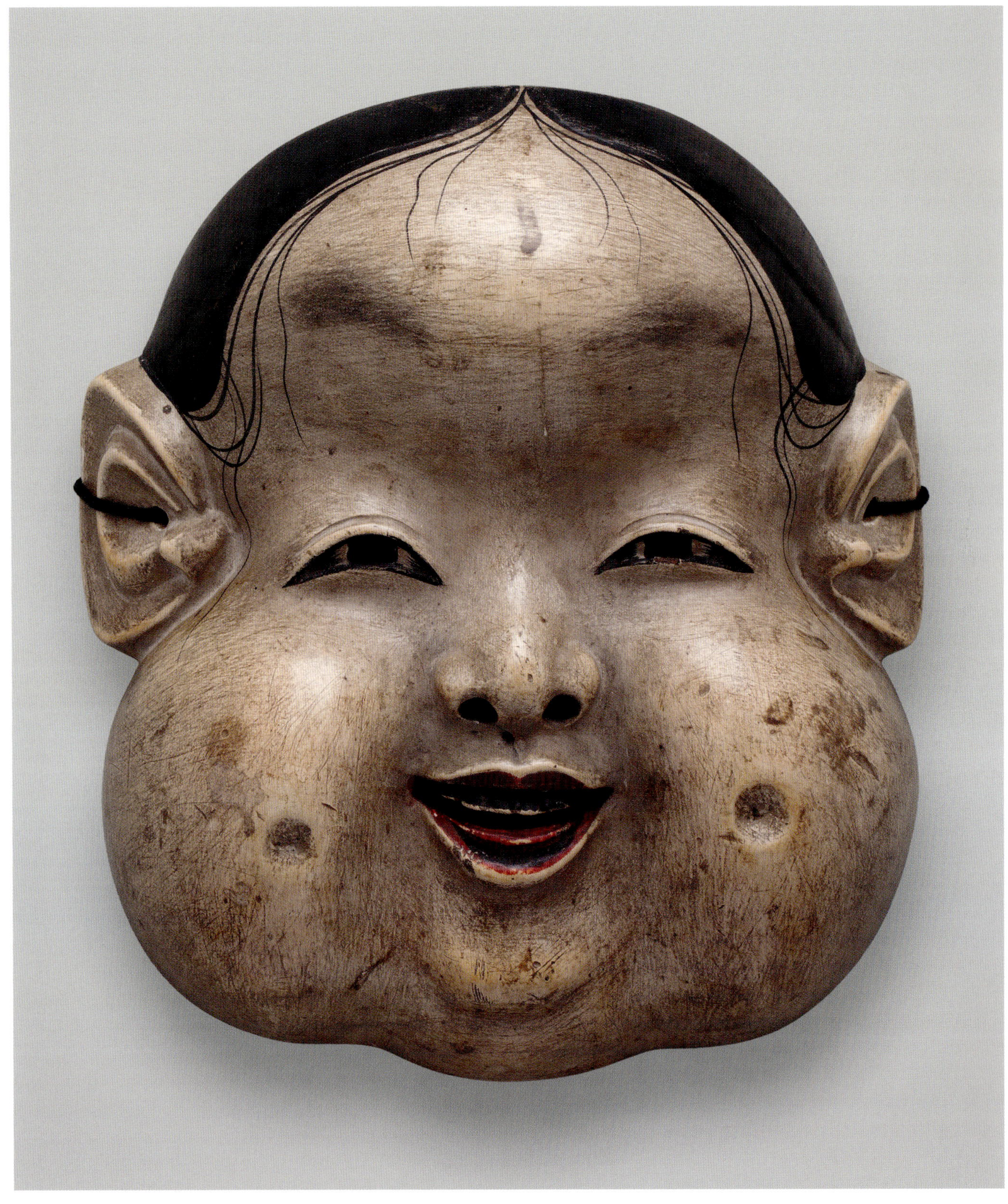

93 *Oto* mask

Edo period, 18th century
National Noh Theatre

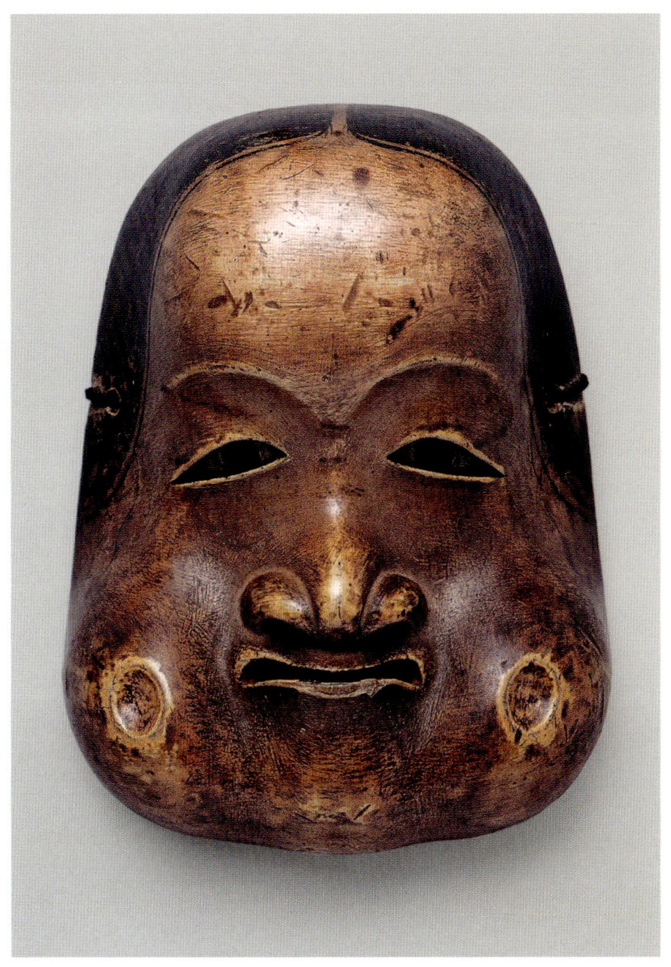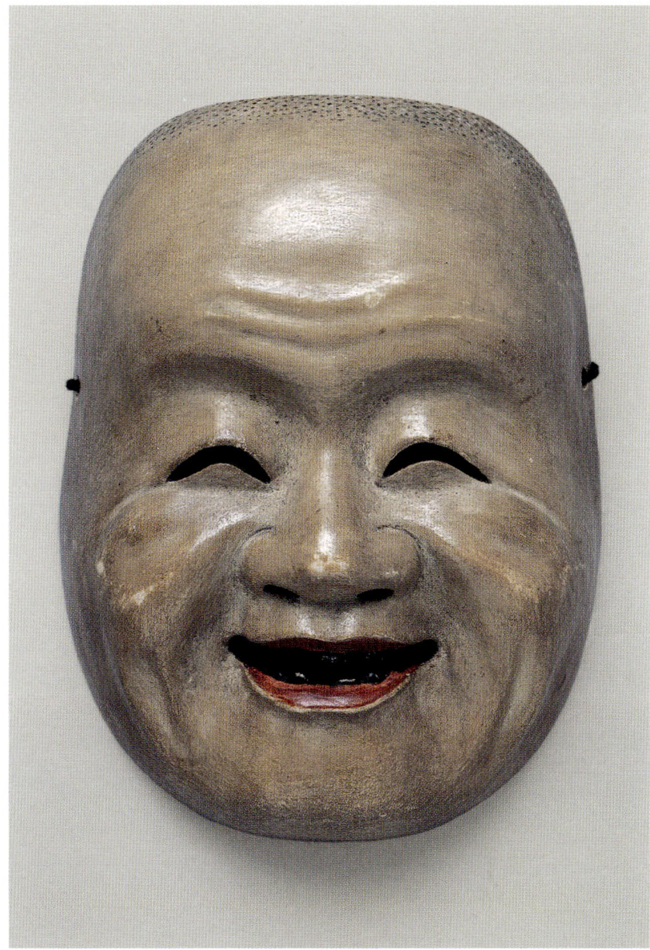

94 *Fukure* mask
Edo period, 18th century
National Noh Theatre

95 *Ama* mask
Edo period, 18th century
National Noh Theatre

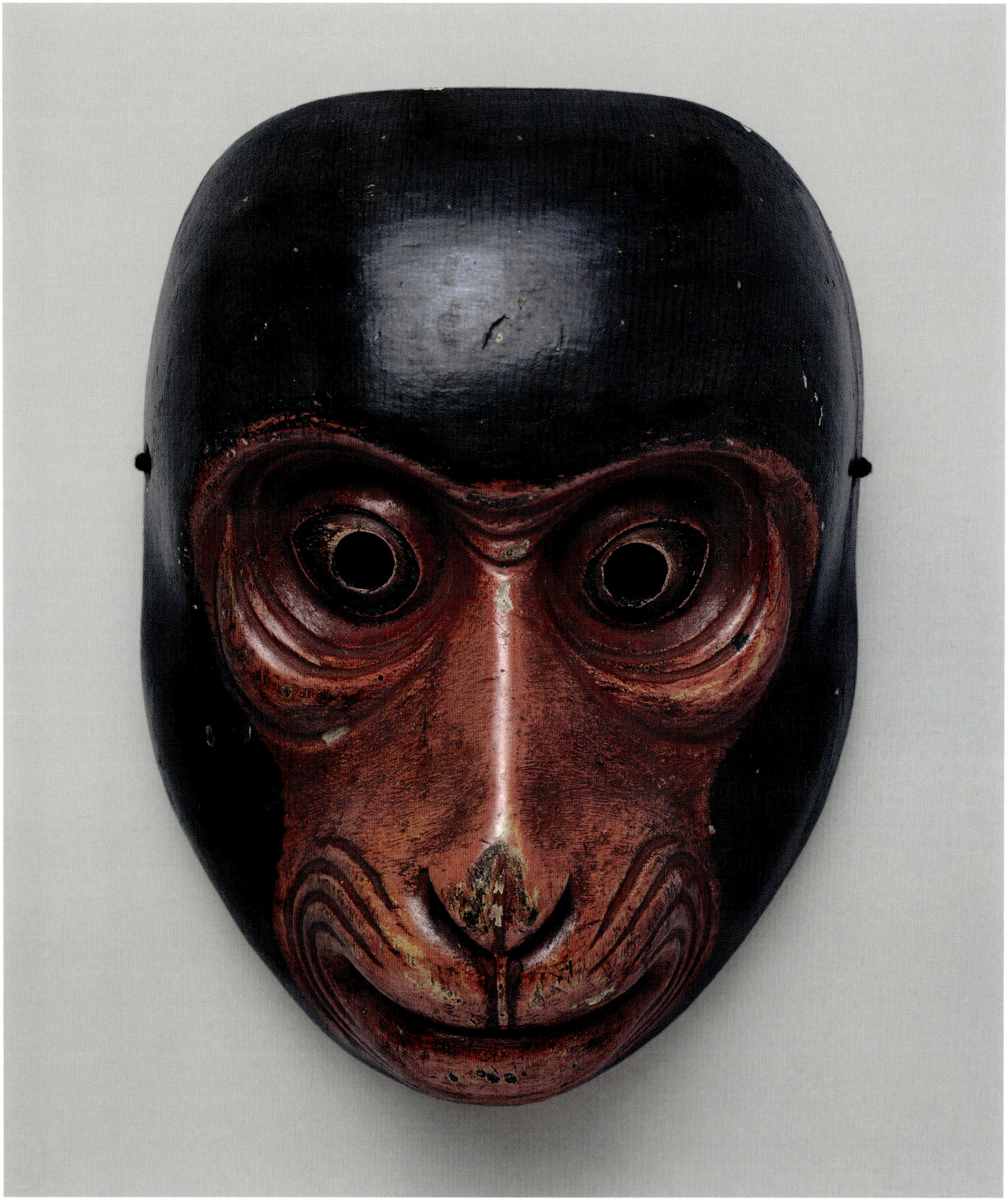

96 *Saru (monkey)* mask

Edo period, 18th century
National Noh Theatre

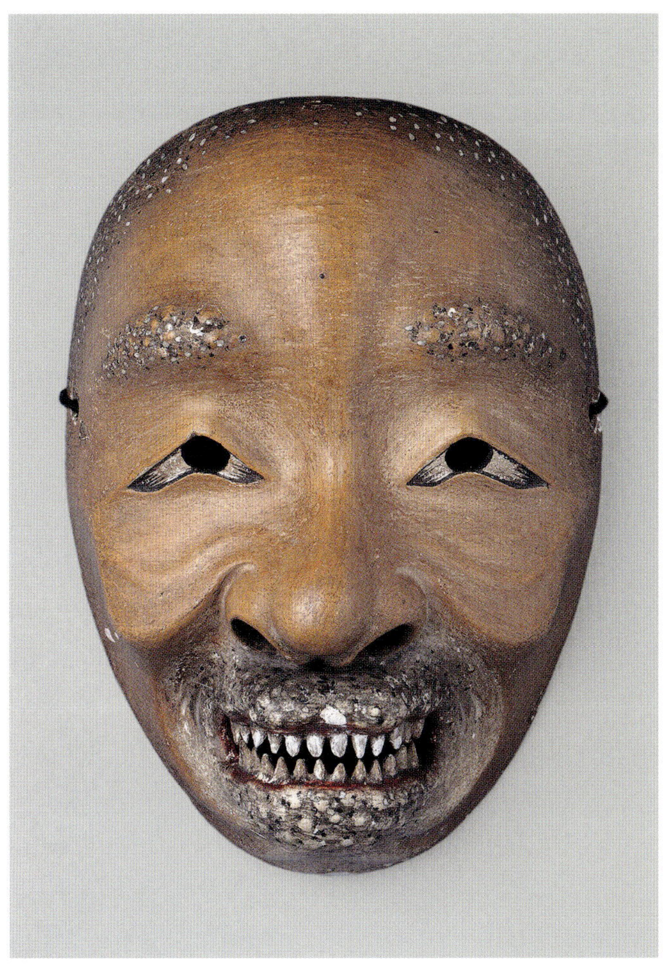

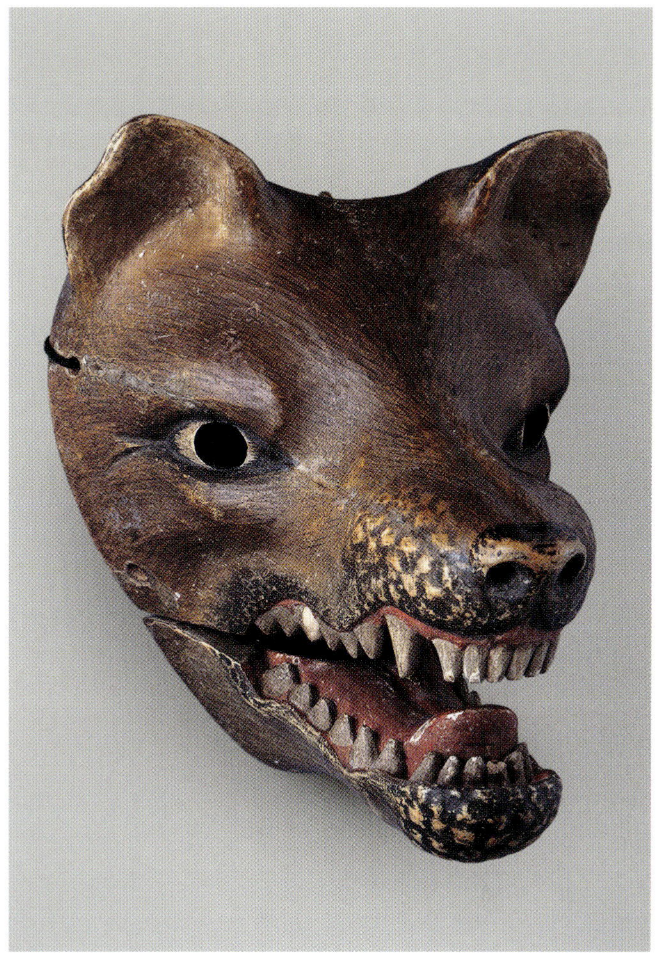

97 *Hakuzōsu* mask
Edo period, 17th century
Agency for Cultural Affairs of Japan

98 *Kitsune (fox)* mask
Edo period, 17th century
Agency for Cultural Affairs of Japan

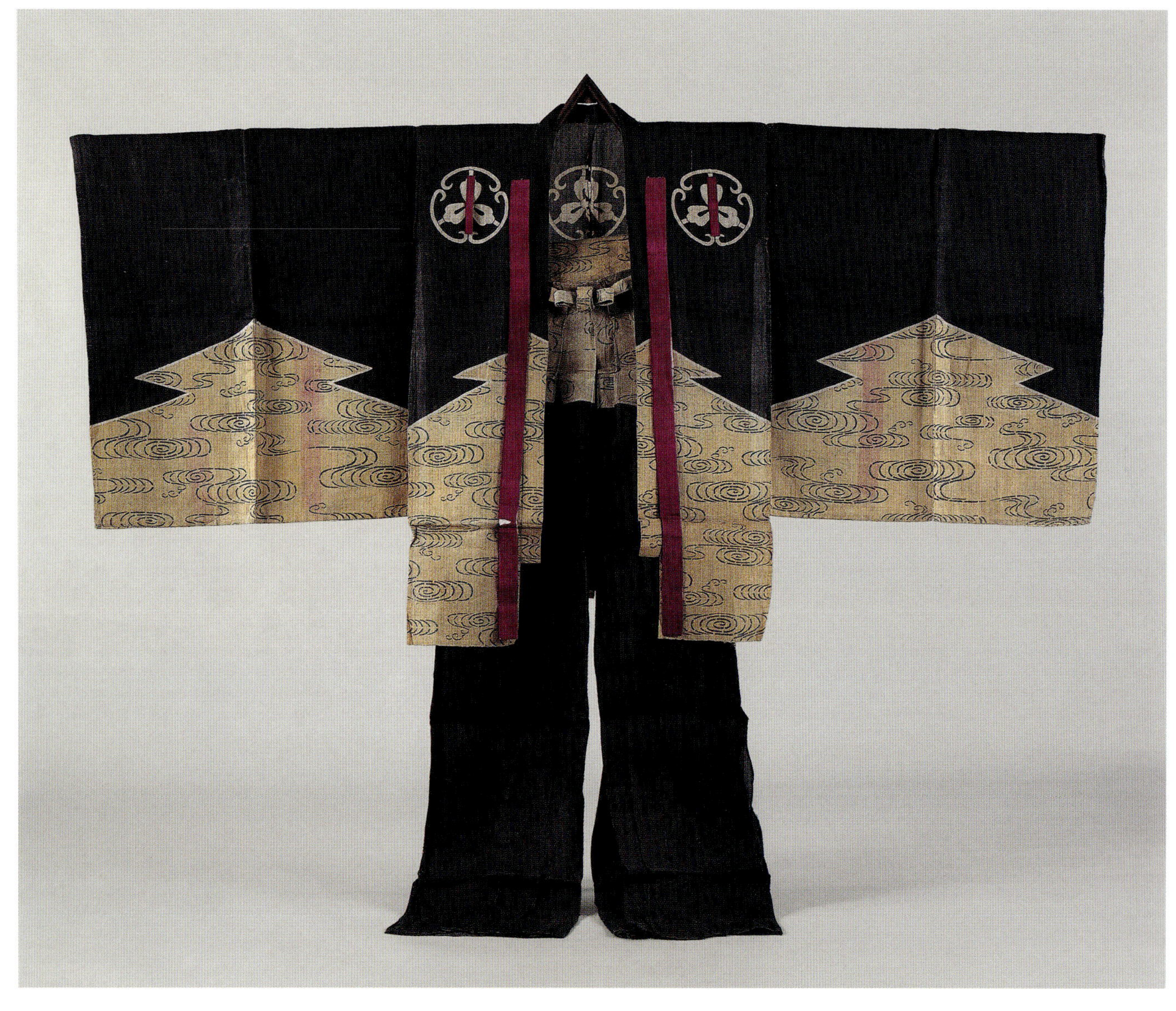

99 *Suō kamishimo* with dye-separated
units of black with design of crests
and tan with design of swirling water

Edo period, 18th–19th century
National Noh Theatre

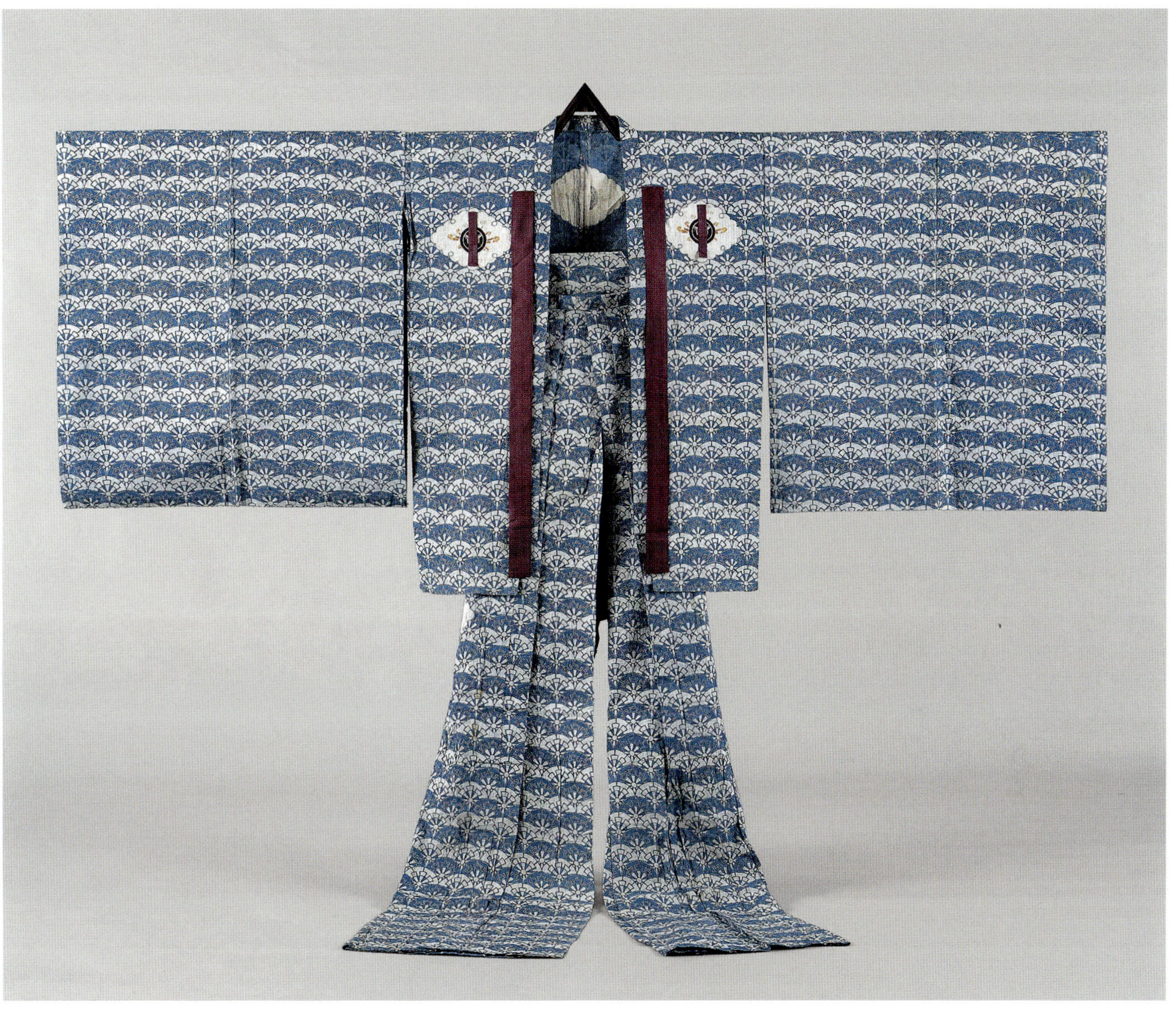

100 *Suō kamishimo* with design of
Genji wheels on indigo ground

Edo period, 19th century
National Noh Theatre

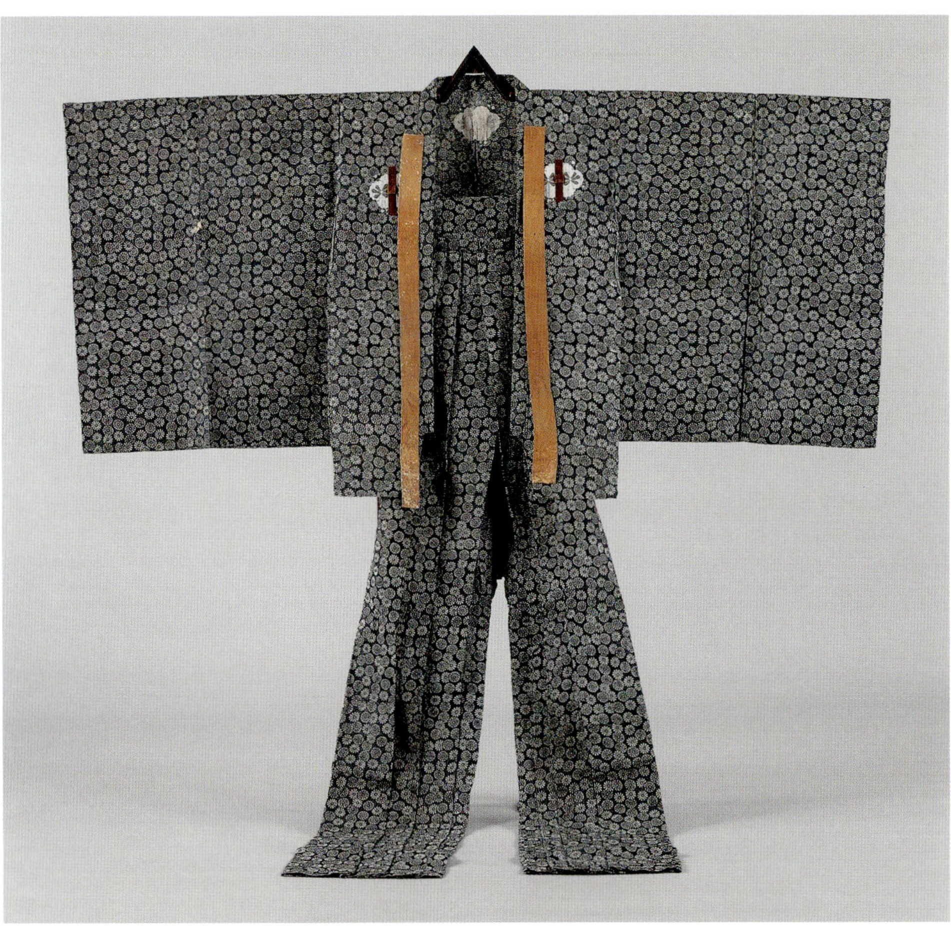

101 *Suō kamishimo* with design
of chrysanthemums on
black ground
Edo period, 19th century
National Noh Theatre

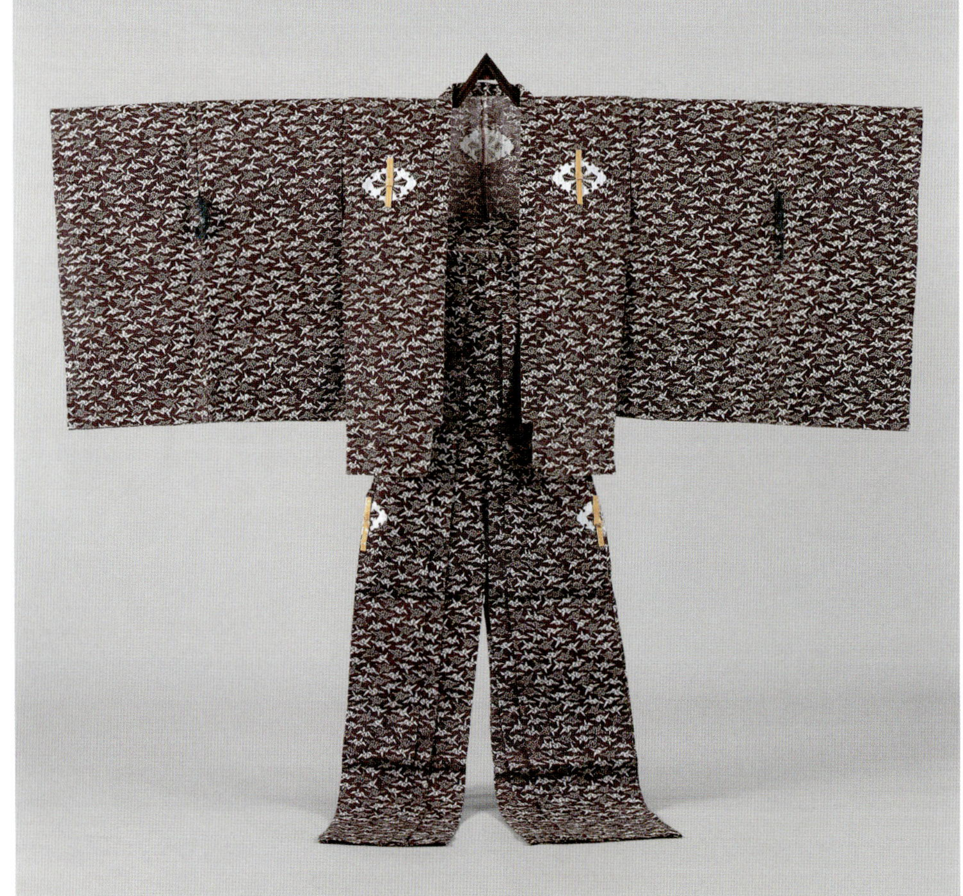

102 *Suō kamishimo* with
design of paper cranes
on maroon ground
Edo period, 19th century
National Noh Theatre

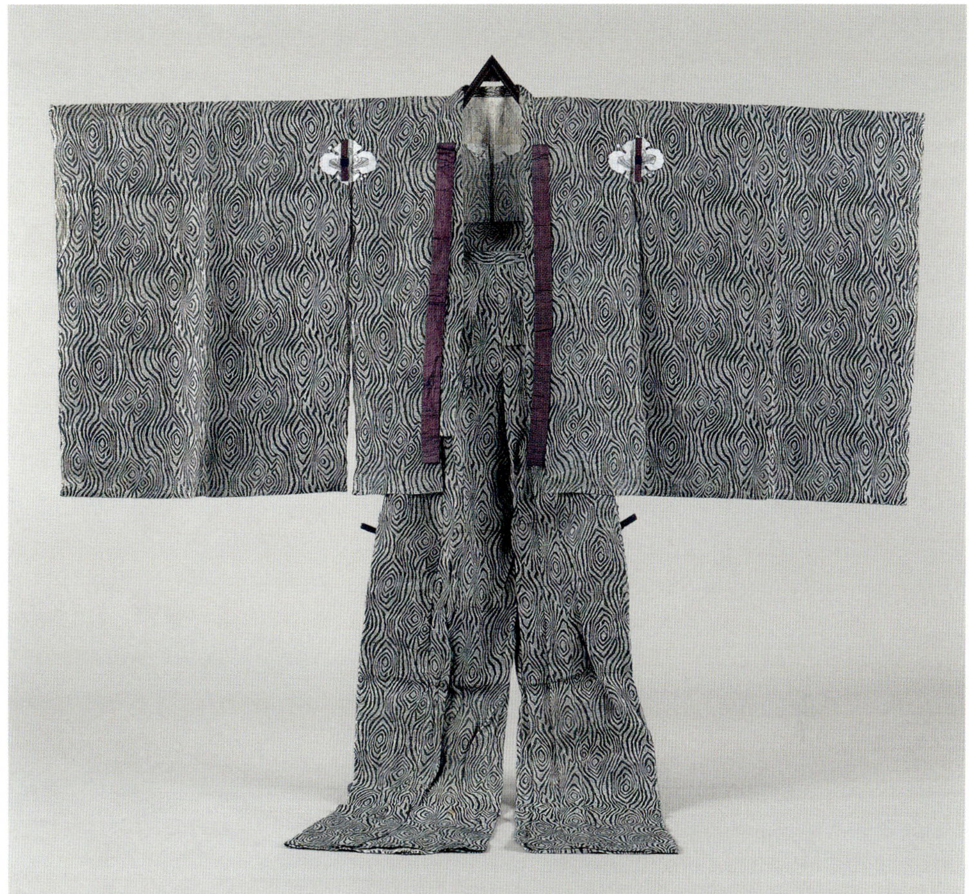

103 *Suō kamishimo* with design of wood-grain pattern on grey ground
Edo period, 19th century
National Noh Theatre

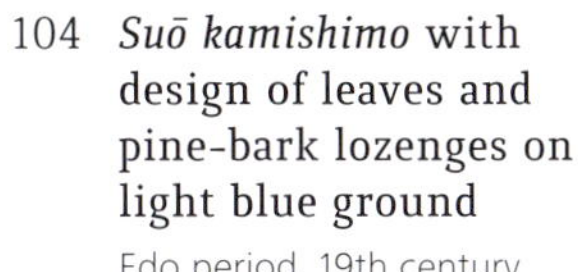

104 *Suō kamishimo* with design of leaves and pine-bark lozenges on light blue ground
Edo period, 19th century
National Noh Theatre

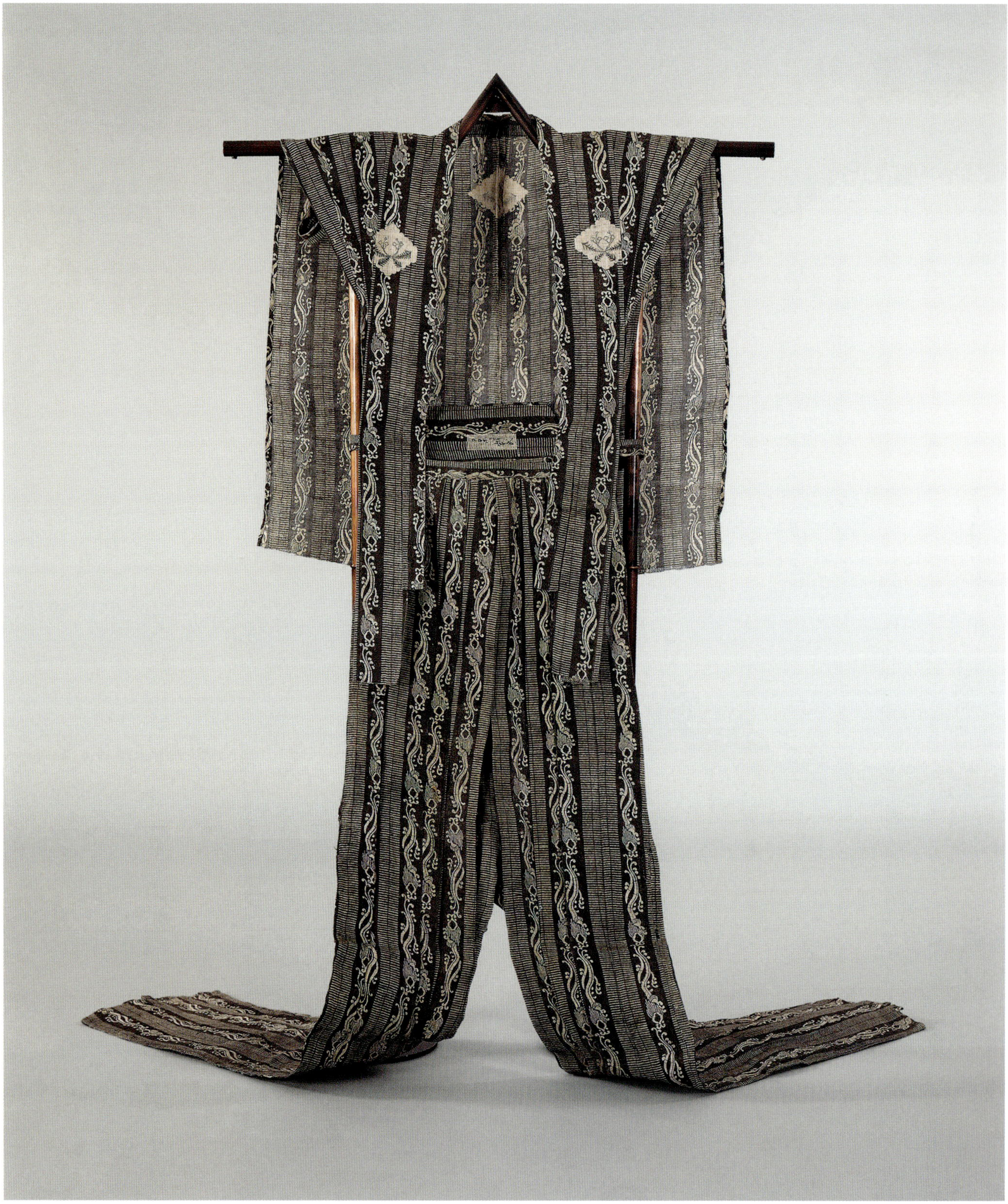

105 *Naga-kamishimo* with design of
rain dragons on brown ground

Edo period, 19th century
Private collection

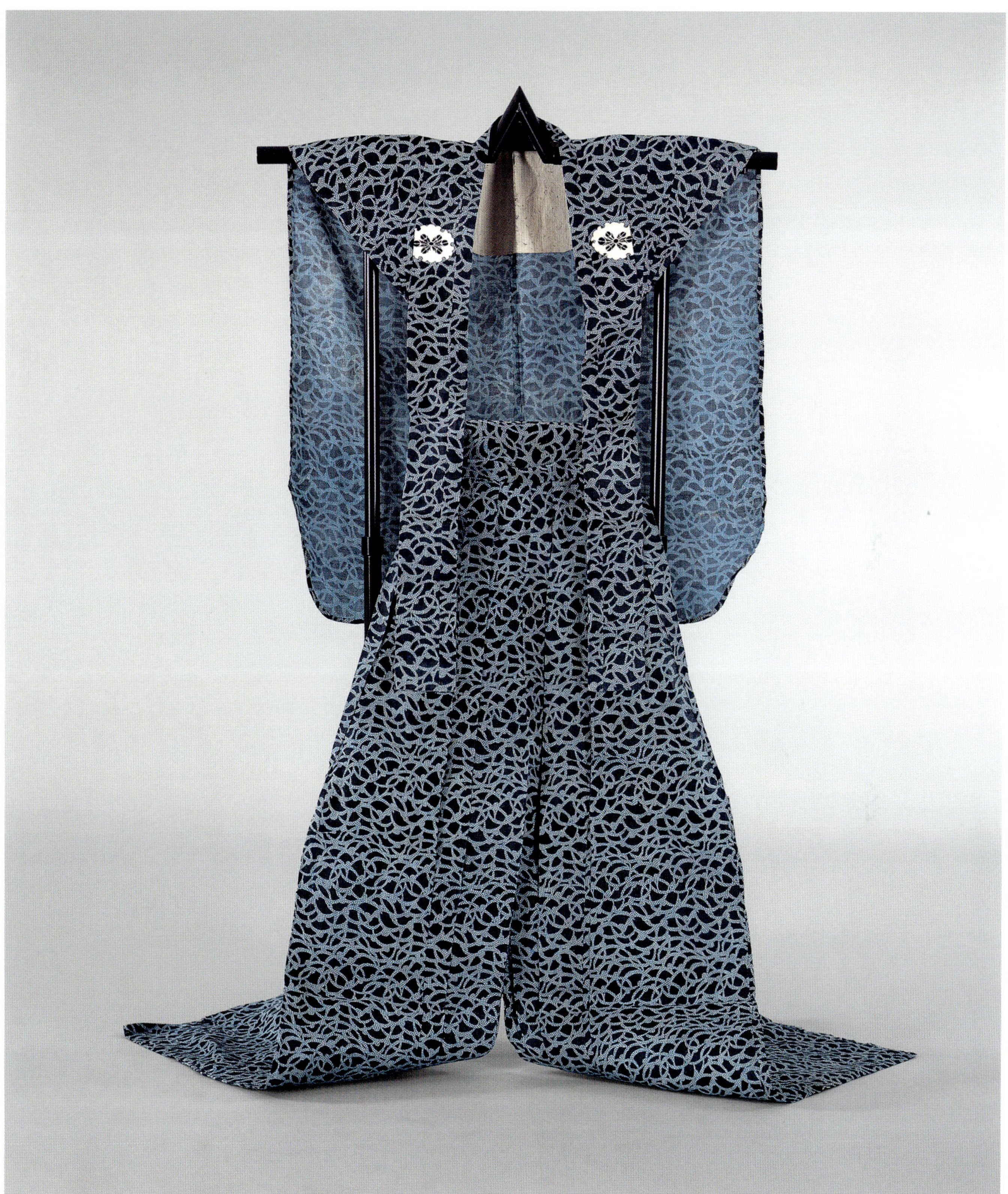

106 *Naga-kamishimo* with design
of interlocking anchors on
dark blue ground

Meiji period, 19th century
National Noh Theatre

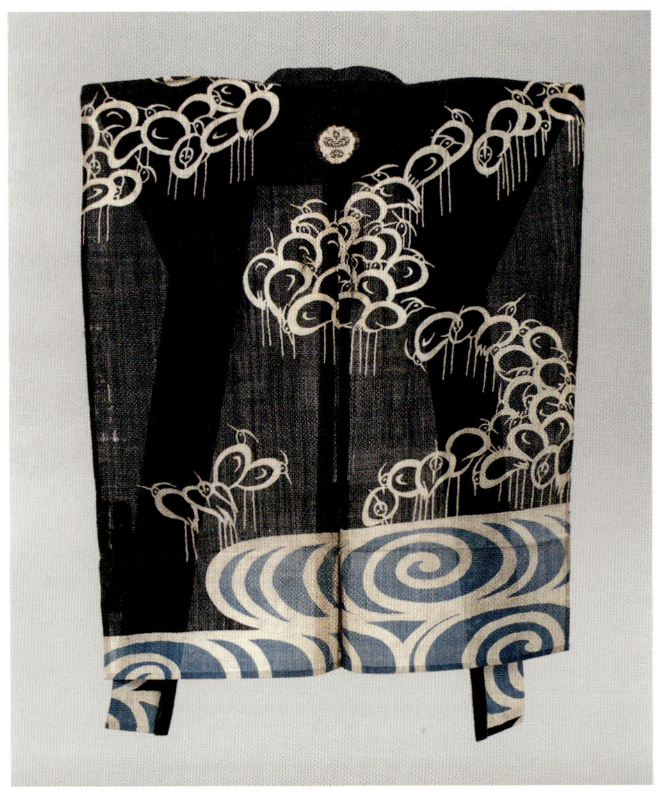

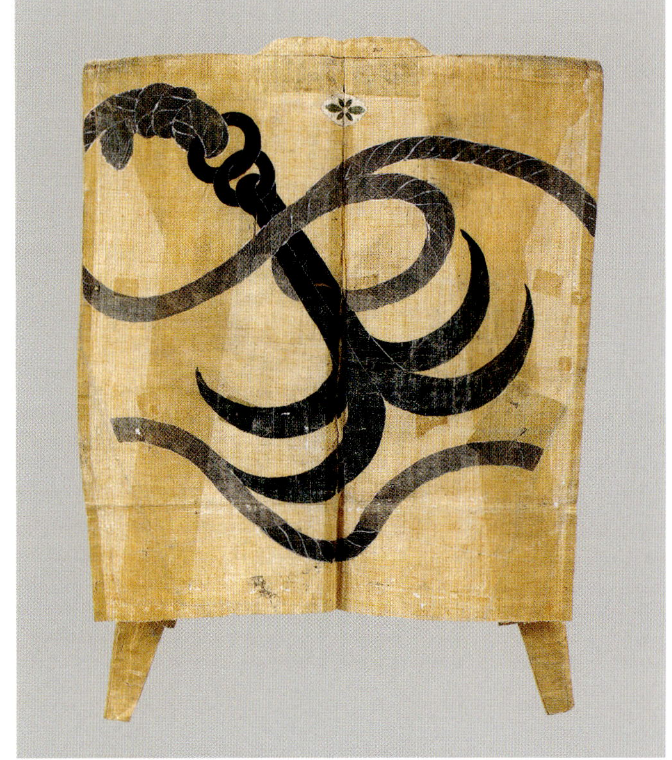

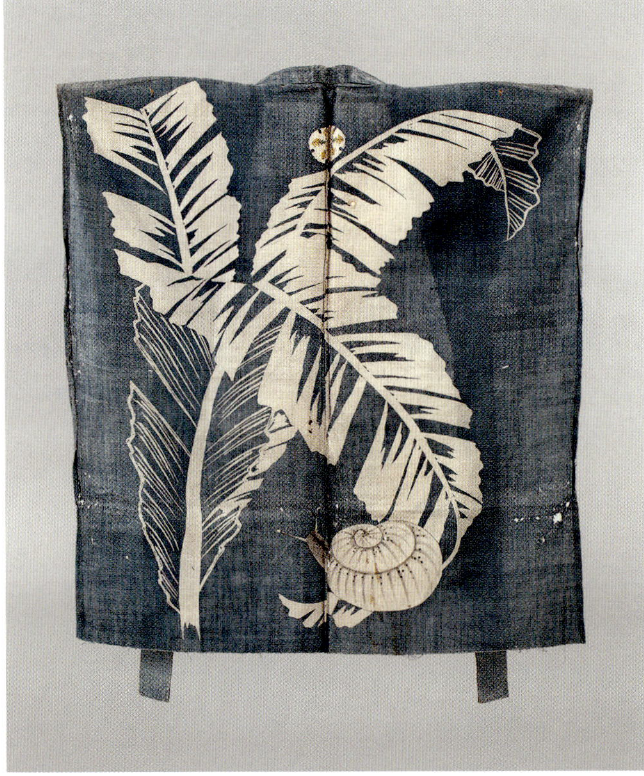

107 *Kataginu* with design of
flowing water and herons
on black ground

Edo period, 18th century
Private collection

108 *Kataginu* with design of
anchor on yellow ground

Edo period, 18th century
National Noh Theatre

109 *Kataginu* with design of
banana leaves and snail
on light blue ground

Edo period, 18th–19th century
National Noh Theatre

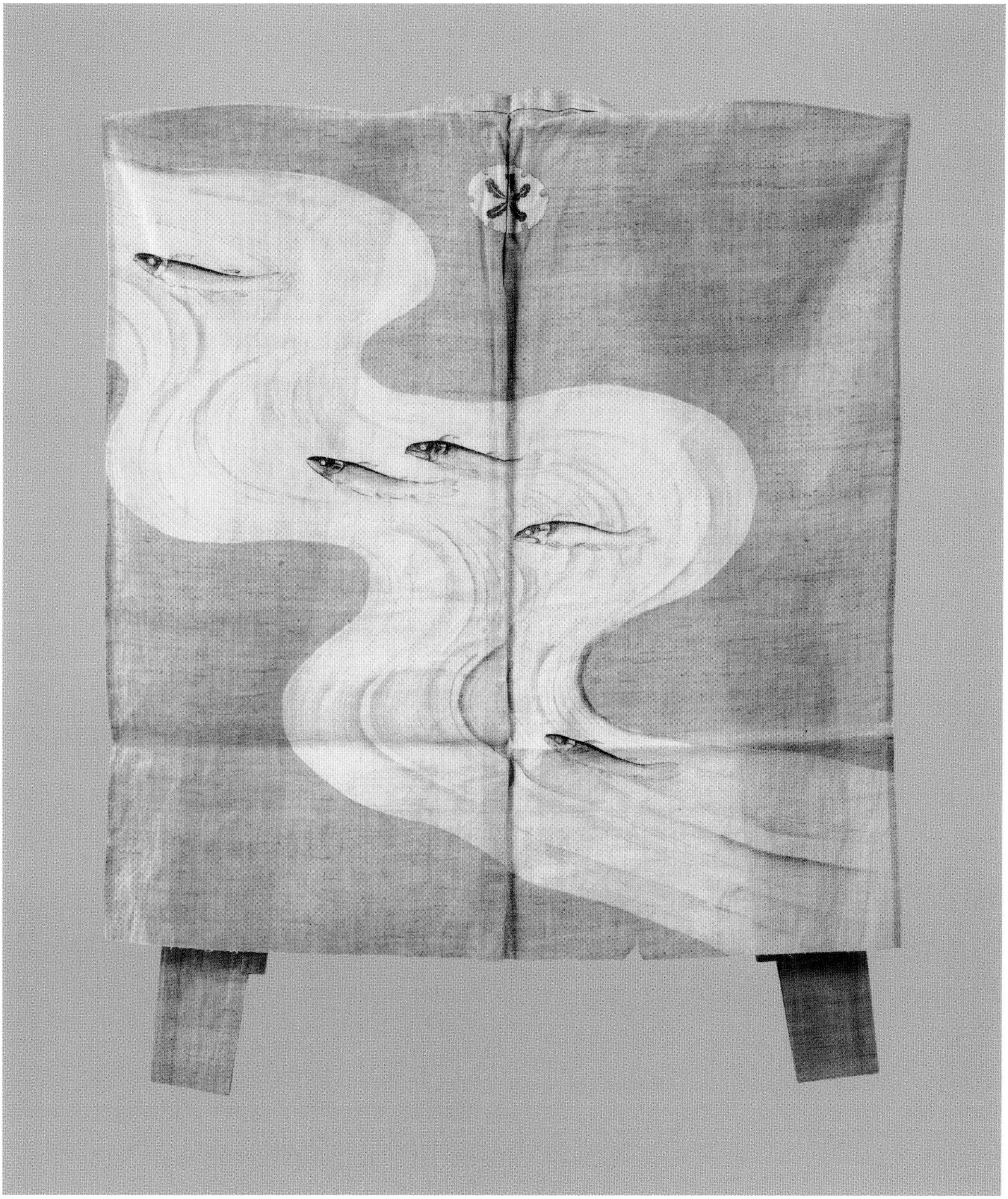

110 *Kataginu* with design of sweetfish
   on yellow ground
Edo period, 19th century
Private collection

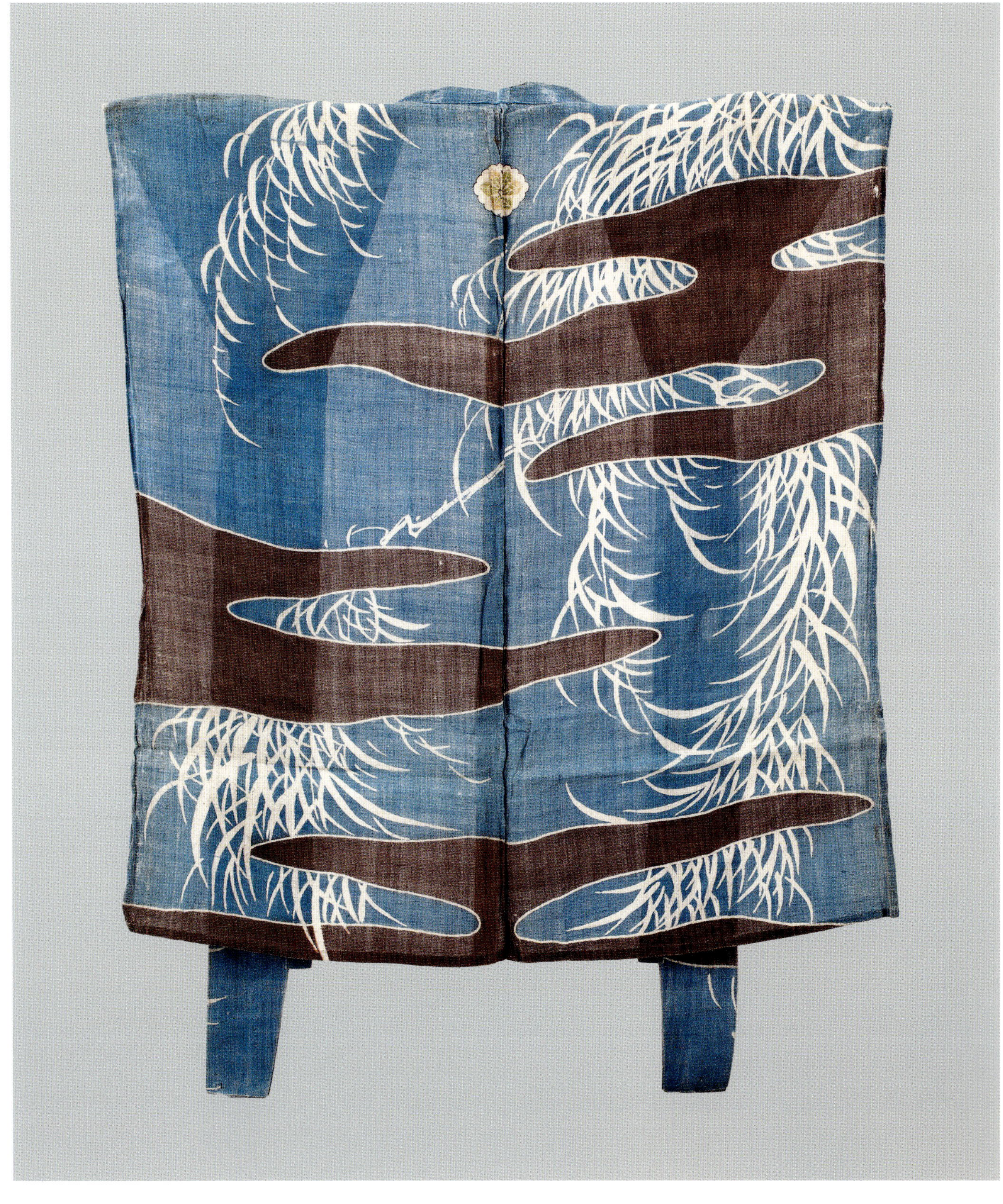

111 *Kataginu* with design of weeping
willow in mist on light blue ground

Edo period, 19th century
National Noh Theatre

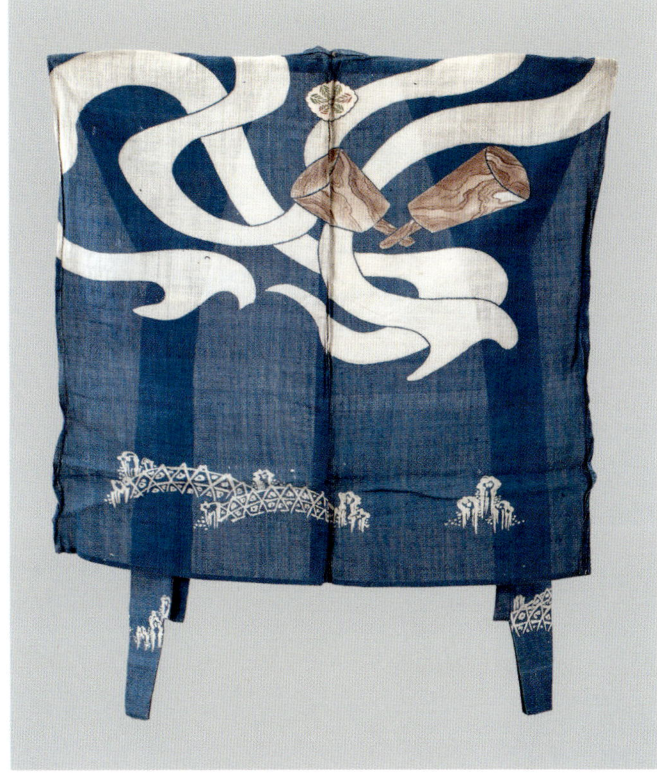

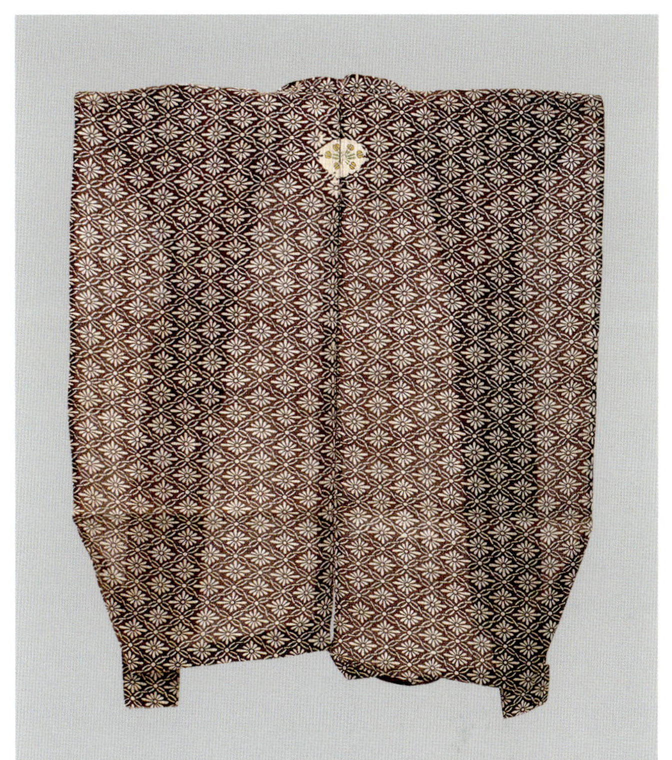

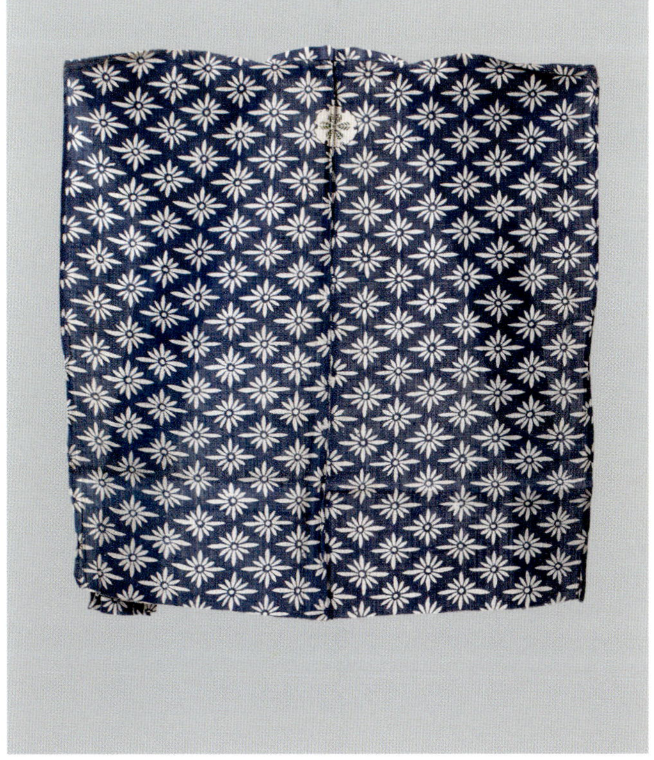

112 *Kataginu* with design of fulling
cloth on indigo ground

Edo period, 19th century
Private collection

113 *Kataginu* with design of interlocking
rings with chrysanthemums
on brown ground

Edo period, 19th century
National Noh Theatre

114 *Kataginu* with design of interlocking
diamonds with chrysanthemums
on dark blue ground

Edo period, 19th century
National Noh Theatre

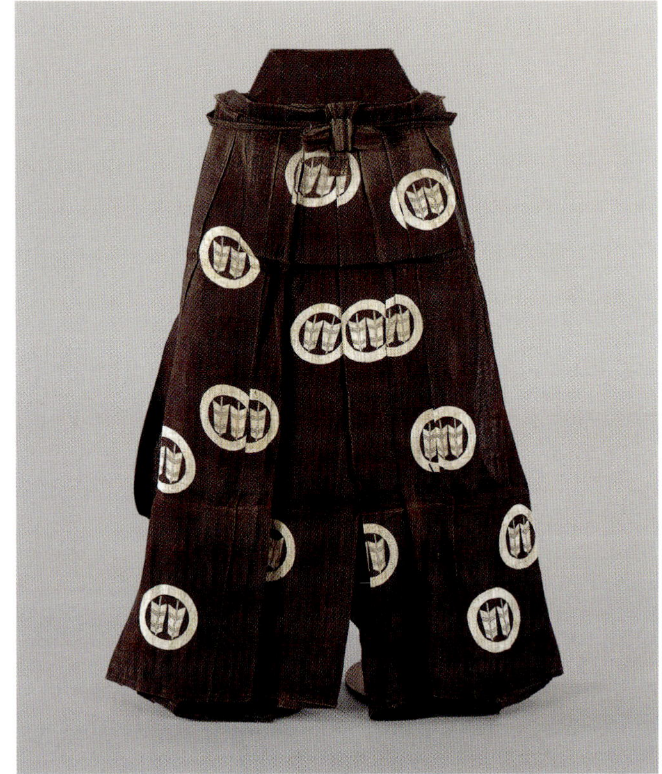

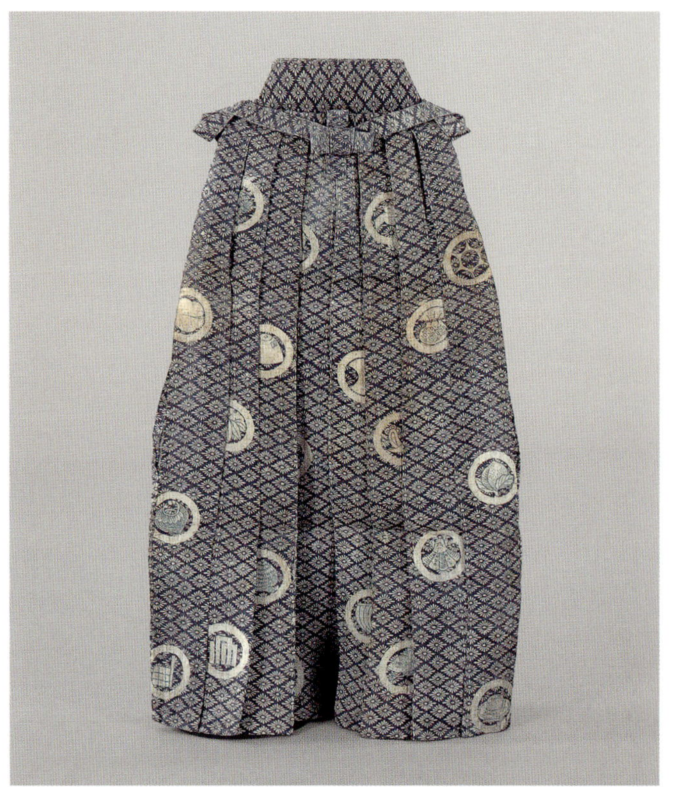

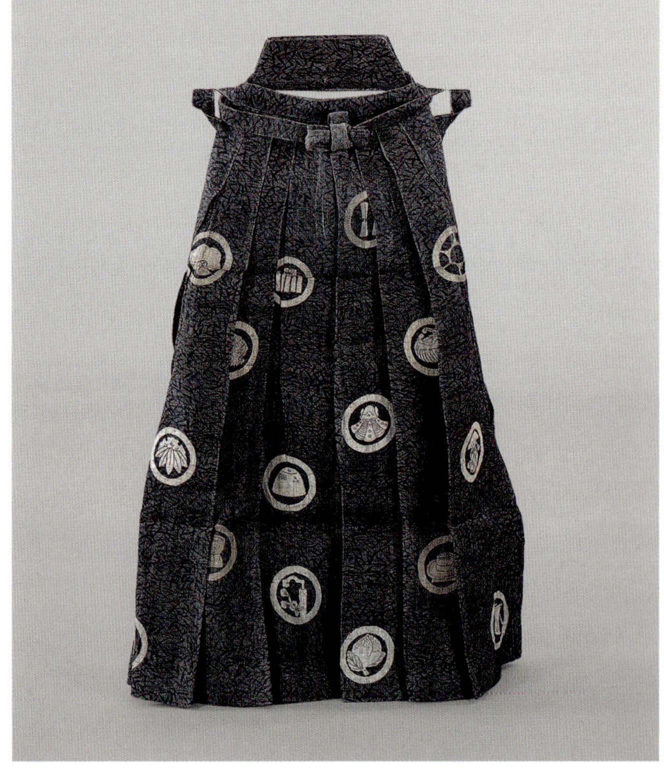

115 *Hanbakama* with design of scattered roundels and arrow feathers on dark brown ground
Edo period, 19th century
National Noh Theatre

116 *Hanbakama* with design of chrysanthemum diamonds and scattered roundels on indigo-grey ground
Edo period, 19th century
National Noh Theatre

117 *Hanbakama* with design of pine needles and scattered roundels on grey ground
Edo period, 19th century
Private collection

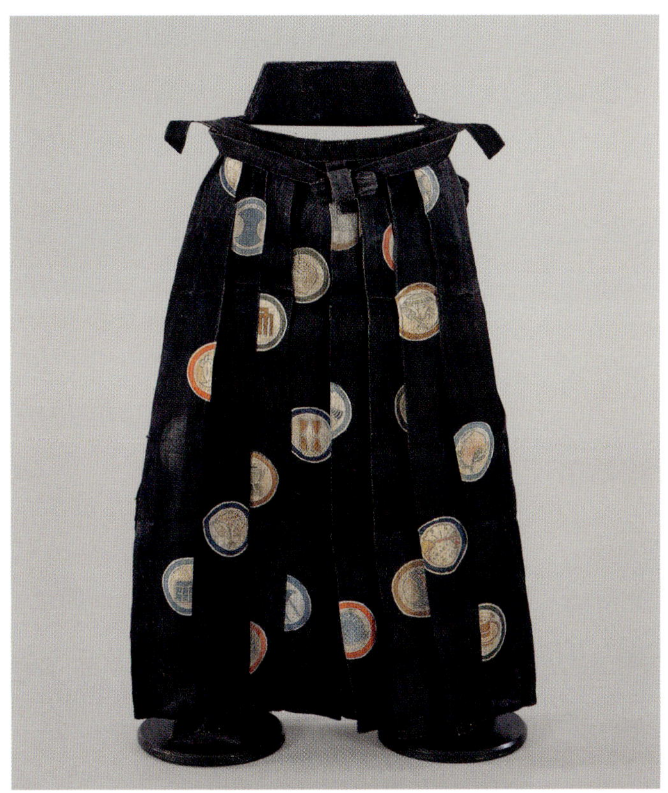

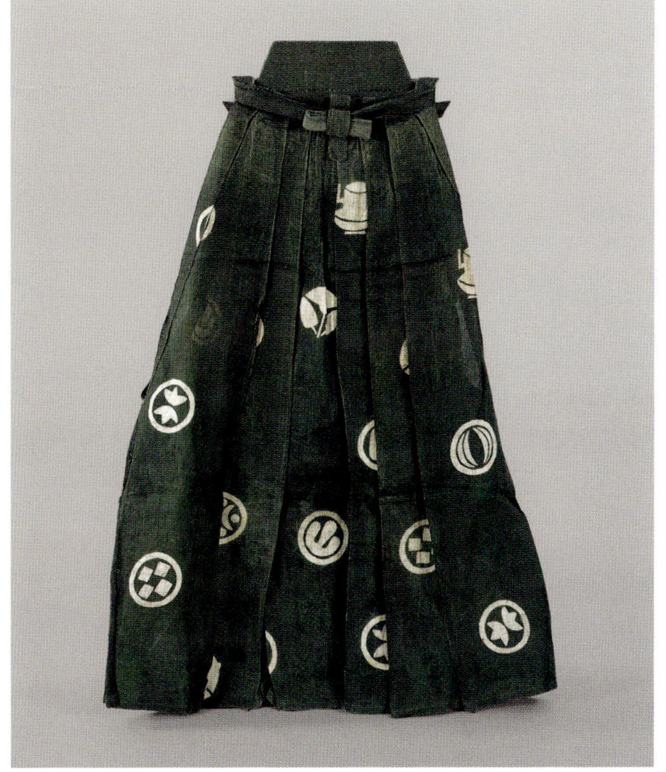

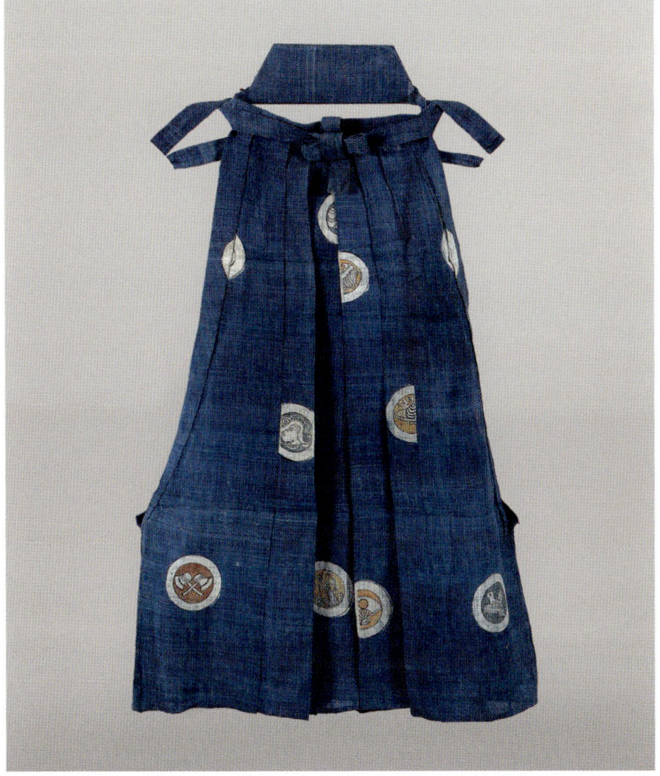

118 *Hanbakama* with design of
scattered roundels on
black ground
Edo period, 19th century
National Noh Theatre

119 *Hanbakama* with design of
scattered roundels on
dark green ground
Edo–Meiji period, 19th century
National Noh Theatre

120 *Hanbakama* with design of
scattered roundels on
indigo ground
Edo period, 19th century
Private collection

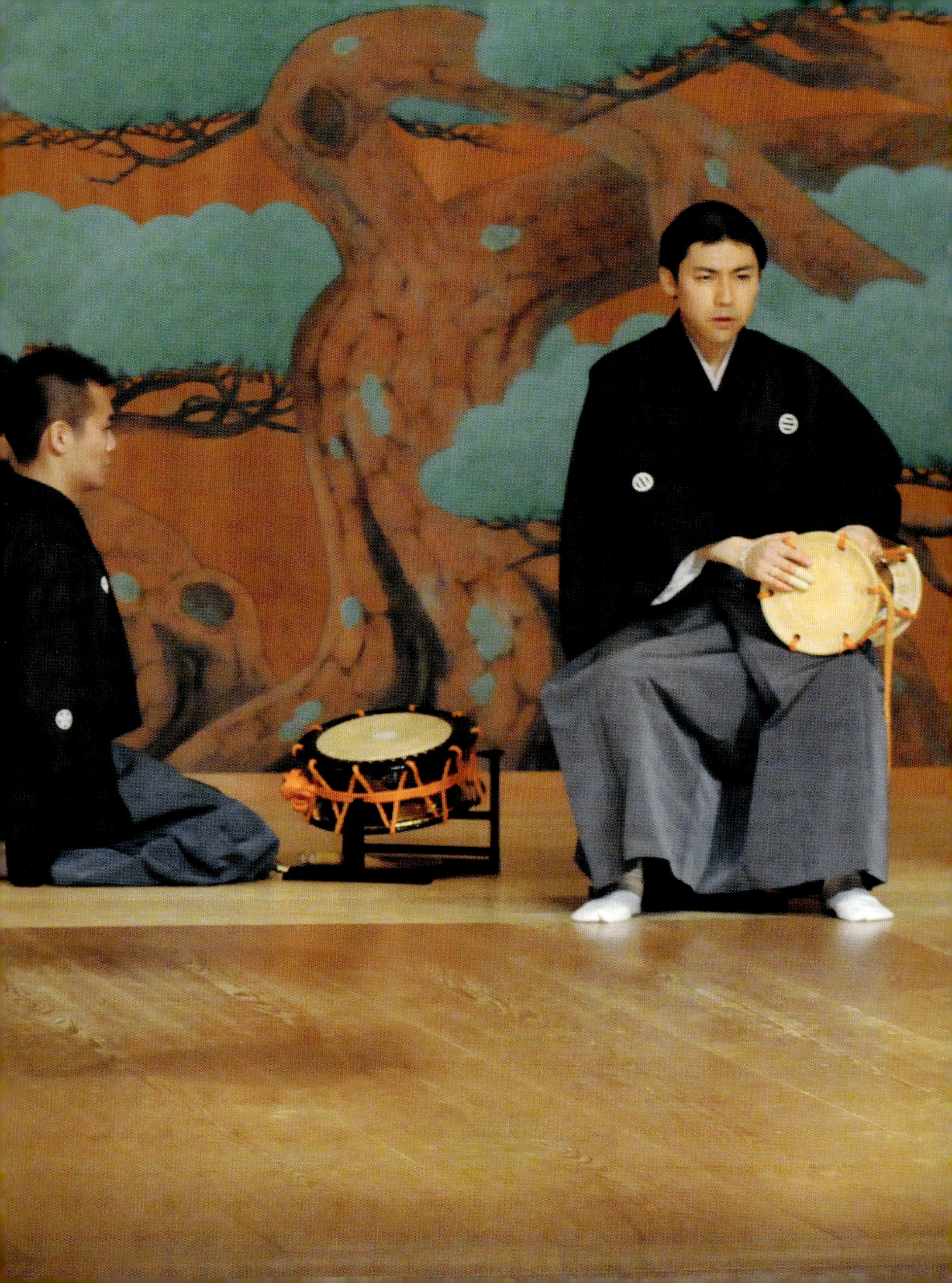

MUSICAL INSTRUMENTS IN NŌ AND KYŌGEN

The nō ensemble consists of a transverse flute and three percussion instruments. The flute is called *fue* or *nōkan*. It is made of bamboo, which is bound with wisteria or birch bark and then lacquered in red on the interior and black on the exterior.

The *kotsuzumi* (shoulder drum) is hourglass shaped and is the smallest of the three percussion instruments. It has a body made of cherry wood, which is lacquered on the exterior with *maki-e* designs in gold and silver. The drum skins (*kawa*) on either end are horsehide and two sets of ropes (*shirabeo*) tie the drumheads together. The drum skins are breathed upon when played to retain a degree of moisture on the skin's surface and to assist in maintaining the instrument's sound.

The *ōtsuzumi* or *ōkawa* (hip drum) is also hourglass-shaped. Its design and materials are similar to the *kotsuzumi*, but the *ōtsuzumi* is larger and has a ring carved in the centre of the drum. Unlike the *kotsuzumi*, the drumheads of the *ōtsuzumi* need to be kept dry during playing in order to produce a harder sound. This is achieved by placing the drumheads over a charcoal burner before use.

The *taiko* (stick drum) differs from both the *kotsuzumi* and *ōtsuzumi*: it is made from one large cylinder that is decorated with lacquer painting on the exterior. *Taiko* are usually made from zelkova (*keyaki*) or Japanese bead tree (*sendan*), and the drum skin is cowhide. Sound is produced by beating the drumhead with two sticks. (NS)

Scene from the nō play *Lady Aoi* (*Aoi no Ue*)

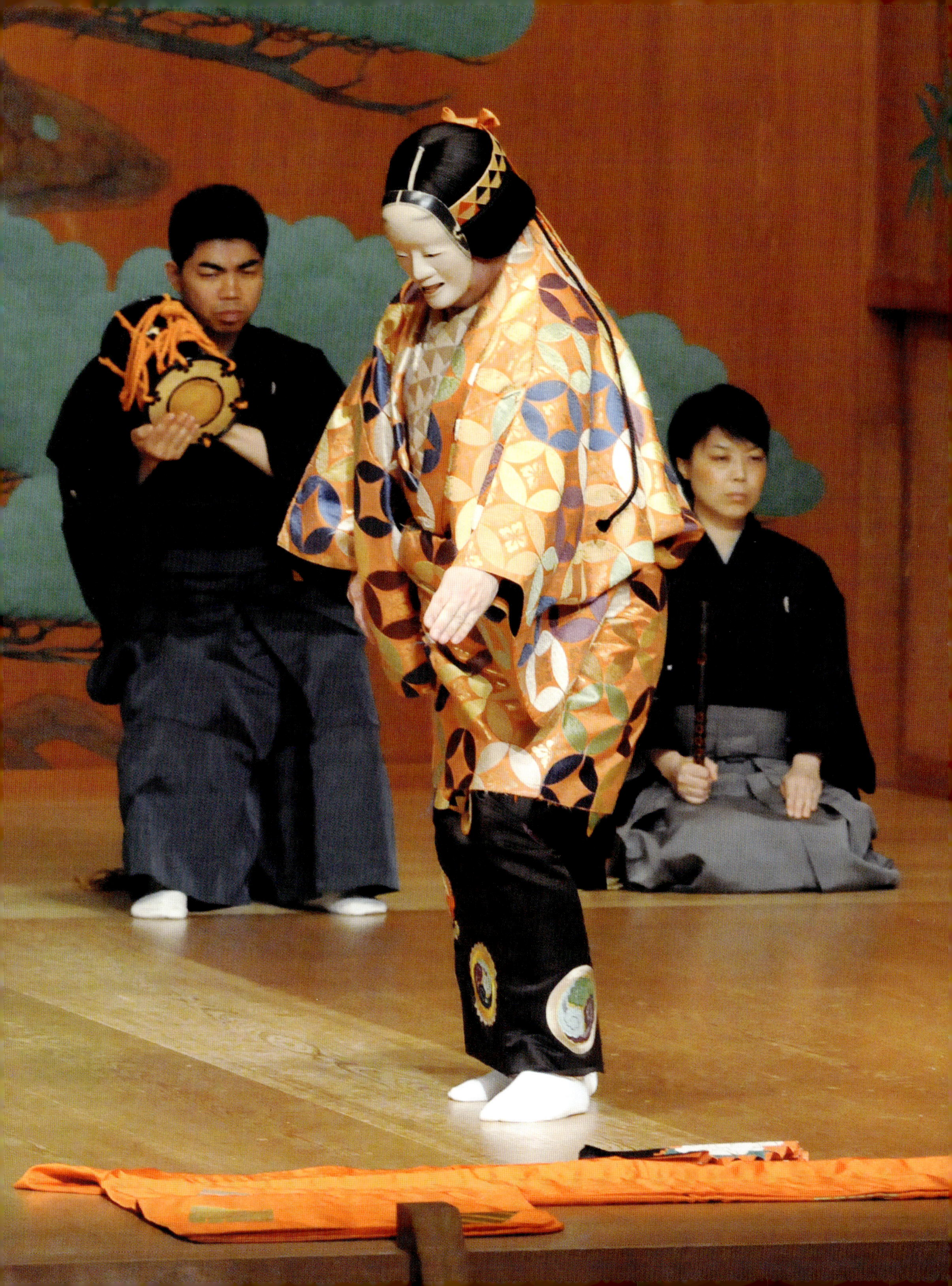

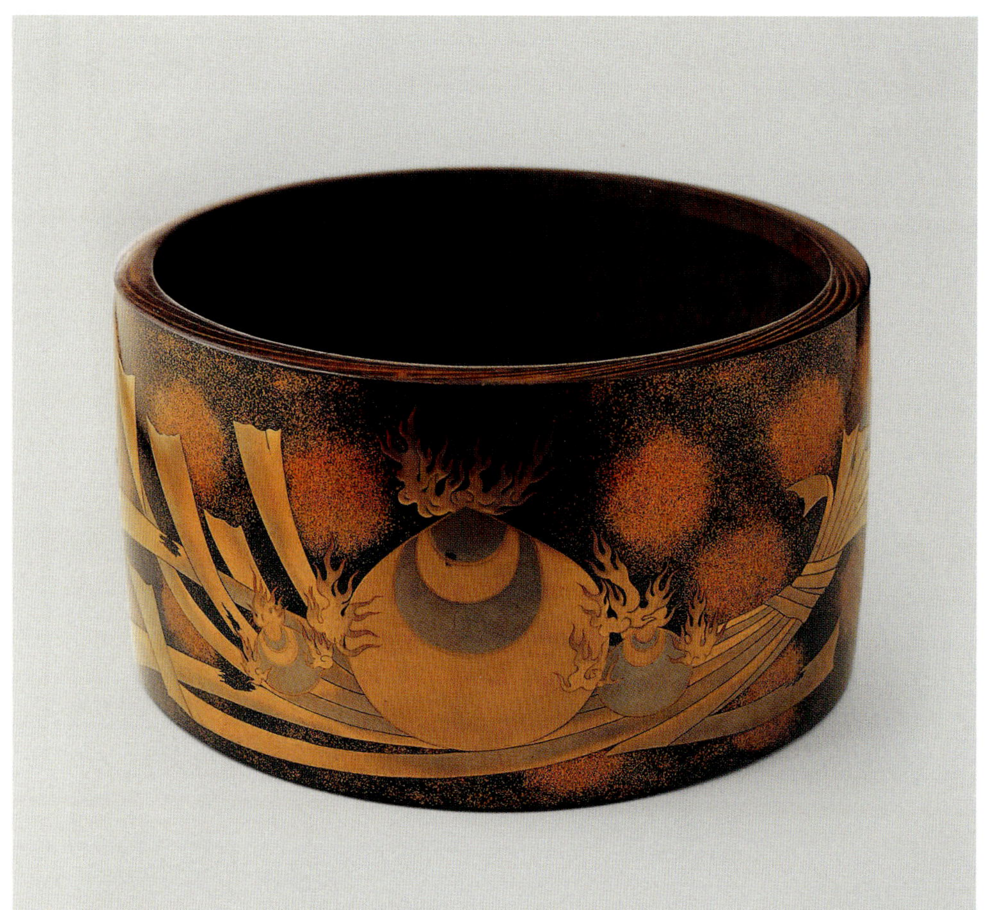

121 *Taiko* drum body with design of flaming jewels
Edo period, 19th century
National Noh Theatre

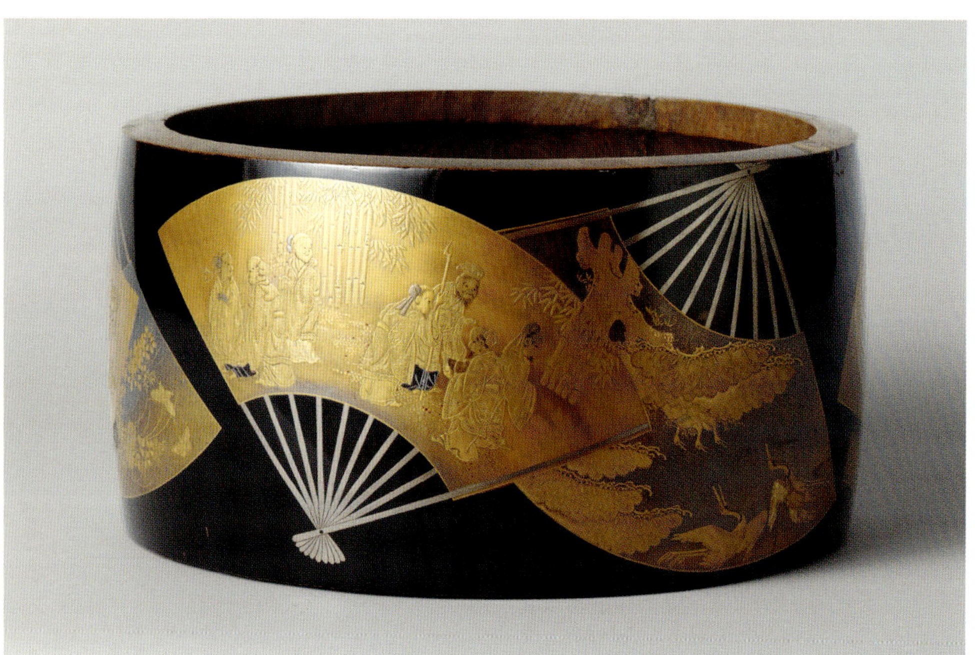

122 *Taiko* drum body with design of fans
Edo period, 19th century
Agency for Cultural Affairs of Japan

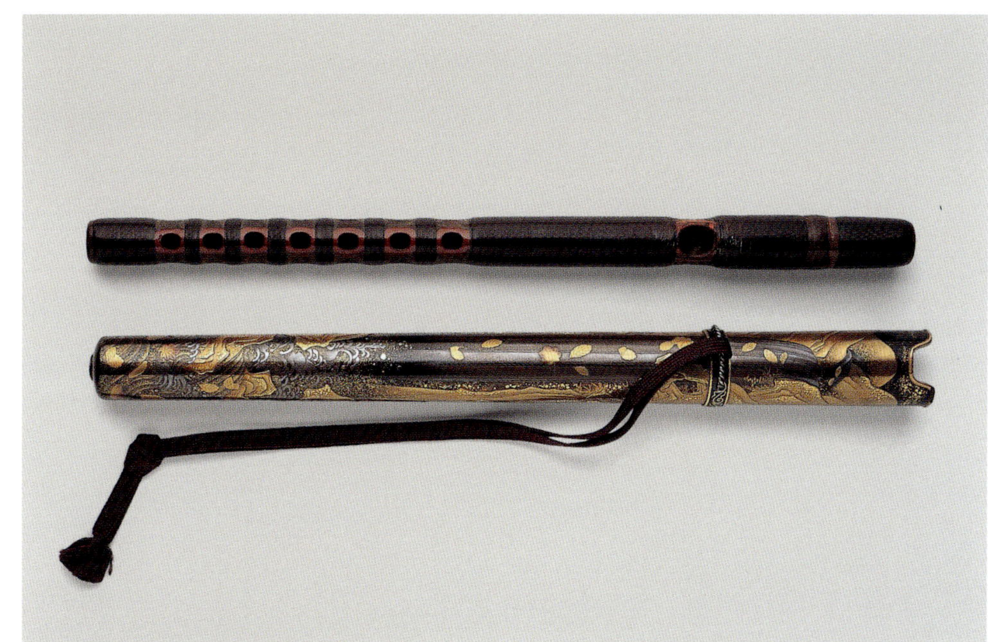

123 Nō flute with design of a warrior on horseback and flute case with design of autumn leaves at Nachi waterfall

Edo period, 19th century
National Noh Theatre

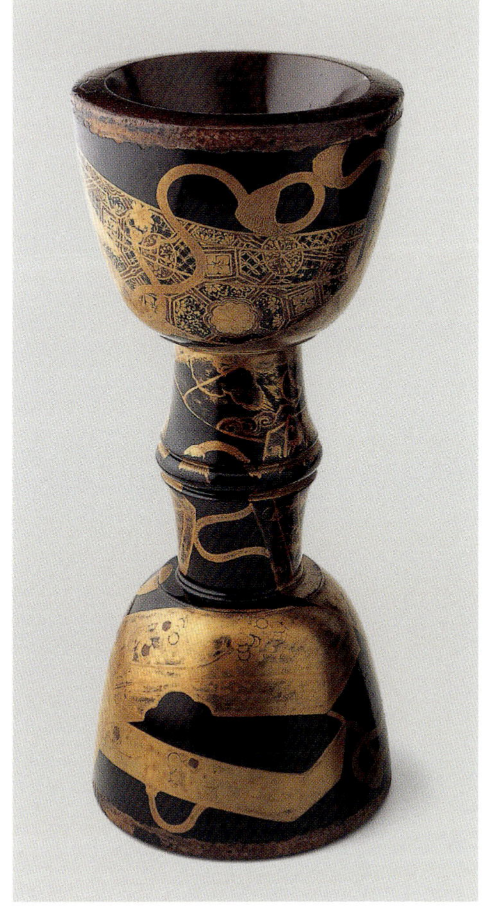

124 *Ōtsuzumi* drum body with design of writing boxes

Edo period, 19th century
National Noh Theatre

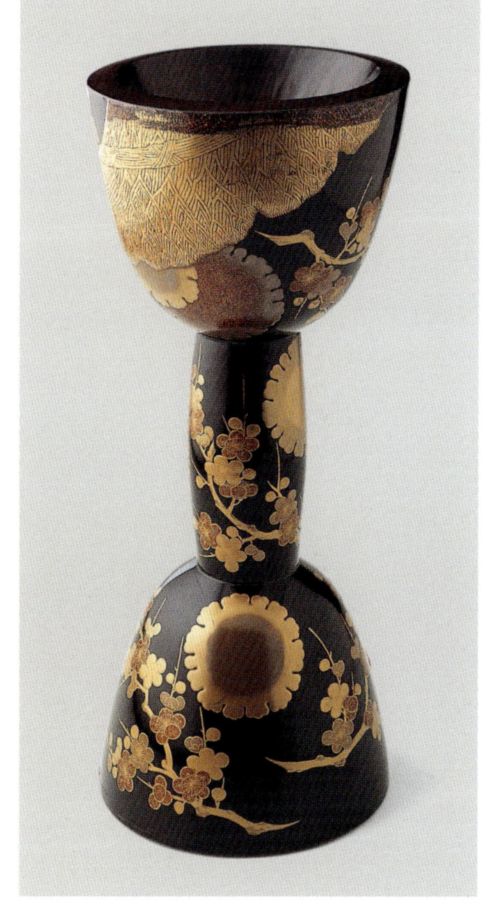

125 *Kotsuzumi* drum body with design of plum branches and brushwood fence

Edo period, 19th century
National Noh Theatre

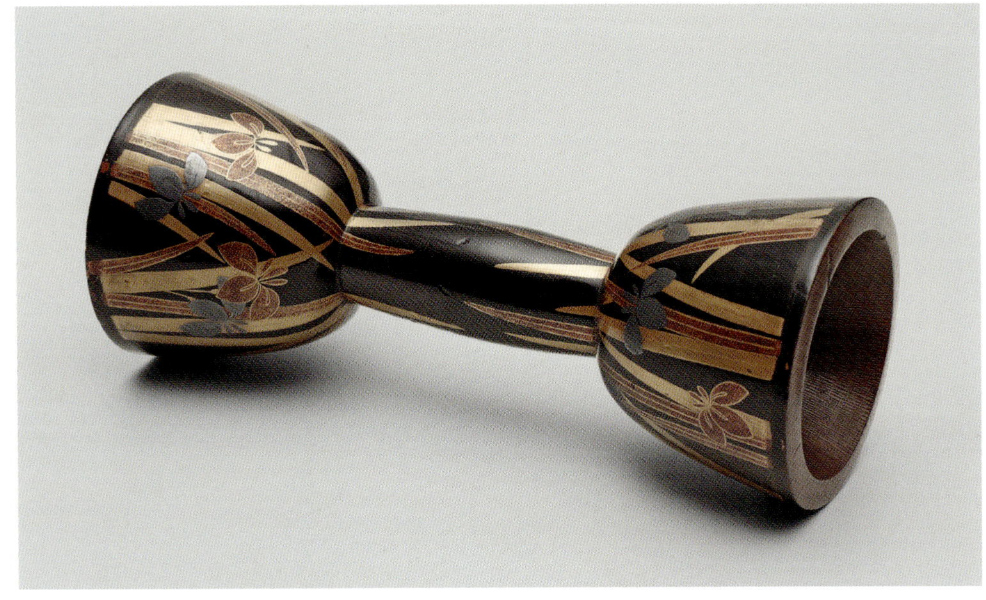

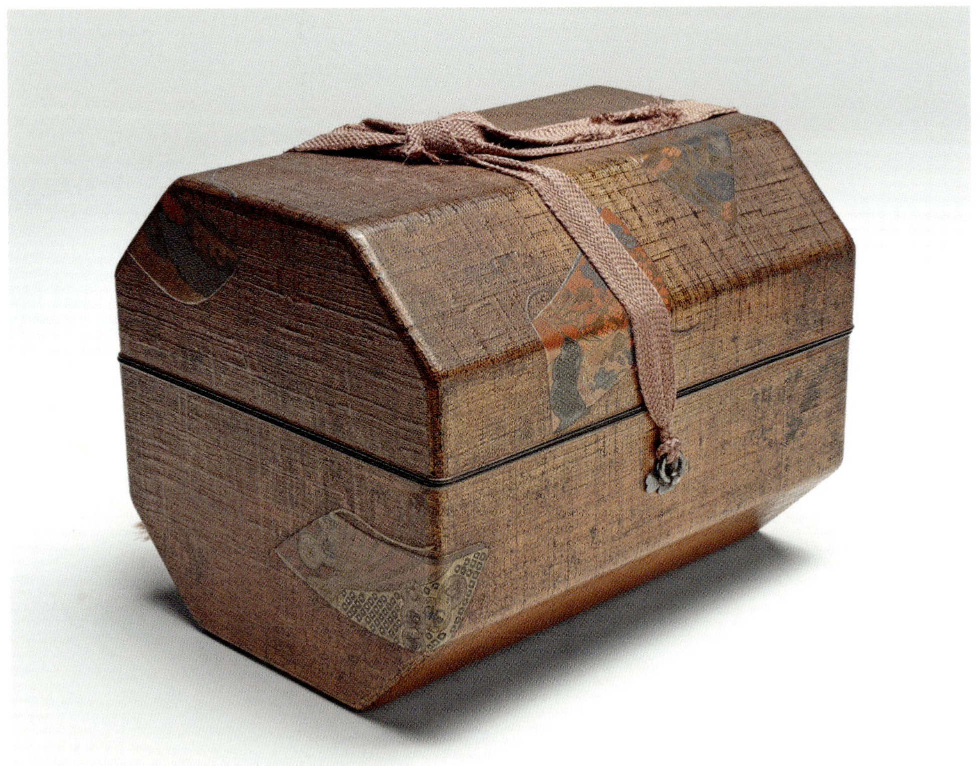

126 *Kotsuzumi* with design of irises and storage
box with design of scattered kimono sleeves

Edo period, 18th century
Art Gallery of New South Wales
Roger Pietri Fund 2013 56.2013a-b

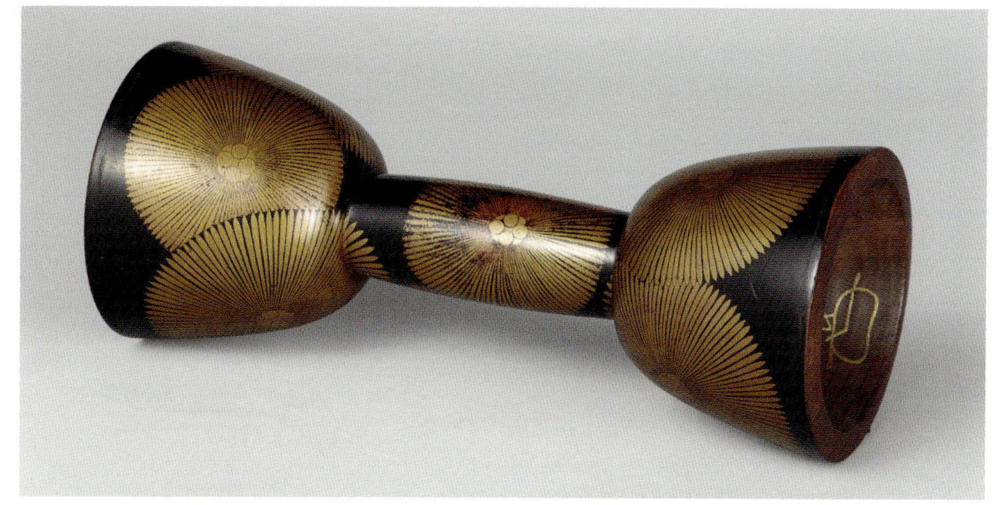

127 *Kotsuzumi* drum body
with design of
Chinese pine

Edo period, 19th century
Agency for Cultural Affairs
of Japan

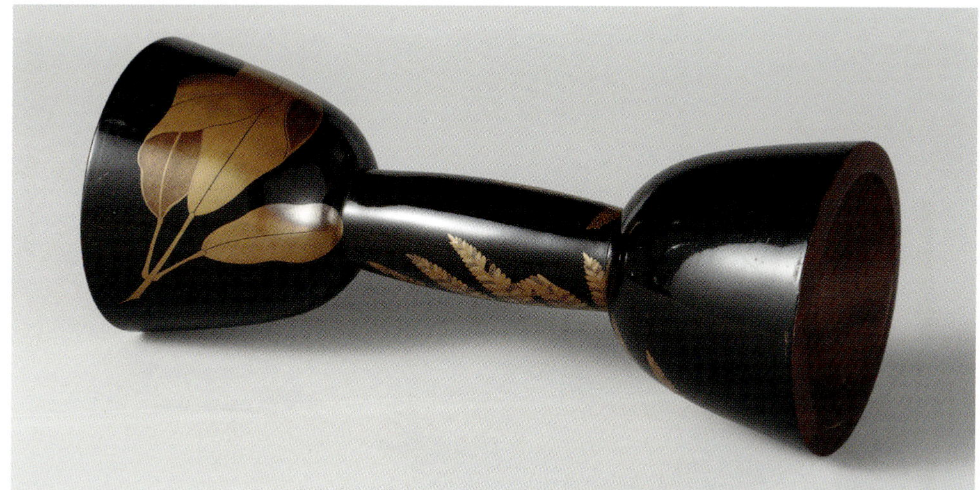

128 *Kotsuzumi* drum body
with design of
false daphne

Edo period, 19th century
Agency for Cultural Affairs
of Japan

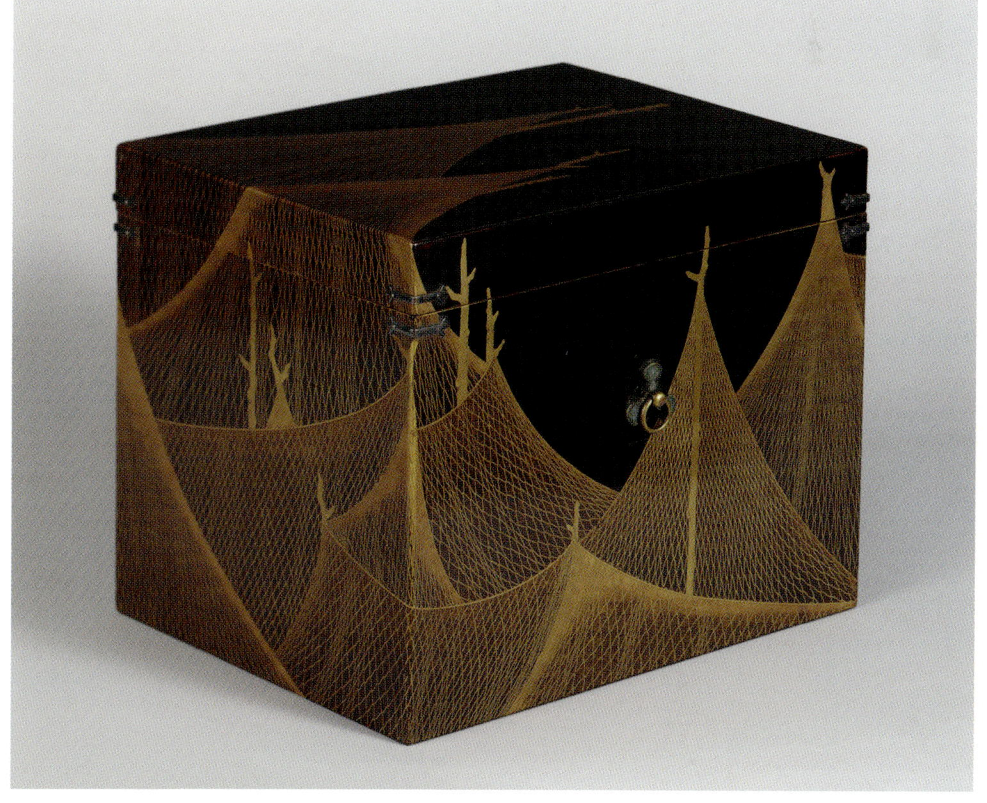

129 Storage box for drum
body with design of
fishing net

Edo period, 19th century
Agency for Cultural Affairs
of Japan

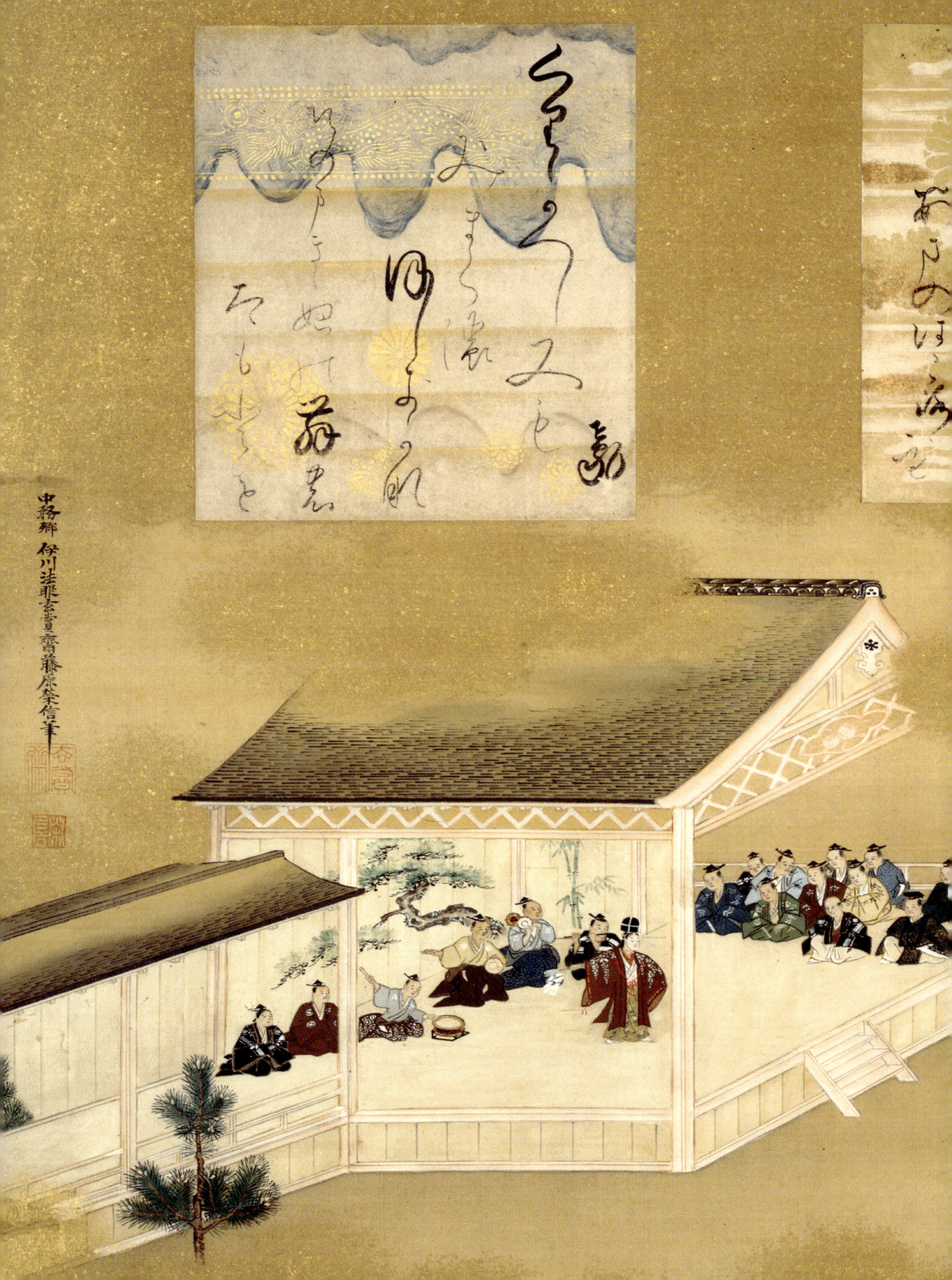

中務卿
伊川法眼玄吾豊實齋藤原栄信筆
あらしのはけしき

NŌ PAINTINGS, PRINTS AND SONGBOOKS

The illustration of nō and kyōgen performances can be divided into two main groups. Works belonging to the first depict the entire stage with the musical ensemble, chorus and actors in performance, as well as the audience, thus providing valuable information on the social context of nō theatre. The second group consists primarily of handscrolls and albums that represent nō and kyōgen plays through the portrayal of their key scenes. The standardised composition focuses on the main characters, their costumes and masks, together with the respective stage properties for each play that are set against a blank background. These artfully conceived works – commissioned by the military aristocracy and during the Edo period by major nō patrons – served as study materials or commemorated important one-day programs that generally consisted of various nō plays and kyōgen interludes. Executed by professional painters in service to the shogunate and local daimyo or by specialised workshops, these handscrolls and albums were treasured as artworks in their own right.

Even though nō was the official theatre and music of the Tokugawa shogunate from the early seventeenth century onwards, the study of unaccompanied nō chants (*su-utai*) was a popular pastime among affluent and cultivated commoners. The result was an increased demand for printed songbooks (*utaibon*) that were widely circulated throughout Japan. The production of these nō libretti was a lucrative business for many Edo-period publishers. Some *utaibon* were luxuriously decorated with sophisticated designs printed in mica on coloured paper and with elegant calligraphy by noted masters. (KT)

162

Detail of Kano Naganobu's
Nō performance at the Imperial palace (see cat 134, p 169)

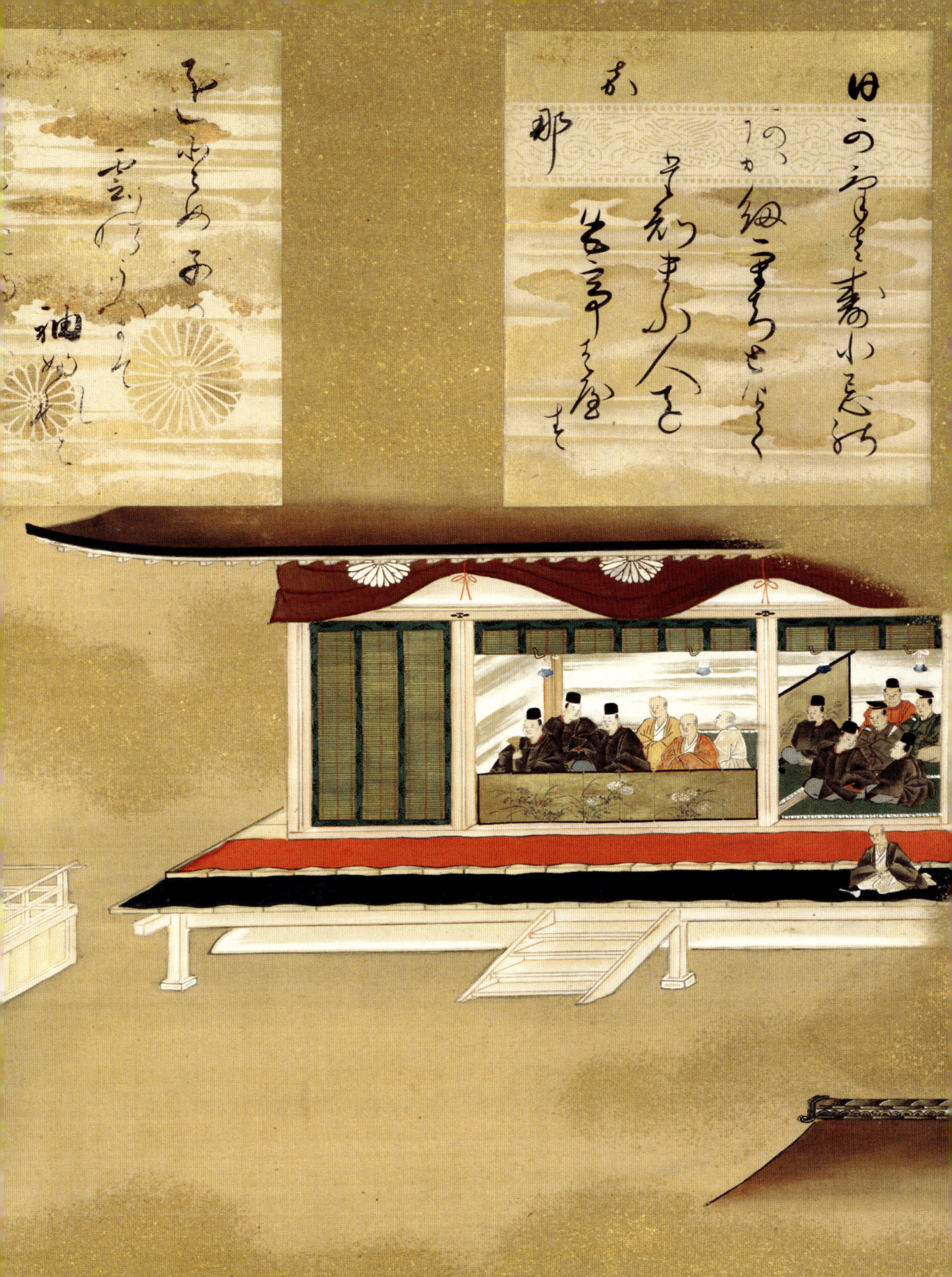

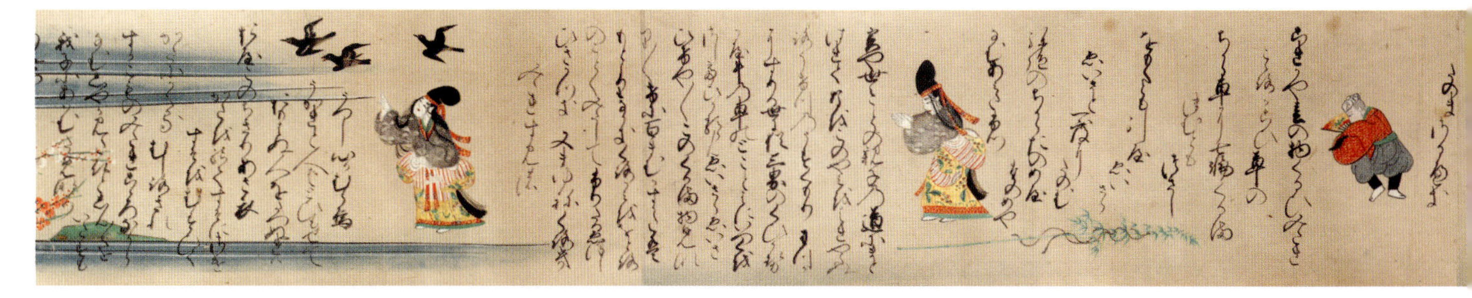

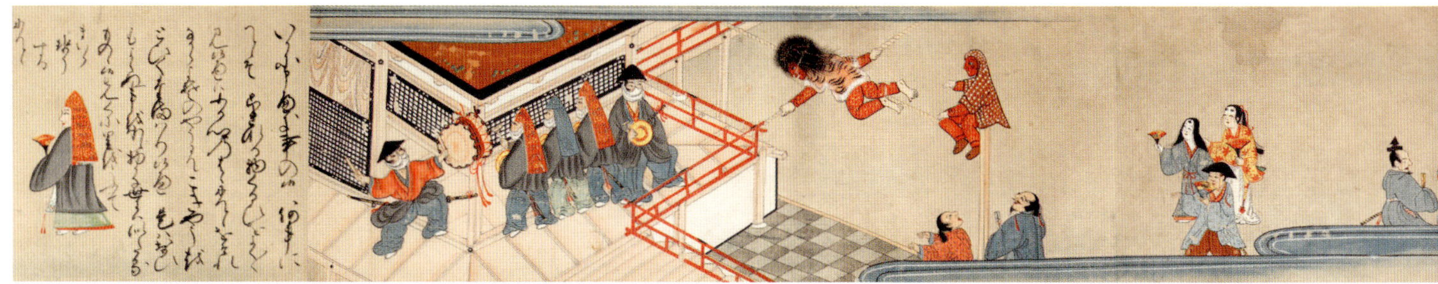

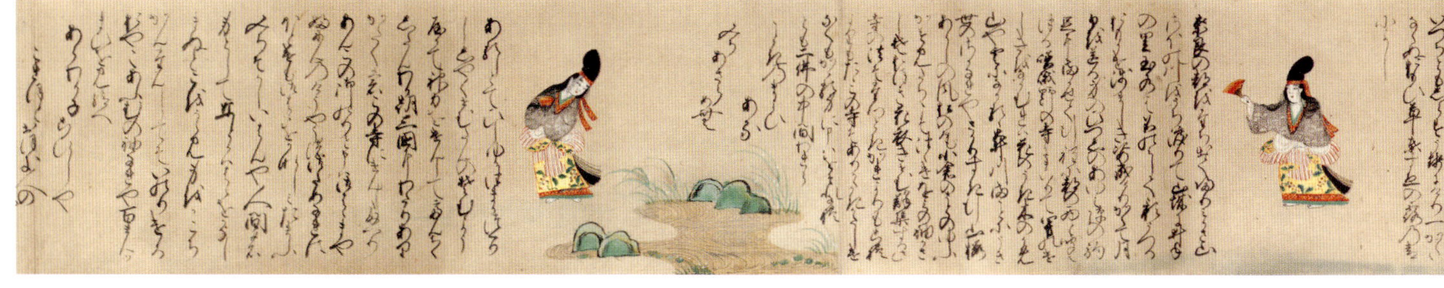

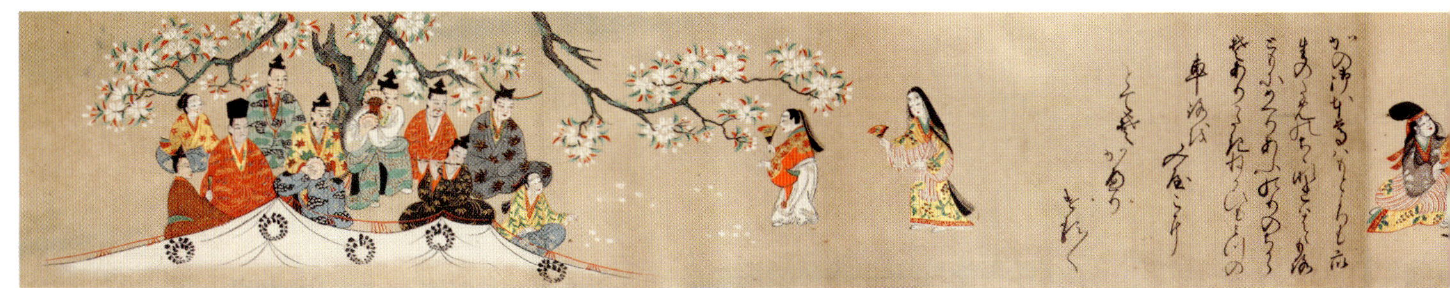

130 Illustrated handscroll of
the nō play *Hyakuman*

Muromachi period, 16th century
National Noh Theatre

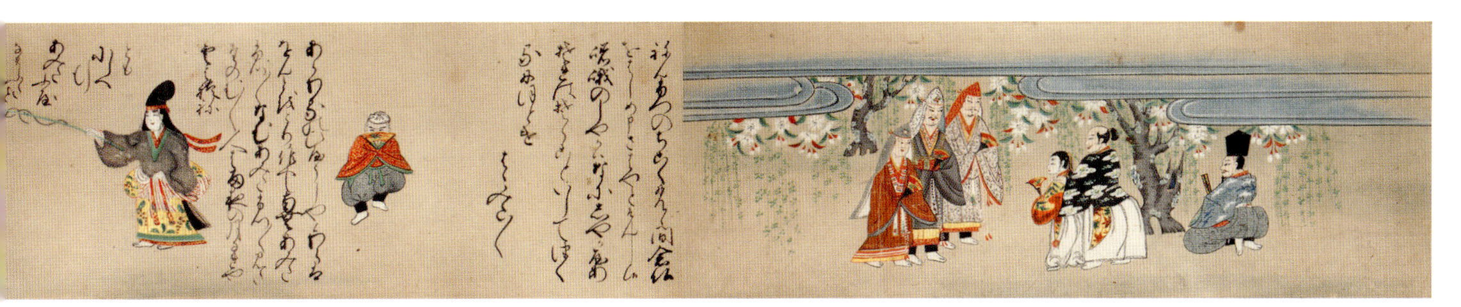

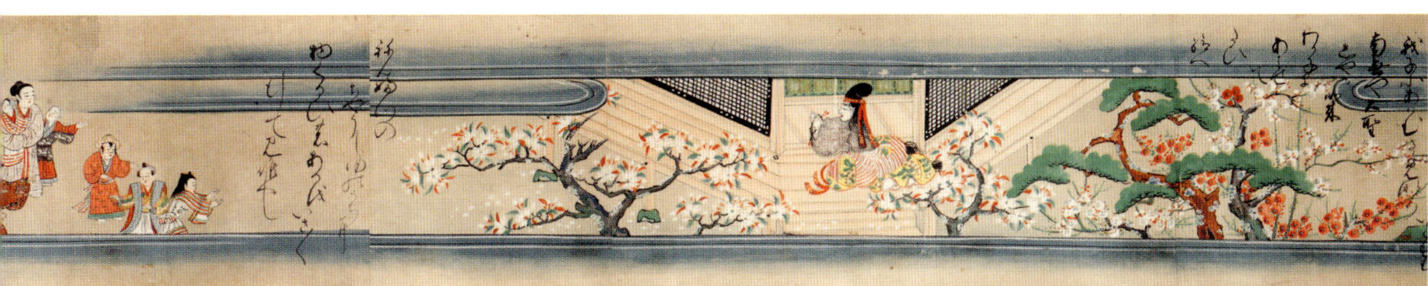

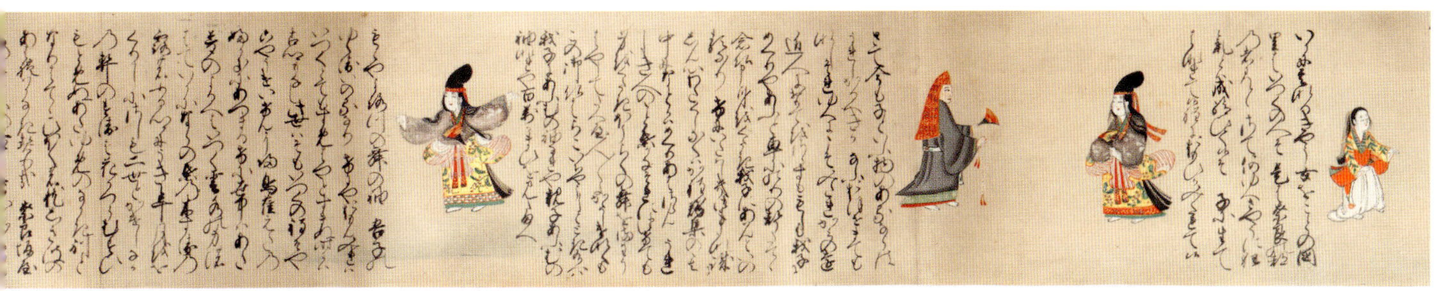

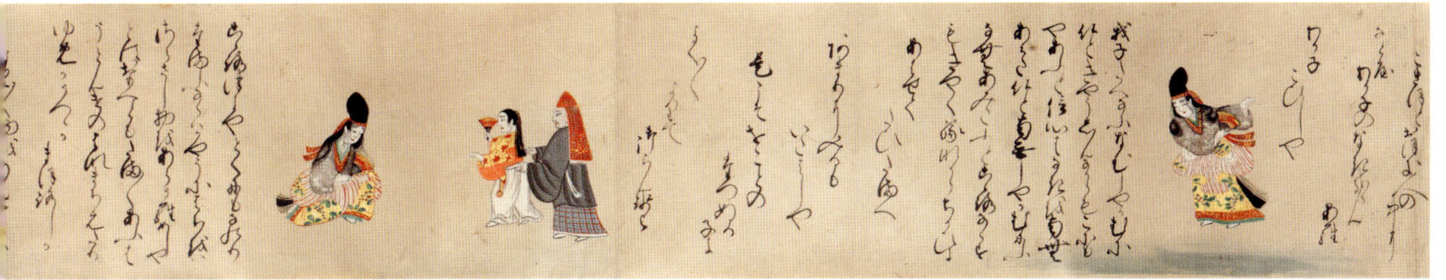

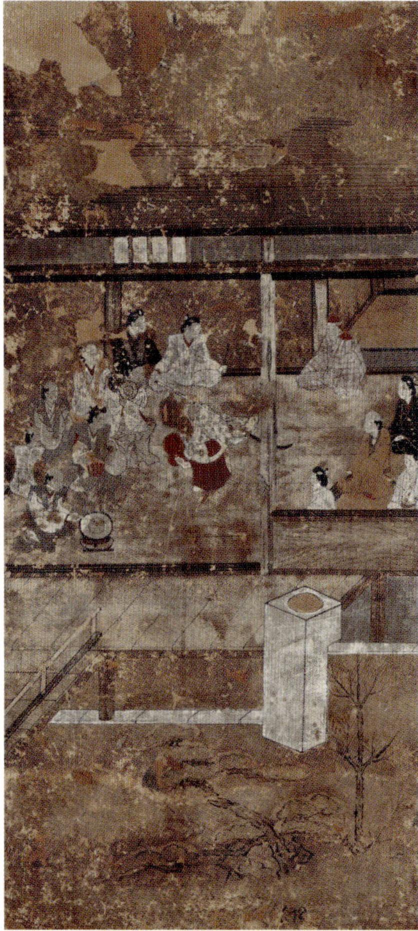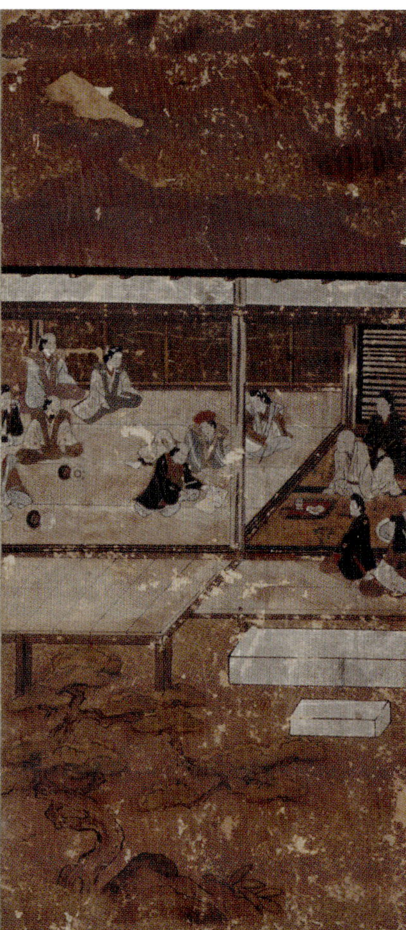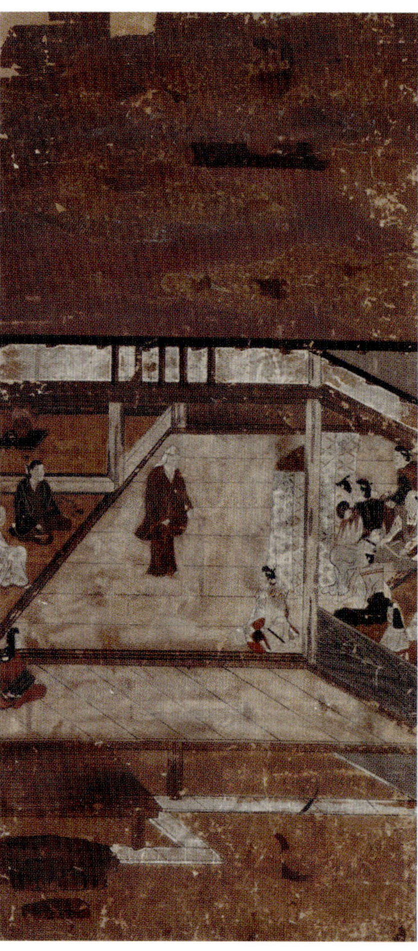

131 Illustrations of old nō performances

early Edo period, Keichō era, 1596–1615
National Noh Theatre

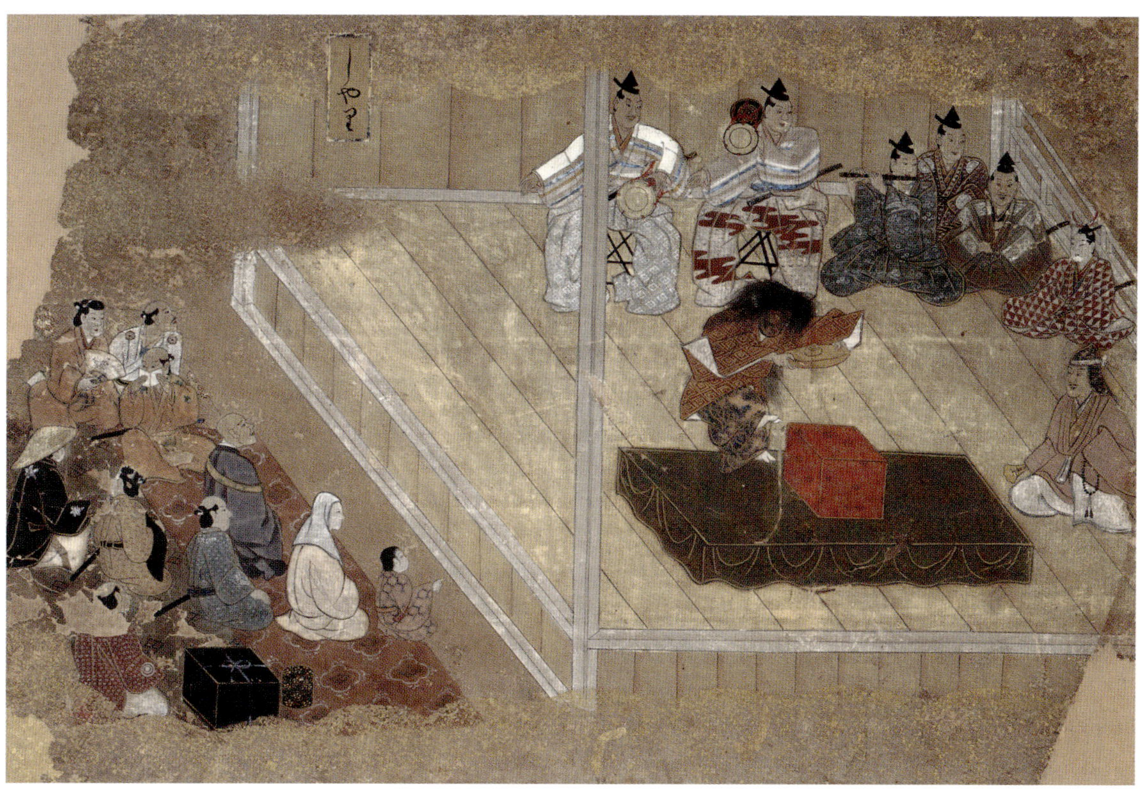

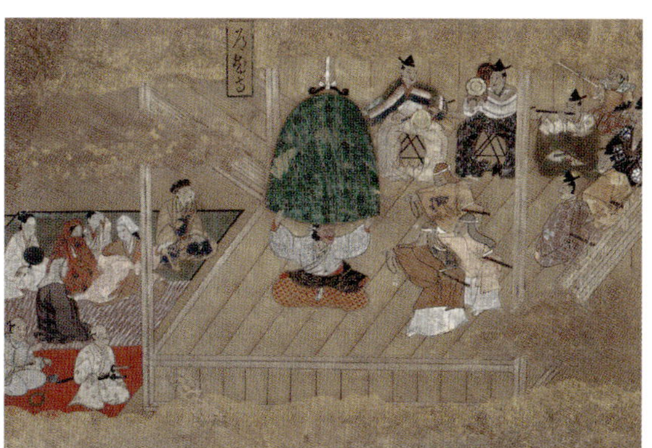

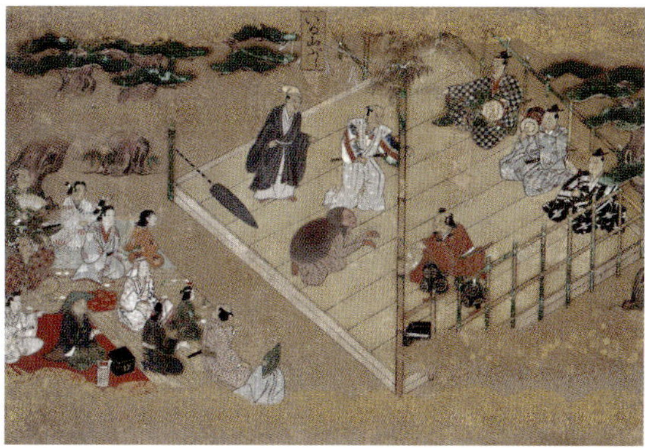

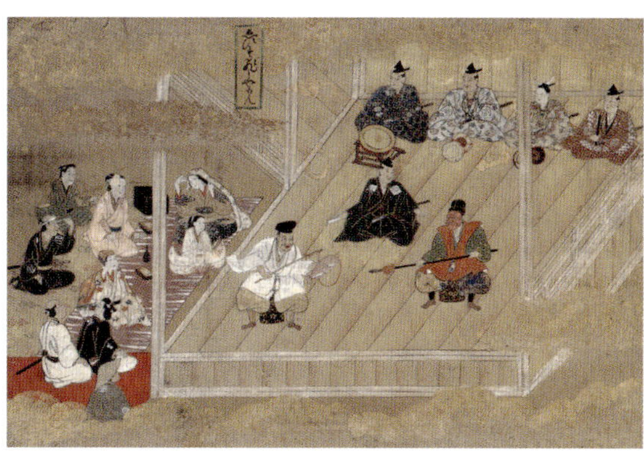

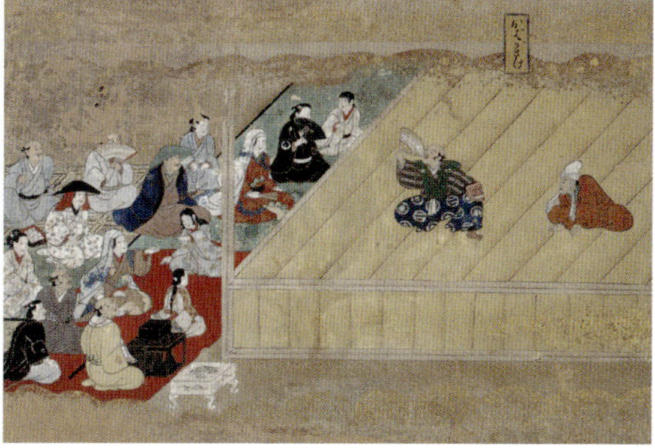

132   Illustrations of old nō and kyōgen
early Edo period, 17th century
National Noh Theatre

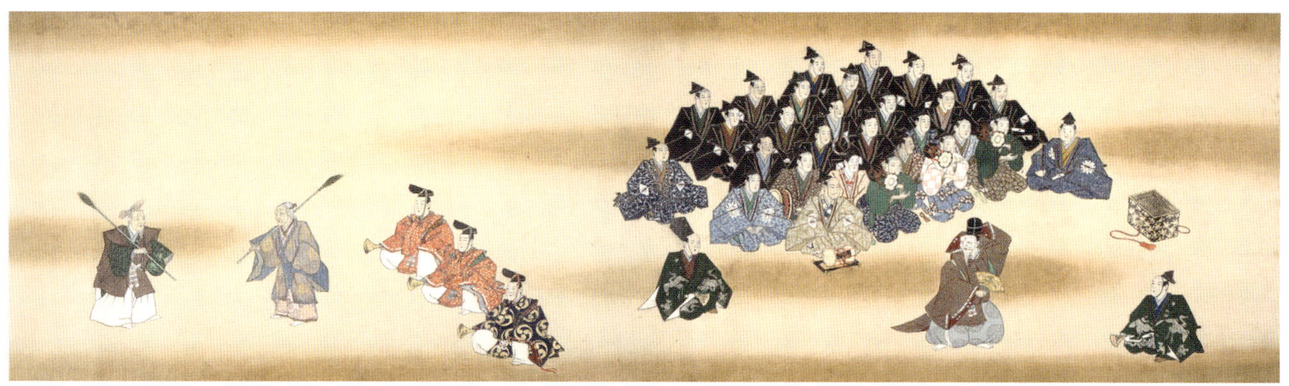

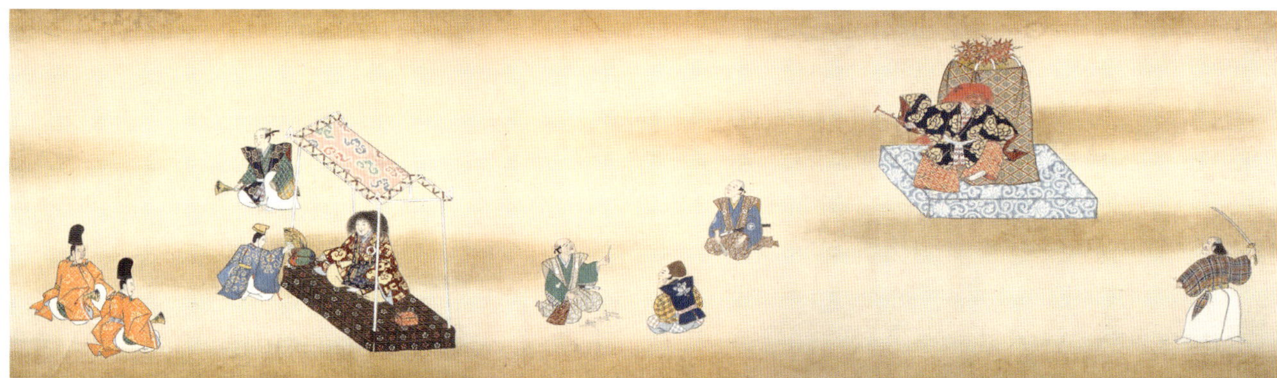

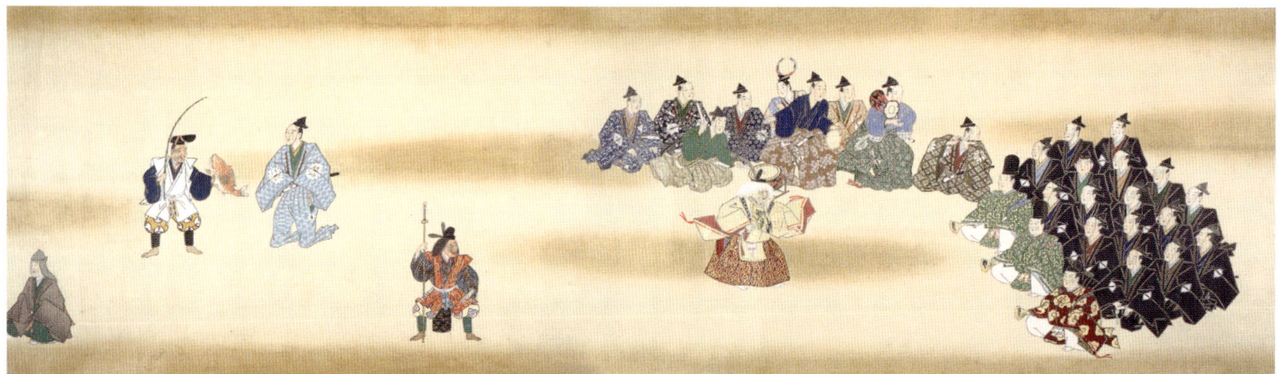

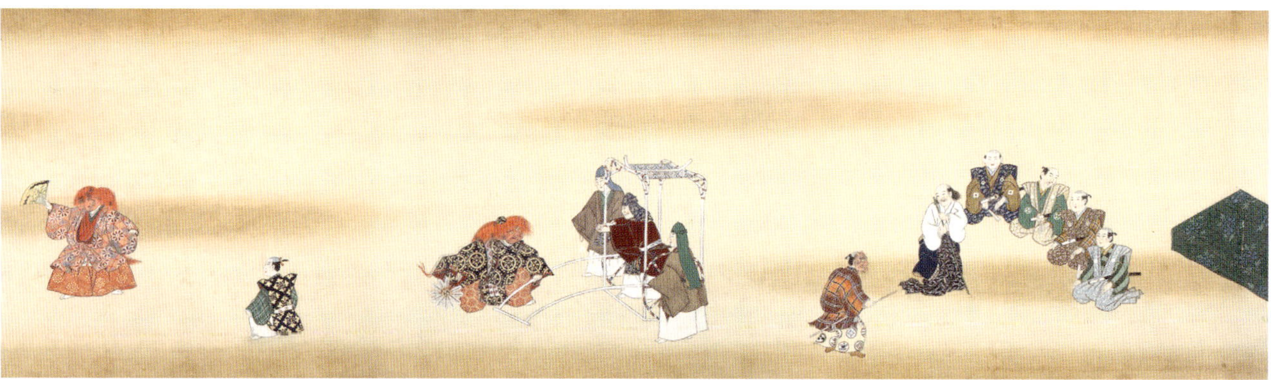

133 Illustrations of nō dances
mid Edo period, 18th century
National Noh Theatre

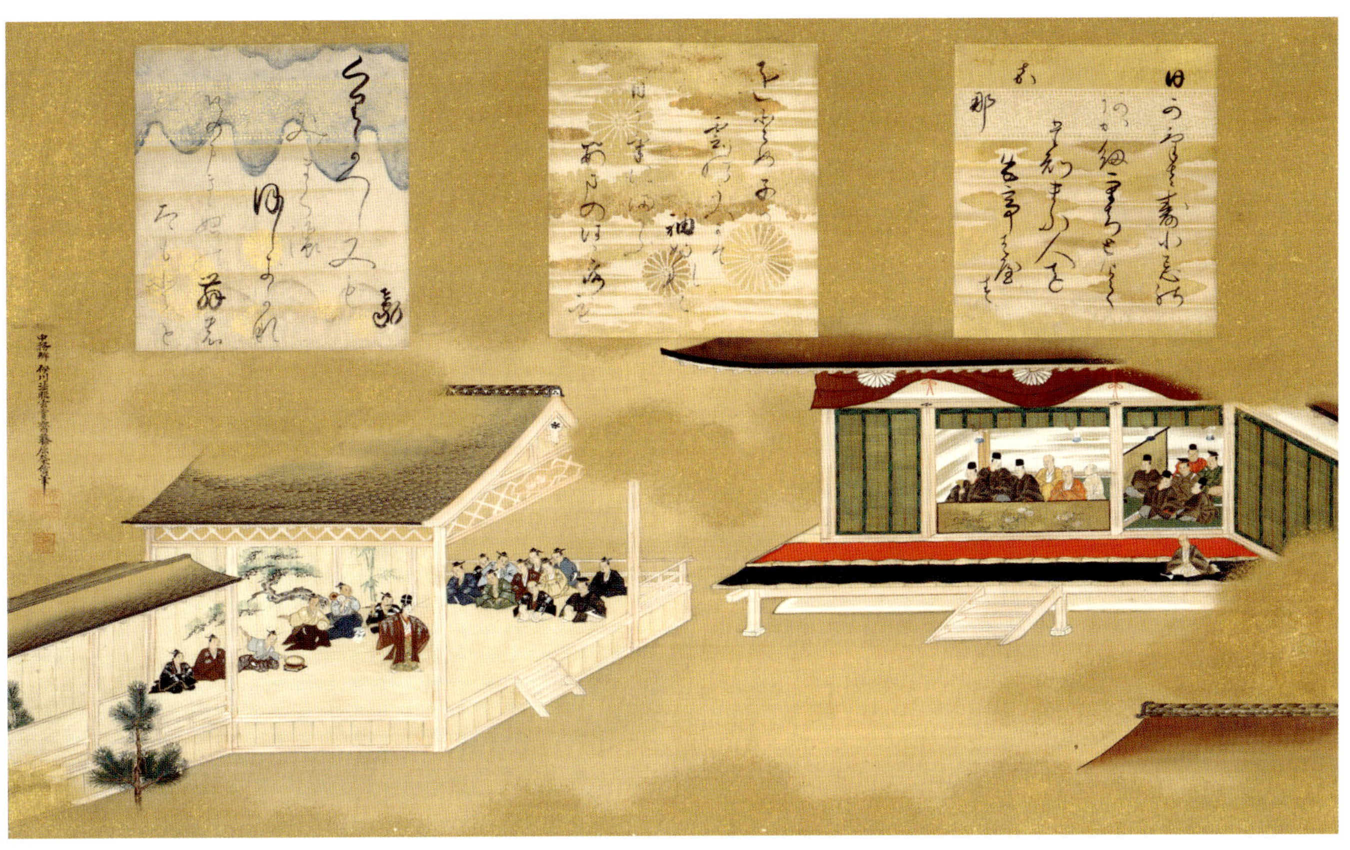

134 Kano Naganobu (1775–1828)
Nō performance at the Imperial palace
after 1802
National Noh Theatre

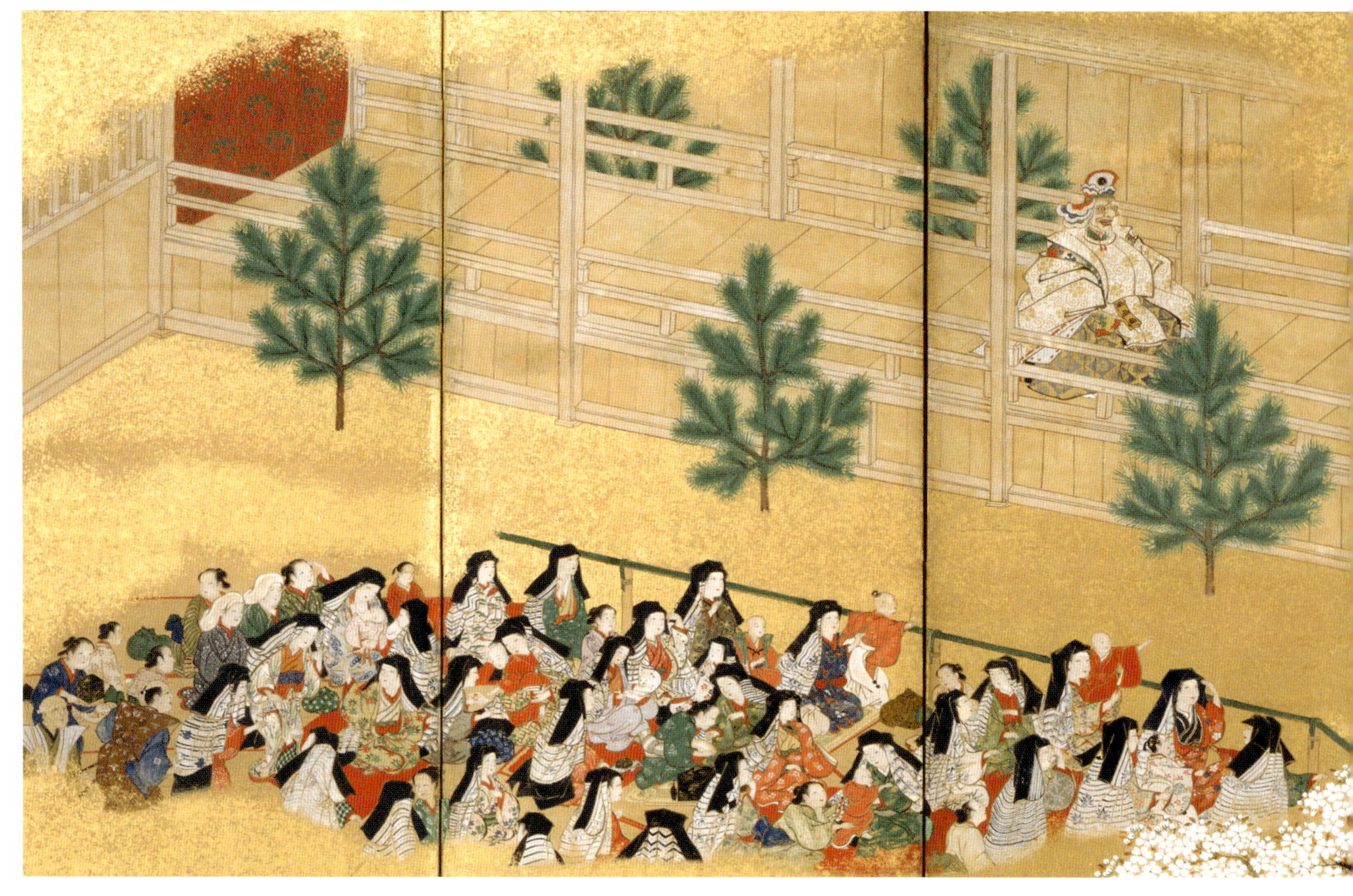

135 Nō performance
mid Edo period, 18th century
National Noh Theatre

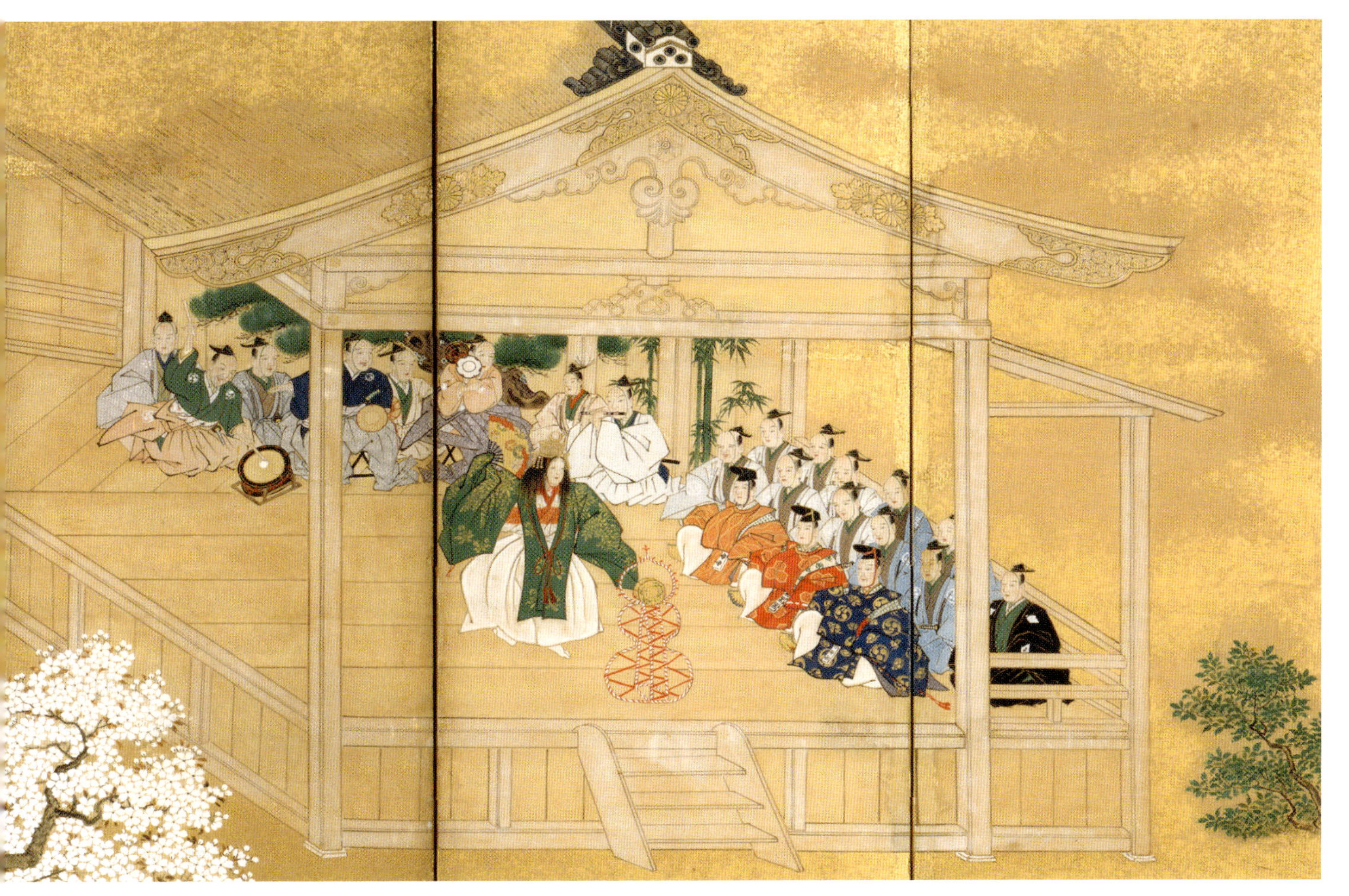

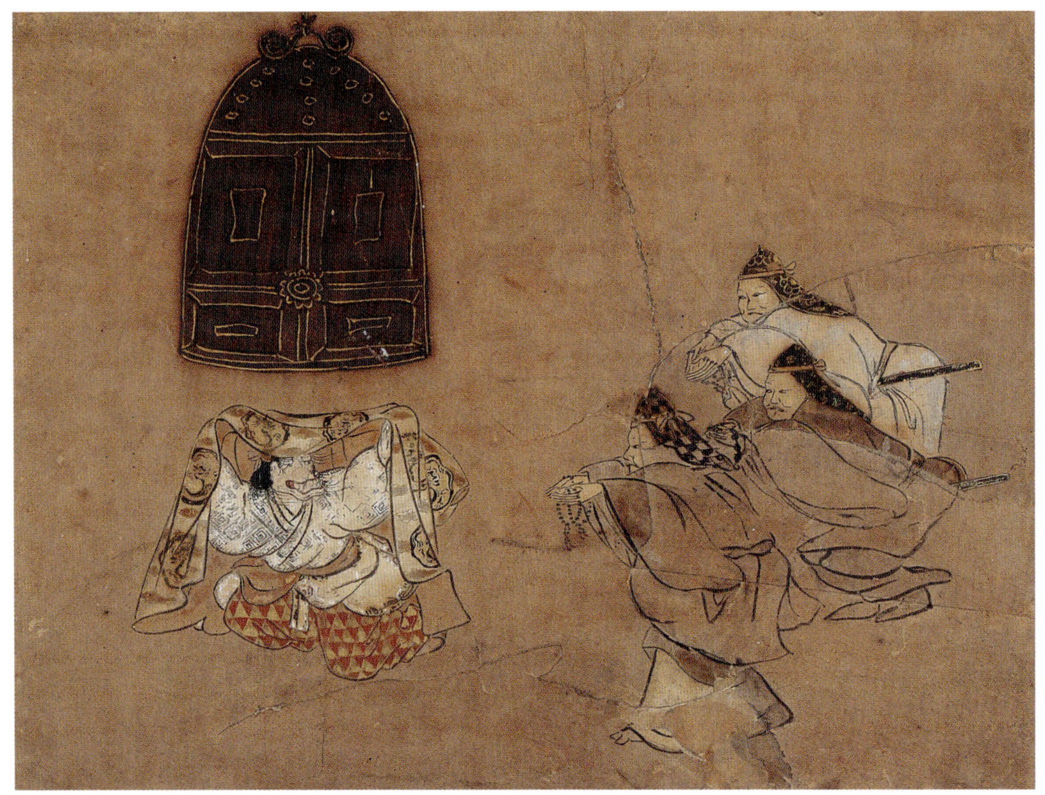

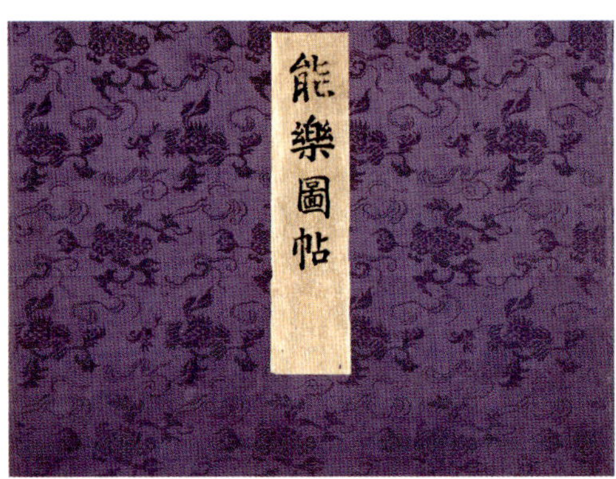

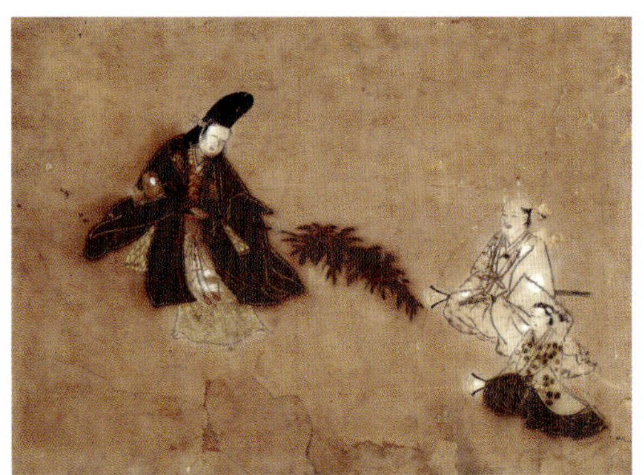

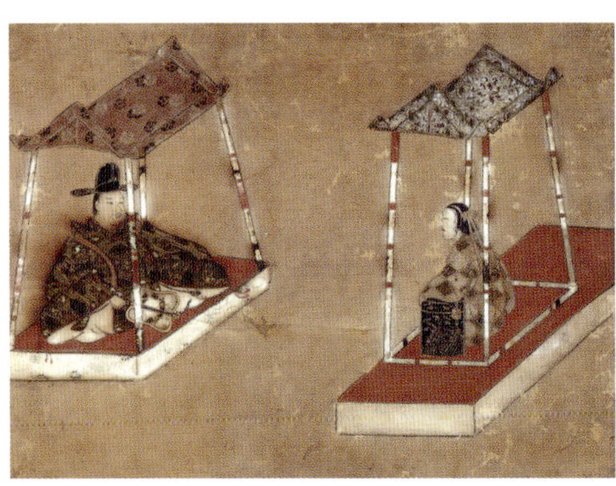

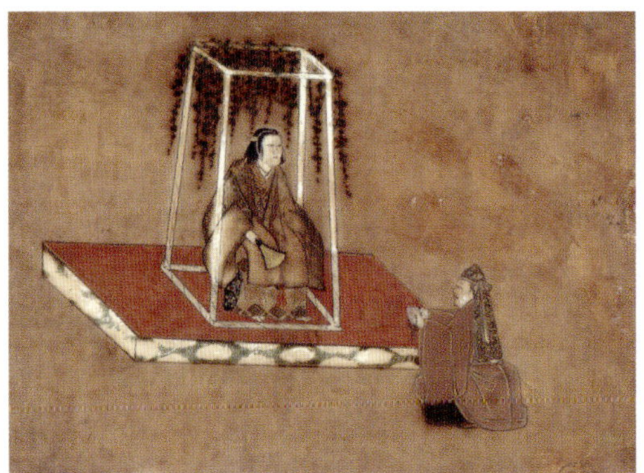

136 Illustrations of nō and kyōgen
Momoyama period, 16th century
National Noh Theatre

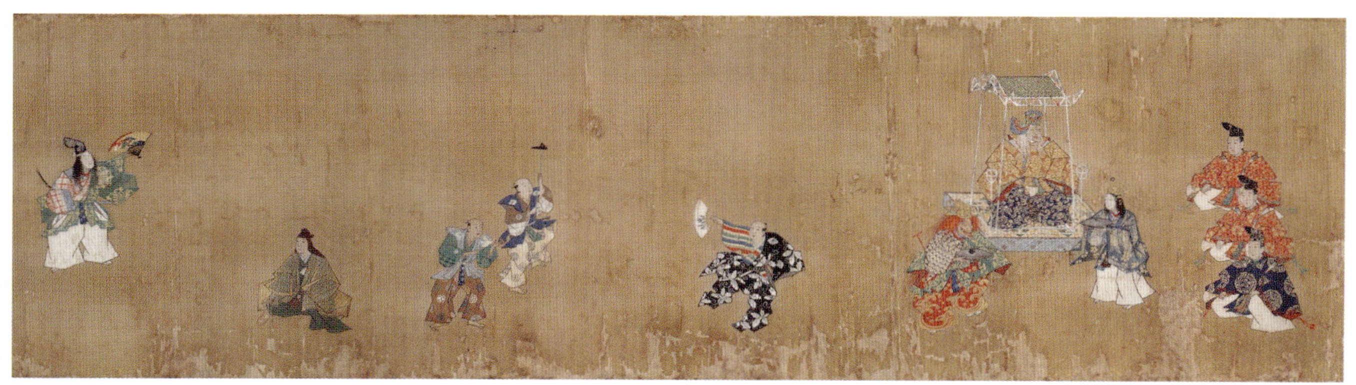

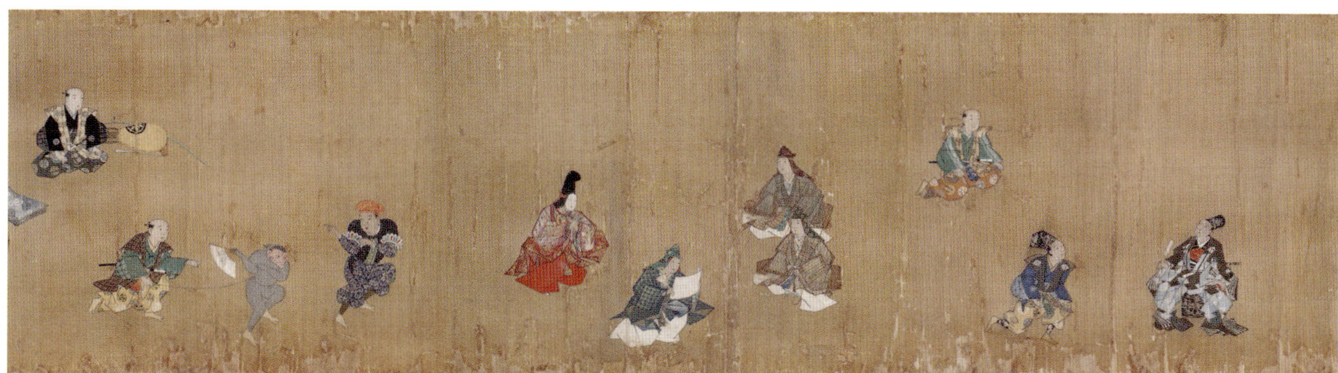

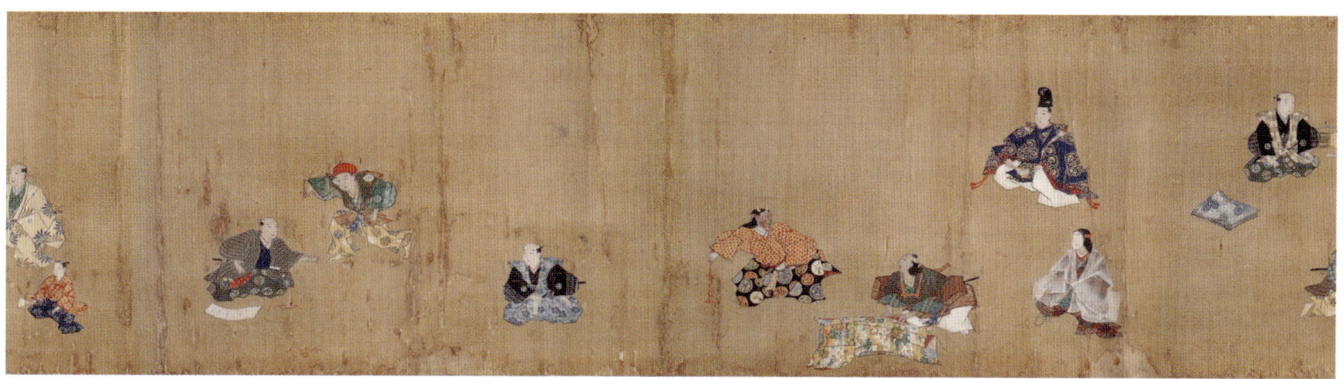

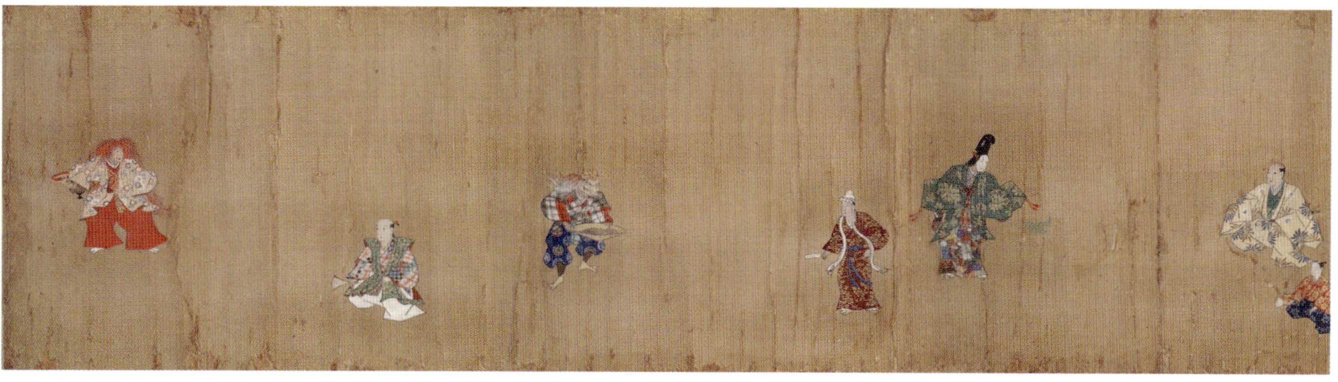

137 Illustrations of nō and kyōgen

early Edo period, 17th century
National Noh Theatre

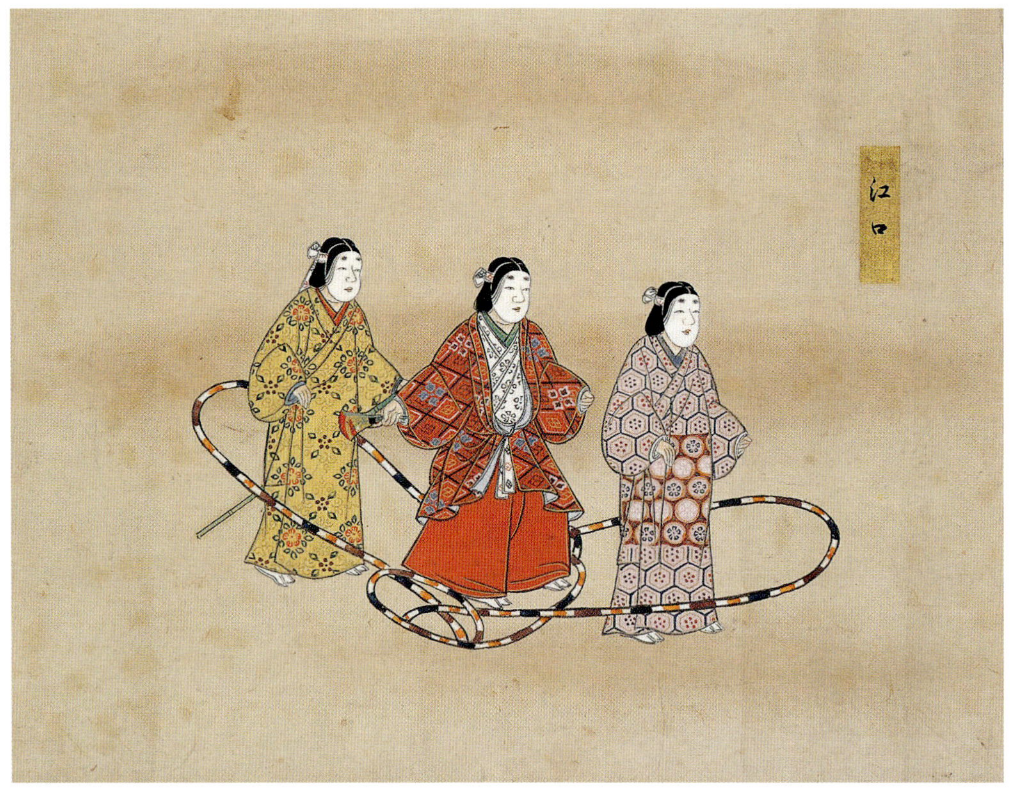
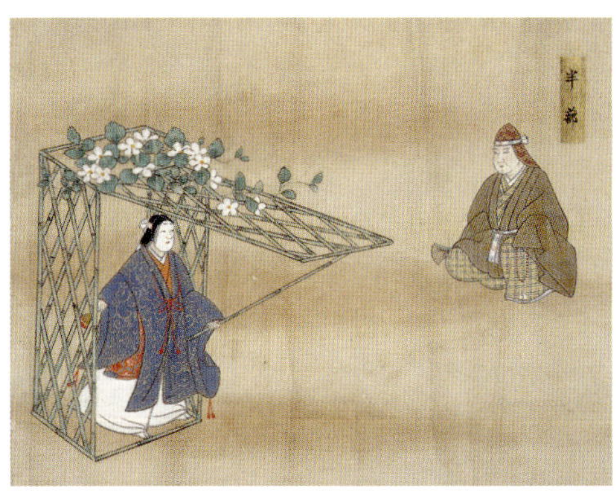
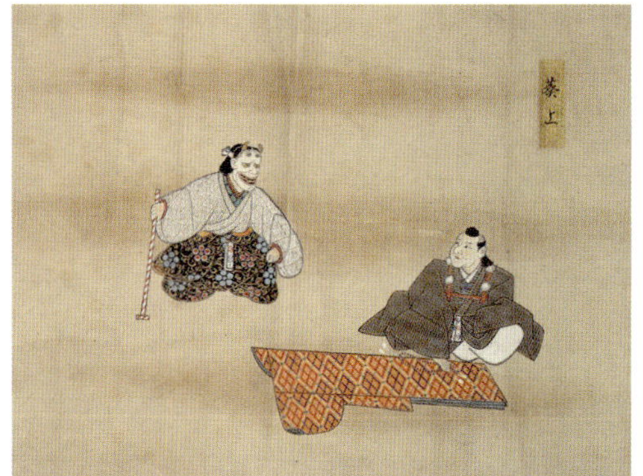
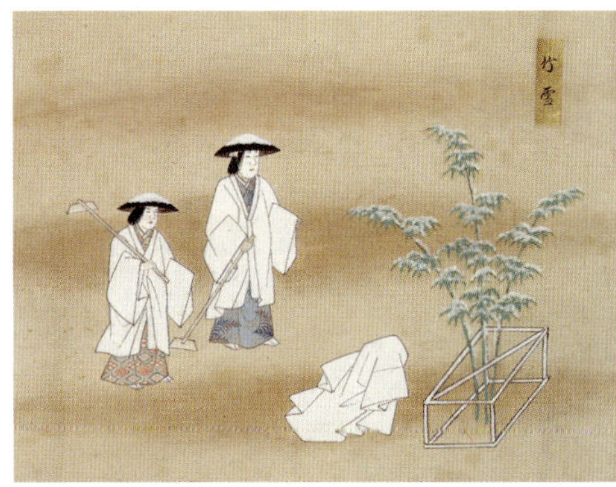
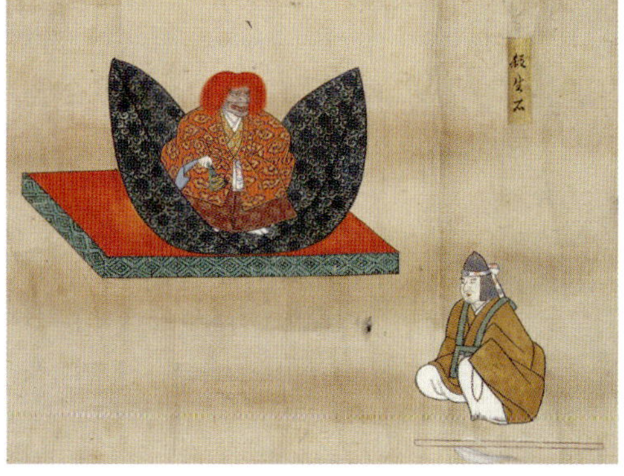

138 Kano Ryūsetsu (1646–1712 or 1729–74)
Illustrations of nō

Edo period, 18th century
National Noh Theatre

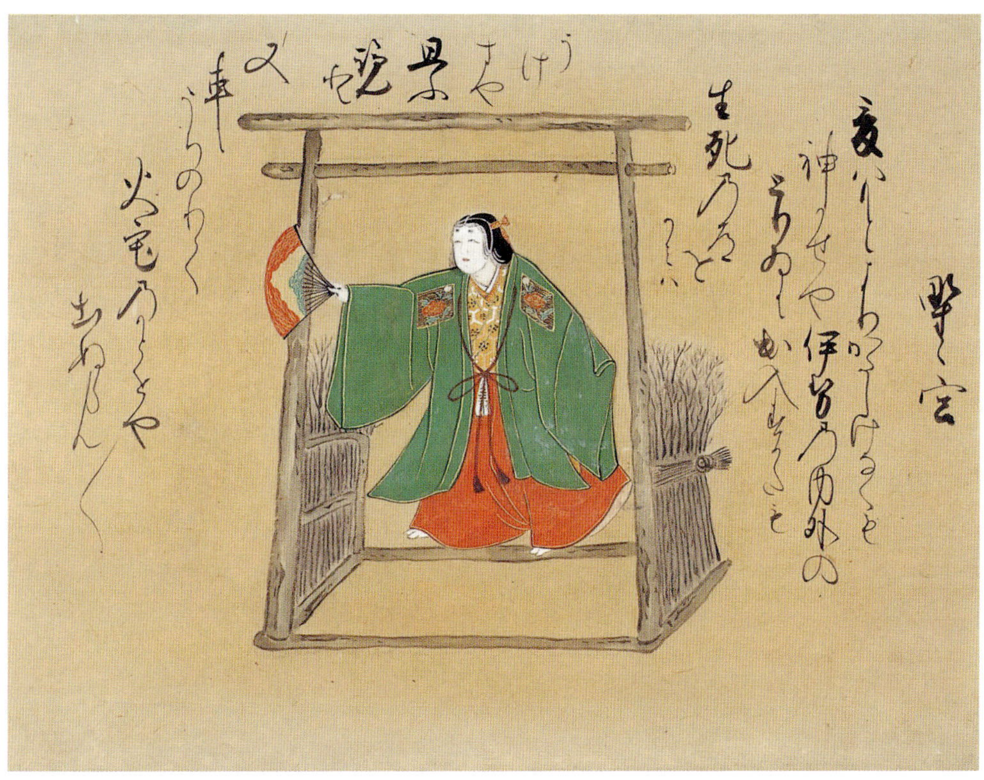

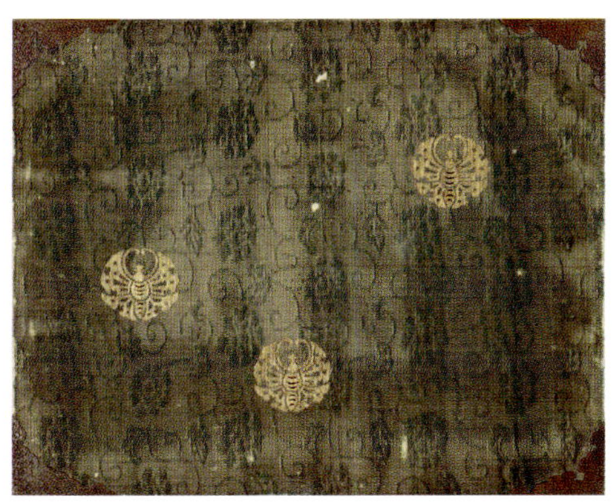

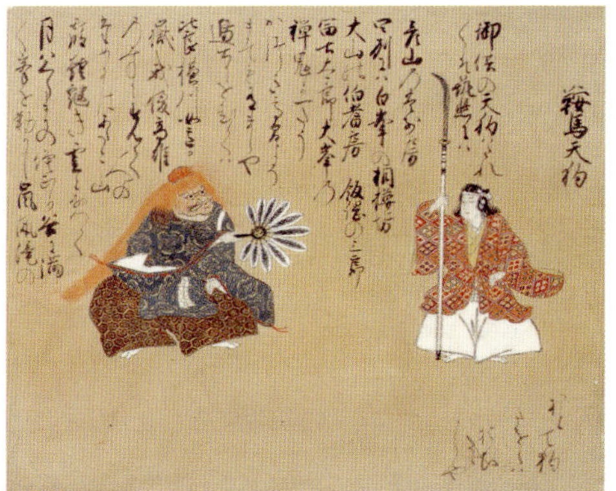

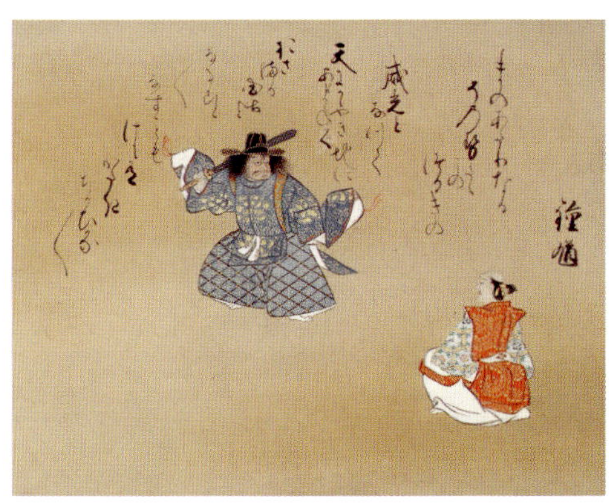

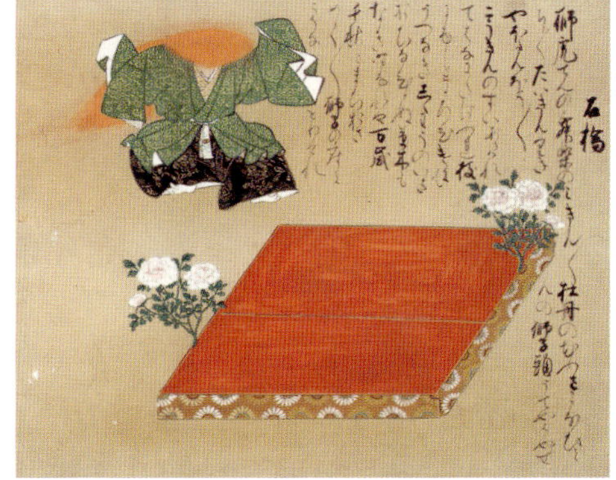

139 Compendium of nō and kyōgen

mid Edo period, 18th century
National Noh Theatre

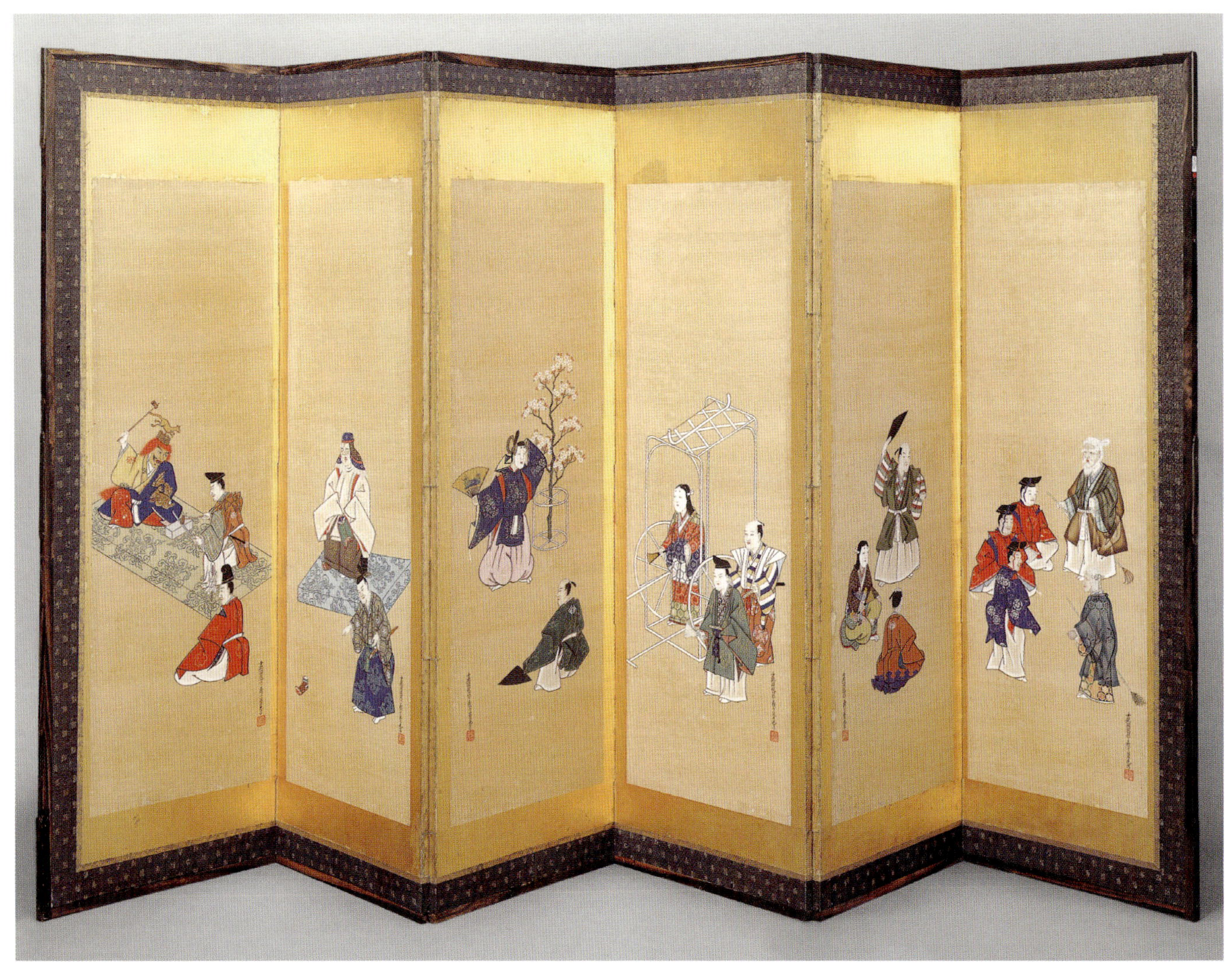

140 Tosa Mitsutaka (1780–1852)
Screen illustrating various nō scenes
Edo period, late 18th–first half of 19th century
six-panel folding screen: ink and colour on silk
National Noh Theatre

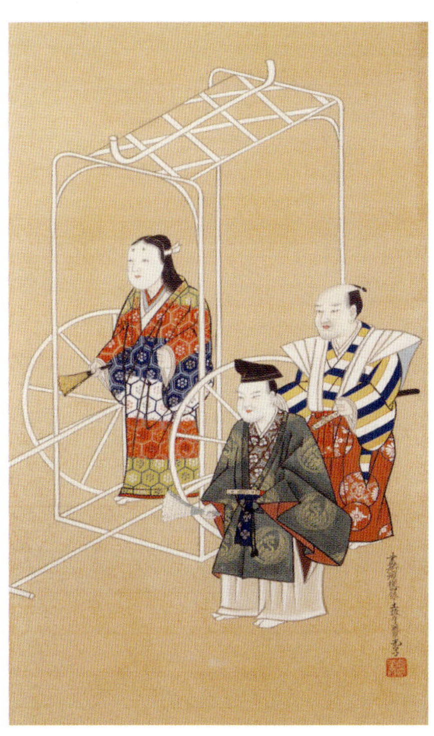
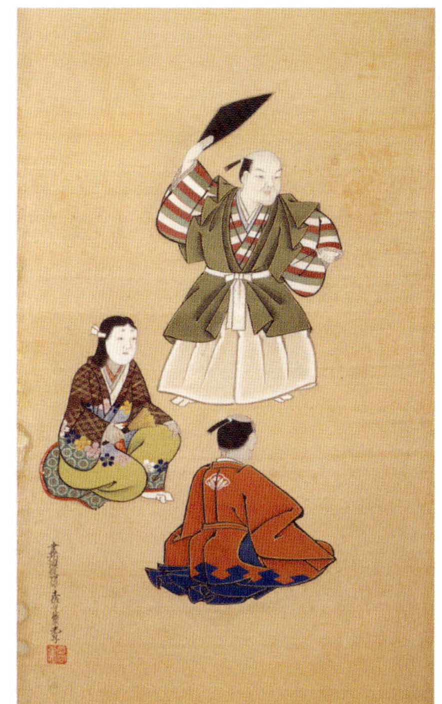
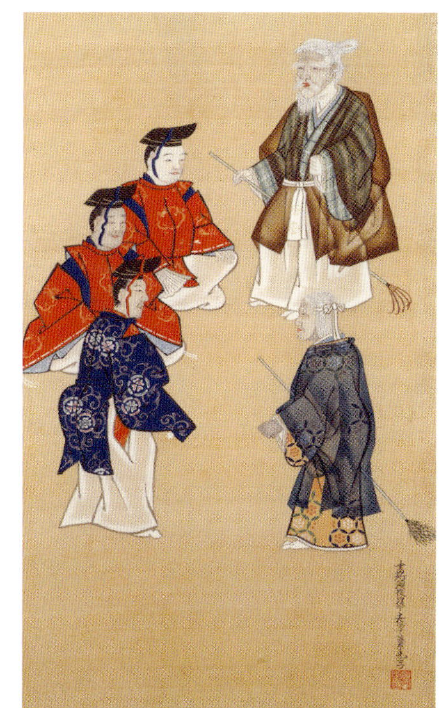
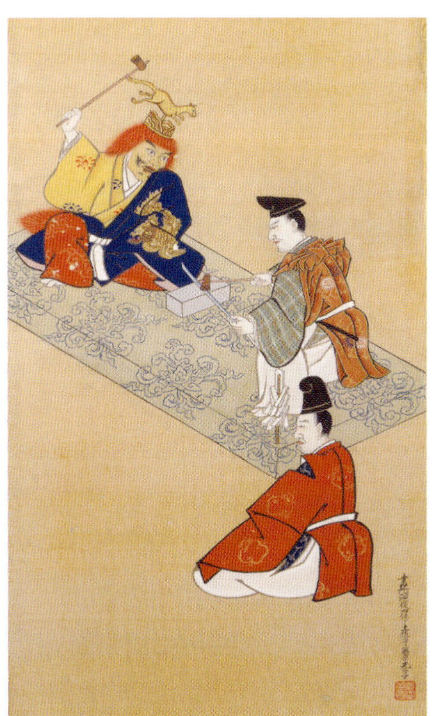
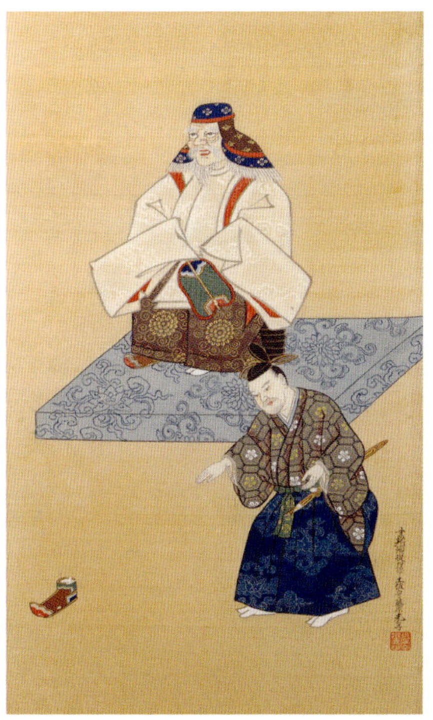
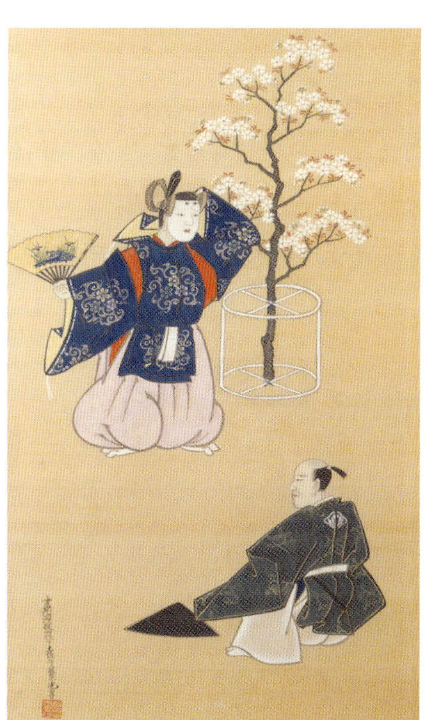

top from right:

Takasago, The reed cutter, Kumano

bottom from right:

The Unrin temple, Chōryō, The swordsmith

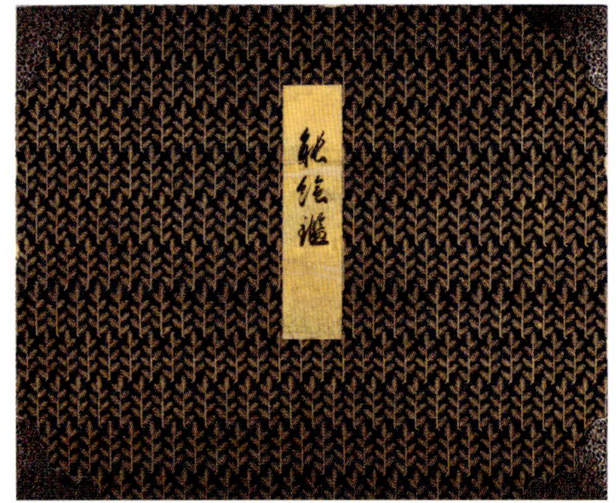
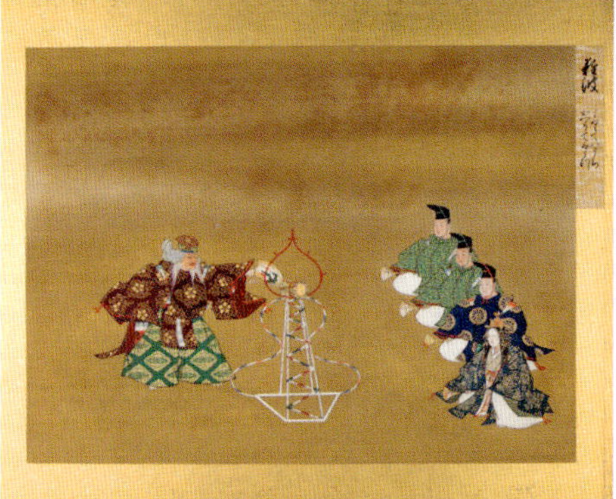
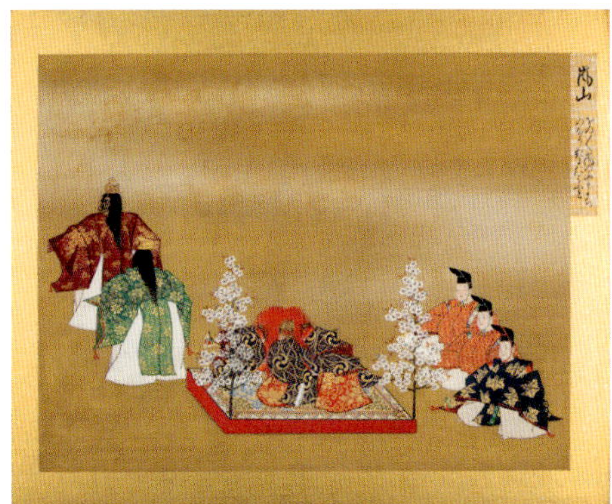
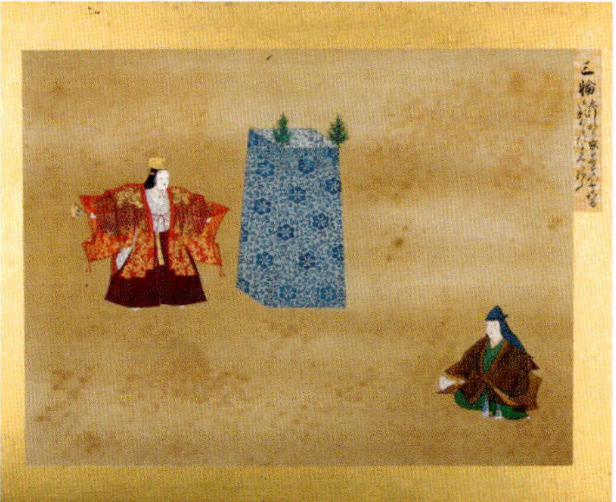
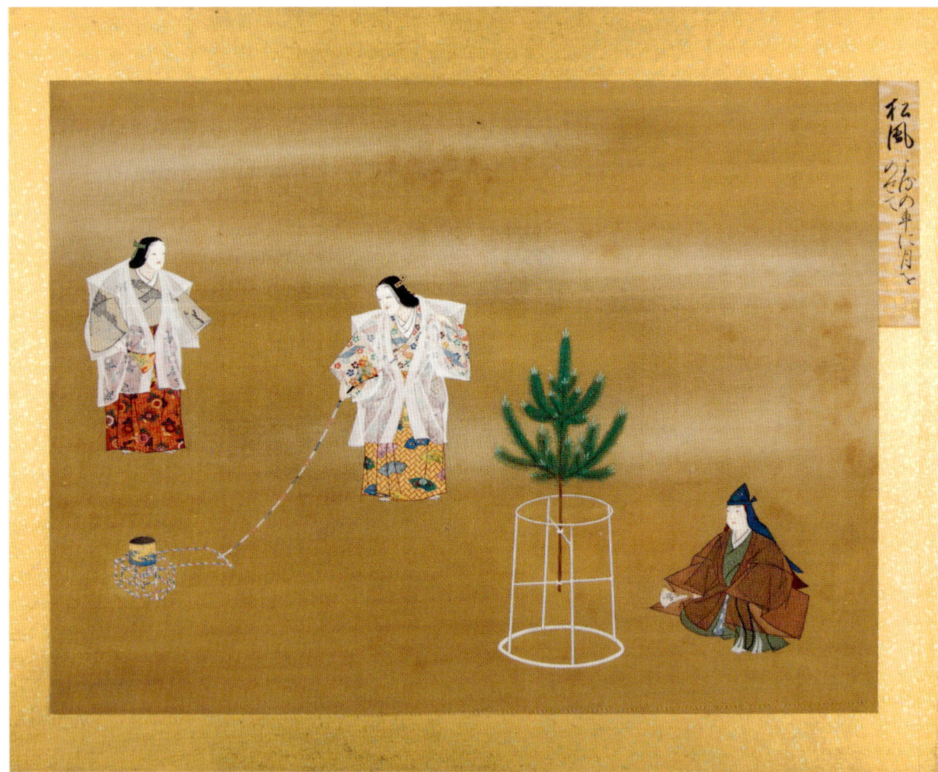

141 Compendium of nō pictures
mid Edo period, 18th century
National Noh Theatre

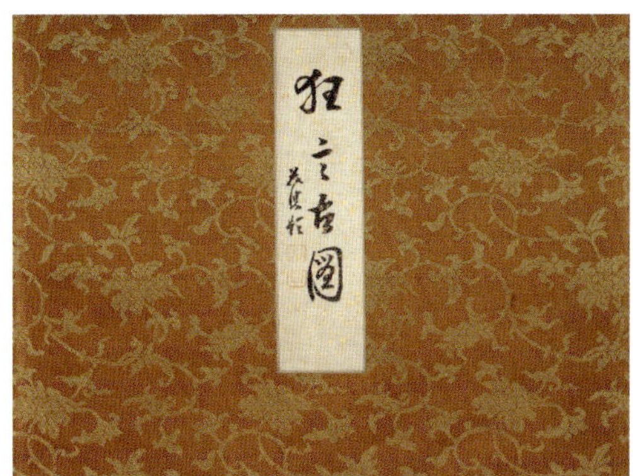

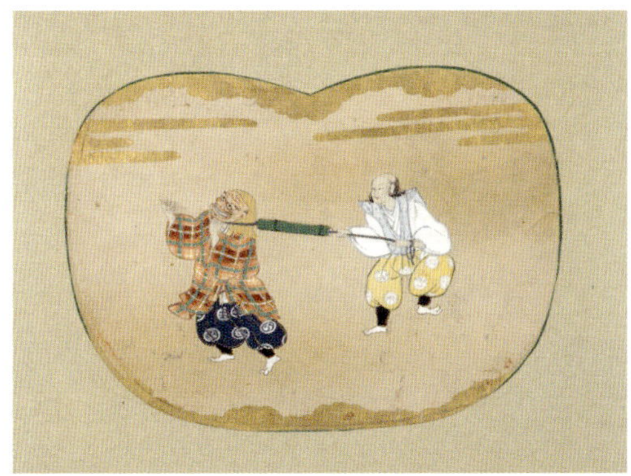

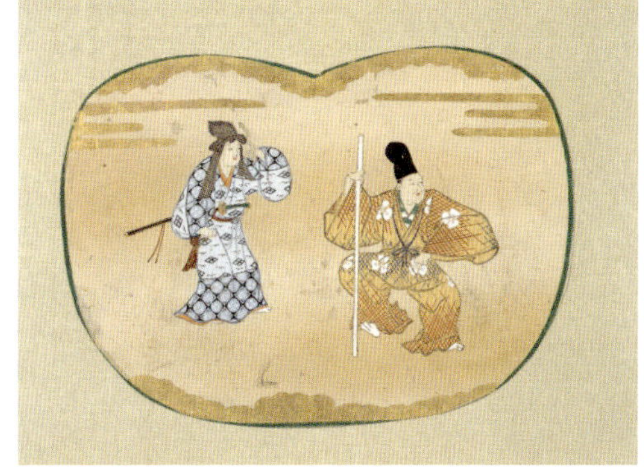

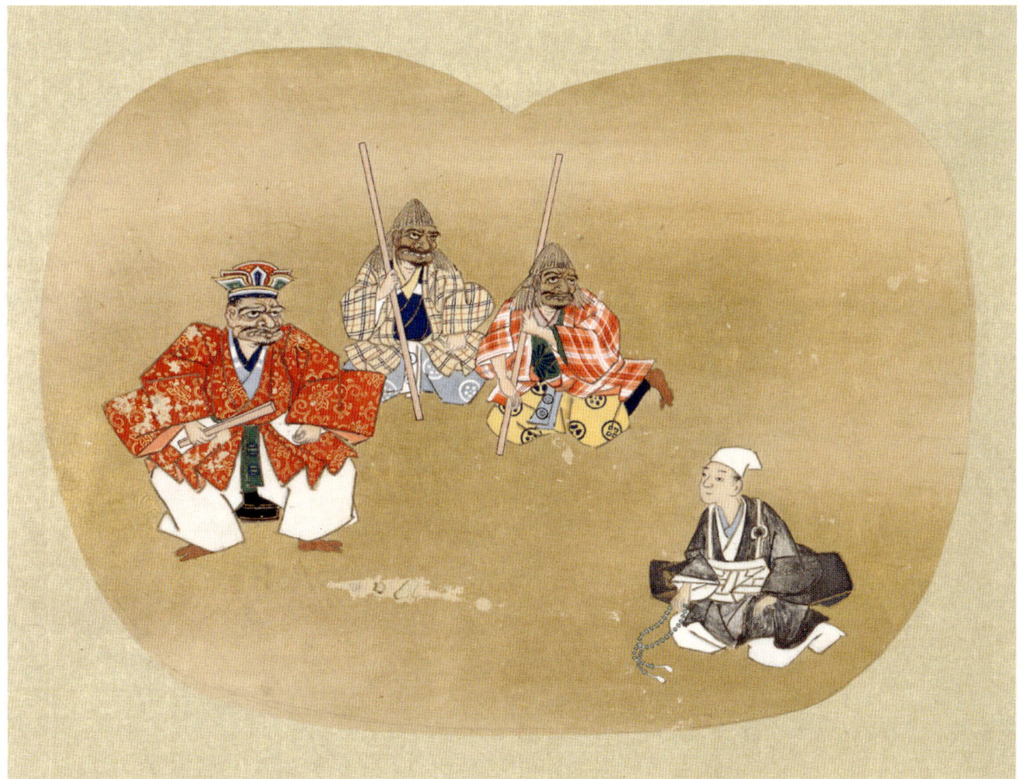

142 Illustrations of old kyōgen performances

early Edo period, 17th century
National Noh Theatre

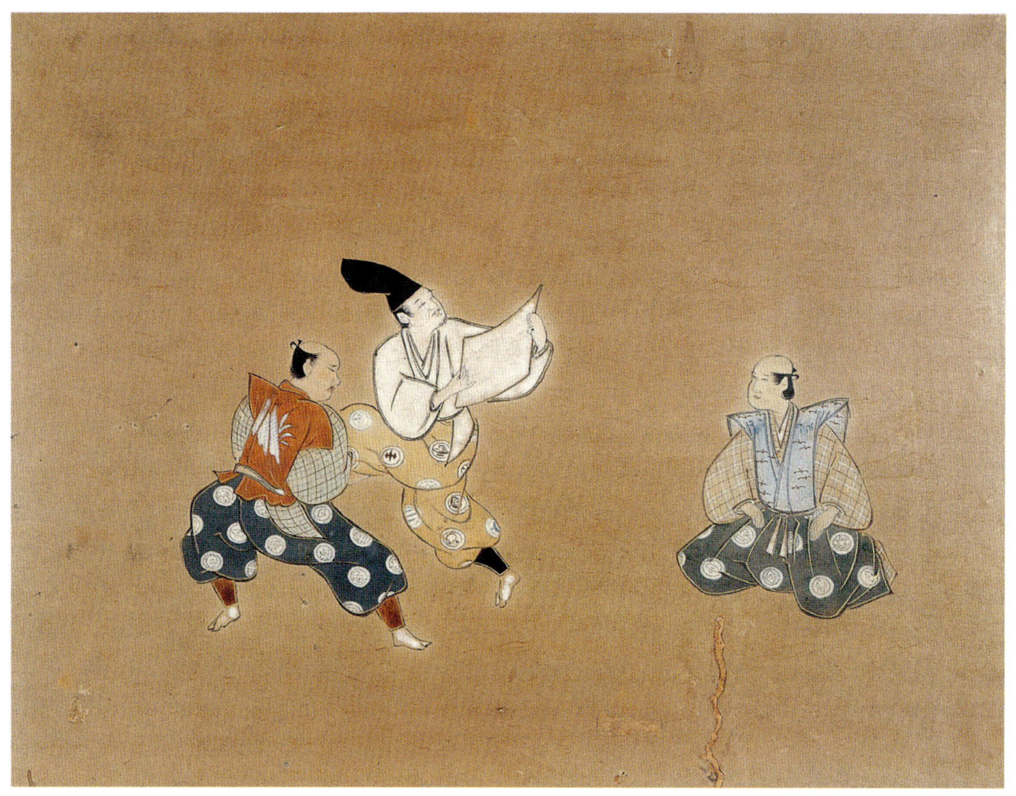

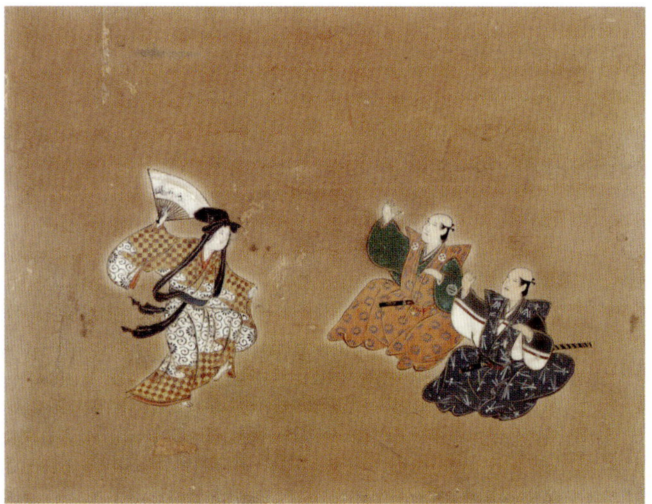

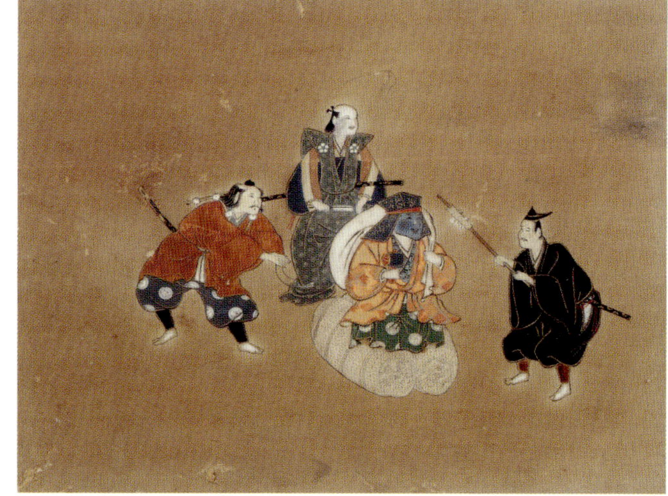

143 Album of old paintings of kyōgen
early Edo period, 17th century
National Noh Theatre

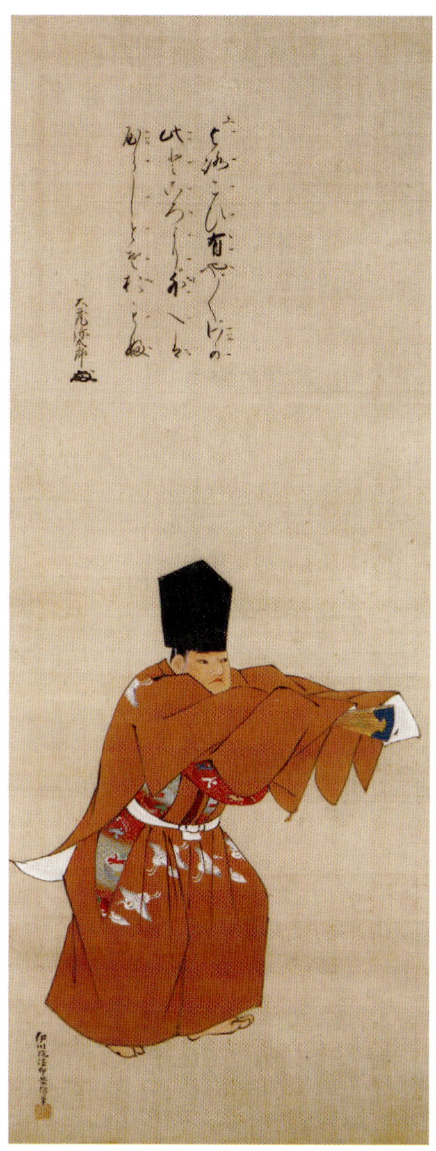

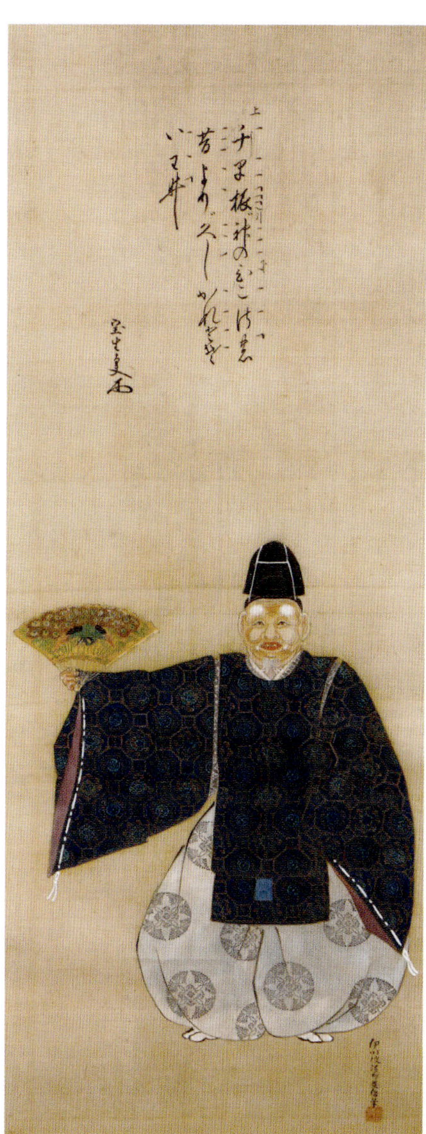

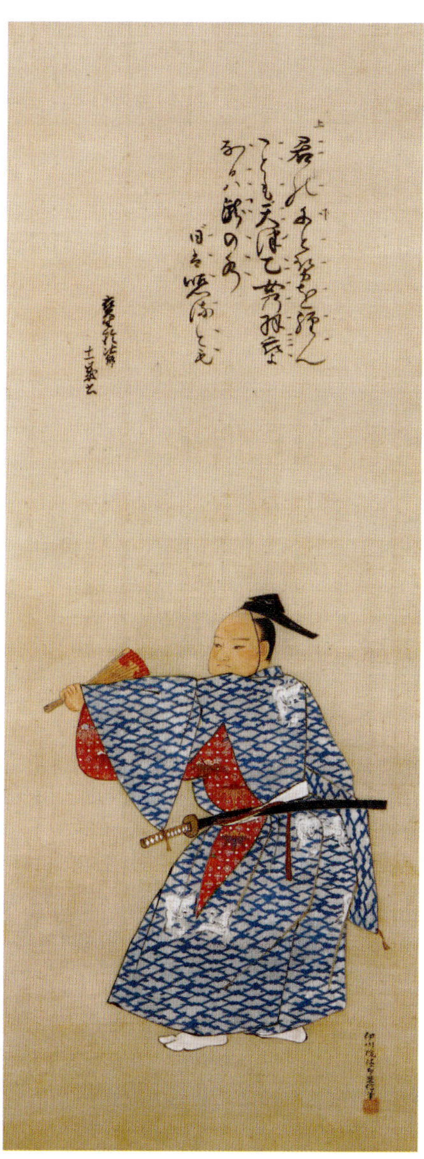

144 Kano Naganobu (1775–1828)
Okina, Sanbasō and Senzai
Edo period, 19th century
National Noh Theatre

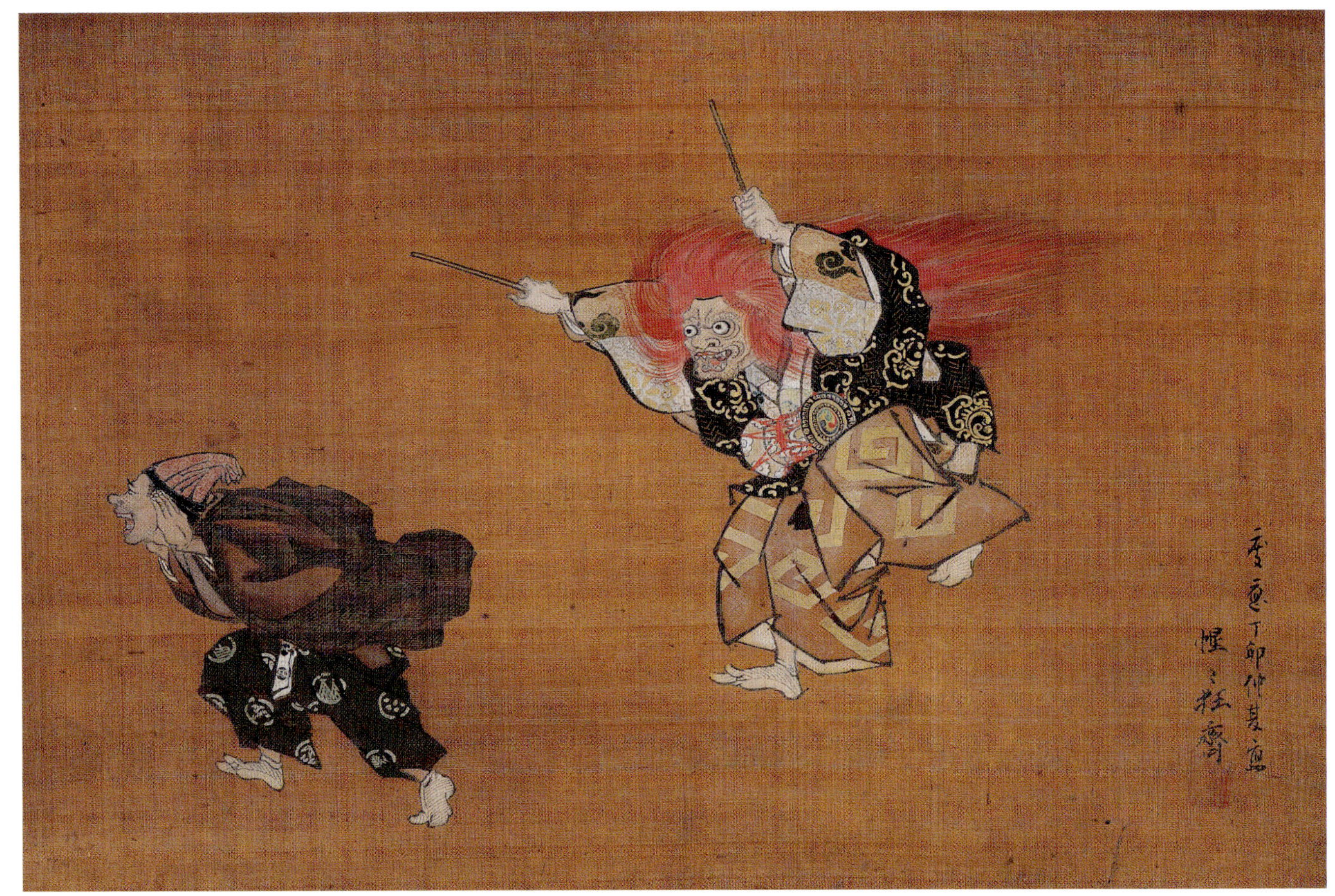

145 Kawanabe Kyōsai (1831–89)
Scene from the play *Thunder* (*Kaminari*)
dated Keiō 3 (1867)
National Noh Theatre

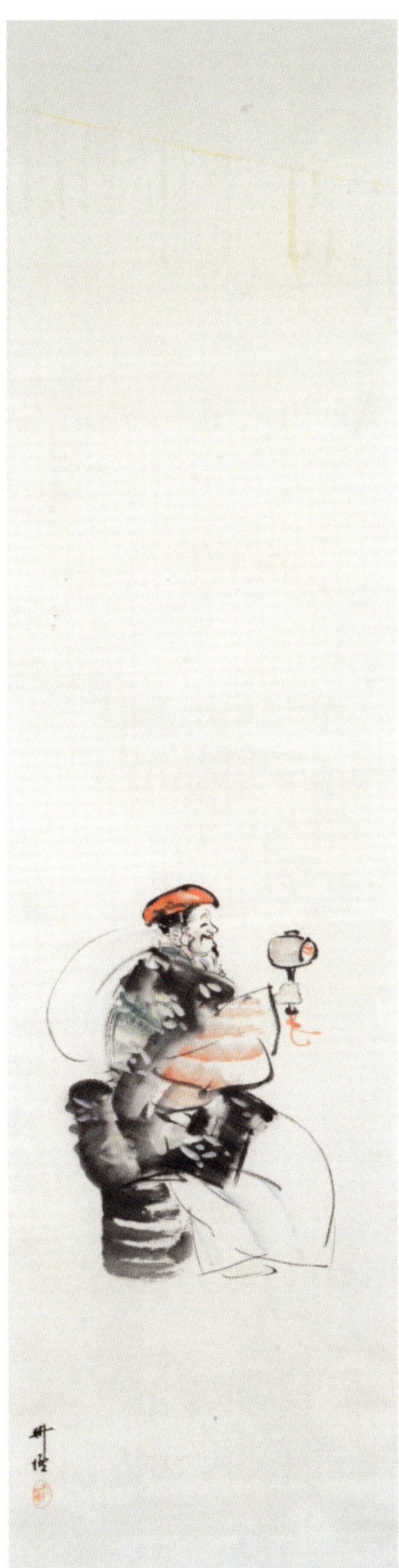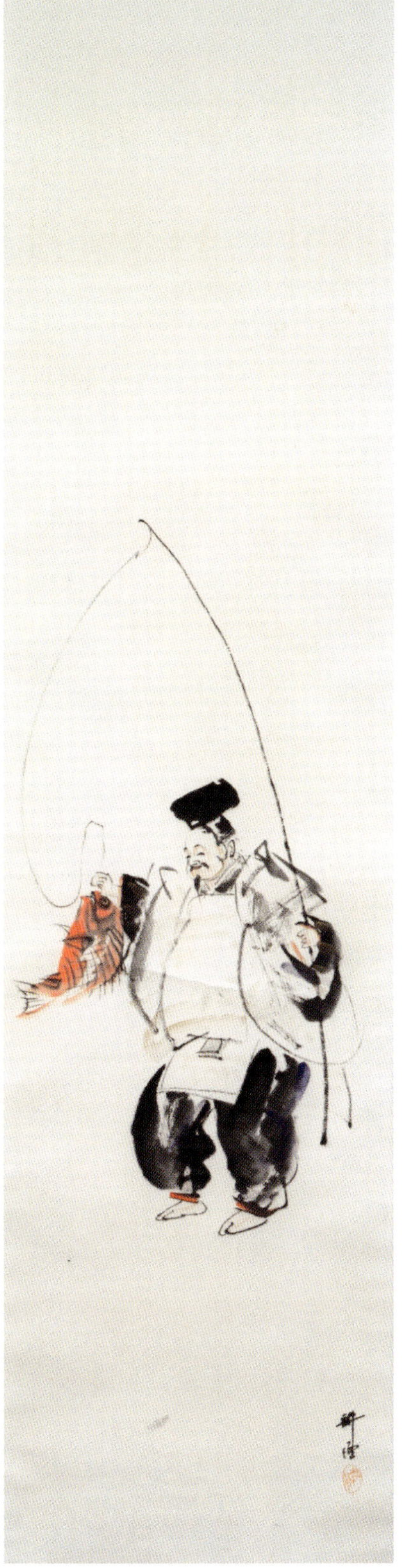

146 Tsukioka Kōgyo (1869–1927)
Daikoku and Ebisu
late 19th–early 20th century
National Noh Theatre

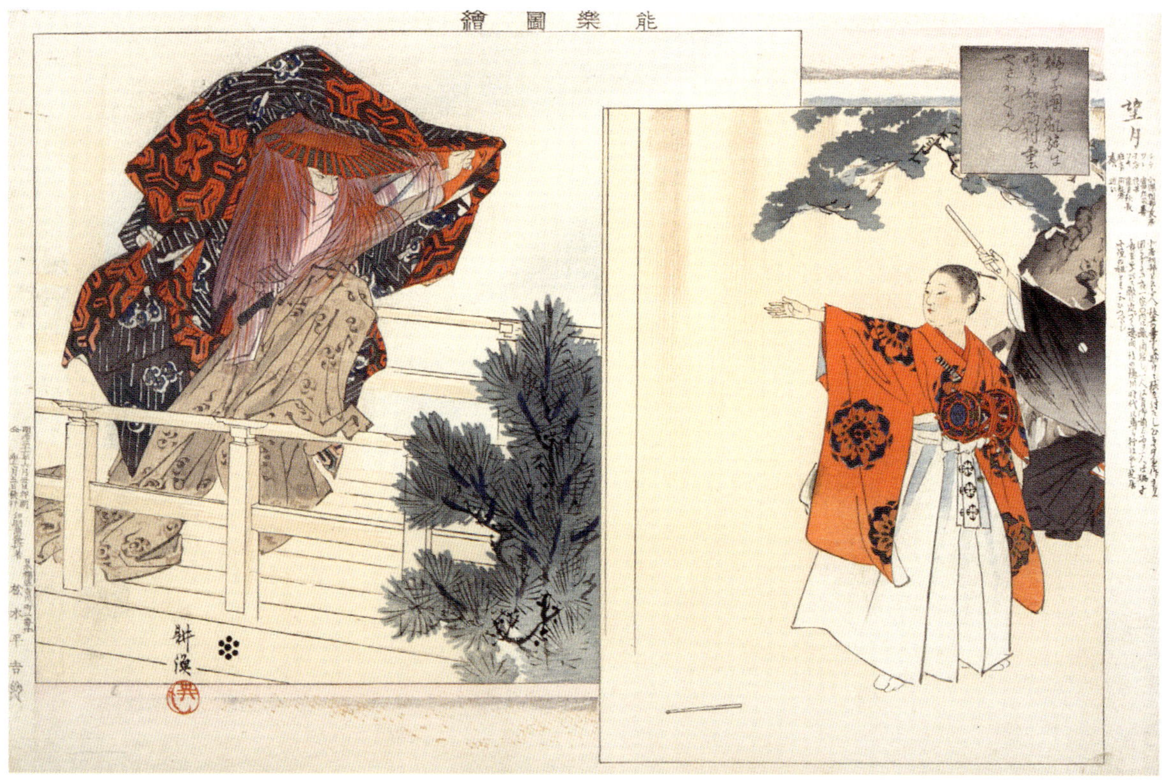

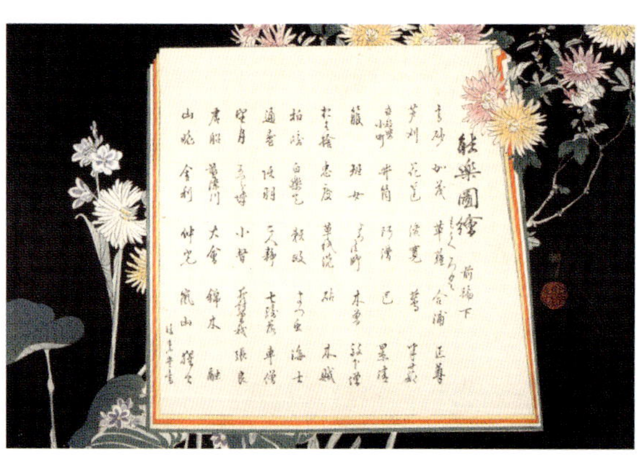

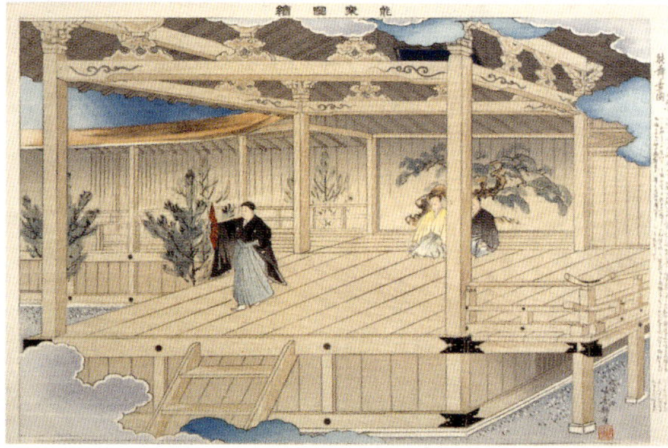

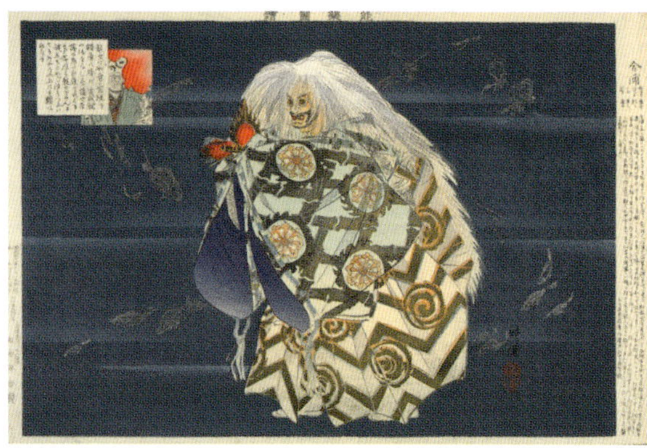

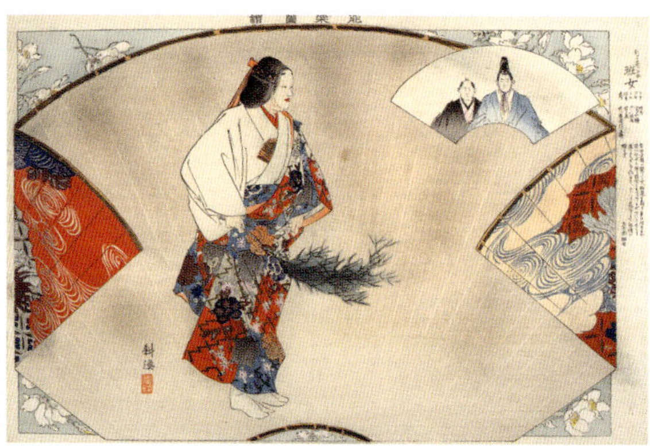

147 Tsukioka Kōgyo (1869–1927)
Pictures of nō plays (Nōgaku zue)
1897–1902
National Noh Theatre

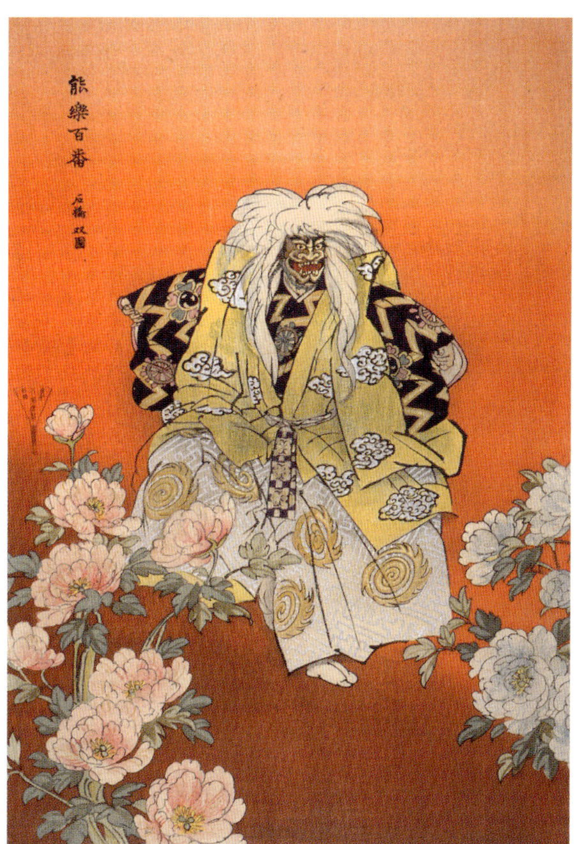

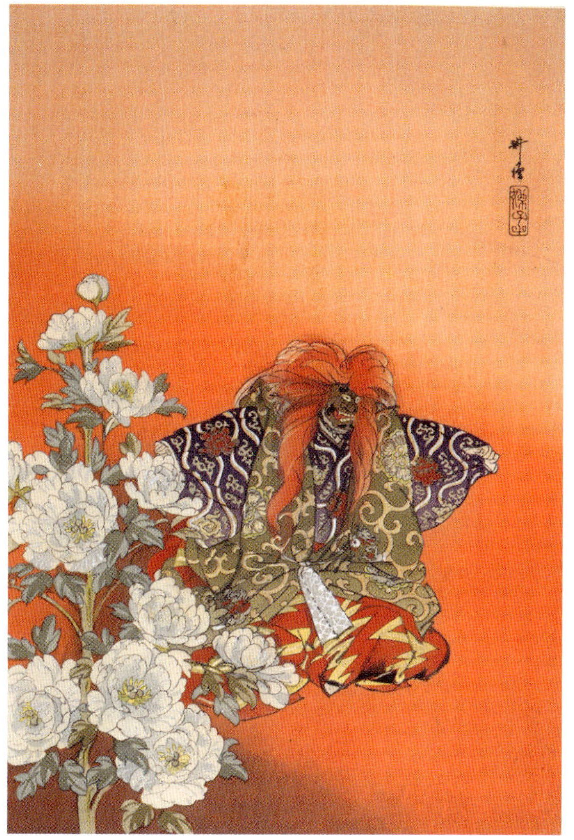

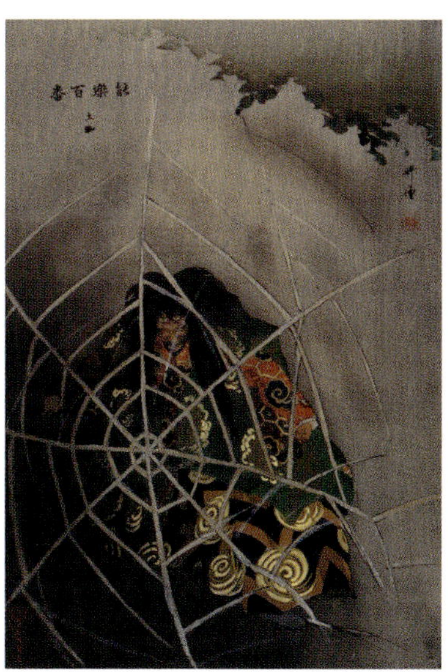

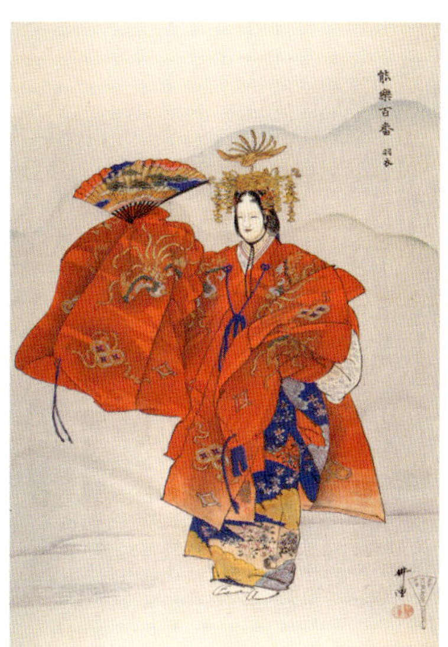

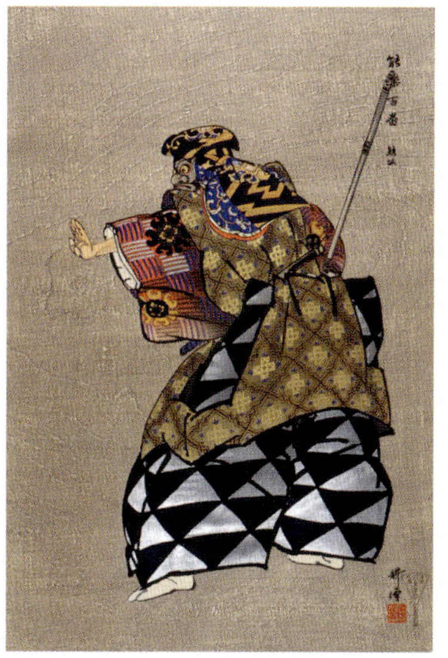

148 Tsukioka Kōgyo (1869–1927)
One hundred nō plays (Nōgaku hyakuban)
1922–27
National Noh Theatre

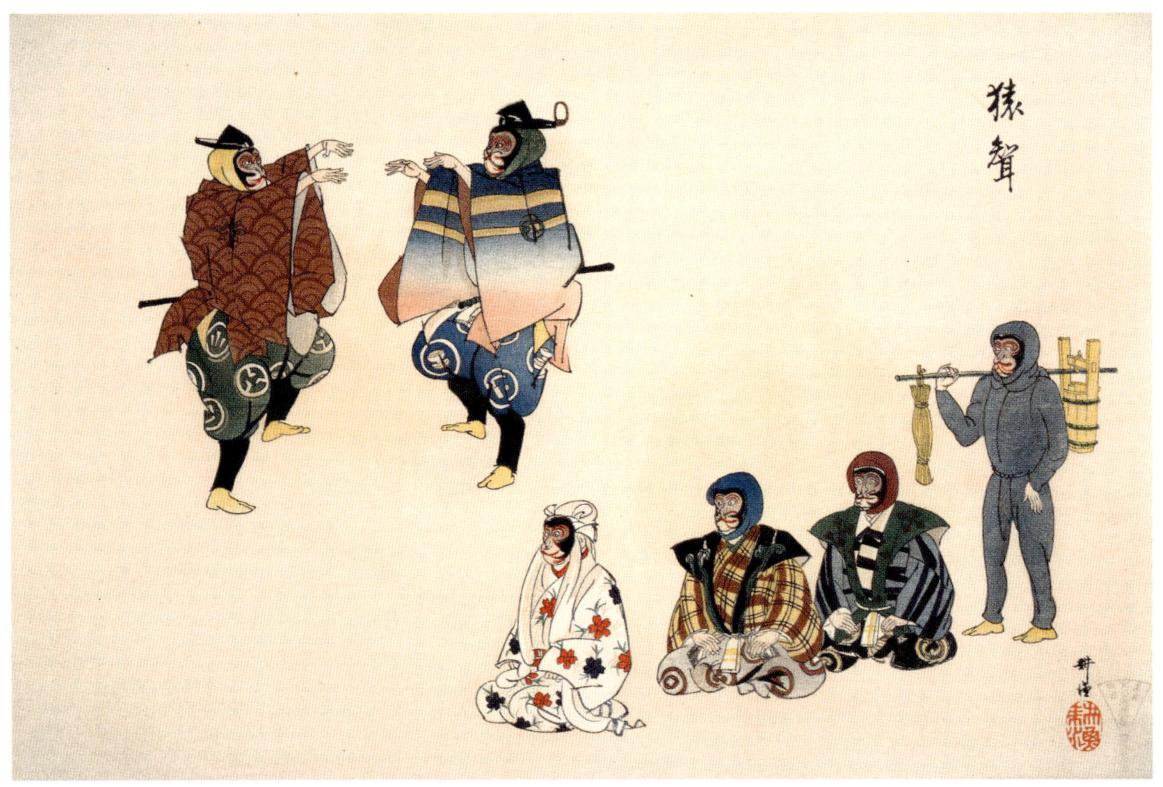

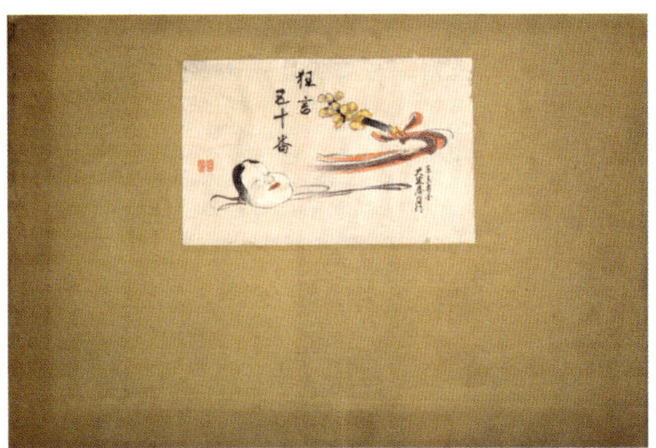

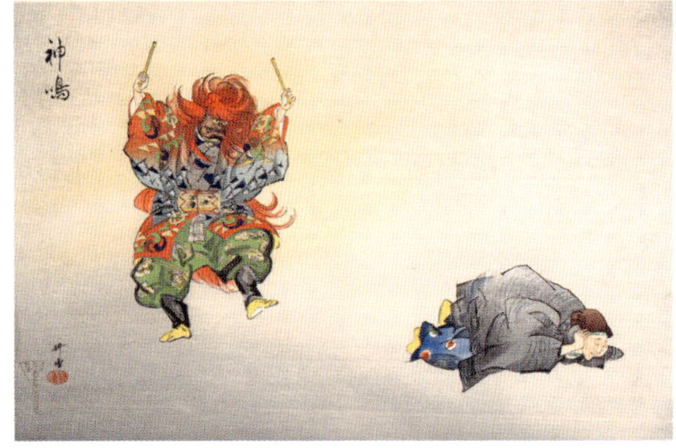

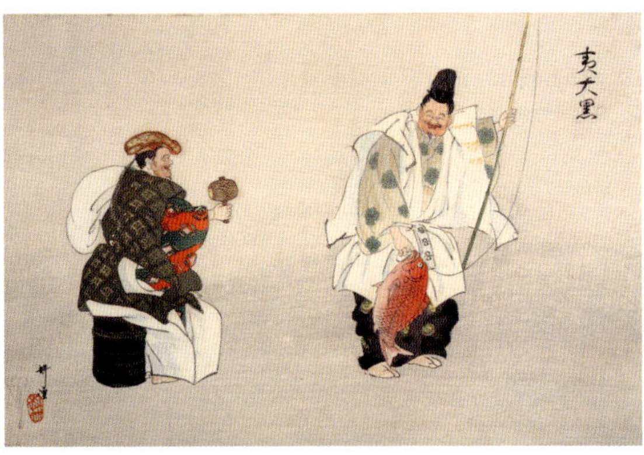

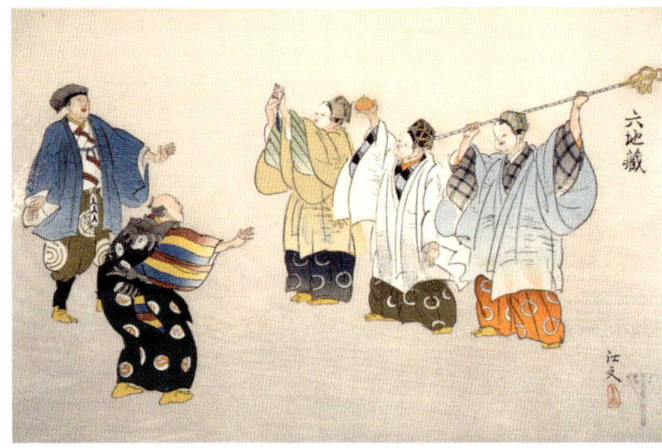

149 Tsukioka Kōgyo (1869–1927) and
Tsukioka Kōbun (1908–94)
Fifty kyōgen plays (Kyōgen gojūban)
1925
National Noh Theatre

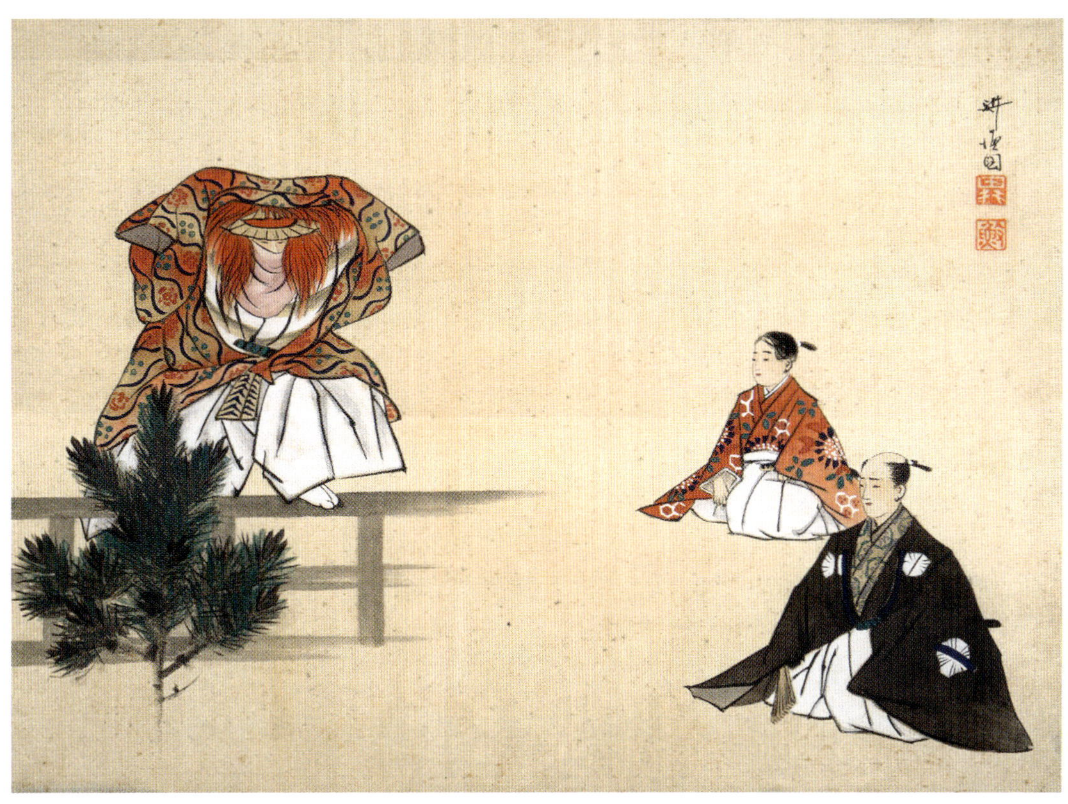

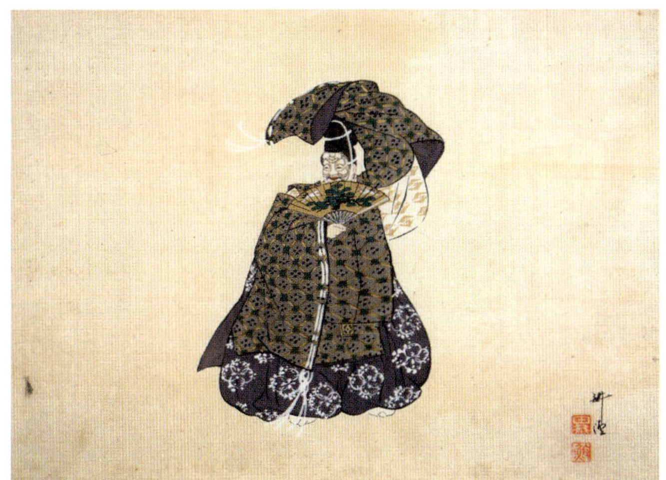

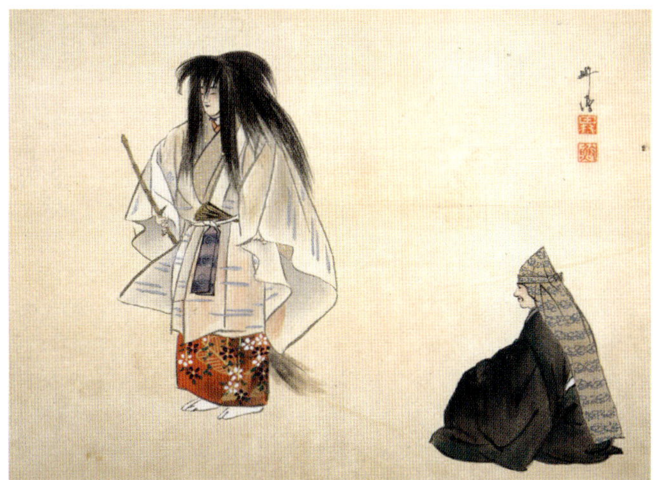

150 Tsukioka Kōgyo (1869–1927)
Pictures of nō and kyōgen plays
(*Nōgaku gachō*)

1920s
National Noh Theatre

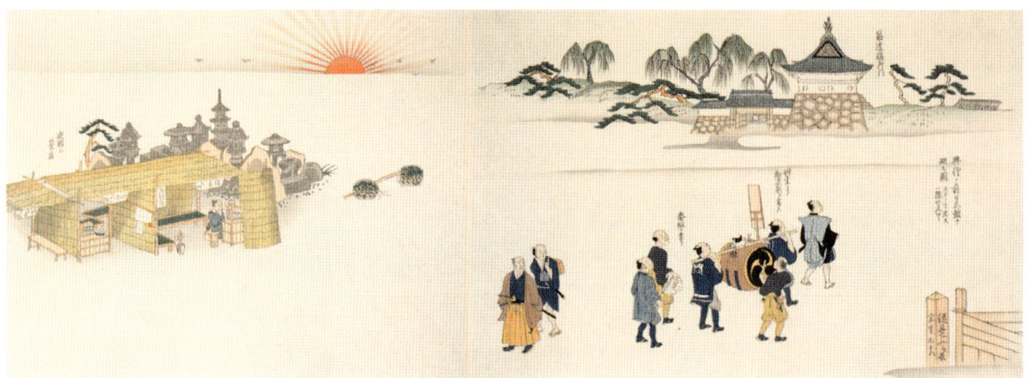

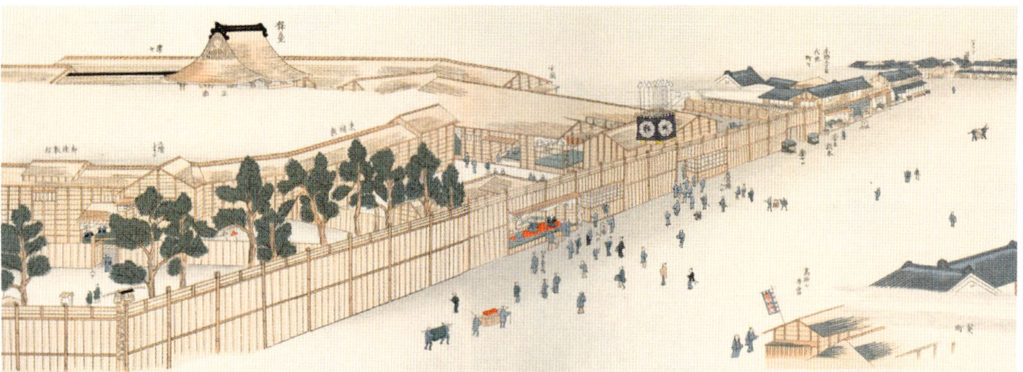

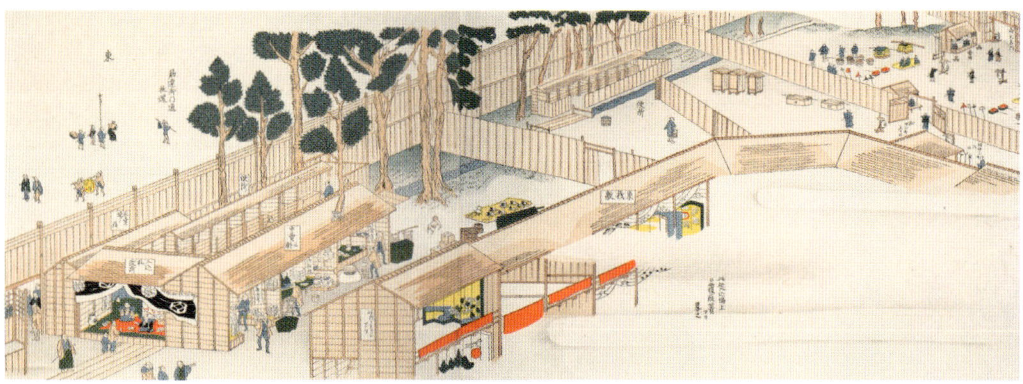

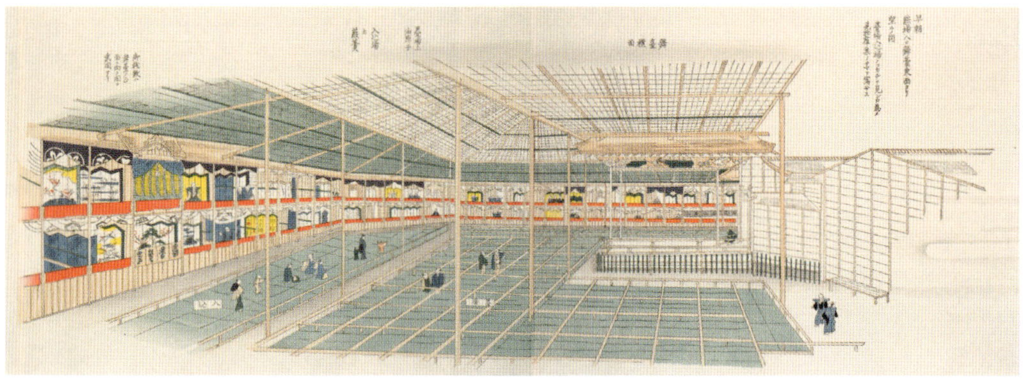

151 Illustrated scrolls of subscription
nō performance in the Kōka era (1844–48)

1909 (later edition)
National Noh Theatre

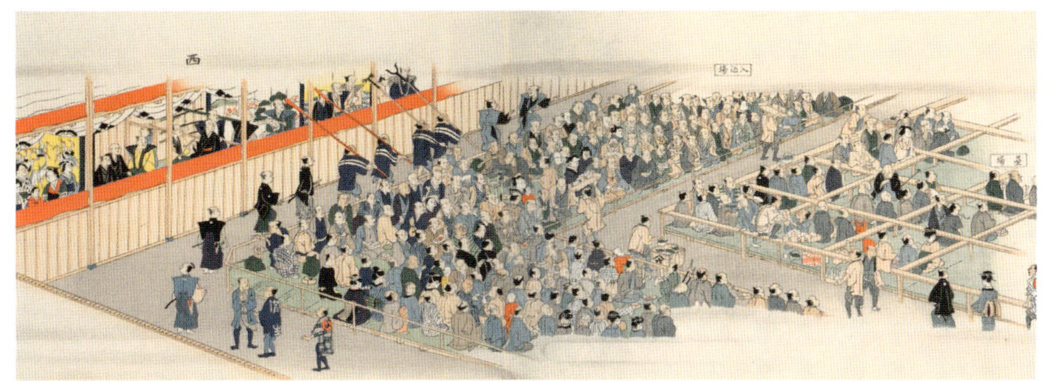

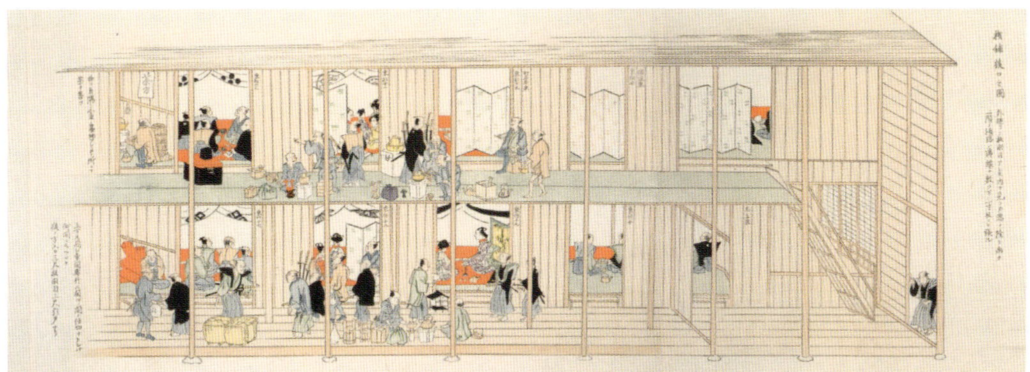

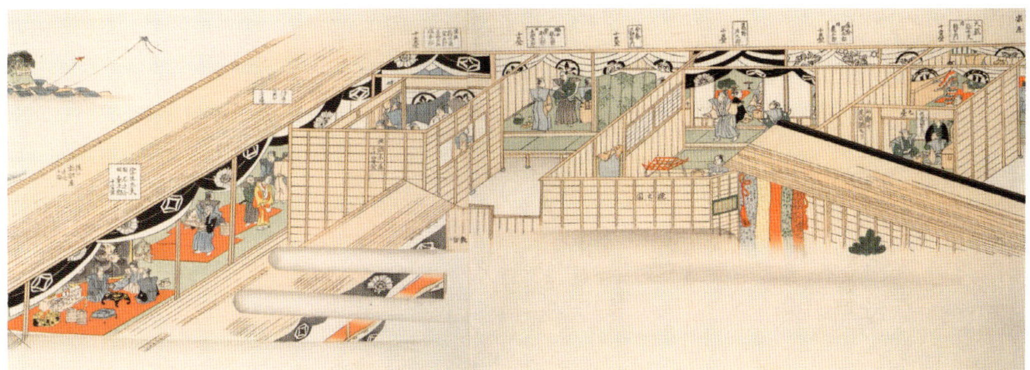

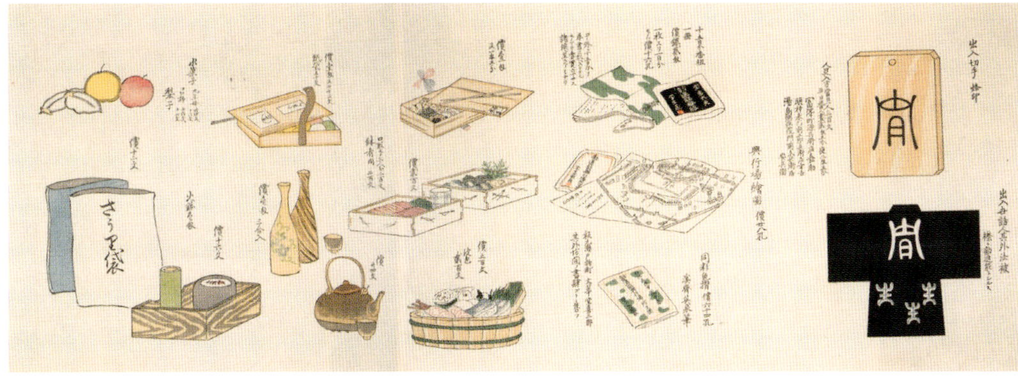

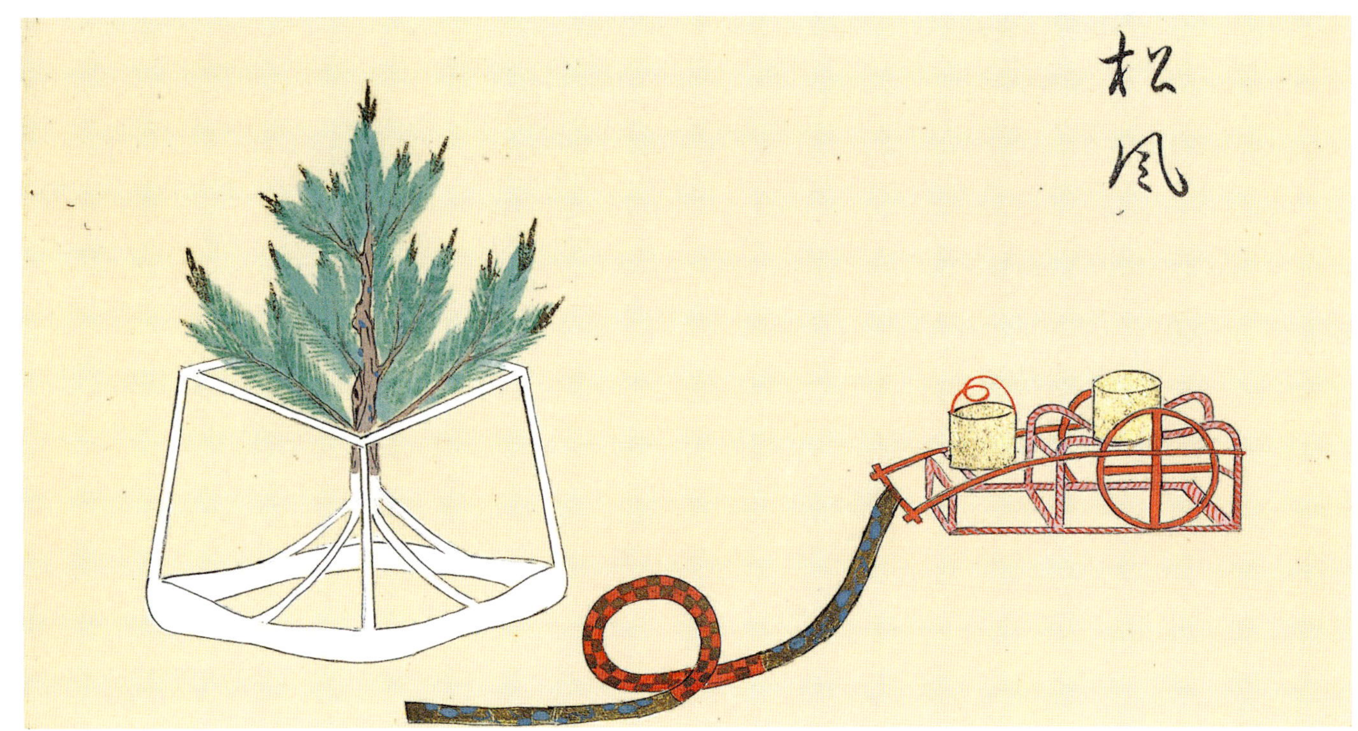

190

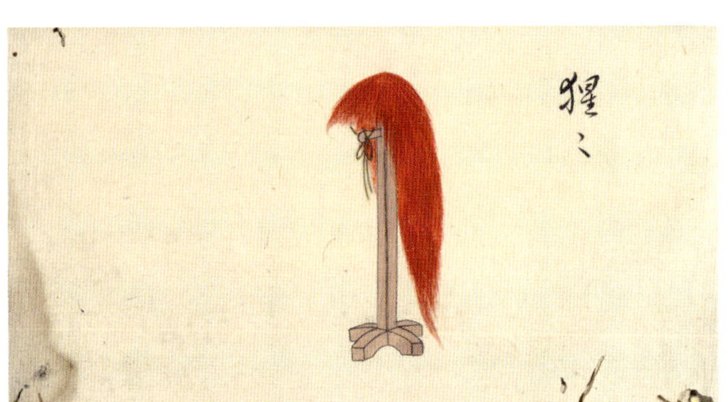

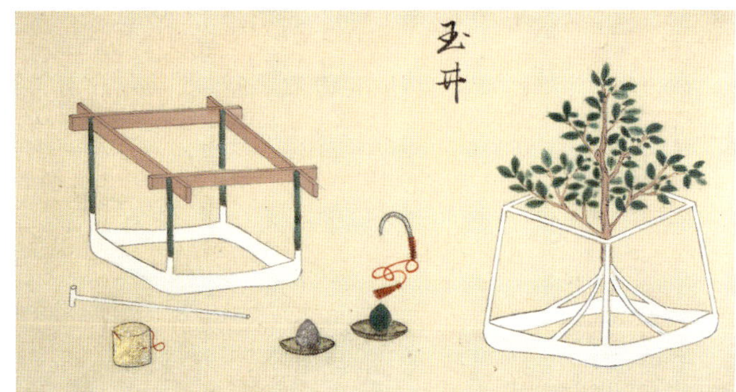

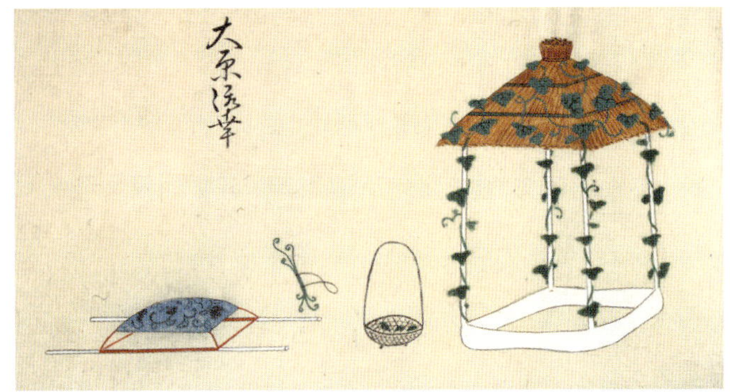

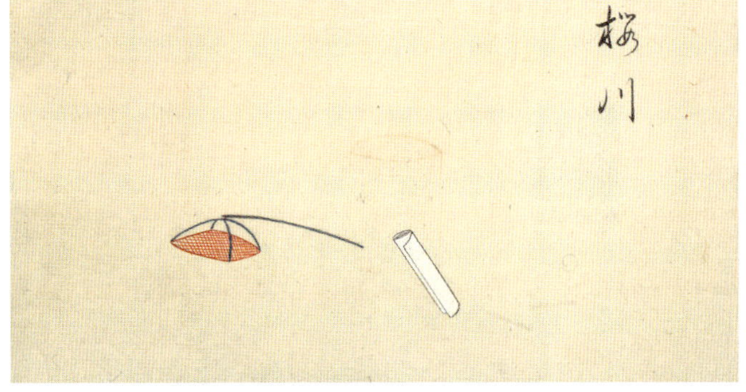

**152 Illustrations of nō properties
and accessories**

late Edo period, 19th century
National Noh Theatre

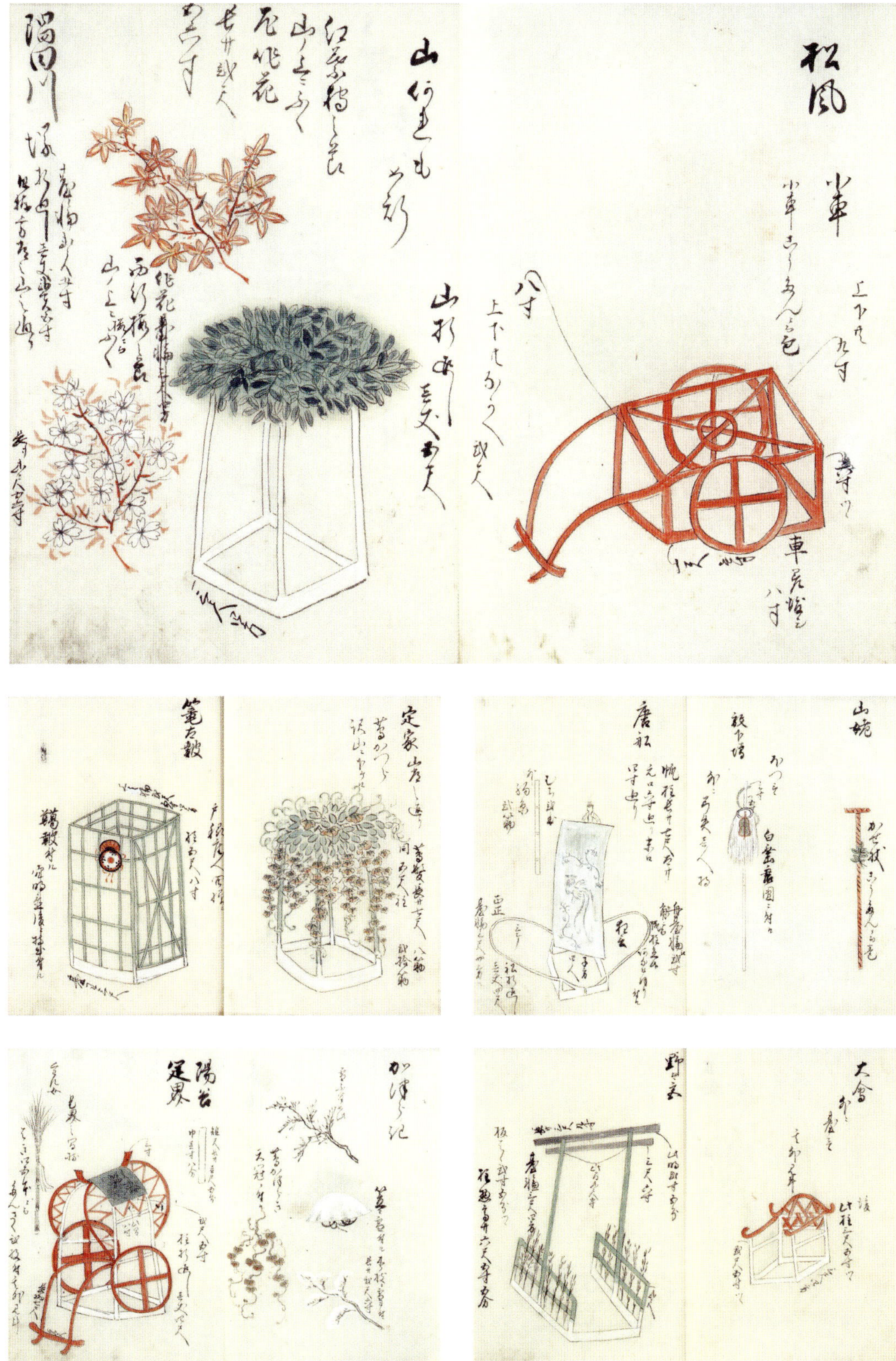

153 Illustrations of nō properties and accessories

late Edo period, 19th century
National Noh Theatre

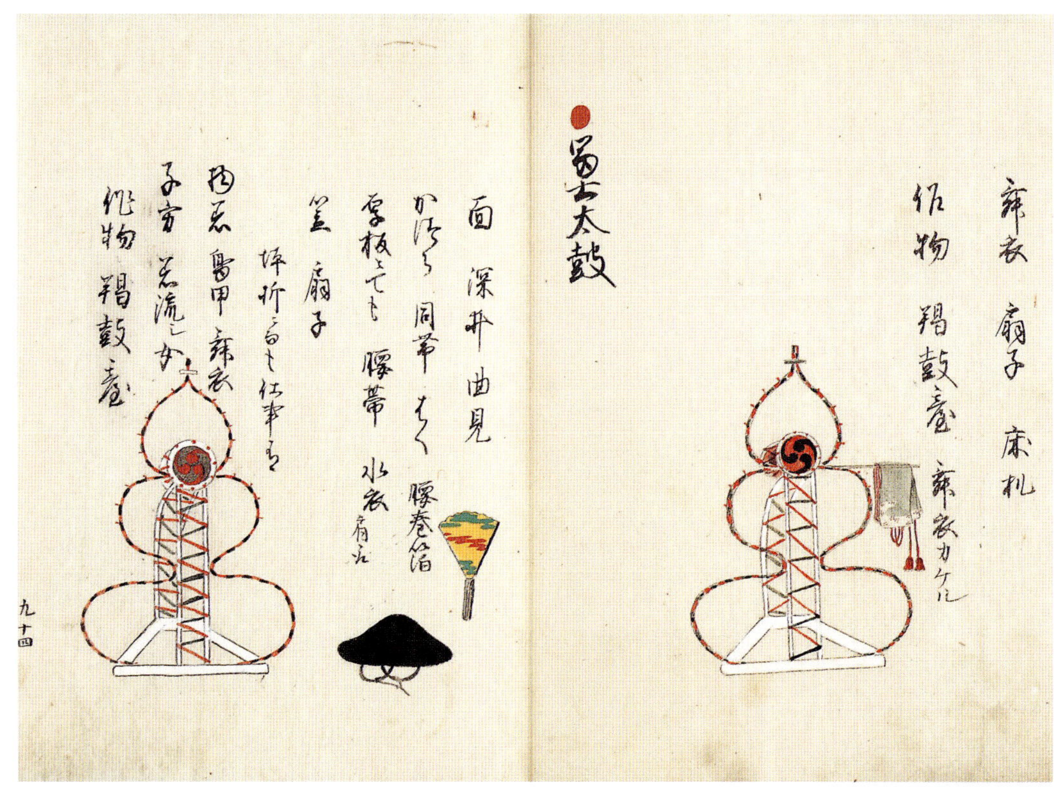

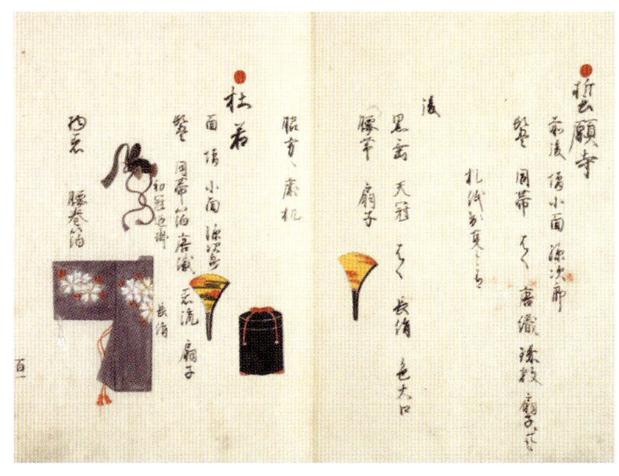

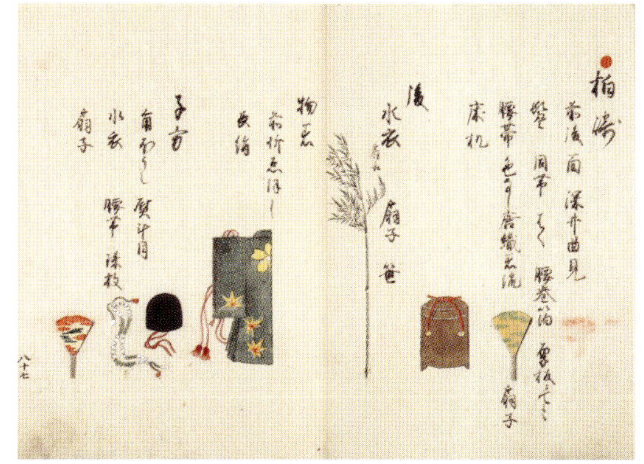

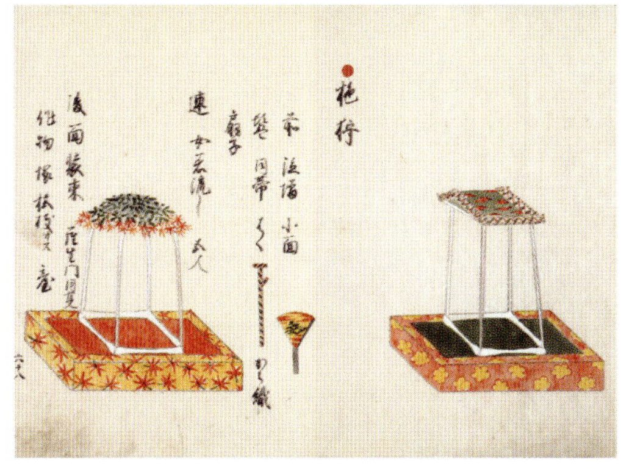

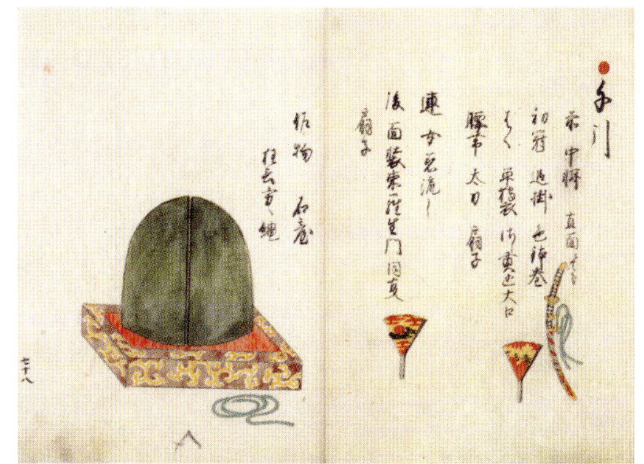

154 Hōshō school index of nō costumes
late Edo period, 19th century
National Noh Theatre

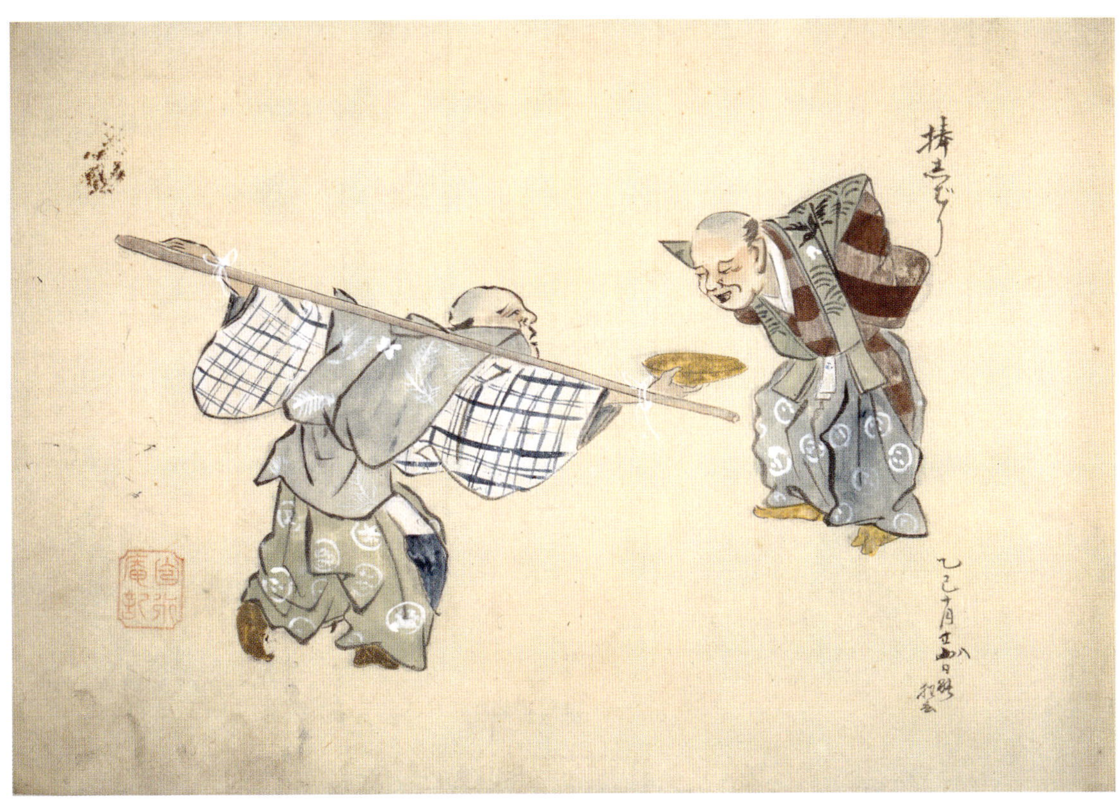

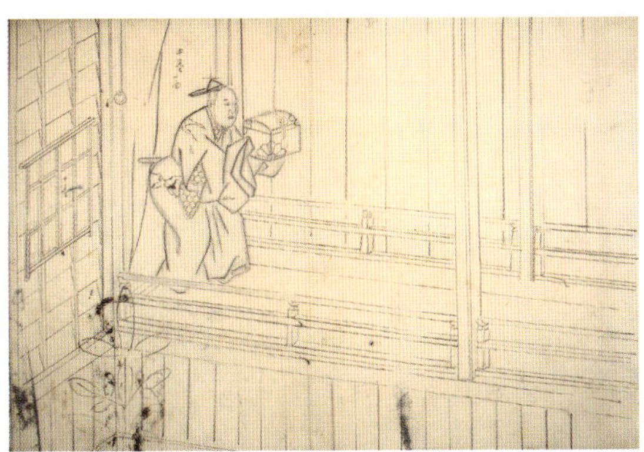

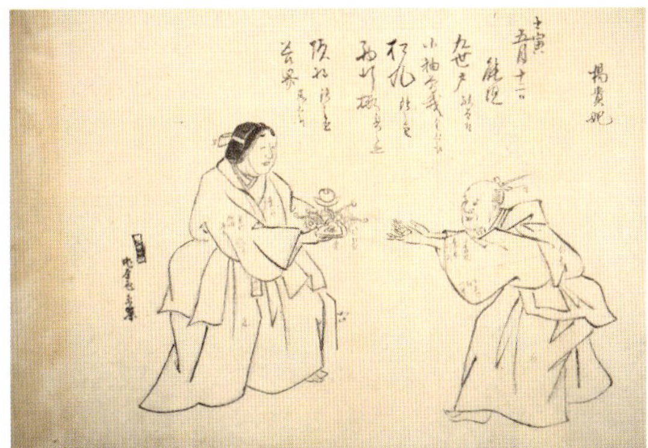

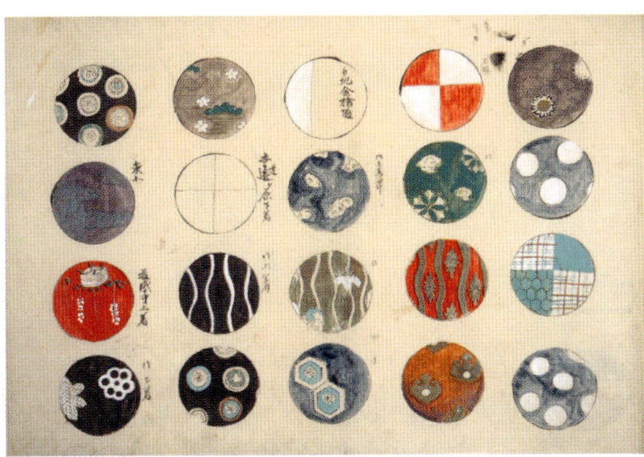

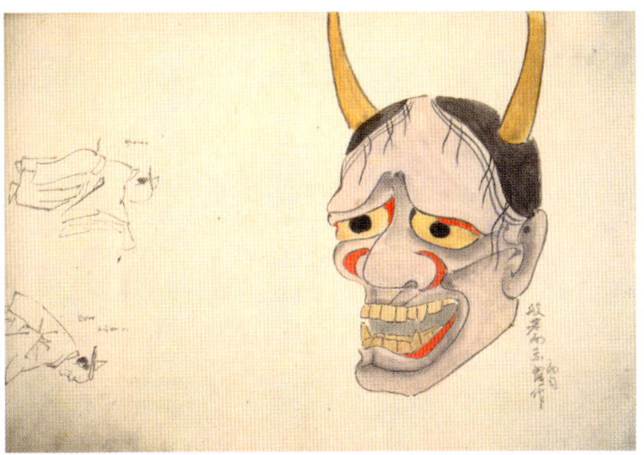

**155 Sketches of Kanze school
nō and kyōgen performances**

late Edo period, 19th century
National Noh Theatre

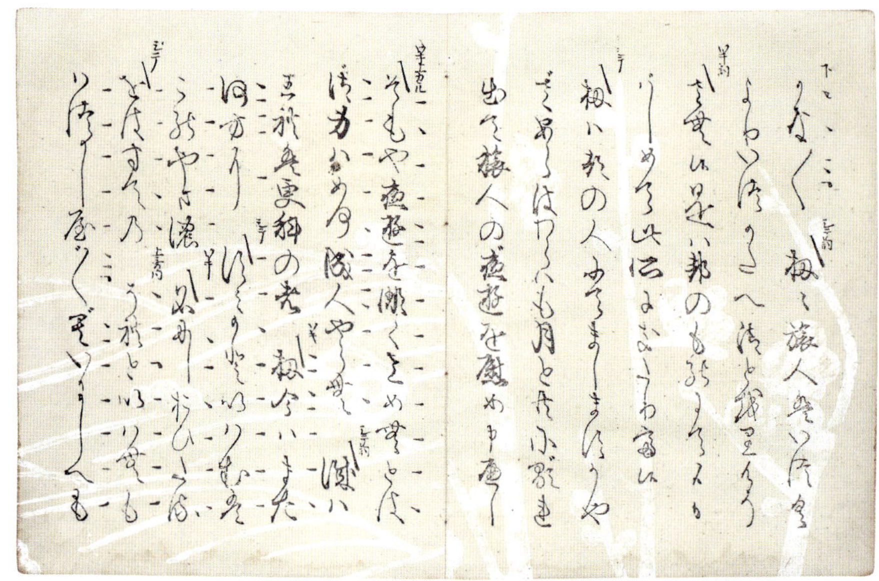

156 Hardcover Kōetsu-style
nō libretto (*utaibon*) for the play
The deserted crone (*Obasute*)

early Edo period, 17th century
National Noh Theatre

157 Multi-coloured Kōetsu-style
nō libretto (*utaibon*) for the play
The layman of the eastern coast (*Tōgan koji*)

early Edo period, 17th century
National Noh Theatre

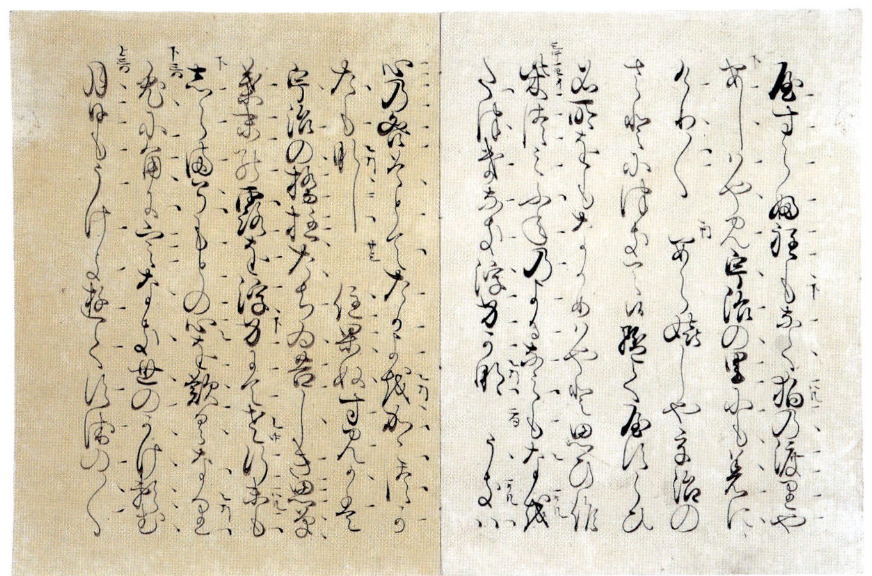

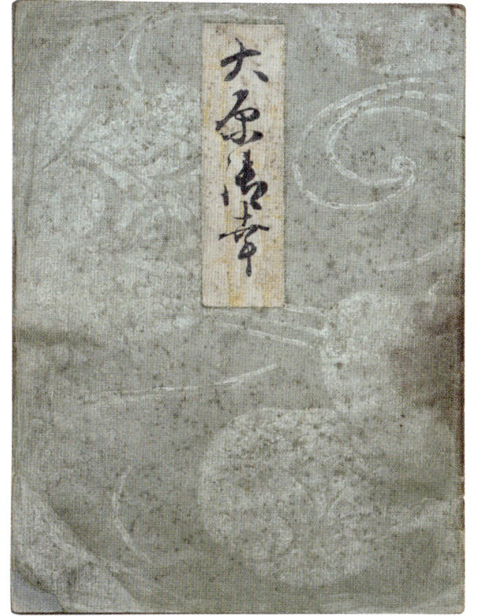

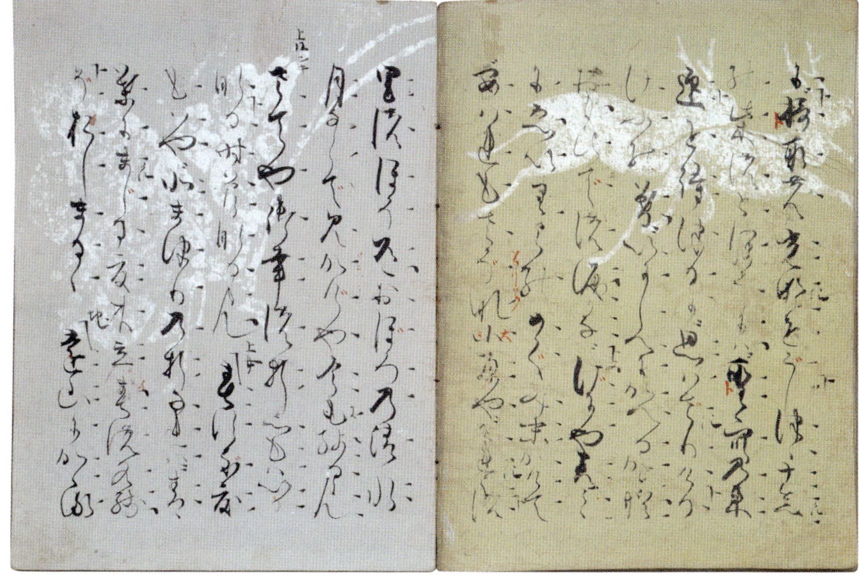

158　Nō libretto (*utaibon*) for the play
A drifting boat (Ukifune)

copy from early Edo period, 17th century
National Noh Theatre

159　Nō libretto (*utaibon*) for the play
Imperial visit to Ohara (Ohara gokō) with
postscript by Kanze Tadachika (1566–1626)

early Edo period, 17th century
National Noh Theatre

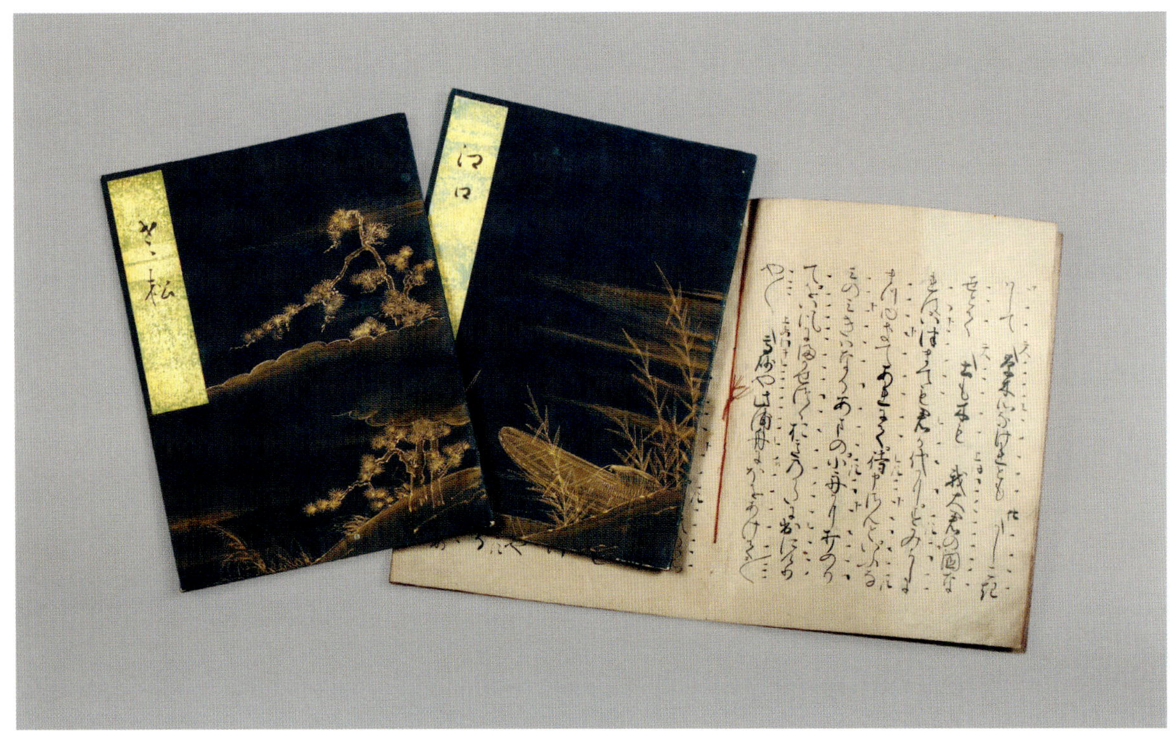

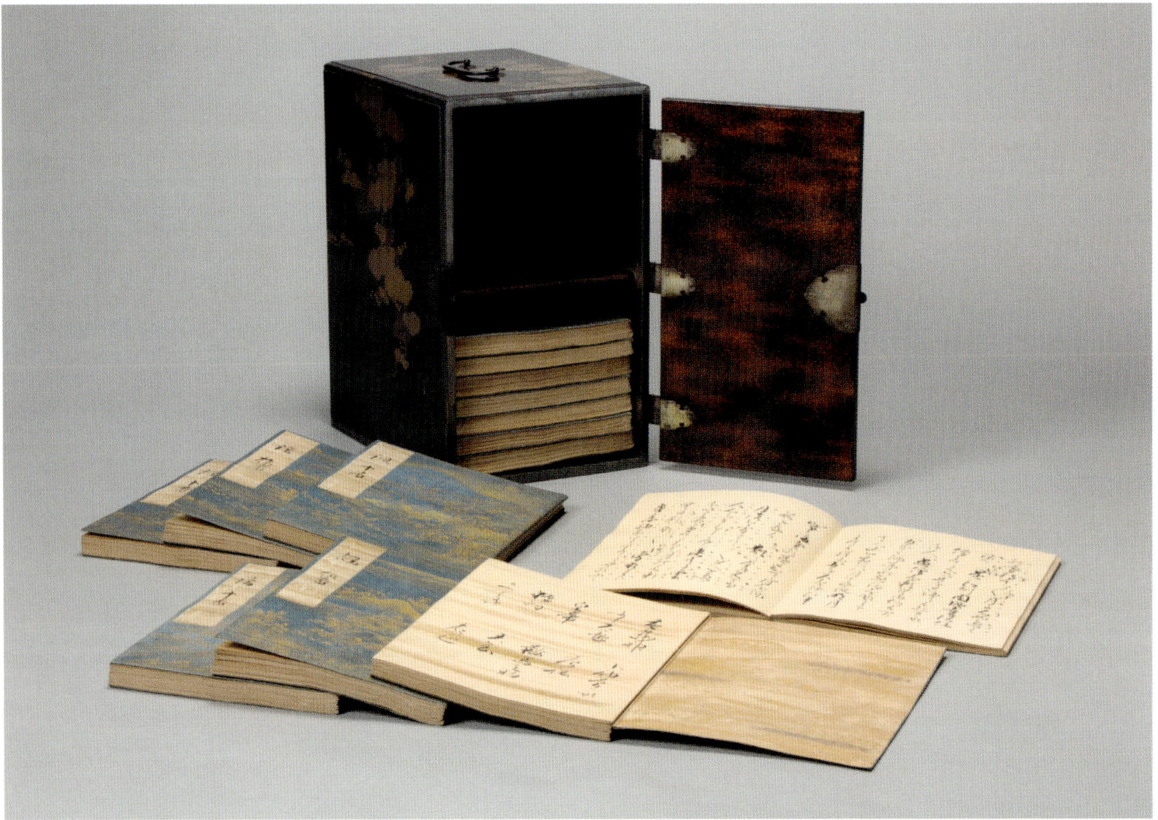

160 **Kanze school dark blue paperback single-play nō libretti (*utaibon*)**
copy from early Edo period, 17th century
National Noh Theatre

161 **Kanze school blue-covered single-play nō libretti (*utaibon*)**
copy from early Edo period, 17th century
National Noh Theatre

List of works and entries

NŌ MASKS

1 白色尉　桃山—江戸時代 16–17世紀
Hakushikijō (okina) mask

Momoyama–Edo period, 16th–17th century
pigment on wood with hair
6.5 x 18 x 13.7 cm
National Noh Theatre

This mask is used in the performance of *Okina* (*Shiki sanban*) when the lead performer (*tayū*) dances as a prayer for peace and stability in the realm. The origins of the *okina* (old man/god) mask lie in the objects of worship kept within Shinto shrines. When the *tayū* takes to the stage wearing the mask, he bestows blessings on the people in his capacity as a deity (*kami*). This example closely resembles the *hakushikijō* ('white old man') mask attributed to the carver Nikkō in the collection of the Kongō family. The open, laughing mouth, prominent eyebrows and the long, trailing beard combine to create an unusually strong impression. The smoothly finished, visible chisel marks on the reverse are covered with lacquer. Characters reading 'Okina, after Nikkō' are embroidered in purple thread on the mask's white satin bag. (KY)

2 黒色尉　桃山—江戸時代 16–17世紀
Kokushikijō mask

Momoyama–Edo period, 16th–17th century
pigment on wood with hair
7 x 17.8 x 13 cm
National Noh Theatre

This role-specific mask is used when the character Sanbasō dances the bell scene in *Okina* (*Shiki sanban*). The actor who dons the *kokushikijō* ('black old man') mask also holds a bell that represents ears of rice as he dances to pray for an abundant harvest. The mask's innocent smile was intended to induce a feeling of calm in viewers. Even though the mask is relatively small, the modelling

is sharp, allowing the actor to convey a broader range of facial expressions by altering the tilt of his head. The chisel marks on the reverse are barely visible and the smoothly finished surface is covered with lacquer. An inscription in red lacquer on the reverse of the forehead reads 'Offering from the Kōno family to Zenshō temple in Umaki village, Wake district, Yoshū (Iyō) province' (present-day Matsuyama city, Ehime prefecture), indicating that it was handed down as a presentation mask. (KY)

3 父尉　室町時代 15–16世紀
Chichinojō mask

Muromachi period, 15th–16th century
pigment on wood with hair
6.6 x 16.8 x 14.2 cm
National Noh Theatre

The *chichinojō* mask is used in the performance of *Okina* (*Shiki sanban*) when Okina performs the solo celebratory dance. Nowadays, the *chichinojō* mask is only utilised in very special performances, meaning that opportunities to view it onstage are rare. The *chichinojō* ('old man') mask is similar to the *hakushikijō* mask [see 1], although the *chichinojō* features a detached jaw and overall has a stiffer facial expression. The bushy eyebrows are made from circles of animal fur glued to the surface of the mask. The chisel marks on the reverse are even and have been covered with lacquer. The reverse also bears an inscription in red lacquer reading '*ichi no san*' (three of one). The National Noh Theatre also houses a *hakushikijō* mask with the inscription '*ichi no ichi*' (one of one) and a *kokushikijō* mask with the inscription '*ichi no ni*' (two of one). Further research is required to decipher the meaning of these inscriptions. (KY)

4 小尉　江戸時代 17世紀
Kojō mask

Edo period, 17th century
pigment on wood with hair
8.9 x 20.9 x 15.7 cm
National Noh Theatre

The *kojō* mask was originally used for roles in which deities transformed themselves from their celestial forms in order to appear in the human world. It later came to be employed for roles depicting distinguished elderly men and the mask's handsome features

are therefore carved to convey an appropriately extra-human sense of dignity and purity. This mask is compact and the features are well ordered. A section of the right ear was damaged at some point and has been repaired by attaching an additional piece of wood to the mask with two strings. A substance resembling *kokuso* (a paste made by adding wood powder to a mixture of flour and lacquer) was applied as filler and then in-painted. There are traces of circular chisel marks that have been smoothly finished and lacquered on the reverse; an impressed branded carver's seal reads 'Yūkan, foremost in the realm' (*tenka'ichi Yūkan*). This piece was handed down through the Yamauchi family. (KY)

5 髭阿瘤尉　江戸時代 17–18世紀
Higeakobujō mask

Edo period, 17th–18th century
pigment on wood with hair
8.7 x 20.7 x 14.7 cm
National Noh Theatre

This work represents a mask type that, while lacking the dignity of the *kojō* mask [see 4], is not uncouth in the same sense as the *sankōjō* mask (the *sankōjō* is an old man mask named after Sankōbō (d1532), a Buddhist monk who first carved a mask of this type). *Akobujō* (meaning 'old man from a foreign country') masks may be carved in a range of facial expressions. This example is identifiable as the *higeakobujō* ('bearded *akobujō*') type owing to the moustache rendered by implanting hair into the wood of the mask. The long face, smooth wrinkle-free skin, deep-set eyes, angular cheekbones and comparatively large jaw conjure up the image of an old man from a distant land. There are traces of chatter marks on the reverse, which is covered with blackish-brown lacquer. There is also an impressed branded carver's seal that reads 'Deme Mitsunori' (Deme Dōsui, d1729) [see also 6, 28 & 30]. (KY)

6 鷲鼻悪尉　江戸時代 18世紀
Washibana akujō mask

Edo period, 18th century
pigment and metal on wood with hair
10.4 x 21.2 x 16 cm
National Noh Theatre

The name of this mask – *washibana akujō* – connotes an old man having strong facial features with an arched, hooked nose resembling an eagle's beak. The fine modelling and refined, simple colouring exemplify the beauty of nō masks at the peak of their development. Moreover, the warm yellowish colouration also imbues the work with a gentle feel. The back of the mask bears traces of the chisel that have been smoothly finished and covered with black lacquer. There is an impressed branded carver's seal that reads 'Deme Mitsunori' [see 5, 28 & 30] and an inscription in red lacquer noting '*Washibana akujō* mask, Kongō school style, a work of supreme workmanship produced in the third month of Kyōhō 17 [1732]'. During the Kyōhō era (1717–36) a large number of masks were kept at the Fushimi residence of the Ikeda family of Inshū, which was located in present-day Kyoto and en route to the daimyo's alternate residence in the capital Edo (present-day Tokyo). This mask was one such example and it is clear from the inscription that it was considered a masterwork. (KY)

7   甘柘榴悪尉　室町時代 16世紀
Amazakuro akujō mask

Muromachi period, 16th century
pigment and metal on wood with hair
9.5 x 21.3 x 16.3 cm
Agency for Cultural Affairs of Japan

The wide, open rounded eyes and mouth of this mask are defining features of the *tobide* ('bulging eyes') category of masks. The expression of the *tobide* mask is also said to relate to 'the appearance of Kan no Shōjō [Sugawara no Michizane, 845–903] spitting out a pomegranate seed' [see also 12]. The Japanese word for pomegranate, '*amazakuro*' (with *ama* written using the character for 'sweet'), was also written with the character for heaven or sky, also read as *ama*, and as a result it is thought that this type of mask was produced for deity roles such as Tenjin (the above Sugawara no Michizane) and the Thunder God (Raijin). The *omoni akujō* mask has very similar features and can be employed in place of the *amazakuro*. In medieval Japan, the term *aku* (bad or evil) was associated with the idea of superhuman strength, and the *akujō* (evil old man) was considered a quasi-god. The gilt wood eyes, upper teeth and cuspids are later additions. Horizontal chisel marks appear on the back, the surface of which is covered in black lacquer. This mask was handed down through the Daishōji branch of the Maeda family. (KY)

8   髭癋見　室町―桃山時代
15–16世紀
Higebeshimi mask

Muromachi–Momoyama period,
15th–16th century
pigment and metal on wood with hair
9.5 x 21 x 17.7 cm
National Noh Theatre

With lips pressed tightly together in a straight line and nostrils flaring, this mask conveys an impression of focused energy. It is normally used for roles such as *tengu* (bird-like goblin) chiefs. At first glance, this mask appears comical, but the richly modelled classical form exudes an extraordinary presence when viewed onstage, making it a tour de force. Traces of the chisel are just visible on the back of the mask; the surface is mostly finished and then covered with lacquer. The gently mellowed wood grain visible on the back of the mask quietly imparts a sense of the mask's antiquity, which contrasts with the energy of its facial expression. (KY)

9   大癋見　室町時代 15–16世紀
Ōbeshimi mask

Muromachi period, 15th–16th century
pigment and metal on wood
10.7 x 22.3 x 17.1 cm
Agency for Cultural Affairs of Japan

The term *beshimi* refers to the facial expression in which the mouth is locked in a tense frown. This type of mask is used for demonic *tengu* roles. Compared with other extant *ōbeshimi* ('large frowning') masks, this example is especially deeply carved. The constricted facial muscles and the strength of the eyes, which are inlaid with gilt bronze rings, generate the force emanating from this mask. The relatively freely executed chisel marks on the back are covered in lacquer. The carved inscription on the reverse of the forehead reads 'A work by Ittō, resident of Kuchi, Sado island' (present-day Niigata prefecture). A legendary carver of demon masks named Shakuzuru (active fifteenth c.) is said to have resided on Sado island. However, as this mask's inscription clearly attributes the work to 'Ittō', more research is required to determine what, if any, connection there may be between this mask and Shakuzuru. The mask was handed down through the Daishōji branch of the Maeda family. (KY)

10   小癋見　江戸時代 19世紀
Kobeshimi mask

Edo period, 19th century
pigment and metal on wood
9.3 x 20.4 x 16 cm
National Noh Theatre

This mask belongs to the *kobeshimi* ('small frowning') category and is used for the demon role in the play *Guardian of the fields* (*Nomori*). The facial muscles are tensed, displaying the power of this character. The depiction of the facial hair on a ground of intentionally darkened red pigment is a trait of this type of mask, but the black ink around the mouth is a later addition. The back of the mask is smooth with no visible chisel marks and is covered with black lacquer. An inscription in red lacquer on the left reverse side of the forehead area reads 'One in a hundred works'. This example was handed down through the Yamauchi family. (KY)

11   泥小飛出　室町時代 15–16世紀
Deikotobide mask

Muromachi period, 15th–16th century
pigment and metal on wood
9.5 x 20.8 x 15.6 cm
National Noh Theatre

The defining features of the *tobide* mask type are the wide, open mouth and eyes, in contrast to the knitting of the brows in the *beshimi* [see 8–10]. The *deikotobide* is used for roles such as spirit foxes, believed to be the messengers of the deity of grain, Inari-myōjin. While remaining faithful to older conventions, over time the imposing countenance of the *deikotobide* acquired an increasingly divine character. The mouth of this mask shares traits with the kyōgen *hakuzōsu* mask [see 97], which illustrates a fox in human form, and as such it is believed that it was especially made for a special performance of the nō play *The swordsmith* (*Kokaji*). The relatively free chisel marks, which are just visible on the reverse of the mask, are covered with lacquer. An inscription in gold on the reverse of the forehead gives the mask type as *kotobide* and the carver as Shakuzuru. However, an inscription in black ink on the mask's inner cover reads '*Kotobide*, carver unknown'. (KY)

12   大飛出　江戸時代 18–19世紀
Ōtobide mask

Edo period, 18th–19th century
pigment and metal on wood
9.6 x 20.6 x 15.4 cm
Agency for Cultural Affairs of Japan

The *tobide* is an imposing deity mask with bulging eyes and a wide, open 'ah-shaped' mouth.[1] The entire surface of this broad featured *ōtobide* ('large *tobide*') is painted in gold; the expression of the open mouth is probably modelled after the face type described as having 'the appearance of Kan no Shōjō spitting out a pomegranate seed' [see also 7]. This mask is suitable for deities such as Zaō Gongen visiting Mount Arashi, or the deity Wake-Ikazuchi of the Kamo shrine, who was believed to cause the thunder that signalled the arrival of a prosperous year. (KY)

1 'Ah' (a) is the sound of the first letter of the Sanskrit alphabet and is voiced with an open mouth (Jp. *agyō*). This contrasts with 'un', which is the last letter of the alphabet and is pronounced with a closed mouth (Jp. *ungyō*). Together they represent the beginning and end of all phenomena. This 'a-un' form is most frequently visualised in the paired sculptures of guardian figures positioned at the entrances of Buddhist temples and Chinese lion guardians of Shinto shrines [see 67].

13　小天神　江戸時代 18世紀
Kotenjin mask

Edo period, 18th century
pigment and metal on wood
8.8 x 20.5 x 14.4 cm
National Noh Theatre

This mask is used for roles such as deities who serve as attendants to the Buddha. The face of this *kotenjin* ('small deity') mask overflows with the power created by the synergy between the fine modelling, the carefully rendered hair and the vibrant skin tone. Both eyes have lost their original gilt copper rings and these areas are now painted with gold pigment. The fine chisel marks on the reverse of the mask are covered with lacquer. An inscription in red lacquer reads 'Kotenjin mask by Deme Genkyū, eighth month of Kyōhō era 16 [1732]'. This mask was handed down within the Ikeda house of Inshū (present-day Tottori prefecture). (KY)

14　黒髭　江戸時代 18世紀
Kurohige mask

Edo period, 18th century
pigment and metal on wood
9 x 20.6 x 14.9 cm
National Noh Theatre

The *kurohige* ('black beard') mask is employed for the role of the dragon deity and this meticulously finished example is unusually fine for the type. The open eyes look upwards, befitting a deity who keeps watch on the terrestrial world from his home element of water. The mask exudes an aura of dignity, appropriate to the swift-moving deity. Some *kurohige* masks are entirely covered in gold and these masks are used for roles where the dragon king is a high-ranking celestial deity. Masks without this gold colouration are utilised for dragons that emerge from the depths of the ocean. The reverse of the mask is covered with lacquer and there are some visible chisel marks. An inscription in red on the reverse of the forehead gives the mask type as *kurohige* and the name of the carver as Himi. (KY)

15　神躰　江戸時代 17−18世紀
Shintai mask

Edo period, 17th–18th century
pigment and metal on wood
8.4 x 20.3 x 14.5 cm
National Noh Theatre

The *shintai* ('body of the *kami*') mask is used for male god roles where the actor dances in a gallant manner. The soft reddish-yellow skin tone and the insertion of gilt copper pupils to the up-turned eyes contribute to the overall impression of a sublime youth. The high forehead, defined cheekbones and firm jaw convey dignity. The chisel marks on the reverse are barely visible and the surface is covered with black lacquer. The carver incised three lines below the nostrils that resemble the marks of a carpenter's plane, apparently as a sort of covert signature. The inscription in red lacquer on the forehead reads 'carved by Echizen Deme, Jirōzaemon'. The artist's written seal (*kao*) 'Deme Gensuke Yoshimitsu' (Eiman, d1705) is on the reverse of the right cheek. (KY)

16　獅子口　室町時代 15−16世紀
Shishiguchi mask

Muromachi period, 15th–16th century
pigment and metal on wood
10.8 x 22 x 17.4 cm
National Noh Theatre

The *shishi* (Chinese lion) is said to appear on Mount Qingliang (Jp. Wutai) in China, where it frolics among peonies. This *shishiguchi* ('Chinese lion's mouth') mask is notable for its dynamic asymmetric modelling and thinly applied gold pigment. The beautiful finish with its patina of age resembles the effect usually achieved through the use of gold foil and effectively conveys the heroic nature of the Chinese lion king. The energetic chisel marks on the back remain unfinished and are simply covered with lacquer. It is believed that the Hōshō family owned the original *shishiguchi* mask upon which this example appears to have been based. The storage bag for this mask has the characters 'shishiguchi' embroidered in gold on a ground of dark blue brocade patterned with peony arabesques. This is consistent with other masks passed down through the Kaga branch of the Maeda family. (KY)

17　小喝食　室町時代 16世紀
Kasshiki (kokasshiki) mask

Muromachi period, 16th century
pigment on wood
7.3 x 20.2 x 13.9 cm
Agency for Cultural Affairs of Japan

Kasshiki refers to a young attendant who announces mealtimes in a Zen monastery. *Kasshiki* masks are divided into three types: large (*ōkasshiki*), medium (*chūkasshiki*) and small (*kokasshiki*). The main actor (*shite*) in *Jinen the lay monk* (*Jinen Koji*) and *The young entertainer* (*Kagetsu*) dons this type of mask. One of the defining differences between types of *kasshiki* masks is in the depiction of the forelocks. In this mask, the fringe fans out to either side in the shape of a ginkgo leaf, such that it is closer in form to the *chūkasshiki* than the *kokasshiki*, in which the hair more usually hangs straight down with no central division. The carver's high level of technical expertise is clear in the delicate portrayal of the hair and eyebrows, the translucent complexion and severe expression. The colouration has been applied in two layers, and the artist's own creativity is evident in the idiosyncratic illustration of the hair and the unconventional use of *gofun* (shell white). The smoothly finished chisel marks on the back of the mask are barely visible and are covered with lacquer. The eyeholes on the reverse of the mask have been filled with gold pigment, and there is an impressed branded carver's seal reading 'Kawachi, foremost in the realm' (*tenka'ichi Kawachi*). Kawachi (d1645) was the best-known carver of the Ōmi Iseki family. This mask was handed down through the Daishōji branch of the Maeda family. (KY)

18　大喝食　江戸時代 19世紀
Ōkasshiki mask

Edo period, 19th century
pigment on wood
7.6 x 21 x 13.7 cm
Agency for Cultural Affairs of Japan

The divided forelocks and unambiguous facial expression of this mask place it within the large *kasshiki* (*ōkasshiki*) category [see 17]. The dimple in the forehead and the unusual undifferentiated teeth are signature features of this mask type. They also appear in the original mask. The smoothly finished chisel marks on the back are barely visible and are covered with clear lacquer. Five vertical strips of hemp are adhered to the reverse, again in close imitation of the original mask. This mask was handed down through the Daishōji branch of the Maeda family. (KY)

19　猩々　江戸時代 18世紀
Shōjō mask

Edo period, 18th century
pigment on wood
6.8 x 20.7 x 13.6 cm
Agency for Cultural Affairs of Japan

A *shōjō* is a sea sprite who emerges from the ocean during the full moon and dances with the waves on the shoreline while drinking sake. A translucent red conveys the flush of slight intoxication and the benevolent nature of this fairy is immediately legible in the facial expression. The hair is illustrated using differing intensities of black ink and red pigment to impart a sense of perspective to the strands on either side of the face, which appear to be blowing in the wind. The fine lines that depict the eyebrows appear to have been drawn from top to bottom, in opposition to the normal direction of growth. The benevolent smile is also noteworthy. The chisel marks on the reverse are bold and are visible through the layer of red lacquer covering the surface. An impressed branded carver's seal reads 'Deme Dōhaku' (Deme Mitsutaka, 1633–1715) [see also 27]. This mask was handed down through the Daishōji branch of the Maeda family. (KY)

20　敦盛　江戸時代 18–19世紀
Atsumori mask

Edo period, 18th–19th century
7.1 x 20.8 x 13.5 cm
pigment on wood
National Noh Theatre

This mask represents the face of Taira no Atsumori (1169–84), who battled Kumagai Jirō Naozane (1141–1208) during the Genpei war (1180–85); it is intended to show Atsumori as a 16-year-old aristocratic youth. The white make-up, high aristocratic eyebrows, blackened teeth and painted red lips might suggest the countenance of a young woman, but the mask belongs to a type that portrays the innocent, youthful nobleman preparing to enter battle. The eyebrows are positioned very high, such that they remain visible during performance when the mask is secured with a headband at the forehead. The smoothly finished chisel marks on the back are covered with lacquer. (KY)

21　邯鄲男　江戸時代 18世紀
Kantan otoko mask

Edo period, 18th century
pigment on wood
8.3 x 19.8 x 13.7 cm
National Noh Theatre

Knitted brows are a feature of the troubled young philosopher Rosei in the nō play *The pillow of Kantan* (*Kantan*). A sense of determination is transmitted through the compact modelling used to depict the thick lips and focused gaze. Though the soiling of the mask and the later addition of colour are unfortunate, this is not conveyed during performance onstage where the features of the mask exude a commanding presence. The smoothly finished chisel marks on the back are inconspicuous and covered with blackish-brown lacquer. An impressed branded carver's seal reads 'Deme Yūsui' (Deme Yasuhisa, d1766). There is also the 'Genji incense sign' associated with chapter 50, 'The eastern cottage' (*Azumaya*), from the eleventh-century novel *Tale of Genji* (*Genji monogatari*), and an inscription reading 'Man from Kantan', both brushed in gold pigment. This work was handed down through the Morioka Nanbu family. (KY)

22　中将　江戸時代 17世紀
Chūjō mask

Edo period, 17th century
pigment on wood
7 x 20.3 x 13.4 cm
National Noh Theatre

This mask is used for roles portraying high-ranking young noblemen and is said to have the features of either the legendary Fifth Rank military commander (*chūjō*) Ariwara no Narihira (825–80) or the Kawahara minister Minamoto no Tōru (822–95). The skin is white and the eyes express a sense of tranquillity, capturing the dignity of a youthful aristocrat. This type of mask was also employed for defeated (eg Taira) warriors in second-category 'warrior' plays. The smoothly finished chisel marks are visible on the back of the mask and are covered with lacquer; the impressed branded carver's seal reads 'Yūkan, foremost in the realm' (*tenka'ichi Yūkan*). Marks resembling those made by a carpenter's plane are visible below the nostrils and are a covert carver's signature. This piece was handed down through the Yamauchi family. (KY)

23　平太　江戸時代 17–18世紀
Heida mask

Edo period, 17th–18th century
pigment on wood
7.8 x 19.9 x 13.4 cm
National Noh Theatre

There are *heida* ('middle-aged man') masks with unrefined, 'sunburnt' facial features (the gold-copper skin colour the result of the character's participation in battle), but this mask represents a heroic young aristocratic military commander. It is also suitable for roles portraying victorious warriors possessing divine traits in plays such as *Tamura*. The black-lacquered reverse of the mask bears an inscription in the upper right in gold that reads 'Konparu Shichirō' and 'Hatano Ujikatsu(?) [*kao*], Heida'. On the left is an artist's written seal (*kao*) and the inscription 'Ōmi' in red lacquer over a gold signature 'By Tokuwaka'. The identity of this individual is not known, but this written seal is seen on many of the masks in the possession of the Kaga branch of the Maeda family. The storage bag is also typical of works handed down through the Maeda. (KY)

24　小面　江戸時代 17世紀
Ko-omote mask

Edo period, 17th century
pigment on wood
7 x 21.7 x 13.7 cm
National Noh Theatre

This mask portrays the features of a sweet young woman. Although the expression appears somewhat hardened due to the damage to the colouration accumulated over many years, the features still have an air of innocence and freshness. One trait of the *ko-omote*

mask is the three strands of hair that
fall naturally from the top of the
forehead. This is not a mask reserved
for fixed roles, rather it is used for
various young woman roles in different
plays depending on the wishes of
the actor. There are slight traces of the
chisel visible on the reverse of the mask
that have been lacquered over. The
impressed branded carver's seal reads
'Yūkan, foremost in the realm' (*tenka'ichi
Yūkan*). Recorded in gold *maki-e* lacquer
next to this are the characters '*Tōkai
gaishi*', an alternate name for Yamauchi
Yōdō (1827–72), the fifteenth head of
the Tosa domain. (KY)

25 万媚　桃山—江戸時代 16–17世紀
Manbi mask

Momoyama–Edo period, 16th–17th century
pigment on wood
7 x 21 x 13.4 cm
Agency for Cultural Affairs of Japan

This mask depicts the features of a
young woman in the first flush of
youth. Shimotsuma Shōjin (Shimotsuma
Nakataka, 1551–1616) and Deme
Gensuke Hidemitsu of Hongan temple
in Kyoto are said to have created the
manbi mask type together. The name
'*manbi*' carries the connotation of
'a heart that outrivals one hundred
flirtations', a claim that the woman's
great beauty surpasses even that of the
celebrated Chinese beauty Yang Guifei.
A single strand of hair is subtly out
of place, giving rise to the impression
that we are glimpsing the private face
of a young woman confused by secret
thoughts. The smoothly finished, barely
visible chisel marks on the reverse are
covered with lacquer. The forehead
section was planed at some point after
the original carving. It bears the written
authentification seal of the thirteenth
head of the Kanze school, Shigeakira
(d1716), in red lacquer. This work was
handed down through the Daishōji
branch of the Maeda family. (KY)

26 泣増　江戸時代 17世紀
Nakizō mask

Edo period, 17th century
pigment on wood
6.9 x 21.4 x 13.7 cm
Agency for Cultural Affairs of Japan

With its translucent white skin and
youthful beauty, this mask also conveys
a sense of resignation that transcends
love or hate. The work possesses a
strange charm generated by the slight
asymmetry of the features and the

ambivalent gaze. The flawlessly smooth
modelling of the wood grain and the
extremely thin application of layers
of *gofun* (shell white) demonstrate
the carver's great skill. The fine chisel
marks on the reverse are well ordered
and covered with blackish-brown
lacquer. The branded seal with the
carver's name impressed on an area
of unlacquered wood and filled with
red pigment reads 'Yamato, foremost
in the realm' (*tenka'ichi Yamato*), a
reference to Ōmiya Yamato Sanemori
(d1672). This mask was handed down
through the Daishōji branch of the
Maeda family. (KY)

27 曲見　江戸時代 17–18世紀
Shakumi mask

Edo period, 17th–18th century
pigment on wood
7.6 x 21.3 x 14.1 cm
National Noh Theatre

This mask is utilised for female
characters, in which a mother leaves
home to search for her child, from
whom she has been separated and
whose whereabouts are unknown.
The expression of the mask is that of a
distraught mother. The pigment used
to cover the surface of the mask has a
slightly yellowish tinge and was applied
using bold brushstrokes. The eyelids and
cheeks are skilfully carved to reveal a
deep sense of interiority and the trials
of advancing age. The skills necessary to
carve a mask were instilled in generation
after generation of carvers through a
training model based on copying an
'original' mask, and this *shakumi* ('oblique
glance') mask is representative of that
practice. Not only do the modelling
and colouration closely follow those
of the original mask, the maker has
even reproduced damaged areas of the
original work, which was handed down
within the Konparu lineage. These areas
include the dents below the left eyebrow
and above the right eye, the line of nicks
that runs along the right dimple and
the blotches on the left side of the jaw.
The smoothly finished chisel marks on
the reverse of the mask are covered with
black lacquer. An impressed branded
carver's seal reads 'Deme Dōhaku'
[see also 19]. (KY)

28 老女　江戸時代 18世紀
Rōjo mask

Edo period, 18th century
pigment on wood
7.8 x 21.2 x 14.2 cm
National Noh Theatre

The features of the *rōjo* ('old woman')
mask exude graceful elegance: the
neatly coiffed hair, the finely painted
eyebrows, the lips tinged with red
and the white skin are hauntingly
beautiful. The overall colouration is
a warm yellowish white. The traces
of the chisel visible on the reverse
of the mask are extremely ordered
and have been covered with lacquer.
An impressed branded carver's seal
reads 'Deme Dōsui' [see also 5, 6 & 30]
and an inscription in red lacquer
reads 'Old woman [mask] created in
the latter part of the third month of
Kyōhō 10 [1725] following the original
type of the Kita school'. This work
was handed down through the Ikeda
house of Inshū. (KY)

29 泥眼　江戸時代 17世紀
Deigan mask

Edo period, 17th century
pigment on wood
6.9 x 20.9 x 13.5 cm
National Noh Theatre

The *deigan* mask is a female mask
that expresses intense resentment.
The single line around the eyelids,
which conveys the impression of
eyes swollen from weeping, is found
only in the *deigan* mask. Stray strands
begin to escape from the neatly coiffed
hair at the temples, transmitting
the sense of a deeply conflicted heart.
The gold pigment used at the eyes
shines like tears and gave rise to the
mask name '*deigan*', meaning 'gold
eyes'. The mask's expression, which
transmits a sense of profound internal
enmity, makes it appropriate for
plays such as *Lady Aoi* (*Aoi no ue*).
The *Menronki*, a treatise on nō masks
written in the early seventeenth
century by the grand master of the
Hōshō school, Hōshō Shigemoto,
records that the *deigan* is 'a mask
employed in the *kiri nō* ['ending nō',
final play of the program] *The diver
(Ama)*'. The mask was originally used
for roles such as the main actor in
The diver and represented women
entering nirvana or Buddhist deities.
The even white features of this
mask impart great dignity and reveal
maternal grief rather than resentment.
The uniform chisel marks on the back
of the mask have been covered with
lacquer. An impressed branded carver's
seal reads 'Kawachi, foremost in the
realm' (*tenka'ichi Kawachi*) alongside
the written seal of 'Nōsei' (Kita
Roppeita XII, d1829). (KY)

30 橋姫　江戸時代 18世紀
Hashihime mask

Edo period, 18th century
pigment on wood
8.5 x 20.5 x 14.8 cm
Agency for Cultural Affairs of Japan

This mask is for the role of a woman who asks the god of the Kibune shrine to transform her into an evil spirit so that she can take revenge on her adulterous husband. Today it is primarily employed in the nō play *The iron crown* (*Kanawa*). It was also formerly used in performances of *Lady of the bridge* (*Hashihime*), leaving open the possibility that the mask was created for that play. This mask replicates the form of the original Hōshō school mask said to have been carved by the fifteenth-century master Yasha. The hair of the Hōshō mask was reportedly painted by the artist Sesshū (1420–1506). The present mask conveys the fierce determination of the character. The large, open eyes inlaid with gilt copper rings and the two-tone teeth – black at the roots graduating to gold at the tips – are indicative of her transformation from mortal woman to supernatural demon. The mask is occasionally deployed for the *ryūnyo* ('dragon woman') role. Brownish lacquer covers the energetic chisel marks on the back of the mask; an impressed branded carver's seal reads 'Deme Mitsunori' [see also 5, 6 & 28]. This mask was handed down through the Daishōji branch of the Maeda family. (KY)

31 山姥　江戸時代 18世紀
Yamanba mask

Edo period, 18th century
pigment and metal on wood
8 x 21.5 x 13.7 cm
National Noh Theatre

This mask is used for *yamanba* ('mountain hag') and mountain fairy roles. The eyes are inlaid with gilt metal rings and the teeth are painted gold to indicate the character's supernatural status. Although the face is entirely smooth and unwrinkled, the hair is greying, suggesting an aged and yet simultaneously ageless being. The eyebrows of the *yamanba* mask may be depicted as naturally growing eyebrows, or as in this case, as the 'aristocratic' eyebrows (*denjō mayu*) that court ladies painted on above their natural eyebrows, which have been shaved. Circular, smoothly finished visible chisel marks on the reverse are covered with blackish-brown lacquer. The artist's written seal in red lacquer in the centre of the forehead reads 'Mitsunaga'. This work was handed down through the Kawachi family. The original mask, upon which this example was based, was carved by Zekan and passed down through the Yamauchi family. (KY)

32 般若　江戸時代 18世紀
Hannya mask

Edo period, 18th century
pigment and metal on wood
9 x 21.3 x 16.7 cm
National Noh Theatre

This mask conveys a sense of obsessive jealousy and anger. The somewhat rounded modelling and only faintly flushed skin tone make this a relatively restrained example of the *hannya* type. Nevertheless, the bulging forehead veins and inlaid metal teeth communicate the character's internal ferocity. The red-lacquered back of the mask bears an inscription recording the mask type and the carver's name of Deme Hanzō (Hokan Mitsunao, d1750). Also attached is an inventory label indicating that this mask belonged to the Ikeda family. (KY)

33 赤般若　江戸時代 18–19世紀
Aka (red) hannya mask

Edo period, 18th–19th century
pigment and metal on wood
9.5 x 21.2 x 16.7 cm
National Noh Theatre

Hannya masks include white, blackish and red types, which are used differently depending on the performance. A comparison with the *hannya* reserved for plays such as *Dōjōji* or *The diver* (*Ama*) reveals that this red *hannya* (*aka hannya*) mask is five millimetres thicker, even though the length and width of the mask is basically the same. The minimal difference in thickness, as well as the colouration, allows the work to convey a surprisingly expanded range of expression. There are only slight traces of the chisel visible on the reverse of the mask. The eye slots have been carved to imitate chrysanthemum flowers with individual 'petals' fanning out in a circle from the central eyehole. The surface has been covered with clear lacquer. There are two marks in red lacquer above the nostrils; an inscription and written seal on the forehead section reads 'After a mask transmitted through Kita Shichidayū, Kōno' (Kita Shichidayū IX, d1829]. (KY)

34 白般若　江戸時代 18–19世紀
Shiro (white) hannya mask

Edo period, 18th–19th century
pigment on wood
9.5 x 21 x 17 cm
National Noh Theatre

Although the *hannya* mask is one of the most striking of all nō masks, the roles for which it is used are quite limited. The white hannya (*shiro hannya*) mask is employed for court lady roles such as Lady Rokujō in *Lady Aoi* (*Aoi no ue*), however, it is unclear when exactly the mask began to be utilised in this particular play. The chisel marks on the reverse have been smoothly finished and the reverse is unlacquered. (KY)

NŌ COSTUMES

35 紺地石畳法螺貝模様袿狩衣
江戸時代 19世紀
Lined *kariginu* with design of cobblestones and conch shells on dark blue ground

Edo period, 19th century
silk, satin weave with gold-leaf paper supplementary weft patterning
152 x 200 cm
Agency for Cultural Affairs of Japan

A pattern of conch shells and cobblestones woven with gold threads are set against the dark blue ground of this lined *kariginu*. The stone patterns do not cover the entire surface of the robe, but have been intentionally split and arranged around large conch shells, whose random placement appears to have been done to accommodate the draping of the garment. Since ancient times, the conch shell has been adopted as an instrument for Buddhist memorial ceremonies and for military use. *Yamabushi* (itinerant Buddhist monks) employed them during their pilgrimages into the mountains to ward off wild animals. This example possesses a regal dignity. (KA)

36 浅葱地竹鶴模様袿狩衣
江戸時代 19世紀
Lined *kariginu* with design of bamboo and cranes on light blue ground

Edo period, 19th century
silk, satin weave with gold-leaf paper supplementary weft patterning
163 x 192 cm
Agency for Cultural Affairs of Japan

Lined *kariginu* are employed for characters such as ministers, noblemen, deities and *tengu*, and many are made of heavy brocade and gold brocade fabrics. This brocade *kariginu* uses gold threads to depict images of dancing cranes, downwards-facing cranes in flight and bamboo, all placed on a light blue satin ground. The resilient, flexible bamboo plant grows swiftly and upright. It is a metaphor for the virtuous, principled man, while the crane is an auspicious bird associated with longevity. The propitious pattern of bamboo and cranes rendered in soft tones, as seen here, is suitable for the robes of deities and aristocrats. (KA)

37 白地丁子立涌桐唐松模様単狩衣
江戸時代 18–19世紀
Unlined *kariginu* with design of undulating vertical lines with clove-shaped crests, paulownia and Chinese pine on white ground

Edo period, 18th–19th century
silk, gauze weave with gold-leaf paper supplementary weft patterning
163.5 x 120 cm
National Noh Theatre

Kariginu were originally worn by the court nobility during outdoor excursions like hunting, and therefore when employed as nō robes for characters of high status, they are frequently decorated with court motifs (*yūsoku monyō*). This *kariginu* is decorated with pine, clove-shaped crest and paulownia patterns woven with gold threads and set against a white ground. The creation of these refined designs without the use of coloured threads makes a robe such as this suitable for an aristocratic character. (KA)

38 萌黄地霞梅花模様単狩衣
江戸時代 19世紀
Unlined *kariginu* with design of plum blossoms in mist on yellow-green ground

Edo period, 19th century
silk, gauze weave with gold-and-silver leaf paper supplementary weft patterning
161.6 x 212 cm
Agency for Cultural Affairs of Japan

Unlined *kariginu* are often made of finely woven silk gauze and gossamer. They are utilised for elegant characters such as aristocrats and spirits. The stylised silver and gold plum blossoms floating amidst mist create a commanding contrast to the rich dark yellow-green silk gauze ground of this unlined *kariginu*.

The austere tonality and the simple individual motifs are refreshing, making this robe suitable for an aristocratic character. The design of floating plum blossoms conjures up the image of fallen, scattered petals, thereby its name, '*kobore ume*', or 'fluttering plums'. (KA)

39 縹地朝鮮錦単法被　江戸時代 18世紀
Unlined *happi* with design of floral arabesques on blue ground

Edo period, 18th century
silk, gauze weave with coloured silk and gold-leaf paper supplementary weft patterning
100.8 x 196 cm
National Noh Theatre

Happi jackets are either lined or unlined, the latter type usually employed for the roles of nobles or unassuming warriors. The floral arabesque designs on this brocaded example are woven with gold and coloured threads and are beautifully positioned on the indigo silk gauze ground. This type of woven brocade with patterns in silver, gold and coloured threads on fine silk gauze or gossamer was frequently an imported item. It is used for various nō robes such as unlined *happi* or 'dancing cloaks' (*maiginu*) [49–52]. (KA)

40 萌黄地卍唐花模様袷法被
江戸時代 19世紀
Lined *happi* with design of Buddhist swastika and arabesques on yellow-green ground

Edo period, 19th century
silk, satin weave with gold-leaf paper supplementary weft patterning
105 x 183 cm
National Noh Theatre

Lined *happi* are suitable for the roles of military commanders. *Happi* worn with *hangiri* [83 & 84] are reserved for roles of demons, powerful deities and fierce warriors, while high-ranking officials and warriors wear them in combination with wide pleated trousers (*ōkuchi*). This *happi* of pale yellow-green satin is woven with gold threads using the 'gold brocade' (*kinran*) technique. Regularly placed Buddhist swastika (*manji*) patterns frame scattered arabesque designs. (KA)

41 紺地雲龍模様側次
江戸時代 18–19世紀
Sobatsugi with design of dragons in clouds on dark blue ground

Edo period, 18th–19th century
silk, satin weave with coloured silk and gold-leaf paper supplementary weft patterning
94.8 x 61 cm
Agency for Cultural Affairs of Japan

A *sobatsugi* is a lined *happi*-style jacket without sleeves and they often have strong, crisp motifs such as peonies, dragons in clouds and phoenixes. When employed as costumes for foreign characters they are decorated with Chinese-style designs such as the *shokkō nishiki* pattern or dragons. This *sobatsugi* depicts two dragons ascending to heaven amidst flames, their bold forms rendered in gold and coloured threads. The contrastive placement of the red and white flames on either side of the garment creates a striking impression. (KA)

42 紺地龍嶮山模様側次
江戸時代 18–19世紀
Sobatsugi with design of steep mountains and dragon on dark blue ground

Edo period, 18th–19th century
silk, satin weave with coloured silk and gold-leaf paper supplementary weft patterning
100 x 63 cm
Agency for Cultural Affairs of Japan

In this masterful work, the magnified form of a dragon occupies much of the upper section, its body twisted to show its imposing head in frontal view. The creature towers above bladelike rocks emerging from the stylised waves at the hem. Originally employed on imperial dragon robes of the Chinese Ming- and Qing-dynasties (1368–1911), this design type was perhaps introduced to Japan during the Edo period (1615–1868), where it was adapted for different uses. The side sections are later additions. (KA)

43 薄萌黄地扁額雪持芭蕉雪持笹模様長絹
江戸時代 18–19世紀
Chōken with design of Japanese banana leaves on a trellis and snow-laden bamboo leaves on light green ground

Edo period, 18th–19th century
silk, gauze weave with gold-leaf paper supplementary weft patterning
101.9 x 205.2 cm
Agency for Cultural Affairs of Japan

Chōken (broad-sleeve outer garment) are either unpatterned silk gauze or gossamer with woven patterns in gold and coloured threads. The open, unstitched sides are a special feature of *chōken*, which are used for both male and female roles. On occasion, the *chōken* is also employed in lieu of an unlined *kariginu*. There are examples in which the principal motif appears on the centre back, on both sleeves and chest section of the front, while smaller designs are scattered evenly at the hem. Others have the same pattern scattered across the entire surface as the principal motif.

A design of snow-laden Japanese banana leaves on a trellis appears on the shoulder and chest of this light green *chōken*. The lower register illustrates snow-laden bamboo grass. These snow-covered motifs are patterned on plants in nature heavily weighed down by snow – they express the sentiment of winter and have auspicious connotations. The design of Japanese banana (*bashō*) plant has autumnal references. According to legend, the Chinese poet and painter Wang Wei (699?–761) painted banana leaves amidst snow, something unlikely to occur in nature and thus imbuing this motif with a fanciful association. This *chōken* is perhaps suitable for the main actor in Act II of the nō play *Bashō* who, as the spirit of the banana plant, performs a dance to lament life's impermanence. (KA)

44 紫地色紙短冊花束芦模様長絹
江戸時代 18–19世紀
Chōken with design of decorative poem cards, flower bouquets and reeds on purple ground

Edo period, 18th–19th century
silk, gauze weave with coloured silk and gold-leaf paper supplementary weft patterning
110.6 x 210.6 cm
Agency for Cultural Affairs of Japan

Patterns of chrysanthemums, bush clover and pampas grass around oblong poem slips (*tanzaku*) and square poem cards (*shikishi*) in the upper section of this purple *chōken* complement the motif of reeds fluttering in the wind in the lower section. The colour variation in weft threads used in the depiction of the autumnal grasses and poem slips creates a sumptuous feel, while the movement of the reed stems and leaves is delicately rendered with only gold threads. The design and pattern configuration of this example is typical of *chōken*. (KA)

45 萌黄地扇地紙牡丹模様長絹
江戸時代 18–19世紀
Chōken with design of fans and peonies on yellow-green ground

Edo period, 18th–19th century
silk, gauze weave with coloured silk and gold-leaf paper supplementary weft patterning
114.5 x 196 cm
National Noh Theatre

Illustrated on the back and chest sections of this yellow-green garment are fans (*ōgi*), fan papers (*jigami*) and peony branches. The lower half of the garment also shows scattered peony boughs, the variegated colours of the weft threads used to depict them creating a textured nuance. In its entirety the garment projects a sense of subdued refinement. (KA)

46 紺地牡丹花舟垣鉄線模様長絹
江戸時代 19世紀
Chōken with design of peony flowers in vases and Chinese clematis on a fence on blue ground

Edo period, 19th century
silk, gauze weave with coloured silk and silver-leaf paper supplementary weft patterning
103.7 x 208.4 cm
Agency for Cultural Affairs of Japan

Peonies in boat-shaped vases are arranged along the top of this *chōken*, while the lower register shows Chinese clematis (*tessen*) entwined around a trellis. Both the *tessen* and peony originated in China, where they were admired and enjoyed. Boat vases, made in metal, ceramic or bamboo, would be hung in decorative alcoves (*tokonoma*), and in this example each contains two resplendent peony blossoms and buds. The *tessen* was a garden cultivar known for its ability to wrap around supports because of its widely spaced stems and flowers. For that reason, and as seen in this example, *tessen* frequently appear as arabesque patterns intertwined around structures such as trellises and fences, establishing a play between the beauty of nature and the beauty of man-made objects. (KA)

47 樺色地枝垂桜鉄線模様長絹
江戸時代 18–19世紀
Chōken with design of weeping cherries and Chinese clematis on birch-coloured ground

Edo period, 18th–19th century
silk, gauze weave with gold-leaf paper supplementary weft patterning
108 x 162 cm
National Noh Theatre

The rich, sombre appearance of this *chōken* lacks showiness in the illustration of the weeping cherries and Chinese clematis, which are produced with gold threads on a brownish ground. Examples such as this are suitable for dance scenes conveying a sense of profound elegance. (KA)

48 浅葱地枝垂柳流水模様長絹
江戸時代—明治時代 19世紀
Chōken with design of weeping willows and flowing water on light blue ground

Edo–Meiji period, 19th century
silk, gauze weave with gold-leaf paper supplementary weft patterning
116 x 215.4 cm
National Noh Theatre

This *chōken* uses gold threads to produce a delicate pattern covering the entire garment. The depiction of the willow on the riverside is refreshing and transmits a beautiful sense of tranquillity. (KA)

49 紫地変青海波若松梅模様舞衣
江戸時代 18–19世紀
Maiginu with design of plums and young pines on ocean waves on purple ground

Edo period, 18th–19th century
silk, gauze weave with coloured silk and gold-leaf paper supplementary weft patterning
149 x 214 cm
Agency for Cultural Affairs of Japan

Maiginu ('dancing cloak') closely resemble the form of *chōken*, but they are slightly longer and have a gusset at the front. Moreover, a tassel is not used to fasten the front panels and the sleeve openings. The designs on *maiginu* are woven in gold and coloured threads on fine fabrics such as silk gauze and unpatterned gossamer. This example is decorated with bouquets of young pine and plum branches scattered over stylised silhouettes of chrysanthemums arranged in repeated rows that simulate the concentric half-arc wave pattern known as *seigaiha* ('blue ocean waves'). While the underlying wave-like pattern is executed with gold threads, the delicate plum blossoms are defined by variously coloured threads to convey an elegant charm. (KA)

50 紅地牡丹銀杏唐草模様舞衣
江戸時代 19世紀
Maiginu with design of peonies and ginkgo arabesques on crimson ground

Edo period, 19th century
silk, plain weave with coloured silk and gold-leaf paper supplementary weft patterning
162 x 212.6 cm
National Noh Theatre

This *maiginu* has a pattern of ginkgo arabesques running from the bottom

third of the sleeves to the hem.
Depicted on the shoulder and chest
are images of peonies and nandina
(heavenly bamboo), graceful motifs that
are suitable for robes worn in dance
scenes by female characters. (KA)

51 濃萌黄地紅葉賀模様舞衣
江戸時代 18–19世紀
Maiginu with design of the
'Autumn excursion' chapter
from the *Tale of Genji* on
dark yellow-green ground

Edo period, 18th–19th century
silk, gauze weave with coloured silk and gold-
leaf paper supplementary weft patterning
141 x 108 cm
Agency for Cultural Affairs of Japan

The sides of this *maiginu* are not
stitched together, instead the front and
back panels are joined by fabric side
straps called *ran*. *Maiginu* are usually
worn belted in the 'waist-wrap' draping
style (*koshimaki*) or tucked up at the
waist (*tsuboori*), and for this reason
examples with *ran* are rare. However,
the mid eighteenth-century *Rinchū's
collection of secrets* (*Rinchū hishō*) notes
the existence of large *maiginu* with *ran*
similar to *happi*.

The pattern on this *maiginu* consists of
headdresses, autumn leaves and 'flame
drums' (*kaen taiko*, drums with flame
patterns) [see also 66 & 83] arranged in
alternating groups against a dark green
ground. The headdresses, known as
torikabuto ('bird helmet'), were worn
by *gagaku* performers. The reference is
thereby understood as being chapter
7, 'Autumn excursion' (*Momiji no ga*),
from the eleventh-century novel
Tale of Genji (*Genji monogatari*). (KA)

52 紅地桐鳳凰模様舞衣
江戸時代 18–19世紀
Maiginu with design of phoenixes
and paulownia on crimson ground

Edo period, 18th–19th century
silk, plain weave with gold-leaf paper
supplementary weft patterning
119 x 188 cm
Agency for Cultural Affairs of Japan

The principal motif on this *maiginu* is
the phoenix, which is represented on
the shoulder, both sleeves and chest
of the garment in a style similar to
chōken [43–48]. Paulownia arabesques
appear below. Like [51], this robe is a
rare variant of the *maiginu* type with
side straps connecting the front and
back panels. The phoenix design on this
work is a tour de force. (KA)

53 紅白段花筏模様唐織
江戸時代 18世紀
Karaori with design of
flower rafts on alternating
blocks of crimson and
white ground

Edo period, 18th century
silk, twill weave with coloured silk
supplementary weft patterning
148.5 x 148 cm
National Noh Theatre

This *karaori*, usually worn as an
outer robe for women's roles,
has a twill ground of alternating
white and red blocks. The pattern
of 'flower rafts' entwined with
boughs of cherry blossoms is woven
with gold and variously coloured
threads. The image of the flower
rafts evokes the appearance of
fallen petals floating on a river
but also communicates the fleeting
beauty of the flowers, as well as
the transition of the seasons.
The clearly delineated shift between
the red and white blocks and the
weft of the garment, which employs
numerous coloured threads, coalesce
in this gorgeous garment. This work
was handed down through the
Ikeda family. (KA)

54 金紅段枝垂桜尾長鳥模様唐織
江戸時代 18世紀
Karaori with design of
weeping cherries and long-tailed
birds on alternating gold and
crimson ground

Edo period, 18th century
silk, twill weave with coloured silk
supplementary weft patterning
148.4 x 137 cm
National Noh Theatre

This *karaori* has an alternating gold
and crimson ground and while the
height of the blocks is smaller than
is customary on these robes, the
areas of gold are still impressive.
The ground is covered with images
of long-tailed fowl (*onagadori*) frolicking
amidst branches of weeping cherry
trees. A design element known
from ancient times, the *onagadori* is
a fantastical animal that resembles
the phoenix. Of the numerous design
categories of cherry blossoms, that
of the weeping cherry best represents
the resplendence of the plant in
full bloom. The *onagadori* delight
in the felicitous, enticing spring
season, and as a whole this *karaori*
is a beguiling work. (KA)

55 紅地雪持椿模様唐織
江戸時代 18–19世紀
Karaori with design of
snow-laden camellias on
crimson ground

Edo period, 18th–19th century
silk, twill weave with coloured silk and gold-
leaf paper supplementary weft patterning
156 x 150 cm
National Noh Theatre

This gorgeous *karaori* is decorated with
snow-covered standing camellia trees
placed against a background of golden
clouds. Each nō school has fixed rules
regarding costume ensemble. For
example, in the *Ken'eirō gasō*, a pictorial
record of cultural history compiled by
the Tayasu branch of the Tokugawa
family, this *karaori* with patterns of
snow-laden camellias was described
as a costume of the head master of
the Hōshō school designated for use in
the nō play *Dōjōji*. In the Meiji period
(1868–1912), the celebrated nō actor
Umewaka Minoru (1828–1909) received
this particular *karaori*, which was
handed down within the family of the
head master of the Hōshō school, from
Hōshō Kurō (1837–1917). (KA)

56 白地七宝繋唐松檜扇模様唐織
江戸時代 18–19世紀
Karaori with design of interlocking
seven jewels with fans and
Chinese pine on white ground

Edo period, 18th–19th century
silk, twill weave with coloured silk and gold-
leaf paper supplementary weft patterning
140 x 130 cm
National Noh Theatre

The geometric 'seven jewels' (*shippō*)
design is rendered with gold thread on
a patterned white ground. It is further
embellished by images of multi-
coloured folding fans and Japanese
larch. The folding fan, made with
strips or 'blades' of cypress wood,
was used by the nobility during
the Heian period (794–1185). It was
considered an auspicious object when
fully opened or closed, and held
together by a decorative binding cord.
The protective paper wrapper for this
karaori records that the designs were
in fact chrysanthemums, not pine.
However, the three dots constituting
the centre of the 'flowers' in this work
indicate that they are indeed Chinese
pine (the centre of chrysanthemums
are distinguished by only one dot).
This robe was handed down through
the Ikeda family. (KA)

57 白萌黄段松藤籠目牡丹模様唐織
江戸時代 19世紀
Karaori with design of pine,
wisteria flowers, peonies and
bamboo baskets on alternating
blocks of white and green ground

Edo period, 19th century
silk, twill weave with coloured silk and gold-
leaf paper supplementary weft patterning
140 x 133 cm
Agency for Cultural Affairs of Japan

The alternating placement of white and
green blocks distinguishes this *karaori*.
The white blocks are decorated with
peony boughs, with superimposed woven
bamboo patterns in gold thread, whereas
the designs on the green blocks show
pines and wisteria along a stylised water
pattern. The peony is the 'king of one
hundred flowers' and symbolises wealth
and high rank. The motif of the peony
overlaid with woven bamboo patterns
originated in China and was inspired by
the bamboo basket vases used to display
cut peony flowers. The pine and wisteria
by flowing water is noted in chapter
57 of the eleventh-century miscellany,
The pillow book (*Makura no sōshi*), by the
court lady Sei Shōnagon: 'Long flowering
branches of beautifully coloured wisteria
entwined about a pine tree'.[1] The
combination of the pine and wisteria
was a Japanese-style decorative pattern
seen on numerous craft objects, as well
as on nō robes. (KA)

1 Translation from *The pillow book of Sei
Shonagon*, Ivan Morris (trans/ed), Penguin
Classics, London, 1971, p 109.

58 濃茶浅葱段秋草麻葉模様唐織
江戸時代 19世紀
Karaori with design of flax leaves,
autumn plants and maple leaves
on alternating blocks of dark
brown and pale blue-green ground

Edo period, 19th century
silk, twill weave with coloured silk and gold-
leaf paper supplementary weft patterning
142 x 138 cm
Agency for Cultural Affairs of Japan

This *karaori* has alternating blocks
in dark brown and pale blue-green,
filled with motifs of autumn
flowers, such as bush clover, Chinese
bellflower, bamboo grass and maple,
in combination with hemp leaves.
The autumnal leaves, which in places
spill over the edges of the blocks, are
later embroidered additions. A robe
with a dark, subdued palette that
does not employ red on the garment is
thought to have been used for female
characters older than middle age. (KA)

59 茶地雲鶴菱模様唐織
江戸時代 19世紀
Karaori with design of clouds and
crane diamonds on brown ground

Edo period, 19th century
silk, twill weave with coloured silk
supplementary weft patterning
152 x 142.6 cm
Agency for Cultural Affairs of Japan

Designs of stylised cranes in diamond
shapes rendered in white, light green
and purple weft threads are set against
a brown ground woven with cloud
patterns. The cranes depicted here are
of two types, one with an opened beak,
that of the other closed, and they are
arranged facing each other to form
a diamond shape. This pattern was
a court motif (*yūsoku monyō*) utilised
during the Heian period.

Depending on the play, each of the
nō schools has their own set of rules
regarding costume ensemble. For
example, *karaori* with diamond-shaped
cranes conceived without the use of
red are worn by actors of the Kongō
and Kita schools for the play *Dōjōji*. By
contrast, Konparu school actors employ
the same motif on robes with red. (KA)

60 紅濃茶萌黄段八橋模様唐織
江戸時代 文化8年2月
Karaori with design of eight-
plank bridge on alternating
blocks of crimson, dark brown
and green ground

2nd month, Bunka 8 (1811)
silk, twill weave with coloured silk and gold-
leaf paper supplementary weft patterning
148 x 151.2 cm
National Noh Theatre

This *karaori* has an alternating pattern of
crimson, dark brown and green blocks
with traditional motifs of the eight-
plank bridge (*yatsuhashi*) and irises
(*kakitsubata*) executed in coloured threads.
The eight-plank bridge and iris appear
in an episode in chapter 9, 'Journey to
the East' (*Azuma-kudari*), from the tenth-
century *Tales of Ise* (*Ise monogatari*). In this
episode, Ariwara no Narihira, en route
from the capital Kyoto to the east, stops
in Mikawa at an iris marsh traversed by
an eight-plank bridge. Moved by the sight
of the blossoming irises, he composes a
poem to express his sadness at leaving
the capital (and the lover he left behind).
Each line of the poem starts with the
five syllables of the word *kakitsubata*
(*ka/ki/tsu/ba/ta*), and in this work the
motifs reference the nō play *The iris*
(*Kakitsubata*) [see also 125]. (KA)

61 紅地舟雪輪福寿草藤袴深見草文筆
模様唐織　　江戸時代 弘化3年5月
Karaori with design of sails,
snowflake rings, adonis,
thoroughwts, peonies, letters and
writing brushes on crimson ground

5th month, Kōka 3 (1846)
silk, twill weave with coloured silk and gold-
leaf paper supplementary weft patterning
146.7 x 138 cm
National Noh Theatre

This *karaori* has raised designs of
thoroughwort, adonis, peonies,
brushes and letters, and a background
with alternating groups of sails and
snowflake rings executed in gold
thread on a crimson ground.
The protective paper wrapper for this
karaori records that it was a garment
made to commemorate an 'auspicious
age' (*uke*). The concept of *uke* is
included within the Japanese system
of esoteric cosmology known as
onmyōdō ('the way of ying and yang')
and refers to a propitious period that
continues for seven years. Included
as part of this auspicious celebration
was the practice of using objects
with names having the character *fu*
(and thus understood as *fuku*, or
'good luck') in the decoration of the
home and as design motifs on gifts.
In this work, sails (*fune*), snowflake
rings (*fuchiyuki*), adonis (*fukujūsō*),
thoroughwort (*fujibakama*), peony (as
alternate name, *fukamikusa*), brushes
(*fude*) and letters (*fumi*) represent the
seven '*fu*'. (KA)

62 薄紅地鱗龍丸雲模様厚板唐織
江戸時代 文化5年
Atsuita karaori with design of
triangles, dragon roundels and
clouds on light red ground

Bunka 5 (1808)
silk, twill weave with coloured silk and gold-
leaf paper supplementary weft patterning
146.7 x 138 cm
National Noh Theatre

The *atsuita* nō robe is generally worn
by male characters. This example has
alternating roundels with cloud and
dragon forms set against a ground
of interlocking square and triangular
vase shapes that create a fish-scale
pattern. The *atsuita karaori* is a composite
garment type: the weaving technique
is typical of *karaori* [53–61], while the
designs are akin to those generally
encountered on *atsuita*. This explains
why it can be utilised as a coat (*uwagi*)
or worn as an undergarment (*kitsuke*).
The term '*atsuita karaori*' therefore

refers to a *karaori* that functions as an *atsuita*. Since this *atsuita karaori* has a fish-scale pattern it was probably used as an undergarment for demon or evil spirit characters. (KA)

63 水浅葱地入子菱丸紋散模様厚板
桃山時代 16–17世紀
Atsuita with design of nested diamonds and scattered floral roundels on pale blue ground

Momoyama period, 16th–17th century
silk, twill weave with coloured silk supplementary weft patterning
134.5 x 125 cm
National Noh Theatre

Patterns of nested diamonds and roundels of mandarin blossoms, two facing cranes and double-petalled, comma-shaped wisteria worked in diversely coloured threads are set against a pale blue ground. The fabric demonstrates the weaving technique characteristic of *karaori*, even though as a nō robe it is thought that it was worn as an *atsuita*. There was a fashion during the Edo period to extend the sleeve width of *kosode* (short-sleeved kimono). Nō robes of this period also reflected this trend, as seen in the wider sleeves of this example. The unnatural widening of the garment from the waist downwards, which results from a loosening of the side seams, indicates that this robe was originally a *kosode* from the Momoyama period (1573–1615) that was later altered for use as a nō costume. (KA)

64 萌黄地雲龍丸模様厚板
江戸時代 17–18世紀
Atsuita with design of dragon roundels and clouds on yellow-green ground

Edo period, 17th–18th century
silk, twill weave with coloured silk supplementary weft patterning
145.5 x 132 cm
Agency for Cultural Affairs of Japan

The yellow-green ground offsets the woven designs of dragons clutching sacred jewels amidst clouds. *Atsuita* frequently have crimson, navy blue and light green grounds with large scattered patterns that convey a powerful, dignified impression. By contrast, this *atsuita* is of a subdued elegance with rather sparsely distributed dragon roundels within wide cloud bands placed on a pale green ground. The shapes and features of the dragons have not been overly stylised, which lends a somewhat realistic feel. (KA)

65 茶地青海波源氏車模様厚板
江戸時代 18世紀
Atsuita with design of ocean waves and Genji wheels on brown ground

Edo period, 18th century
silk, twill weave with coloured silk and gold-leaf paper supplementary weft patterning
146 x 137 cm
National Noh Theatre

This work shows an overlapping pattern of concentric half-arcs (*seigaiha*) against a brown ground, with variously coloured 'Genji wheels' in black, navy blue, yellow-green, pale blue-green and purple. The 'Genji wheel' motif is derived from the wheels of ox-drawn carriages used as transport for the aristocracy during the Heian period. The association of designs related to flowing water (eg the *seigaiha*) with that of the carriage wheel evolved from the practice of soaking carriage wheels as a means to protect them from drying out and splitting. The 'Genji wheel' motif is already encountered on lacquerware from the Heian period. (KA)

66 濃萌黄地綾杉牡丹巴丸模様厚板
江戸時代 18世紀
Atsuita with design of 'flame drums' and peonies over cedar pattern on dark green ground

Edo period, 18th century
silk, twill weave with silk supplementary weft patterning
152 x 144 cm
Agency for Cultural Affairs of Japan

The dark green ground of this *atsuita* is almost completely concealed by raised weft patterning of zigzags in crimson, white, navy blue and green. Scattered across the surface are 'flame drums' (*kaen taiko*) [see also 51 & 83] with three comma-shaped crests and peonies. The 'flame drum' is a large drum used in *bugaku* (court dance and music) and as the name suggests, it is decorated with flame patterns. The blazing flames convey a sense of vibrant force and the heroic. Robes for male roles, such as *hangiri*, *happi* and *atsuita*, employed this design. (KA)

67 茶納戸段毘沙門亀甲繋獅子丸模様厚板
江戸時代 18世紀
Atsuita with design of Chinese lion roundels over interlocking tortoiseshell pattern on alternating blocks of brown and greyish blue ground

Edo period, 18th century
silk twill weave with coloured silk and gold-leaf paper supplementary weft patterning
137 x 137 cm
National Noh Theatre

The alternating blocks of brown and greyish blue ground of this *atsuita* are decorated with *bishamon-kikkō* ('Bishamon tortoiseshell'), a motif illustrating the armour of the Buddhist guardian deity Bishamonten [see 87]. The *bishamon-kikkō* is so called because of its resemblance to a pattern that combines three sections of hexagonal tortoiseshell shapes. Gold and coloured threads are used for the roundels depicting Chinese lions, whose forms are surrounded by flame patterns. Two types of Chinese lions are illustrated here, each conveying lively movement: the first has an opened mouth (*agyō*), while that of the second is closed (*ungyō*) [see 12]. Chinese lions are the 'kings of animals' and are seen as sacred, symbolically powerful creatures. The subdued palette of this work conceals the dynamism underlying this work. (KA)

68 紺紅段花入亀甲繋桐打板模様厚板
江戸時代 18世紀
Atsuita with design of paulownia crests and cloud-shaped gongs over interlocking hexagonal lozenges with flower motif on alternating blocks of dark blue and crimson ground

Edo period, 18th century
silk, twill weave with coloured silk supplementary weft patterning
142.5 x 146 cm
National Noh Theatre

This *atsuita* has a ground of alternating blocks in dark blue and crimson. The entire garment is covered with raised hexagonal shapes that resemble a tortoiseshell pattern. These are overlaid with bold, striking paulownia leaf and temple gong motifs. Many collections of nō robes house similar *atsuita*, which depict large showy designs of paulownia, peonies, chrysanthemums, clouds, gongs, as well as Buddhist swastikas and wheels, set against a ground of alternating blocks in red, dark blue, white and yellow-green. This robe is reported to have been handed down through the Hongan temple in Kyoto, the location of the oldest documented nō stage. (KA)

69 紅白段腰替桐巴格子模様厚板
江戸時代 18–19世紀
Atsuita with design of paulownia
crests and comma-shaped motifs,
checks and cobblestones on
alternating blocks of crimson
and white ground

Edo period, 18th–19th century
silk, twill weave with coloured silk
supplementary weft patterning
129 x 136.8 cm
National Noh Theatre

In *atsuita* like this example the same
pattern appears on the shoulders
and hem, while the body of the
garment has either a different pattern
or is blank. This type of decoration
is known as *katasuso* ('shoulders and
hem'). Here, the shoulders and hem
are decorated by linearly arranged
paulownia and comma shapes (*tomoe*)
set against a ground comprising
alternating blocks of crimson and white
with blue, green and brown checks.
The waist section of the garment
has a cobblestone design in white and
pale yellow. When worn with *happi*
and *hangiri* this waist section is
generally concealed, and only the
crimson ground and the lattice
patterns are visible. This costume
is suitable for the main characters
of military commanders in second-
category 'warrior' plays. (KA)

70 白萌黄段格子蔦模様厚板
江戸時代 19世紀
Atsuita with design of ivy and
lattices on alternating blocks
of white and green ground

Edo period, 19th century
silk, twill weave with coloured silk
supplementary weft patterning
149 x 146 cm
National Noh Theatre

A ground with alternating blocks
in white and yellowish green
characterise this *atsuita*. The areas
of white ground are decorated with
a woven crimson and light yellowish-
green lattice motif; the blocks of
yellow-green illustrate ivy. Ivy was
long used as an arabesque design,
but it was also employed as a design
element that embodied the charm
and beauty associated with autumnal
colours. The subdued palette and
the absence of the usual scattered
raised pattern means that this *atsuita*
would be appropriate for the main
actor in Act II of a fifth-category
'ending nō' play. (KA)

71 白地草木禽獣御所車扇模様縫箔
桃山時代 16世紀
Nuihaku with design of plants
and animals on white ground

Momoyama period, 16th century
silk, plain weave with stencilled gold foil
and silk embroidery
150 x 114 cm
Agency for Cultural Affairs of Japan

This robe combines the techniques
of embroidery (*nui*) and stencilled
metallic silver or gold foil (*haku*).
In this robe the shoulder and hem
sections, worked in the *nuihaku*
technique, are connected to the
waist section of white plain weave
silk. Gold foil covers the white plain
weave ground on the embroidered
shoulder and hem areas. In addition
to various types of animals and
plants, such as cherries, wisterias,
camellias, pines, shells, chickens,
cranes, long-tailed tortoises and deer,
other motifs on the robe include
wave crests, fans, poem slips and
royal carriages that represent scenery
of the four seasons. The principal
embroidery technique on this work
is the float stitch (*watashi-nui*, see
also 75), in which the stitches move
from one edge of the design to the
other without the thread appearing on
the underside. This type of restrained
embroidery was characteristic of the
Momoyama period. (KA)

72 鬱金地雲尾長鳥丸模様縫箔
江戸時代 18世紀
Nuihaku with design of clouds
and long-tailed bird roundels
on yellow ground

Edo period, 18th century
silk, satin weave with stencilled gold foil
and silk embroidery
147.8 x 138 cm
National Noh Theatre

In this *nuihaku* cloud shapes outlined
with coloured threads are scattered
against a vivid turmeric-coloured
satin ground. They are filled with
interlocking Buddhist swastika motifs
and other abstract designs produced
with the *surihaku* (stencilled metallic
patterning) technique. Overlapping
the clouds are scattered roundels
that illustrate facing long-tailed
birds clutching floral branches (Jp.
hanakuidorimon) in their beaks. This bird
motif has its origins in the art of the
Persian Sasanian court and can be seen
on objects from China's Tang dynasty
(618–907) that are stored in the Shōsōin
repository in Nara. The birds depicted

on these objects include large parrots,
phoenixes, mandarin ducks and long-
tailed fowl holding jewelled necklaces,
arabesque designs, ornamental bands
of cloth and branches. As seen here,
these symbolic, auspicious motifs were
also adopted by Japanese artists and
craftsmen. (KA)

73 薄黄地露笹唐扇地紙松皮菱模様縫箔
江戸時代 18世紀
Nuihaku with design of fans and
pine-bark lozenges over bamboo
leaves on yellow ground

Edo period, 18th century
silk, plain weave with stencilled gold
pattern and silk embroidery
143 x 132 cm
Agency for Cultural Affairs of Japan

The yellow ground of this example
has designs of bamboo grass created
through the use of gold metallic
stencilling, over which are scattered
motifs of 'Chinese fans' (*tōsen*), abstract
pine-bark lozenges (*matsukawabishi*)
and fan papers (*jigami*). The Chinese
kidney-shaped fans are filled with
images of pines or maple leaves in
clouds, the folding fan-shaped papers
contain motifs of autumn flowers,
including patrinia, bush clover, pampas
grass and thoroughwort, and the
pine-bark lozenges are filled with
tortoiseshell, interlocking diamond and
hemp-leaf patterns. All are meticulously
rendered with sumptuous embroidery.
The Chinese flat fan is, as the name
suggests, Chinese in origin, and the
fan papers are affixed to the spines of
Japanese-style folding fans. In nō, the
fan was an indispensable accessory
employed in most plays, and not
surprisingly, the Chinese flat fan was
utilised for Chinese characters. (KA)

74 紅地流水鴛鴦桜花枝垂桜鳳凰模様縫箔
江戸時代 18–19世紀
Nuihaku with design of weeping
cherries, phoenixes and
mandarin ducks over waves
on crimson ground

Edo period, 18th–19th century
silk, plain weave with stencilled gold foil
and silk embroidery
149 x 134 cm
Agency for Cultural Affairs of Japan

The crimson ground of this robe
is divided by bold, showy diagonal
sections, a compositional design that
is rare among nō *nuihaku* robes.
The decoration in upper left half shows
phoenixes in flight among weeping

cherry blossoms, while the lower right half depicts mandarin ducks swimming between waves interspersed by scattered cherry blossoms. Sections of the weeping cherries and waves are highlighted through the use of metallic stencil patterning that in terms of decoration are as magnificent as *karaori*. The intricate embroidery for each of the motifs further contributes to the brilliance of this dazzling work, which conveys a perfect harmony between the straight and curved lines. (KA)

75 紺地立浪水犀桶模様縫箔
江戸時代 19世紀
Nuihaku with design of waves, *kirin* and buckets on dark blue ground

Edo period, 19th century
silk, satin weave with silk embroidery
142 x 141 cm
National Noh Theatre

This nō robe was handed down through a wealthy Osaka merchant family named Hirase. Embroidered wave crests, mythical *kirin* and buckets are set against a rich navy blue satin ground in the upper and lower sections. The embroidery is worked in a float stitch (see also 71). The outlines of the waves and buckets exhibit the use of a couching stitch (*koma-nui*), an embroidery technique believed to date to the early Edo period that involves affixing gold or thick twisted threads to the satin ground by stitching thinner threads over it. This technique may have been taken up for nō costumes in around the nineteenth century. The *kirin* with a carapace on its back possesses the spiritual power of a deity (*kami*) and is a sacred Chinese creature that is said to love murky waters. (KA)

76 紅地白鷺太藺模様縫箔
江戸時代 安政5年
Nuihaku with design of herons and bulrushes on crimson ground

Ansei 5 (1858)
silk, satin weave with stencilled gold foil and silk embroidery
156 x 144 cm
National Noh Theatre

The design on this *nuihaku* shows a flock of white herons gathering by a riverbank. Billowing clouds and gold mist are seen on the shoulders and sleeves, while the lower section depicts bulrushes in flowing water. The protective paper wrapper for this *nuihaku* records that it has a design

of *fūhyō kōshi futoi* ('bulrush with a nobleman's demeanour'). The term '*fūhyō*' connotes an elegant refinement in outward appearance and '*kōshi*' refers to a high-ranking nobleman or the son of an aristocrat. This work expresses the graceful bearing of the white herons, the sumptuous embroidery underscoring their beauty. (KA)

77 紺地丸紋散模様縫箔
江戸時代 19世紀
Nuihaku with design of scattered roundels on dark blue ground

Edo period, 19th century
silk, satin weave with appliqué silk embroidery
141.5 x 126 cm
National Noh Theatre

Originally this robe was made from different fabric, but due to tearing the crest sections have been cut out and sown onto a new dark blue satin ground. Circular crests with designs, including paulownia, facing butterflies, long-tailed tortoises, lupines, peonies and arrow wheels, as well as roundels of flowering quince and tortoiseshells filled with comma shapes, are illustrated using coloured threads. The empty spaces in each roundel are filled with applied gold foil. *Nuihaku* with scattered circular patterns are worn over *surihaku* with fish-scale designs by the main actor in Act II of the play *Dōjōji*. The largely undecorated body of *nuihaku* results from the fact that it is worn in the 'waist-wrap' draping style (*koshimaki*), with the sleeve slipped off the shoulder and the upper part folded down at the waist. This explains why the design in the unseen waist section of the garment can be dispensed with. (KA)

78 紺地丸紋散模様縫箔
江戸時代 18世紀
Nuihaku with design of scattered roundels on dark blue ground

Edo period, 18th century
silk, satin weave with silk embroidery
141 x 138 cm
Agency for Cultural Affairs of Japan

This *nuihaku* is decorated with diverse scattered roundels set against a deep blue satin ground. Motifs in the large and small roundels include paulownia, oak, ginkgo, wood sorrel, ginger, bellflower, mandarin orange, hemp palm, Buddhist swastikas, gongs, wave crests, Chinese lions and dragons embroidered in variegated threads. The blank spaces within the roundels are filled with

applied gold foil. The assemblage of many designs of the same type is referred to as *tsukushi*, which includes motifs such as *takara-zukushi* (treasures or auspicious symbols), *senmen-zukushi* (fans) or, as here, roundels (*marumon-zukushi*). Sumptuously conceived assemblages of roundels filled with various motifs were fashionable on women's *kosode* in the early Edo period. They are used on nō robes for characters of vengeful, jealous women whose spirits have been transformed into serpents; they are commonly combined with *surihaku* decorated with triangular scale designs. (KA)

79 浅葱地青海波松入松皮菱模様摺箔
江戸時代 18世紀
Surihaku with design of ocean waves and pine-bark lozenges on light blue ground

Edo period, 18th century
143 x 140 cm
silk, plain weave with stencilled silver and gold-leaf
Agency for Cultural Affairs of Japan

The technique of *surihaku* involves the application of paste through stencils cut in the form of the desired designs, over which gold and silver foil is affixed and pressed. The name of the technique also refers to the robe type. *Surihaku* were worn by female characters and only the upper part of the robe is generally seen. This explains why the designs at the waist or running from the waist to the bottom are at times simplified. There are numerous *surihaku* with motifs such as floral crests, dew and grass, the 'seven treasures' (*shippō*), overlapping concentric half-arcs (*seigaiha*) and latticed wickerwork. This *surihaku* employs both gold and silver metallic foils, and onstage would have created an impression of splendid, yet subtle, gracefulness. (KA)

80 白地青海波紅葉模様摺箔
江戸時代 18世紀
Surihaku with design of ocean waves and autumn leaves on white ground

Edo period, 18th century
silk, plain weave with stencilled silver-leaf and hand painting
143.5 x 146 cm
National Noh Theatre

This work exhibits an overlapping pattern of concentric half-arcs (*seigaiha*) rendered using stencilled silver leaf against a white ground, over which are scattered delicate designs of autumn leaves. The autumn foliage – in red, blue, yellow-green, yellow and pale blue-green – exhibit a gradated colouring, the stalks and veins of the leaves delineated in black ink and silver pigment. The protective paper wrapper containing this robe records that it was handed down through a daimyo family. In nō performance *surihaku* are worn as undergarments (*kitsuke*) and are therefore generally covered, with only the upper half of the robe visible. The beautiful patterning on the entire garment is perhaps characteristic of the extravagance of a daimyo household, in this case the Ikeda family. (KA)

81 白地鱗模様摺箔
江戸時代 18–19世紀
Surihaku with design of triangular scales on white ground

Edo period, 18th–19th century
silk, satin weave with stencilled gold-leaf
142.5 x 139.6 cm
Agency for Cultural Affairs of Japan

The white ground of this robe is brilliantly decorated with a repeating pattern of triangular gold fish-scale motifs. The fish-scale design has been known in world cultures since ancient times. In Japan it assumed a simple, uncomplicated representation, with interlocking scales said to resemble the scales on fish, dragons or serpents. The use of gold metallic stencil patterning for fish-scale patterns on nō robes expresses female implacability and was suitable for characters of ogresses, witches, or spirits of vengeful, jealous women transformed into serpents. (KA)

82 白地鱗模様摺箔　　江戸時代 18–19世紀
Surihaku with design of triangular scales on white ground

Edo period, 18th–19th century
silk, satin weave with stencilled gold-leaf
144.8 x 135.6 cm
Agency for Cultural Affairs of Japan

Similar to [81], the white ground of this *surihaku* robe is beautifully embellished with repeating triangular scale patterns produced with gold metallic foil and placed against a white ground. A broad band of pine-bark lozenges divide the top and bottom of the garment in a parallel zigzag pattern. This type of *surihaku* with fish-scale patterns would be worn under a *nuihaku* with embroidered roundels, which would be turned down at the waist

in what is referred to as the 'waist-wrap' draping style (*koshimaki*). This revealed the top half of the *surihaku*, but covered the waist section. This means that the differences in designs between the waist and the top and bottom sections of the *surihaku* would not be readily evident. With time (and depending on the draping of the *surihaku*) the patterning on the unseen waist area became simplified, leading to a generally more modest appearance. (KA)

83 紅地亀甲繋火焔太鼓模様半切
江戸時代 19世紀
Hangiri with design of interlocking hexagonal lozenges and 'flame drums' on crimson ground

Edo period, 19th century
silk, satin weave with gold-leaf paper supplementary weft patterning
107.8 x 78.5 cm
Agency for Cultural Affairs of Japan

Hangiri, a type of broad pleated trousers, are frequently made from gold brocade. They are furnished with two strap-like belts that are attached at the back, folded and tied several times at the front. The colour of *hangiri* vary, but crimson and dark blue are the most common. *Hangiri* are often worn together with *happi* [39 & 40] and for that reason they share similar crisp, showy woven motifs such as waves, diamonds, parallel zigzags, arabesques, fish scales and undulating vertical lines (*tatewaku*). This *hangiri* displays interlocking tortoiseshell designs on a crimson ground, with three comma shapes encircled by cloud and flame patterns, a representation of a 'flame drum' [see also 51 & 66]. (KA)

84 白地唐花入丁字立涌模様半切
江戸時代 19世紀
Hangiri with design of undulating vertical lines and clove-shaped crests with flowers on white ground

Edo period, 19th century
silk, twill weave with gold-leaf paper supplementary weft patterning
101 x 80 cm
Agency for Cultural Affairs of Japan

The motif of undulating vertical lines known as *tatewaku* [see also 83] is said to recreate the form of water vapour rising from the earth's surface, and the inclusion of diverse patterns between the thick curved lines of the *tatewaku* has led to numerous design variations. Here the woven *tatewaku* are clove-shaped motifs filled with colourful arabesques

set against the robe's white ground. Cloves were an imported commodity utilised as a medicine, spice, dye and oil. Due to their rarity, they were considered a 'treasure' (*takara*) and were included in the pictorial assemblage referred to as 'takara-zukushi' [see 78]. The combination of white, gold and various light-coloured threads coalesce in this work of elegant refinement. (KA)

KYŌGEN MASKS

85 登髭　　江戸時代 17世紀
Noborihige mask

Edo period, 17th century
pigment on wood with hair
7.7 x 18.7 x 14.6 cm
National Noh Theatre

This kyōgen mask is employed for roles of deities affiliated with Shinto branch shrines. Although a branch shrine is subordinate to a main shrine, its deity is nevertheless a powerful figure. The name *noborihige* ('climbing beard') comes from the sideburns, which appear to grow upwards. The symmetrical facial features coalesce into a dignified smile. The mask's colouration has suffered significant damage over time, but the mask nevertheless retains its expressivity. The smoothly finished chisel marks on the back of the mask are barely visible, and the unlacquered surface means the wood grain is apparent. The use of high-quality, late sixteenth-century Momoyama-period *karaori* and *nuihaku* fabrics for the mask's storage bag indicates that its historical owner was most likely a daimyo. (KY)

86 武悪　　江戸時代 18世紀
Buaku mask

Edo period, 18th century
pigment and metal on wood
9.4 x 19 x 16.1 cm
National Noh Theatre

This demon mask is used in kyōgen plays. It was not only worn by actors performing demon roles, but was also employed as a stage prop to scare other characters. At first glance, the mask appears simply to be frightening, but when seen onstage it can be deployed to convey a whole spectrum of emotions. After the *oto* mask [see 93], *buaku* are one of the most representative of all kyōgen masks. They are produced in a range of colours, including red and white, but black masks such as this example are rare. The lacquer-covered chisel marks on the reverse of the mask have a rough beauty. There is evidence that the reverse of the mask was re-carved at some point in the past to achieve a better fit. (KY)

87　毘沙門　江戸時代 18–19世紀
Bishamon mask

Edo period, 18th–19th century
pigment on wood
8.9 x 19.7 x 15.4 cm
National Noh Theatre

Bishamon is one of the four guardian deities of Buddhist doctrine and the name is an abbreviated form of Bishamonten, an alternate name for the deity Zōchōten [see 67]. His wrathful expression reflects his calling to banish the demons that attempt to obstruct Buddhism. This example is rather small for a *Bishamon* mask, but the intense red colouration and the generously modelled features fully convey the authority of the deity. This mask is used in kyōgen performances for the role of Bishamonten, the principal deity of the Kurama temple in Kyoto. (KY)

88　通円　江戸時代 18世紀
Tsūen mask

Edo period, 18th century
pigment on wood
8.6 x 20.2 x 15 cm
National Noh Theatre

The main actor wears this mask in the kyōgen play *Tsūen*. Tsūen is the name of the owner of a teashop near the foot of the Uji bridge close to Byōdōin temple. Beside himself with the large number of worshippers coming to the temple, Tsūen throws himself into making tea for them all and dies of exhaustion. His ghost asks for spiritual release from a Buddhist priest. *Tsūen* is performed as a parody of the nō play *Yorimasa* and the mask was also created with this nō play in mind. The carver has succeeded brilliantly in producing a work that vividly references the *Yorimasa* nō mask, while at the same time conveys the fact that Tsūen is a teashop owner, not a military commander. Rather than expressing regret or frustration, this dignified mask projects pride in Tsūen's sacrifice. Chisel marks, covered with reddish-brown lacquer, are just visible on the reverse of the mask. The mask's storage bag is made from blue *nerinuki* (plain weave) silk and the red inscription reads 'Tsūen, work of Moku *tayū*'. (KY)

89　鼻引　江戸時代 18–19世紀
Hanahiki mask

Edo period, 18th–19th century
pigment on wood
8.6 x 19.2 x 15.7 cm
National Noh Theatre

This mask is used for roles that portray the ghosts of old men. In many ways it is similar to the *noborihige* mask [see 85], but the small nose of the *hanahiki* flares more widely, creating a strong facial expression. Unlike the *noborihige* mask, it is rarely utilised for branch shrine deity roles, instead it is often employed for roles in which the characters display strong human traits. (KY)

90　賢徳　江戸時代 18世紀
Kentoku mask

Edo period, 18th century
pigment on wood
7.7 x 19 x 14 cm
Agency for Cultural Affairs of Japan

This mask is employed for characters such as crab spirits, and animals such as cows and horses. Similar to the *usofuki* [see 91], it is suitable for a broad range of roles and as such, like many kyōgen masks, is not limited to use in a single set role. The 'skin' of this example is a lustrous red-brown colour, and the upward-staring eyes are also vaguely reminiscent of a crab. The horizontal chisel marks on the back of the mask are coated with a reddish lacquer, reflecting the colouration of the front of the mask. A circular branded seal is impressed on the forehead and traces of bluish-green pigment are visible in the crevices of the illegible seal. (KY)

91　空吹　江戸時代 19世紀
Usofuki mask

Edo period, 19th century
pigment on wood
7.8 x 19.4 x 14.5 cm
Agency for Cultural Affairs of Japan

This mask is used for numerous roles, from mosquito spirits, octopus ghosts and mushrooms to scarecrows. The flattened ears, downturned eyes, and the lips drawn together as if whistling are all typical features of the *usofuki* ('whistler') mask. In this case, the majority of the colouration is a later addition, though this is not noticeable onstage where the mask's rich expressivity captures the viewer's attention. The carefully finished traces of the chisel visible on the back have been lacquered over. (KY)

92　祖父（貝杓子）　江戸時代 18世紀
Ōji (kaijakushi) mask

Edo period, 18th century
pigment on wood
8.9 x 19 x 15 cm
Agency for Cultural Affairs of Japan

This old man mask depicts the face of an elderly man that shows the passage of time. The *kaijakushi* ('shell ladle') is one type within the category of mask known as *ōji* ('old man'), but in this case the aged appearance is strongly conveyed. The mask encapsulates the description of a decrepit old man in the kyōgen piece *Grandfather in love (Makura monogurui)*, in which the old man's face is said to be very dark, his mouth distorted and his eyes 'decaying'. The collapsing bone structure is captured precisely. Rough traces of the chisel on the reverse of the mask are covered with black lacquer. (KY)

93　乙　江戸時代 18世紀
Oto mask

Edo period, 18th century
pigment on wood
8.7 x 20.4 x 17.5 cm
National Noh Theatre

In kyōgen, female roles are generally performed without a mask, but the *oto* ('strange' or 'comic') mask is used for roles where the woman is unattractive. The female characters in kyōgen are often talkative or nagging women, and as such the *oto* mask has the representative features of a robust woman of the commoner class. The charm of the strong, energetic townswoman has been magnificently rendered. This mask is also employed for Buddha and mushroom spirit roles. The utilisation of one mask in a number of different roles is a peculiar feature of kyōgen. (KY)

94　ふくれ　江戸時代 18世紀
Fukure mask

Edo period, 18th century
pigment on wood
7.4 x 19.8 x 14.7 cm
National Noh Theatre

This mask belongs to the category of masks known as *oto* [see 93], but because it represents a woman of more advanced years than the *oto*, it is also used for the role of the elderly nun in the plays *The plum blossom hut (Iori no ume)* and *An old nun names a young man (Bikusada)*. At first glance, the mask conveys a peaceful rather than brilliant feel, but the knowing eyes and the mouth in fact seem to impart a variety of expressions. Circular traces of the chisel arranged horizontally are visible over the entire surface of the back of the mask, which is covered with blackish-brown lacquer. A single incised line between the nostrils appears to be a covert carver's signature. The characters for 'iori' (hut) are inscribed in black on the mask. (KY)

95 尼　江戸時代 18世紀
Ama mask

Edo period, 18th century
pigment on wood
8.6 x 19.8 x 15 cm
National Noh Theatre

This mask portrays an elderly nun (*ama*). Her advanced age is indicated by numerous wrinkles and missing teeth, but the general impression is of a plump, healthy face that is wreathed in smiles. This mask is used by the main actor of the kyōgen piece *Bikusada* in which the happy nun is asked to name a child. The hair is appropriately tonsured. The smoothly finished, almost invisible, chisel marks on the reverse are covered with lacquer. (KY)

96 尼　江戸時代 18世紀　尼
Saru (monkey) mask

Edo period, 18th century
pigment on wood
7.9 x 18.8 x 14 cm
National Noh Theatre

This mask is used for the role of the monkey son-in-law who moves into his monkey father-in-law's residence in the kyōgen piece *A monkey wedding (Sarumuko)*, which is performed as an interlude between the two acts of the nō play *Mount Arashi (Arashiyama)*. This handsome young male monkey has lively eyes, shiny skin and fur, and a straight nose. The entire surface of the back of the mask is covered with thick, circular chisel marks covered by brownish-black lacquer. A covert carver's signature of a straight line is incised between the nostrils. (KY)

97 白蔵主（伯蔵主）　江戸時代 17世紀
Hakuzōsu mask

Edo period, 17th century
pigment on wood
8.1 x 20 x 13.9 cm
Agency for Cultural Affairs of Japan

The main actor in Act I of the kyōgen play *Fox trapping (Tsurigitsune)* wears this mask. It was conceived as one half of a pair with the *kitsune (fox)* mask [see 98], which was made by the same carver. The protagonist of *Fox trapping*, an old fox, knows that a trapper is setting snares for him and transforms himself into the form of the trapper's uncle, the priest Hakuzōsu, to visit the trapper in order to persuade him to desist. At first glance, this mask looks human, but in fact the mouth and teeth are clearly those of a fox. The angular cheeks, sharp nose and pointed chin also resonate with the image of the fox and the vigilant eyes seem to be on the watch for the trapper. Only a single strand of the original implanted whiskers survives near the left-hand side of the mouth, suggestive of the carver's determination to create a thoroughly fox-like mask. The mask is very thinly carved and a piece of lacquered hemp has been attached to the entire reverse side of the mask to provide structural reinforcement. (KY)

98 狐　江戸時代 17世紀
Kitsune (fox) mask

Edo period, 17th century
pigment on wood
17.7 x 18.7 x 17.5 cm
Agency for Cultural Affairs of Japan

The main actor in Act II of the play *Fox trapping (Tsurigitsune)* utilises this mask, which is a pair with the *hakuzōsu* mask above [see 97]. The modelling and the colouration of this mask are extremely skilful and extremely attractive. The shaping of the ears and the depiction of the muscles around the eyes suggest careful observation of real foxes, which adds a richness to the character onstage. The lower jaw was carved separately and is joined to the upper portion of the mask with metal fittings. The construction is such that when the actor 'barks' during a performance, the mouth of the mask opens. The rough circular chisel marks on the reverse are lacquered over. (KY)

KYŌGEN COSTUMES

99 染分地観世水模様素襖
江戸時代 18–19世紀
Suō kamishimo with dye-separated units of black with design of crests and tan with design of swirling water

Edo period, 18th–19th century
hemp, plain weave with stencilled paste-resist decoration
jacket: 90.2 x 194 cm;
trousers: 142.3 x 24.2 (waist) cm
National Noh Theatre

Suō kamishimo are matched hempen suits with broad-sleeved upper jackets (*suō*) and long pleated trousers (*nagabakama*). During the medieval era this type of garment represented the daily dress for samurai, but over time it evolved into formal attire. By the Edo period, it was utilised as ceremonial dress for middle-ranking samurai and daimyo retainers. The kyōgen theatre, which had a strong populist element, employed *suō* as a robe for characters with social position.

The black and tan dyed upper and lower sections on this jacket and trouser suit are divided by an area of pine-bark lozenge patterns. *Suō* are normally embellished with small, simply conceived repeating dyed motifs or with medium-sized stencilled dyed patterns, but there are also a number of kyōgen costumes like this example that are dye separated. The whirling design set against the whitish ground is known as *Kanze-mizu* ('Kanze water'), a motif derived from the family crest of the head master of the Kanze school [see also 107]. The *Kanze-mizu* was initially used for songbook (*utaibon*) covers and nō costumes, and later became a common decorative pattern on non-nō related art and craft objects. (KA)

100 縹地源氏車青海波模様素襖
江戸時代 19世紀
Suō kamishimo with design of Genji wheels on indigo ground

Edo period, 19th century
hemp, plain weave with stencilled paste-resist decoration
jacket: 81 x 200 cm;
trousers: 165 x 25 (waist) cm
National Noh Theatre

This suit of indigo hempen cloth is decorated with a motif known as *seigaiha* ('blue ocean waves'). *Seigaiha* are generally composed of repeating concentric half-arc shapes, but variants do exist in which the arcs are replaced by other forms such as chrysanthemum flowers, dots or, as in this example, the wheels of ox-drawn carriages. The arrangement of the slightly darker blue and white of the carriage wheels results in a work of refreshing appeal. (KA)

101　黒地菊花模様素襖　江戸時代 19世紀
Suō kamishimo with design of chrysanthemums on black ground

Edo period, 19th century
hemp, plain weave with stencilled
paste-resist decoration
jacket: 65.5 x 168 cm;
trousers: 163 x 24.5 (waist) cm
National Noh Theatre

The decoration on this work shows chrysanthemum blossoms on a dyed black ground. The arrangement of the scattered blossoms is not systematic, instead it is characterised by random, overlapping groupings. While some flowers are completely white, others have only white outlines, leaving the black ground to shine through. (KA)

102　海老茶地折鶴模様素襖
江戸時代 19世紀
Suō kamishimo with design of paper cranes on maroon ground

Edo period, 19th century
hemp, plain weave with stencilled
paste-resist decoration
jacket: 67.5 x 180.4 cm;
trousers: 150 x 24.8 (waist) cm
National Noh Theatre

The maroon colour of this example is known as _ebicha_ ('lobster/prawn brown') from the fact that the reddish colour – one associated with the Japanese spiny lobster (_Ise-ebi_) – is tinged with ashen brown. Irregularly positioned on the _ebicha_ ground of this suit are designs of scattered, folded paper cranes. The tradition of folding paper (_origami_) evolved from the custom of making standardised paper shapes as ritual decorations or as gift packaging. The establishment of _origami_ as a pastime, which led to the creation of many shapes, is thought to have occurred from the Edo period onwards. The simple, straight lines of the folded paper crane forms here are striking. (KA)

103　鼠地杢目模様素襖　江戸時代 19世紀
Suō kamishimo with design of wood-grain pattern on grey ground

Edo period, 19th century
hemp, plain weave with stencilled
paste-resist decoration
jacket: 77.6 x 184 cm;
trousers: 161.7 x 23.5 (waist) cm
National Noh Theatre

In this matched suit, overlapping, undulating ellipses resembling wood grain are set against a dyed grey ground. The use of a wood-grain motif as a design detail can be found on _kosode_, but it is rare to find it stencil dyed on the entire surface of a _suō kamishimo_, as seen in this example. This is a showy ensemble for a _kyōgen_ costume. (KA)

104　浅葱地松皮菱葉模様素襖
江戸時代 19世紀
Suō kamishimo with design of leaves and pine-bark lozenges on light blue ground

Edo period, 19th century
hemp, plain weave with stencilled
paste-resist decoration
jacket: 67.5 x 172 cm;
trousers: 159 x 24.8 (waist) cm
National Noh Theatre

This matched suit has a repeating pattern of pine-bark lozenges dyed in light blue with an overlaid design of fluttering white leaves created through the technique of stencilled paste-resist dyeing. The process of stencil dyeing (_katazome_) is labour intensive, requiring two stencil applications. In this _suō_, small white dots suggesting dewdrops appear in the spaces between and inside each lozenge on the dark blue ground. Arranged over these are delicately depicted motifs of fallen leaves that seem to dance, as if stirred by a gust of wind. (KA)

105　茶地雨龍模様長裃
江戸時代 19世紀
Naga-kamishimo with design of rain dragons on brown ground

Edo period, 19th century
hemp, plain weave with stencilled
paste-resist decoration
vest: 64.5 x 66 cm;
trousers: 150.3 x 24.2 (waist) cm
Private collection

This _naga-kamishimo_, a matched suit consisting of long pleated trousers (_nagabakama_) and a sleeveless vest (_kataginu_), is used for roles of minor daimyo, household heads or small landowners. Here, mythical Chinese 'rain dragons' (_amaryō_), so called because they reportedly ascend to heaven to cause rain, and lateral stripes are alternatively placed against a brown ground. The forms of the rain dragons have been simplified to accommodate the process of stencil dyeing, but they still retain

characteristic traits such as the sinuous, undulating body, the separated claws and tail. The body of the rain dragon is slimmer than other dragon types, its hornless form resembling a large lizard. It is also said to be a water spirit that inhabits muddy waters. (KA)

106　紺地碇繋模様長裃
明治時代 19世紀
Naga-kamishimo with design of interlocking anchors on dark blue ground

Meiji period, 19th century
hemp, plain weave with stencilled
paste-resist decoration
vest: 65.1 x 70 cm;
trousers: 141.7 x 24 (waist) cm
National Noh Theatre

The decoration of this _naga-kamishimo_ comprises interlocking anchors against a blue ground. The ocean was a particularly important source of livelihood for the island nation of Japan, and ships and their related objects were frequent motifs in the visual arts. The interlocking anchors on this _naga-kamishimo_ draw inspiration from the form of anchor tips, which have been overlapped in a complex manner in order to picture them from different angles. They are intriguing as designs of interlocking rings. (KA)

107　黒地流水鷺模様肩衣
江戸時代 18世紀
Kataginu with design of flowing water and herons on black ground

Edo period, 18th century
hemp, plain weave with paste-resist
decoration
73.4 x 31 cm
Private collection

Worn together with the _hanbakama_, the sleeveless vest (_kataginu_) was utilised for commoner and servant (eg Tarō Kaja) roles. The hem section of this example has been dyed in pale blue and illustrates a large whirling _Kanze-mizu_ ('Kanze water'), a pattern associated with the Kanze troupe of nō actors [see also 99]. A flock of herons gather along the riverbank in a zigzag formation. The rotund forms of the herons provide a striking contrast to the lines delineating their diminutive heads and long, stick-like legs. Though simplified, the heads, bodies and feathers of the herons coalesce to create a magnificent composition. (KA)

108 黄地碇模様肩衣　　江戸時代 18世紀
Kataginu with design of
anchor on yellow ground

Edo period, 18th century
hemp, plain weave with paste-resist
decoration
59.6 x 54.2 cm
National Noh Theatre

The placement of the black anchor
shape against the bright yellow ground
of this costume produce a striking,
effective contrast. In this cleverly
conceived, very kyōgen-like costume,
the creative handling of the subject
gives the impression that the anchor
has been flung onto the surface. The
anchor is utilised as a prop having
connotations of the ocean, and the term
for a depiction of an anchor 碇図 (*jōzu*)
is a wordplay on the homophonically
sounding word上手 (*jōzu*), which means
'skilful' or 'dexterous'. (KA)

109 浅葱地芭蕉蝸牛模様肩衣
江戸時代 18–19世紀
Kataginu with design of
banana leaves and snail on
light blue ground

Edo period, 18th–19th century
hemp, plain weave with paste-resist
decoration
72 x 34.1 cm
National Noh Theatre

The dyed forms of banana leaves and
a snail outlined in black ink create
a beautiful contrast to the pale blue
ground of this vest. The rambling
snail clutches onto one banana leaf.
The front and back of the leaves change
from white to pale blue. The banana
plant originated in southern lands and
its characteristic elliptically shaped
leaves were a common design motif.
This *kataginu* is essentially void of
any colouration and the snail adds a
peaceful, subdued note to the robe's
ornamentation. (KA)

110 黄地若鮎模様肩衣　　江戸時代 19世紀
Kataginu with design of
sweetfish on yellow ground

Edo period, 19th century
hemp, plain weave with paste-resist
decoration
71.3 x 67.8 cm
Private collection

The pattern on this sleeveless vest
shows young sweetfish swimming
in a river and set against a yellow
ground. In the autumn sweetfish swim
downstream to spawn and in the spring
the young fish or fry swim upstream

from the ocean. On this *kataginu*, the
meandering river flows from the left
shoulder to the right hem, and the fry
are depicted with their heads directed
to the left, beautifully suggesting their
journey upstream against the current.
Created without stencils, rather with
freehand painting, this piece imparts a
feeling of tranquil springtime. (KA)

111 浅葱地枝垂柳霞模様肩衣
江戸時代 19世紀
Kataginu with design of
weeping willow in mist on
light blue ground

Edo period, 19th century
hemp, plain weave with paste-resist
decoration
76.2 x 34.4 cm
National Noh Theatre

The forms of brown mist and a weeping
willow outlined in white on a light
blue ground conjure up an image of a
willow silhouetted against a night sky,
but the scene might also be interpreted
as a trompe l'oeil, in which the blue
ground is a flowing river and the
willow's swaying branches are seen
as reflections on the water's surface.
The composition conveys a sense of
refreshing charm. (KA)

112 縹地砧模様肩衣
江戸時代 19世紀
Kataginu with design of fulling
cloth on indigo ground

Edo period, 19th century
hemp, plain weave with paste-resist
decoration
71.8 x 76 cm
Private collection

The upper section of this *kataginu*
depicts strips of cloth and mallets,
while the lower section can perhaps
be viewed as an abstracted landscape
design of what appears to be a cliff-
side bridge or thatched hedge. From
ancient times in Japan, the pounding,
beating or 'fulling' of silk cloth was
carried out to straighten and soften
the fabric and to bring out the lustre
of the silk. This practice was referred
to as 'pounding or beating the fulling
block' (*kinuta-uchi*). In the nō play
The fulling block (*Kinuta*) a wife,
waiting impatiently for the return of
her husband, borrows a mallet from
villagers and beats cloth to assuage
her sense of longing. The light-hearted
feel of this vest is reinforced by the
use of an object from everyday life
as the principal design, a particular
feature of kyōgen costumes. (KA)

113 茶地菊輪繋模様肩衣
江戸時代 19世紀
Kataginu with design of
interlocking rings with
chrysanthemums on brown
ground

Edo period, 19th century
hemp, plain weave with stencilled
paste-resist decoration
65.7 x 81.7 cm
National Noh Theatre

This *kataginu* has a pattern of diamond-
shaped chrysanthemum blossoms
encircled by interlocking chain-like rings.
The rings not only allude to the 'seven
treasures' (*shippō*), but their intertwined
forms also create a polished and refined
look. Kyōgen *kataginu* have comparatively
more freehand designs produced
with *kaki-e* (painting with a brush) or
tsutsugaki (hand-drawn paste-resist
decoration) than with stencils (*katazome*).
This example was probably intended
as the top part of a *naga-kamishimo*
matched suit [see 105 & 106]. (KA)

114 紺地菊菱繋模様肩衣
江戸時代 19世紀
Kataginu with design of
interlocking diamonds with
chrysanthemums on dark
blue ground

Edo period, 19th century
hemp, plain weave with stencilled
paste-resist decoration
68.4 x 70.6 cm
National Noh Theatre

Adjoining chrysanthemums in a diamond
shape constitute the pattern on this
kataginu. The chrysanthemum originated
in China where it was valued for its
beauty and special fragrance. One of
the five annual festivals in China also
included the Chrysanthemum festival
on the ninth day of the ninth month,
when individuals drank sake infused
with chrysanthemum petals as a wish
for long life. Chinese customs and
aesthetics such as these were adapted
in Japan, where the chrysanthemum
was widely employed as a design motif
from the Heian period onwards. (KA)

115 濃茶地丸文散模様半袴
江戸時代 19世紀
Hanbakama with design of
scattered roundels and arrow
feathers on dark brown ground

Edo period, 19th century
hemp, plain weave with paste-resist
decoration
82.5 x 24 (waist) cm
National Noh Theatre

The ankle-length *hanbakama* (short trousers) is combined with the *kataginu* and *suō* jackets for use in peasant, merchant and servant (eg Tarō Kaja) roles. Designs on *hanbakama* comprise scattered roundels; here each of the roundels on the dark brown ground contains two arrow feathers side by side. The arrow is a symbol of samurai military prowess, and ceremonial arrows (*hamaya*) would also have been well known as amulets to ward against evil or as talismans. *Hanbakama* decorated with scattered roundels filled with only one motif, as seen here, were quite rare. (KA)

116　藍鼠地菊菱丸文散模様半袴
江戸時代 19世紀
Hanbakama with design of chrysanthemum diamonds and scattered roundels on indigo-grey ground
Edo period, 19th century
hemp, plain weave with paste-resist decoration
92.1 x 24.7 (waist) cm
National Noh Theatre

This *hanbakama* has an indigo-grey ground ornamented with stylised diamond-shaped chrysanthemum flowers overlaid by scattered roundels. The roundels illustrate diverse motifs, including sparrows, *kemari* balls, pouches, clove shapes, weights, shells, sails, straw rain coats, 'Genji incense signs' and plum blossoms. (KA)

117　鼠地丸文散模様半袴
江戸時代 19世紀
Hanbakama with design of pine needles and scattered roundels on grey ground
Edo period, 19th century
hemp, plain weave with paste-resist decoration
87.3 x 22.5 (waist) cm
Private collection

The roundels in this example illustrate various motifs, such as sails, fulling blocks, peaches, 'Genji incense signs', headdresses worn by *gagaku* dancers and pouches, scattered on a black tinged grey ground. There are many darkly coloured *hanbakama*, but the decoration of the grey ground with the designs of pine needles in this example sets it apart from the usual monochromatic robes of this type. (KA)

118　黒地丸文散模様半袴
江戸時代 19世紀
Hanbakama with design of scattered roundels on black ground
Edo period, 19th century
hemp, plain weave with paste-resist decoration
82.6 x 24 (waist) cm
National Noh Theatre

The scattered roundels on this *hanbakama* are delineated by a white outer circumference inside of which are rings of red, brown, navy blue, pale blue-green, green and so forth. The inside of the roundels display differing motifs such as straw umbrellas, fulling blocks, peaches, 'Genji incense signs', weights and pouches, distinguishing this charming work from other *hanbakama*. (KA)

119　濃萌黄地丸文散模様半袴
江戸―明治時代 19世紀
Hanbakama with design of scattered roundels on dark green ground
Edo–Meiji period, 19th century
hemp, plain weave with paste-resist decoration
89 x 23.5 (waist) cm
National Noh Theatre

Roundels with designs of umbrellas, bamboo and gentian, weights and other motifs are scattered against a dark green ground. Even though *hanbakama* and *kataginu* [107–114] are different types of garments, their shape and the designs used on them are generally similar, and in this case they are referred to as *kyōgen-bakama* ('kyōgen trousers'). (KA)

120　縹地丸文散模様半袴
江戸時代 19世紀
Hanbakama with design of scattered roundels on indigo ground
Edo period, 19th century
hemp, plain weave with paste-resist decoration
75.8 x 21.3 (waist) cm
Private collection

Light yellowish-green, brown and yellow roundels, defined by a white outer ring, are scattered against an indigo ground. Each roundel is filled with motifs including birds, fans, crossed axes, conch shells and butterflies. It is thought that this *hanbakama* was a child's robe in that the side openings are large and the garment is short. (KA)

121　火焔宝珠蒔絵太鼓胴
江戸時代 19世紀
Taiko drum body with design of flaming jewels
Edo period, 19th century
red and gold lacquer *maki-e* on black lacquer ground
14.5 x 26 (diameter) cm
National Noh Theatre

The *taiko* is a percussion instrument that is set on a stand and struck with drumsticks. The drumheads are stretched with leather and the instrument's sound is determined by the rhythm used in beating the drumheads. The *taiko* is not used during the entire nō performance, rather it principally announces the entrance of characters such as deities, benevolent and evil spirits in first-category 'god' plays and fifth-category 'ending nō' plays. The black-lacquered body of this example is decorated with a composition of flaming sacred jewels (*hōju*) on a bound sheaf of paper. The sacred jewel is believed to have the power to fulfil wishes, while the bound sheaf is associated with longevity: together they are seen as congratulatory, auspicious designs. The fiery force emanating from the flaming treasured jewels is conveyed through the sprinkled gold *maki-e* in the background. (KA)

122　扇蒔絵太鼓胴　江戸時代 19世紀
Taiko drum body with design of fans
Edo period, 19th century
gold lacquer *maki-e* on black lacquer ground
14 x 25.5 (diameter) cm
Agency for Cultural Affairs of Japan

The black lacquer ground of this *taiko* drum body is decorated with elegantly scattered fan shapes rendered through various *maki-e* techniques. The designs on the fans are diverse. Two of particular note depict the traditional pictorial themes of the 'Seven sages of the bamboo grove' (Jp. *Chikurin no shichiken*), a reference to the seven literati recluses who gather in a bamboo grove to escape the world and to engage in philosophical discourse, and two hermits (seen here). One hermit washes his ears in a waterfall and the other leads an ox. Together they would have represented the tale of the Chinese recluses Xuyou and Chaofu (Jp. Kyoyū and Sōho), who exemplify the aversion to worldly fame and high social status. Further designs on the fans include fallen autumn leaves floating on a stream, Chinese lions and peonies, cranes in pines, trough shells and phoenixes with paulownia. (KA)

123 能管「騎馬武者図」・那智紅葉蒔絵能管筒　江戸時代 19世紀
Nō flute with design of a warrior on horseback and flute case with design of autumn leaves at Nachi waterfall

Edo period, 19th century
gold *maki-e* on black lacquer ground
flute: 39 (length) x 2.7 (diameter) cm;
case: 39 (length) x 4.2 (diameter) cm
National Noh Theatre

The four types of musical instruments in nō (*hayashi*) – transverse flute (*fue* or *nōkan*), small and large hand drums (*kotsuzumi*, *ōtsuzumi*) and drum (*taiko*) – are collectively known as *shibyōshi* ('four rhythms'). Together with the actor's dancing and chanting, the *shibyōshi* is an essential element in a nō performance.

The *fue* is made of dried bamboo (*susutake*) with seven finger holes and a mouth hole. The sound is subtly regulated by the tilting of the flute. A small tube, called *nodo* (throat), is inserted on the inside between the mouth hole and the first finger hole. This reduces the diameter of the *fue* and produces the high pitched sound that is characteristic of nō flute music. The head section of this nō flute has carved inlaid gold work depicting a warrior on horseback playing a flute. The design on the flute case, rendered in gold and silver *maki-e*, illustrates an autumnal scene along the cascading Nachi waterfall, which is located within the precincts of the Kumano Nachi shrine on Mount Nachi in Wakayama prefecture. (KA)

124 文箱蒔絵大鼓胴　江戸時代 19世紀
Ōtsuzumi drum body with design of writing boxes

Edo period, 19th century
gold *maki-e* on black lacquer ground
28.5 (length) x 11.8 (diameter) cm
National Noh Theatre

The hourglass shaped *ōtsuzumi* (large hand drum) is a percussion instrument. The leather drumheads are stretched onto either end of the drum body, which is positioned on the left knee, held with the left hand and beaten with the right. The *ōtsuzumi* and the *kotsuzumi* are roughly the same shape, but the centre section of the *ōtsuzumi* body has a carved ring. The *ōtsuzumi* differs from the *kotsuzumi* in that the leather drumheads are heated over a charcoal brazier before performance; they are then tightly lashed to the body with hempen cords known as *shirabeo*. The *ōtsuzumi* is noted for producing a crisp, high and sharp pitched sound when forcibly hit. This example is decorated with the design of various boxes for storing writing utensils, created by areas of sprinkled metal powder using the lacquer techniques of *hiramaki-e* (flat *maki-e*) and *e-nashiji* ('pear skin'). The two cords of the boxes are depicted as ornamental loops. (KA)

125 柴垣梅折枝蒔絵小鼓胴　江戸時代 19世紀
Kotsuzumi drum body with design of plum branches and brushwood fence

Edo period, 19th century
gold *maki-e* on black lacquer ground
24.7 x 9.5 (diameter) cm
National Noh Theatre

Like the *ōtsuzumi* above [124], the hour-glassed shaped *kotsuzumi* (small hand drum) is a percussion instrument. The leather drumheads are stretched onto either end of the drum body, which would be held with the left hand over the right shoulder and beaten with the right hand. The drumheads of *kotsuzumi* are lashed to the body with *shirabeo* cords, and the tightening or loosening of the *shirabeo* can change the tension of the heads so as to produce the desired sound. It is important to maintain a degree of moisture in the horse-hide drumheads at all times and this is regulated during performance. Although the *shirabeo* cords generally conceal the drum body, there are nevertheless many examples that depict beautiful designs executed in gold *maki-e* against a black lacquer ground. The imagery on this work includes a brushwood fence, blossoming plum branches and fluttering snowflakes, all pointing to an early spring scene. They are worked in *takamaki-e* (raised *maki-e*) and *bokashi maki*, the latter a type of the *hiramaki-e* (flat *maki-e*) shading

technique in which two types of gold powder are sprinkled through a bamboo sieve and dusted on the surface. The inside of this work has not been turned on a lathe, rather it has been fashioned by hand. (KA)

126 杜若蒔絵小鼓胴　江戸時代 18世紀
Kotsuzumi with design of irises and storage box with design of scattered kimono sleeves

Edo period, 18th century
drum body: silver, red and gold *maki-e*, *kirigane* on black lacquer ground; storage box: silver and red *maki-e* on gold ground, textile, wood
drum: 25.1 x 10 x 20.2 (diameter) cm;
box: 23.4 x 30.8 x 24 cm
Art Gallery of New South Wales
Roger Pietri Fund 2013　56.2013.a–b

The decoration on this elegant *kotsuzumi* depicts blossoming water irises, which are finely worked in gold and silver *hiramaki-e* and *e-nashiji* to create a striking, sumptuous contrast to the black lacquer ground. The manner in which the irises have been cropped creates the impression that the drum rim is the surface of the pond from which the plants emerge. The splendid colour and form of the water iris led it to being among the most popular design motifs on Japanese lacquerware, textiles and painting. The water iris is associated with summer, specifically the fifth month, and the image of these flowers in bloom is often linked to the episode of the 'Eight bridges' in chapter 9, 'Journey to the East' (*Azuma-kudari*), in the tenth-century *Tales of Ise* (*Ise monogatari*). This literary episode was adapted for the nō play *The iris* (*Kakitsubata*), thought to be by the eminent actor, playwright and theorist Zeami Motokiyo (c1363–c1443) [see also 60]. (KT)

127 唐松蒔絵小鼓胴　江戸時代 19世紀
Kotsuzumi drum body with design of Chinese pine

Edo period, 19th century
gold *maki-e* on black lacquer ground
L25 x 10.2 (diameter) cm
Agency for Cultural Affairs of Japan

This gorgeous *kotsuzumi* drum body has a design of overlapping Chinese pine leaves rendered in gold *maki-e* on a black lacquer ground. Chinese pine are generally depicted as stylised floral forms, with the needle-like leaves presented in a circular arrangement and enclosing a centrally placed carpel. (KA)

128 ゆずり葉蒔絵小鼓胴
江戸時代 19世紀
Kotsuzumi drum body
with design of false daphne
Edo period, 19th century
gold *maki-e* on black lacquer ground
25 x 10.1 (diameter) cm
Agency for Cultural Affairs of Japan

The black lacquer ground of this *kotsuzumi* is ornamented with a pattern of false daphne and white back ferns of the type that would have been employed as an embellishment on a congratulatory gift or as a decoration for the home at the new year. The extensive black ground, a composition that delicately shifts between an alternating placement of design motifs and the superb *maki-e* contribute to the refined feel of this work. (KA)

129 網干蒔絵鼓箱　江戸時代 19世紀
Storage box for drum body
with design of fishing net
Edo period, 19th century
gold *maki-e* on black lacquer ground
24.1 x 30 x 23 cm
Agency for Cultural Affairs of Japan

This box is used to store the *kotsuzumi* drum bodies decorated with designs of Chinese pine and false daphne seen above [127 & 128]. In this example a scene of fishing nets hung on poles to dry is rendered in gold *maki-e*. The marks on the box indicates that metal clasps on the side appear to have originally been circular, but here they are stylised wave shapes, perhaps an association with coastal scenery. The interior of the box is lined with *karaori* brocade that has a pattern of scattered chrysanthemum blossoms and a bamboo fence on a purple ground. This fabric is thought to be a section recycled from a nō robe. (KA)

NŌ PAINTINGS, PRINTS, AND SONGBOOKS

130 百万絵巻　室町時代 16世紀
Illustrated handscroll of
the nō play *Hyakuman*
Muromachi period, 16th century
handscroll: ink and colour on paper
16.6 x 738.1 cm
National Noh Theatre

This charming handscroll, composed of 16 text excerpts with 16 images, is an early, very rare visualisation of a nō play using the pictorial and compositional conventions of medieval illustrated narrative handscrolls (*emakimono*). Zeami's *Hyakuman* is a fourth-category 'miscellaneous' play that is based on an older piece entitled *The crazed woman of Saga* (*Saga monogurui*) by his father Kan'ami (1333–84). In the play, a priest from Yoshino accompanies a young boy to the Seiryō temple in Saga to attend an incantation ceremony (*dai-nenbutsu*) for the Amida Buddha. As seen in this handscroll, the temple is also host to various other activities and entertainments such as acrobatic performances, but it is a madwoman dancing and chanting that draws the attention of many visitors and worshippers. The man speaks to the madwoman, who confesses that her deranged emotional state is due to her grief over the loss of her son and that her dancing and chanting is a supplication to the Buddha to ensure her child's safe return. The priest then realises that the boy in his company is in fact the madwoman's son and the play ends with their joyful reunion. (KT)

131 古能楽図　江戸時代 慶長期
Illustrations of old nō
performances
early Edo period, Keichō era, 1596–1615
three panels: ink and colour on paper
117 x 47 cm each
National Noh Theatre

Today mounted as individual works, these three panels might originally have belonged to one or various folding screens with diverse scenes on each panel. Illustrated here are the nō plays *Kumasaka* [left] and *Miwa* [right], and the kyōgen piece *Igui* [centre]. The portrayal of spectators seated in a tatami room adjacent to the actors and musicians suggests that these are private, exclusive performances hosted by a wealthy patron at his residence. The painting style and compositional mode resemble other works belonging to the genre depicting amusements in aristocratic residences (*teinai yūrakuzu*) [see also 132] from the early Edo period. (KT)

132 古能狂言之図　江戸時代 17世紀
Illustrations of old nō and kyōgen
early Edo period, 17th century
album leaves: ink and colour on paper
44.4 x 59.5 cm each
National Noh Theatre

These 20 leaves, bound together in a concertina album, illustrate 13 nō and seven kyōgen plays that would have been performed as popular entertainments at Buddhist temple and Shinto shrine festivals. The staging of such performances for a broad audience predates the patronage of nō as the official theatre of the Tokugawa shogunate in the early Edo period. The lively depictions of the nō and kyōgen theatre in these album leaves share similarities with genre scenes dating from the Kan'ei (1624–43) to early Genroku (1688–1704) eras, especially those showing amusements in aristocratic residences (*teinai yūrakuzu*) [see also 131]. Further, the compositional device of capturing both the action onstage and the audience from a bird's-eye view has parallels with early images of the kabuki theatre. The careful brushwork, the attention to detail and the degree of realism imbue these works with a highly refined aesthetic value; they are also important resources in the study of nō performance history. These album leaves must have been part of a larger set, however, the circumstances surrounding their commission and the artist(s) who created them are still unclear. This is a topic awaiting future research. (KT)

133 能舞之図　江戸時代 18世紀
Illustrations of nō dances
mid Edo period, 18th century
two handscrolls: ink and colour on paper
1st scroll: 31.4 x 547.3 cm; 2nd scroll: 31.6 x 509.8 cm
National Noh Theatre

This work by an unknown artist comprises 25 images (13 in the first scroll/12 in the second) and is presumably a visual record of various plays staged in a one-day program. The first scroll begins with the depiction of the auspicious play *Okina*, which usually marks the start of the day's performances. The representation of the most important dance scene from nō plays belonging to each of the five categories is interspersed by illustrations of kyōgen pieces. The picturing of the orchestra, chorus and stage assistants in only the first image of each scroll is noteworthy. (KT)

134 狩野栄信筆　宮中能楽図
Kano Naganobu (1775–1828)
Nō performance at the
Imperial palace
after 1802
hanging scroll: ink and colour on silk
116 x 173 cm
National Noh Theatre

Commissioned to commemorate a special banquet hosted at the Imperial palace, this hanging scroll pictures a nō performance held for an illustrious group of guests (courtiers and Buddhist monks). The three elegant square poem cards (*shikishi*) pasted along the top of the composition further underscore the dedicatory character of the work. Each of the cards is inscribed with a 31-syllable Japanese-style poem (*waka*) composed by the banquet's participants as poetic responses to the performance, in this case the fourth-category 'miscellaneous' play *Rolls of silk* (*Makiginu*). Naganobu used the honorific title *hōgen* ('Eye of the law') in his signature on this work, enabling a dating to after 1802. (KT)

135　能楽図屏風　江戸時代 18世紀
Nō performance

mid Edo period, 18th century
six-panel folding screen: ink and colour
on gold ground
72 x 227 cm
National Noh Theatre

This screen illustrates a highlight from Act II of the first-category 'god' play *Naniwa*, when the goddess Konohana Sakuyahime and the ghost of the scholar Ōnin perform a celebratory dance to orchestral accompaniment. Four stage assistants, the chorus, the subsidiary actor (*tsure*) and his two companions also appear onstage. In the Edo period, special nō performances were staged in the spring and autumn at the Imperial palace for court ladies and their children. The blossoming cherry trees in the garden, as well as the audience of numerous noblewomen (identifiable by their cloak-like veils or *goshokazuki*) and young children, indicate that this work records such an occasion. (KT)

136　能楽図帖　桃山時代 16世紀
Illustrations of nō and kyōgen

Momoyama period, 16th century
album with 24 illustrations: ink and
colour on paper
25.6 x 31.7 cm each
National Noh Theatre

The compositions of the 24 leaves in this concertina album are characterised by a somewhat naïve brushwork and a limited palette; they are believed to be among the earliest known nō representations. The tailoring and the draping of the costumes reflect then current fashions, while the designs on the shoulders and hems document *karaori* robes during their initial stage of development. Even though the pictorial elements are sparse, the depicted plays are easily identifiable by the masks, costumes and stage

properties. This restrained compositional mode became the standard in illustrations of nō and kyōgen. (KT)

137　御能狂言図巻　江戸時代 17世紀
Illustrations of nō and kyōgen

early Edo period, 17th century
handscroll: ink and colour on silk
28.6 x 431 cm
National Noh Theatre

Opening with the key scene from the first-category 'god' play *White beard* (*Shirahige*), this scroll continues with illustrations of five nō plays and five kyōgen interludes that together would comprise a full day's program. The scroll – and by extension the day's performances – concludes with the fifth-category 'ending nō' play *The tipster sprite* (*Shōjō*). The placement of the characters against a blank background serves to enhance the detailed representation of the sumptuous costumes and masks. The high artistic quality and the use of expensive materials suggest that this work was by a member of one of the orthodox painting schools patronised by the court or military aristocracy. (KT)

138　狩野柳雪筆　能之図
Kano Ryūsetsu (1646–1712 or 1729–74)
Illustrations of nō

Edo period, 18th century
two handscrolls: ink and colour on paper
1st scroll: 22.1 x 864.4 cm;
2nd scroll: 22.1 x 865.9 cm
National Noh Theatre

The over 60 images now mounted on these two handscrolls were most likely originally collected into an album. A colophon at the beginning of each scroll lists the plays illustrated and records Kano Ryūsetsu as the artist. There were at least two members of the long-standing Kano lineage who used the art name Ryūsetsu, most notably, Hidenobu (1646–1712) and Nakanobu (1729–74), however, a firm attribution of these handscrolls to either artist has yet to be established. Executed with careful brushwork and high-quality pigments, each scene is presented in the formulaic compositional manner that isolates the actors and their props from the surrounding stage. The identification of the plays is facilitated by the inclusion of their titles written in ink on gold-leaf labels and positioned in the upper right-hand corner of each scene. (KT)

139　能楽手鑑　江戸時代 18世紀
Compendium of nō and kyōgen

mid Edo period, 18th century
album with 20 illustrations: ink and
colour on silk
30.4 x 37.5 cm each
National Noh Theatre

This album depicts the most characteristic scenes from 20 nō plays. The title and synopsis of each play are written in elegant calligraphy and are artfully arranged around the image. The album's silk cover and frontispiece feature the stylised butterfly crest of the Ikeda house of Inshū. The inscription on the album's wooden storage box further confirms this illustrious provenance. Gorgeously executed anthologies of nō and kyōgen plays like this were popular among daimyo and wealthy commoners who studied nō. (KT)

140　土佐光孚筆　演能図屏風
Tosa Mitsutaka (1780–1852)
Screen illustrating various nō scenes

Edo period, late 18th–first half of
19th century
six-panel folding screen: ink and
colour on silk
155 x 310.8 cm
National Noh Theatre

Each of the six panels on this folding screen depicts a key scene from the following six plays (from right): *Takasago*, *The reed cutter* (*Ashikari*), *Kumano* (also known as *Yuya*), *The Unrin temple* (*Unrin'in*), *Chōryō* and *The swordsmith* (*Kokaji*). Even though all the scenes are painted separately, they are rendered from the same vantage point, their arrangement on the six panels creating a unified composition. The signature 'Tosa Mitsutaka, lower fourth rank of the Imperial painting office [*edokoro*]' appears on every panel. (KT)

141　能絵鑑　江戸時代 18世紀
Compendium of nō pictures

mid Edo period, 18th century
album with 50 illustrations: ink and
colour on silk
37 x 45.5 cm each
National Noh Theatre

Striking for its use of delicate brushwork, vibrant pigments and meticulous attention to detail, this luxuriously bound album illustrates 50 popular nō and kyōgen plays. This work is one of the most impressive examples of a nō compendium known whose production resulted from daimyo sponsorship. The album was originally in the collection of the Mizuno clan, lords of the Okazaki domain (present-day Aichi prefecture) and later handed down to a well-respected Kyoto family. A written document accompanying and transmitted with the album identifies Sumiyoshi Gukei (1631–1705) as the painter, and while this cannot be substantiated it is quite possible that the artist was a member of the Sumiyoshi studio in Kyoto. In keeping with the pictorial conventions used for nō imagery, the stage setting is omitted, the focus firmly on the main characters, their costumes and stage props. (KT)

142　狂言古図　江戸時代 17世紀
Illustrations of old kyōgen performances

early Edo period, 17th century
album with 16 illustrations: ink and
colour on paper
24 x 30.9 cm each
National Noh Theatre

The 16 lively compositions in this album reflect the dynamic nature of kyōgen. Originally painted on kidney-shaped fans made from robust *torinoko* paper, the individual leaves were later pasted onto rectangular album leaves. The selection of the plays (the titles are listed on the back) and the image sequence appear to be random, the differences in brushwork indicating that this is a collaborative work by members of a specialised painting studio. Recent research has established that the leaves in this album belong to a larger set of over 200 illustrations formerly in the possession of Enoshima Ihei (1895–1975), a kyōgen aficionado and publisher of Hōshō school libretti. This album is a valuable document of nō performance history, since some of the plays illustrated here were staged only by the Sagi school, which disappeared after the Meiji Restoration of 1868. (KT)

143　狂言古画帖　江戸時代 17世紀
Album of old paintings of kyōgen

early Edo period, 17th century
album with 13 illustrations: ink and
colour on paper
21.5 x 28 cm each
National Noh Theatre

Different from the album discussed above [see 142], all of the 13 illustrations in this example were painted directly onto a rectangular album leaf. The painting style also varies slightly, exhibiting less detail in the brushwork and fewer colours. The album includes

some plays that were very rarely performed, even in the early Edo period. This suggests that the individual who commissioned it had a very specific knowledge of and interest in kyōgen. Recent research indicates that members of a studio located in the Kyoto area created this piece, and like the artists of the previous album they probably based their paintings on the same printed model book. Nevertheless, it is not clear to what extent these scenes represent contemporary performance styles or are the products of artistic imagination. (KT)

144　狩野栄信筆　翁・三番三・千歳
Kano Naganobu (1775–1828)
Okina, Sanbasō and Senzai

Edo period, 19th century
hanging-scroll triptych: ink and
colour on silk
78.6 x 29 cm each
National Noh Theatre

Okina – also known as *Shiki sanban* ('Three rituals') – is not actually a nō play but a highly sophisticated ceremonial performance that has its origins in Shinto rites praying for peace and prosperity. *Okina* is often performed during the new year season, at particular festivals and on auspicious occasions when it would be the opening play for a one-day nō program. It features the dance of three figures: the white-masked old man Okina, the black-masked old man Sanbasō and the youthful Senzai. The inscriptions above the figures identify Yagorō Tomoyuki *tayū* (1795?–1865), the fifteenth head of the Hōshō nō actor lineage, as Okina (centre scroll); Ōgura Yatarō Torafumi (1791–1824), the twentieth head of the Ōgura kyōgen actor lineage, as Sanbasō (left scroll); and the 11-year-old Hōshō Rinjirō as Senzai (right scroll). Based on the birth and death dates of the performers, as well as surviving performance records, it can be conjectured that this triptych documents a unique performance that took place at the inner citadel of Edo castle between 1820 and 1822. (KT)

145　河鍋暁斎筆　雷
Kawanabe Kyōsai (1831–89)
Scene from the play
Thunder (Kaminari)

dated Keiō 3 (1867)
hanging scroll: ink and colour on silk
26 x 38 cm
National Noh Theatre

Thunder is categorised as a 'demon' kyōgen play and here the Thunder god (Kaminari) is rendered as a fierce figure. Initially conned into believing the efficacy of a cure by a quack doctor, Kaminari unleashes his true wrathful nature when it comes to negotiating payment. Vividly captured here is the final scene in the play when Kaminari chases the petrified doctor away. Kawanabe Kyōsai is acknowledged as one of the most versatile and colourful artists of the Meiji period. In addition to his activity as painter, print designer and instructor, Kyōsai was also known as an ardent student and amateur actor of kyōgen. (KT)

146　月岡耕漁筆　大黒・夷
Tsukioka Kōgyo (1869–1927)
Daikoku and Ebisu

late 19th–early 20th century
hanging-scroll diptych: ink and
colour on paper
199 x 44.8 cm each
National Noh Theatre

A student of Tsukioka Yoshitoshi (1839–92) and Ogata Gekkō (1859–1920) – arguably two of the best-known Meiji-period painters and print designers – Kōgyo excelled in the traditional genres of landscape, nature scenes, as well as imagery of the Sino-Japanese (1894–05) and Russo-Japanese (1904–05) wars. However, Kōgyo's favourite subject was the nō theatre; he produced more than 70 paintings, five sets of prints (totalling over 700 individual designs) and hundreds of magazine illustrations and postcards relating to nō.

Kōgyo demonstrates his mastery of the subject in this hanging-scroll diptych, which is executed in an abbreviated manner with brisk, dynamic brushstrokes and adeptly placed colour accents. These scrolls depict two of the 'Seven gods of good fortune' (*Shichifukujin*): Daikoku, who stands on a rice bale holding a mallet, and Ebisu with his fishing rod and sea bream. The two figures wear masks, indicating that this work portrays two kyōgen actors performing a play of the same name and is not simply an illustration of these two popular deities. (KT)

147　月岡耕漁筆　能楽図絵
Tsukioka Kōgyo (1869–1927)
Pictures of nō plays (Nōgaku zue)

1897–1902
five albums: colour woodblock prints
24.2 x 35.8 cm each
National Noh Theatre

Pictures of nō plays was not only Kōgyo's most ambitious undertaking in nō imagery, but it perhaps represents the largest series within the tradition of Japanese woodblock prints (*ukiyo-e*) with over 260 prints. Each album illustrates 50 nō and kyōgen plays, with additional prints showing architectural elements of the theatre, the audience seating area, backstage, masks, accessories and other stage properties. There is no apparent order, alphabetically according to play or thematic, in the sequence of the prints.

The majority of the images follow the conventional compositional mode adopted for nō imagery, with a focus on the figure of the main actor in a key scene from the play and set against a blank background. Some images are more fanciful with the inclusion of small insets in the form of square poem cards or fans that contain excerpts from the play or illustrations of the preceding or following scenes. Others employ the device of a split-screen view to portray multiple scenes or utilise a trompe l'oeil effect. The use of colour is sparse, often gradated to emulate the appearance of a watercolour painting. Expensive metallic pigments and the technique of blind-printing accentuate the beauty of the designs. It has been posited that this deluxe edition demonstrates a concerted effort on the part of publisher and artist to generate renewed interest in traditional art forms – *ukiyo-e* prints and nō theatre – in an age of increasing modernisation. (KT)

148 能楽百番　月岡耕漁筆
Tsukioka Kōgyo (1869–1927)
One hundred nō plays
(Nōgaku hyakuban)
1922–27
two albums with 120 colour
woodblock prints
42.3 x 29.8 cm each
National Noh Theatre

In July 1922, 20 years after the release of *Pictures of nō plays* [147], the Tokyo publisher Daikokuya embarked on Kōgyo's second major series, *One hundred nō plays*. Stylistically and in terms of format, the prints in this set differ greatly from *Pictures of nō plays*. Here Kōgyo opts for a vertical, rather than horizontal, orientation. The compositional plane is thus narrower, prompting a reduction in pictorial elements, and the emphasis on the magnified figure of the main actor

creates a monumental, authoritative presence. The backgrounds in the designs of *One hundred nō plays* are rarely blank. They are defined by an area of richly gradated colour or abstracted landscape and nature motifs drawn with broad, sweeping washes that impart a heightened sense of drama. (KT)

149 月岡耕漁/月岡江文筆　狂言五十番
Tsukioka Kōgyo (1869–1927) and
Tsukioka Kōbun (1908–94)
Fifty kyōgen plays (Kyōgen gojūban)
1925
album with 50 colour woodblock prints
39.7 x 41.5 cm each
National Noh Theatre

This album, launched in 1925 by the publishing house Daikokuya, is most likely Kōgyo's last work, and it is his only set devoted to kyōgen. The artist signed 16 of the 50 illustrations; the remaining 34 bear the signature 'Kōbun', the art name of his daughter and student Tsukioka Gyokusei. The painting style and composition of the prints are similar to those in *One hundred nō plays* [148]: the main characters are magnified within the picture plane and isolated from the stage setting. The backgrounds are largely left blank and colour washes are applied sparingly to suggest landscape elements or to create a more dramatic visual effect. Kōbun's designs harmonise well with her father's style, providing a seamless stylistic transition throughout the album. The striking similarities in style and composition, as well as the proximity of the production dates, suggest that *Fifty kyōgen plays* was conceived as a companion set to *One hundred nō plays*. (KT)

150 月岡耕漁筆　能楽画帳
Tsukioka Kōgyo (1869–1927)
Pictures of nō and kyōgen plays
(Nōgaku gachō)
1920s
album with ten colour woodblock prints
24.7 x 32.2 cm each
National Noh Theatre

This set – illustrating ten nō and kyōgen plays – appears to be a privately commissioned work that may have been produced in more than one album. The individual prints are generally conventional in compositional approach, nevertheless they exhibit excellent brushwork with great attention to

detail in the rendition of the costumes. The album begins with the representation of *Okina* and ends with *The tipster sprite (Shōjō)*, which suggests that it was intended as a visual chronicle of a one-day program. (KT)

151 弘化勧進能絵巻（模刻）　明治時代
Illustrated scrolls of subscription nō performance in the Kōka era (1844–48)
1909 (later edition)
two handscrolls: colour woodblock print
1st scroll: 26.6 x 1178.6 cm;
2nd scroll: 26.6 x 983.1 cm
National Noh Theatre

Subscription (*kanjin*) nō performances were traditionally staged by religious institutions or local administrations as fund-raising events for the renovation of Shinto shrines, Buddhist temples or bridges. Subscription nō performances were logistically complicated events to orchestrate: they required the construction of not only a stage but an outdoor theatre area equipped with all the necessary amenities such as toilet facilities, restaurants, teahouses, stalls selling various goods and so forth. This meant that a subscription nō performance was a once in a lifetime project for the head master of one of the five principal nō schools, and in fact only 12 such events took place during the Edo period. The twelfth and last Edo-period subscription nō was organised in 1848 by the fifteenth head of the Hōshō nō actor lineage, Yagorō Tomoyuki *tayū*. For this a showground was built on the fire evacuation area at the Sujikai bridge in Kanda and performances continued for 15 days. The entire event was accurately recorded by the painter Saitō Gesshin (1804–78) and his work was handed down through the main Hōshō family. Even though Gesshin's painting was later lost during a fire, woodblock-printed versions were produced from the late 1800s onwards. The two handscrolls in the collection of the National Noh Theatre are later copies issued by the publisher Ōkubo Hasetsu in 1909. (KT)

152 能装図　江戸時代 19世紀
Illustrations of nō properties and accessories
late Edo period, 19th century
album: ink and colour on paper
11.3 x 20 cm
National Noh Theatre

153 能作物・道具図　江戸時代 19世紀
Illustrations of nō properties and accessories

late Edo period, 19th century
colour woodblock-printed books
27.2 x 20.6 cm
National Noh Theatre

With the canonisation of nō performance in the Edo period, it became necessary for each of the five main schools – Kanze, Konparu, Hōshō, Kongō and Kita – to record in detail the choreography, the use of music, costumes, mask types and stage properties for each of the over 200 plays in the entire nō repertoire. The records took the form of handbooks as seen in these two well-preserved examples. The former illustrates only the props employed in each play, while the latter has precise construction sketches with measurements and other specifications. (KT)

154 宝生流能装束付　江戸時代 19世紀
Hōshō school index of nō costumes

late Edo period, 19th century
two volumes: ink and colour on paper
23.5 x 17.6 each
National Noh Theatre

The Hōshō lineage of nō actors received the highest recognition with its appointment as the official instructor (*shinan'yaku*) to the fifth Tokugawa shogun Tsunayoshi (1649–1709), the sixth shogun Ienobu (1662–1712) and the tenth shogun Ieharu (1737–86). The Hōshō also served as nō instructors to the Tayasu and Hitotsubashi clans, two branch families of the ruling Tokugawa shoguns. In accordance with this high office, much effort was invested in the production of paintings and other visual documents that recorded the school's teachings. Beautifully crafted compilations of costumes and stage props, such as the volumes here, were usually made for and handed down through daimyo families or through the family of the school's head. (KT)

155 観世座能狂言写生帖
江戸時代 19世紀
Sketches of Kanze school nō and kyōgen performances

late Edo period, 19th century
three volumes: ink and colour on paper
27.7 x 40.4 cm each
National Noh Theatre

These three volumes are invaluable resources in our understanding of the performance style of the Kanze school in the nineteenth century. They comprise over 100 pages with sketches of nō and kyōgen performances, masks, stage props and costume patterns that are at times hastily drawn in ink or embellished with colour. Performance dates are noted on certain pages. The unfinished, unpretentious nature of the illustrations indicates that they were probably done impromptu as study materials or as preparatory sketches for later paintings or handbooks. (KT)

156 光悦謡本特製本「姨棄」
江戸時代 17世紀
Hardcover Kōetsu-style nō libretto (*utaibon*) for the play *The deserted crone (Obasute)*

early Edo period, 17th century
woodblock-printed book with mica
23.9 x 18 cm
National Noh Theatre

157 光悦謡本色替り本「東岸居士」
江戸時代 17世紀
Multi-coloured Kōetsu-style nō libretto (*utaibon*) for the play *The layman of the eastern coast (Tōgan koji)*

early Edo period, 17th century
woodblock-printed book
23.9 x 18 cm each
National Noh Theatre

158 謡本「浮舟」　江戸時代初期書写
Nō libretto (*utaibon*) for the play *A drifting boat (Ukifune)*

copy from early Edo period, 17th century
woodblock-printed book with mica
24.1 x 18 cm
National Noh Theatre

159 観世身愛奥書謡本「大原御幸」
江戸時代 17世紀
Nō libretto (*utaibon*) for the play *Imperial visit to Ohara (Ohara gokō)* with postscript by Kanze Tadachika (1566–1626)

early Edo period, 17th century
woodblock-printed book with mica
23.7 x 17.4 cm
National Noh Theatre

160 観世流一番綴紺表紙本
江戸時代初期書写
Kanze school dark blue paperback single-play nō libretti (*utaibon*)

copy from early Edo period, 17th century
twenty volumes: woodblock-printed books
23.2 x 17.1 cm
National Noh Theatre

161 観世流一番綴縹色表紙謡本
江戸時代初期書写
Kanze school blue-covered single-play nō libretti (*utaibon*)

copy from early Edo period, 17th century
ten volumes: woodblock-printed books
24.2 x 17.8 cm
National Noh Theatre

Songbooks with musical notations – generally referred to as *utaibon* – were already known in the late fourteenth century when nō was formalised under Zeami. Medieval students of nō chanting relied on handwritten manuscripts that were usually in the handscroll format. The popularisation of nō recitation among affluent and cultured merchants (*machishū*) in Kyoto in the late sixteenth century resulted in an increased demand for *utaibon*. Benefiting from the introduction of printing with moveable type, many publishers saw a lucrative market in the production of printed songbooks and issued luxurious editions of nō libretti using expensive coloured paper for the inside pages [157] and delicate designs of landscape, flora and fauna painted or printed with gold or silver pigment on both the cover [160 & 161] and inside pages [158 & 159]. Occasionally sumptuously decorated lacquer boxes were custom made to store these books, and both the books and their storage boxes became highly sought-after collector's items [161]. Among the most appreciated deluxe editions of *utaibon* are those by the celebrated artist Hon'ami Kōetsu (1558–1637) in collaboration with Suminokura Sōan (1571–1632), an extremely wealthy and influential Kyoto merchant. Representative examples of the Kōetsu-style libretti are distinguished by the master's elegant calligraphy and the abstract designs of plants and animals printed with *mica* [156]. (KT)

Notes

THE HISTORY OF NŌ: AN ENDURING TRADITION

1 Today, images such as that of *sangaku* drawn on a bow (*Dangū sangaku zu*) and the *Shinzei scroll of old performances* (*Shinzei kogaku zu*) housed in the Shōsōin in Nara, are thought to depict *sangaku* in China.

2 As its names suggests, *dengaku* was originally connected with celebrations surrounding the rice harvest; it was later incorporated into court entertainment.

3 In *genzai nō*, the main character is an individual living in the real world and the principal theme is the depiction of the character's inner feelings, with the drama developing in essence through spoken dialogue. See also: http://www2.ntj.jac.go.jp/unesco/noh/en/ (accessed 30 September 2013).

4 His excellent understanding and perception of Zeami's theory regarding *nōgaku* and its dramatic interpretation are evident in the four-volume *Collective works of Kanze Hisao* (*Kanze Hisao chosaku shū*), Heibonsha, Tokyo, 1980–81.

NŌ THEATRE, PAST AND PRESENT

1 Nippon Gakujutsu Shinkōkai (ed), *Japanese noh drama: ten plays selected and translated from the Japanese*, vol 2, Nippon Gakujutsu Shinkōkai, Tokyo, 1959, p 93.

2 Nippon Gakujutsu Shinkōkai (ed), 1959, p 95.

3 Nippon Gakujutsu Shinkōkai (ed), 1959, pp 95–96.

4 Nippon Gakujutsu Shinkōkai (ed), 1959, p 101.

5 Nippon Gakujutsu Shinkōkai (ed), 1959, p 102.

6 Among the many books available on the history and aesthetics of nō, one of the very best is Konparu Kunio, *Noh theater: principles and perspectives*, first published by Weatherhill/ Tankosha in 1983 and in subsequent paperback editions by other publishers.

7 See Zeami, 'Style and the flower', in J Thomas Rimer & Yamazaki Masakazu (trans), *On the art of the nō drama: the major treatises of Zeami*, Princeton Library of Asian Translations, Princeton University Press, Princeton, 1984, p 47.

8 See Zeami, 'Disciplines for joy', in Rimer and Yamazaki (trans), 1984, p 119.

NŌ, THE MASKED DRAMA

1 Omote Akira & Amano Fumio (eds), *Nō no rekishi*, vol 1 of *Iwanami kōza nō kyōgen*, Yokomichi Mario, Koyama Hiroshi & Omote Akira (eds), Iwanami Shoten, Tokyo, 1987, p 64.

2 Tokuda Rinchū, *Rinchū hishō*, vol 2 of *Nōgaku shiryō*, Sakamoto Setchō (ed), Wan'ya Shoten, Tokyo, 1967, p 8.

3 Nakamura Yasuo, *Noh: the classical theater*, Don Kenny (trans), Walker/ Weatherhill, New York, 1971, p 159.

4 *Hachijō kadensho*, in Hayashiya Tatsusaburō et al (eds), *Kodai chūsei geijutsuron*, pp 511–665, vol 23 of *Nihon shisō taikei*, Iwanami Shoten, Tokyo, 1995, pp 588–92.

5 Gotō Hajime, *Nihon no kamen*, Mokujisha, Tokyo, 1989, p 160.

6 Miyake Noboru, *Nōgaku geiwa*, Hinoki Shoten, Tokyo, 1976, p 212. Miyake wrote about a *ja* mask in the collection of the Kongō school, which is visually similar to the *shinja* mask in fig 3.4. Technically, *ja* and *shinja* are different types of masks, but they are hard to distinguish from one another.

7 Nakamura Yasuo, *Kamen to shinkō*, Shinchō Sensho, Tokyo, 1993, p 56.

8 The story and a colour image of the mask appears in Eric C Rath, *The ethos of noh: actors and their art*, Harvard East Asian Monographs 232, Harvard University Asia Center, Cambridge, MA, 2004, p 90, pl 5.

9 Tokuda, 1967, pp 68–69.

10 Nakamura, 1971, p 35.

11 For further discussion of medieval mask legends and the 'Three rituals', see Rath, 2004, pp 18–33, 226–38.

12 For an extensive and well-illustrated discussion of the varieties of nō masks, see Stephen E Marvin, *Heaven has a face, so does hell: the art of the noh mask*, Floating World Editions, Warren, CT, 2010.

COLOUR, TEXTURE AND TAILORING: THE ROLE OF COSTUME IN NŌ AND KYŌGEN

1 *Fūshi kaden* (*Teachings on style and the flower*, 1400), in *Zeami Zenchiku*, Iwanami Shoten, Tokyo, 1974, pp 21–27; Tom Hare (trans), 'Transmitting the flower through effects and attitudes', in *Zeami performance notes*, Translations from the Asian Classics, Columbia University Press, New York, 2008, pp 31–36; and *Sarugaku dangi* (*An account of Zeami's reflections on art*, 1430), in *Zeami geijutsu ronshū*, Shinkosha, Tokyo, 1976, pp 232–36; Erika de Poorter (trans), *Zeami's Talks on sarugaku: an annotated translation of the Sarugaku dangi, with an introduction on Zeami Motokiyo*, Japonica Neerlandica 2, J C Gieben, Amsterdam, 1986, pp 116–19.

2 Examples include *Sarugaku dangi*, 1976, pp 219, 235, and De Poorter (trans), 1986, pp 108–109, 118.

3 *Sarugaku dangi*, 1976, pp 229, and De Poorter (trans), 1986, p 115. This is not a warning against use of gold per se, since in the previous section Zeami suggests that wearing a gold-brocaded (*kinran*) bag would add a needed accent to a performance. Rather, glitter is inappropriate for the ritual nature of *Okina*.

4 The nō *kariginu* derives from the 'hunting cloak' worn on informal occasions by courtiers, but later adopted as a ceremonial garb in the shogunal court.

5 Open, or gauze, weaves give a gossamer effect due to holes created by crossing adjacent warps. Two common types are the simple gauze weave (*sha*), where adjacent warps alternately cross and uncross, and a variant (*ro*), where three, five or seven plain weave weft shots intercede between each warp crossing. In either case, supplementary wefts of gold and possibly coloured silk create the pattern. The term *chōsen nishiki* refers both to the textile originating in Korea (Chōsen) and the many colours (*nishiki*) used in the patterning, not to a compound weave (another reading of *nishiki*).

6 The Edo-period nō actor Tokuda Chikatada (1679–?) mentions this variant tailoring of the *maiginu* employed by the Kisshū branch of the Tokugawa in his *Things heard and seen by Tokuda Chikatada* (*Rinchū kenmonshū*).

7 Today the manipulation of the pattern heddles is operated by a jacquard system using punch cards.

8 Translated by Donald Keene in both Donald Keene (ed), *Twenty plays of the nō theatre*, Columbia University Press, New York, 1970, pp 237–52, and in Karen Brazell (ed), *Traditional Japanese theater: an anthology of plays*, Translations from the Asian Classics, Columbia University Press, New York, 1998, pp 193–206.

9 The Kanze school uses the fan shown here; other schools prescribe different designs.

10 *Atsuita* can also be draped as an outer robe for male and female roles.

11 Technically speaking, *atsuita* tend to have a six-harness twill ground, while *karaori* usually have a finer three-harness twill ground, but this is not a hard and fast rule.

12 Spontaneous stripping of garments to donate to good actors dates back to Zeami's time, when it formed a major form of income. Payment could also be in bolts of cloth or actual garments.

VISUALISATIONS OF NŌ IN PAINTINGS AND PRINTS

1 The sketches are contained in the text entitled 'Figure drawings for the three modes in two plays' (*Nikyoku santai ningyōzu*), compiled in 1421. Nishino Haruo, 'Kawanabe Kyōsai no nōga kyōgenga', in Nishino Haruo et al., *Tokubetsuten Kawanabe Kyōsai no nō kyōgenga*, exh cat, Mitsui Memorial Art Museum, Tokyo, 2013, p 10.

2 The screen has been variously identified as a performance hosted by Toyotomi Hideyoshi at his mansion Jūrakudai in 1588 or 1592 on the occasion of an imperial visit or as a celebratory presentation hosted by Emperor Go-Yōzei (r1586–1611) at his palace to honour Hideyoshi's receipt of the title '*kanpaku*' (Chief advisor to the emperor) in 1575. Ozawa Hiromu, *Fūzokuga – sairei, kabuki*, vol 13 of *Nihon byōbu-e shūsei*, Takeda Tsuneo, Yamane Yūzō & Yoshikawa Chū (eds), Kodansha, Tokyo & New York, 1980, p 101, no 80, and Amano Fumio, 'Kobe Shiritsu Hakubutsukan shozō "Kan nō zu byōbu" no toki to ba – Azuchi Momoyama jidai nōgakushi kenkyū no tame ni', in *Nihon bungaku shiron – Shimazu Tadao sensei koki kinen ronshū*, Sekai Kisōsha, Kyoto, 1997, pp 282–95.

3 See Fujioka Michiko, 'Kyōgen no kaiga shiryō no kōsatsu – Kokuritsu Nōgakudō shuzōhin o chūshin ni', in [*Noh theatre*] *Kokuritsu Nōgakudō chōsa kenkyū*, vol 7, Mar 2013, p 14.

4 There is evidence that Kano painters in service to the Tokugawa shogunate and daimyo were ordered to attend nō performances and thereafter to produce nō pictures. See Nishino et al, 2013, p 11.

5 Kōno Motoaki, 'Rinpa and nō', in *Hosomi korekushon – Rinpa ni miru nō*, exh cat, National Noh Theatre, Tokyo, 2009, p 7.

6 On nō chanting as a diversion for the general population, see Nishiyama Matsunosuke, *Edo culture: daily life and diversions in urban Japan, 1600–1868*, Gerald Groemer (trans/ed), University of Hawai'i Press, Honolulu, 1997, pp 185–88.

7 On the strong connection between the works of the Rinpa artists Kōetsu, Sōtatsu and Kōrin and the nō theatre, see Kōno, 2009, pp 4–7.

8 See Robert Schaap, 'A "silent beauty" in *ukiyo-e*: printed imagery of the nō theatre', in Robert Schaap & J Thomas Rimer, *Beauty of silence: Japanese nō and nature prints by Tsukioka Kōgyo 1869–1927*, Hotei Publishing, Leiden, 2010, pp 21–27.

9 For the most recent comprehensive studies on Kyōsai's achievements in the genre of nō imagery, see the essays by Nishino Haruo, Kawanabe Kusumi and Higuchi Kazutaka in Nishino et al, 2013.

Glossary

For a breakdown of the categories of nō and kyōgen masks and the nō costumes types see pp 40 and 45, respectively.

J Thomas Rimer has compiled the descriptions for the categories of nō plays.

bunraku 文楽 puppet theatre evolving principally in the seventeenth and eighteenth centuries; together with nō, kyōgen and kabuki, one of Japan's classical theatre forms

gigaku 伎楽 a masked dance-drama performed from the seventh to late twelfth century as part of religious processionals at Buddhist temples

hashigakari 橋掛り the roofed bridge that links the main and backstage areas of a nō stage

hayashi 囃子 a reference to both the musical instruments and the musicians of the nō theatre

Hōshō 宝生 one of the five main schools of nō actors

kabuki 歌舞伎 a flamboyant theatre form that evolved in the seventeenth century, with urban, historical and fantastical themes; different from nō, kabuki actors do not wear masks and have heavy make-up

kagami ita 鏡板 'mirror board', the back wall on the nō stage with a large painted pine tree

kagami no ma 鏡の間 'mirror room', offstage area where actors prepare for their entrances

kagura 神楽 broad designation for folk performing arts, ranging from masked costumed dramas enacted on Shinto shrine stages to dancing lions in festival parades

Kanze 観世 one of the five main schools of nō actors founded by Kan'ami (1333–84) and his son, Zeami Motokiyo (c1363–c1443)

kao 花押 an artist's 'written' seal

Kita 喜多 one of the five main schools of nō actors

Kongō 金剛 one of the five main schools of nō actors

Konparu 金春 one of the five main schools of nō actors

kyōgen 狂言 'wild words', short comic plays often appearing as interludes between the acts of nō plays; the plots are derived from folk tales or deal with daily life

maki-e 蒔絵 technique of lacquer decoration, in which the designs are painted with gold or coloured lacquer on lacquered ground; types include *hiramaki-e* (flat *maki-e*) and *takamaki-e* (raised *maki-e*)

nō (noh) 能 'talent' or 'skill', traditional form of Japanese theatre originating in the fourteenth century under official patronage: male actors, who also play female characters, chant and sing to the accompaniment of an orchestra and a chorus. Stage props are limited; some actors wear masks and the robes are often sumptuous. There are five main schools of nō actors, and there are five categories of nō plays (*shin-nan-nyō-kyō-ki*):

> **first**: 'god' plays (*kami nō* 神能 or *waki nō* 脇能); these often deal with the history of a Shinto shrine and with miracles associated with its deity

> **second**: 'warrior' plays (*shura nō* 修羅能); these frequently handle incidents in epics such as *Tale of the Heike* (*Heike monogatari*) and portray ghosts of warriors who remember their suffering

> **third**: plays concerning women (*katsura nō* 鬘能, 'wig play'); these stress the elegiac, generally picturing women abandoned by their lovers and other similar situations

> **fourth**: 'miscellaneous' plays (*zatsu nō* 雑能) with a wide range of subject matter and including plays with more realistic dialogue found in present-day life (*genzai nō*); plays about madness (*kyōran* or *monogurui mono*) and vengeful spirits (*onryō mono*) are sub-categories

> **fifth**: 'ending nō' (*kiri nō* 切能) or the final play in a day's program; these have rapid tempos and the main character is often a demon

nōga 能画/*nō-e* 能絵 'nō pictures', painting, prints and illustrated material depicting nō and kyōgen performances

nōgaku 能楽 a term adopted in 1881 for both nō and kyōgen; previously known as *sarugaku*

Okina 翁 (also known as *Shiki sanban* 式三番, 'Three rituals'), not actually a nō play, *Okina* is a highly sophisticated ceremonial performance that has its origins in Shinto rites praying for peace and prosperity

sangaku 算額 a performance tradition from Tang-dynasty China known as *baixi* ('one hundred entertainment arts'); together with *bugaku* (court dance and music) was the only form of court entertainment in Japan before the Nara period

sarugaku 猿楽 'monkey music' or 'monkey entertainment', a courtly form of dancing, singing and music evolving from *sangaku* that was popular in the Heian and Kamakura periods; it later developed into nō and kyōgen and was the collective name for them until the Meiji period

shibyōshi 四拍子 'four rhythms', a reference to the four types of musical instruments used in nō – transverse flute (*fue or nōkan*), small and large hand drums (*kotsuzumi, ōtsuzumi*) and drum (*taiko*) – and the musicians who play them

Shiki sanban see *Okina*

shite シテ 'the one who does', the main actor in a nō play; there is only one *shite* in a play and he generally wears a mask

tayū 大夫 (or *dayū* when inflected), originally a pseudo-official title given to promising performers by the samurai affiliated with major temples; troupe leaders adopted the title for themselves in the sixteenth century

tsure ツレ 'to accompany', subsidiary actors in a nō play, who may accompany the *shite* or *waki*

ukiyo-e 浮世絵 'pictures of the "floating world"', a reference to the paintings, woodblock prints and illustrated books illustrating the *ukiyo*, or 'floating world', associated with popular culture in the Edo period

utaibon 謡本 nō libretto or songbook, with lyrics and musical notation

waki ワキ 'to the side', supporting or secondary role to the *shite* actor in a nō performance; they play roles of Buddhist monks, Shinto priests and warriors and do not wear masks

yūgen 幽玄 'profound mystery', an aesthetic concept originating in China that expresses a sense of mystery and depth, calling on a gentle, saddened understanding of the mystery of human existence; Zeami applied *yūgen* in his formulation of a nō performance style that conveys tranquil, sublime beauty

Chronology

Prehistoric age
Jōmon period 12 000–400 BCE
Yayoi period 400 BCE–250 CE
Kofun period 250–6th C

Ancient age
Asuka period 6th C–710
Nara period 710–94
Heian period 794–1185

Medieval age
Kamakura period 1185–1333
Nanbokuchō period 1333–92
Muromachi period 1392–1573

Early modern age
Momoyama period 1573–1615
Edo period 1615–1868

Nineteenth/twentieth century
Meiji period 1868–1912
Taishō period 1912–26
Shōwa period 1926–89
Heisei period 1989–present

Note: The dates of Japanese historical periods can differ according to scholarly opinion, and in some cases, in relation to subject matter.

Bibliography

Amano Fumio. 'Kobe Shiritsu Hakubutsukan shozō "Kan nō zu byōbu" no toki to ba – Azuchi Momoyama jidai nōgakushi kenkyū no tame ni', in *Nihon bungaku shiron – Shimazu Tadao sensei koki kinen ronshū*, Sekai Kisōsha, Kyoto, 1997

Bethe, Monica & Nagasaki Iwao. *Patterns and poetry: nō robes from the Lucy Truman Aldrich collection*, exh cat, The Museum of Art, Rhode Island School of Design, Providence, 1992

Brandon, James R et al. *Japanese theater in the world*, exh cat, Japan Foundation and Japan Society, New York with The Tsubouchi Memorial Theatre Museum, Waseda University, Tokyo, 1997

Brazell, Karen (ed). *Traditional Japanese theatre: an anthology of plays*, Translations from the Asian Classics, Columbia University Press, New York, 1998

De Poorter, Erika (trans). *Zeami's Talks on sarugaku: an annotated translation of the Sarugaku dangi, with an introduction on Zeami Motokiyo*, Japonica Neerlandica 2, J C Gieben, Amsterdam, 1986

Fujioka Michiko. 'Kyōgen no kaiga shiryō no kōsatsu – Kokuritsu Nōgakudō shuzōhin o chūshin ni', in *[Noh theatre] Kokuritsu Nōgakudō chōsa kenkyū*, vol 7, Mar 2013

Gotō Hajime. *Nihon no kamen*, Mokujisha, Tokyo, 1989

Hayashiya Tatsusaburō et al (eds). *Kodai chūsei geijutsuron*, vol 23 of *Nihon shisō taikei*, Iwanami Shoten, Tokyo, 1995

Keene, Donald (ed). *Twenty plays of the nō theatre*, Columbia University Press, New York, 1970

Kōno Motoaki. 'Rinpa and nō', in *Hosomi korekushon – Rinpa ni miru nō*, exh cat, National Noh Theatre, Tokyo, 2009

Konparu Kunio. *Noh theater: principles and perspectives*, Jane Corddry and Stephen Comee (trans), Weatherhill/Tankosha, New York & Kyoto, 1983

Marvin, Stephen E. *Heaven has a face, so does hell: the art of the noh mask*, Floating World Editions, Warren, CT, 2010

McKinnon, Richard N. *Selected plays of kyōgen*, Uniprint Inc, Tokyo, 1968

Miyake Noboru. *Nōgaku geiwa*, Hinoki Shoten, Tokyo, 1976

Nishiyama, Matsunosuke. *Edo culture: daily life and diversions in urban Japan, 1600–1868*, Gerald Groemer (trans/ed), University of Hawai'i Press, Honolulu, 1997

Nakamura, Yasuo. *Noh: the classical theater*, Don Kenny (trans), Walker/Weatherhill, New York, 1971

Nakamura Yasuo. *Kamen to shinkō*, Shinchō Sensho, Tokyo, 1993

Nishino Haruo et al. *Tokubetsuten Kawanabe Kyōsai no nō kyōgenga*, exh cat, Mitsui Memorial Art Museum, Tokyo, 2013

Omote Akira & Amano Fumio (eds). *Nō no rekishi*, vol 1 of *Iwanami kōza nō kyōgen*, Yokomichi Mario, Koyama Hiroshi & Omote Akira (eds), Iwanami Shoten, Tokyo, 1987

Omote Akira. *Kanzeryū shi sankyū*, Hinoki Shoten, Tokyo, 2008

Ozawa Hiromu. *Fūzokuga – sairei, kabuki*, vol 13 of *Nihon byōbu-e shūsei*, Takeda Tsuneo, Yamane Yūzō & Yoshikawa Chū (eds), Kodansha, Tokyo & New York, 1980

Rath, Eric C. *The ethos of noh: actors and their art*, Harvard East Asian Monographs 232, Harvard University Asia Center, distributed by Harvard University Press, Cambridge, MA, 2004

Rimer, J Thomas & Yamazaki Masakazu (trans). *On the art of nō drama: the major treatises of Zeami*, Princeton Library of Asian Translations, Princeton University Press, Princeton, 1984

Schaap, Robert & J Thomas Rimer. *Beauty of silence: Japanese nō and nature prints by Tsukioka Kōgyo 1869–1927*, Hotei Publishing, Leiden, 2010

Suzuki Masahito. *Nōgakushi nenbyō: kōdai, chūsei hen*, Tōkyōdō Shuppan, Tokyo, 2007

Suzuki Masahito. *Nōgakushi nenbyō: kinsei hen, jō kan*. Tōkyōdō Shuppan, Tokyo, 2008

Takeda, Sharon Sadako, in collaboration with Monica Bethe, with contributions by Hollis Goodall et al. *Miracles & mischief: noh and kyōgen theatre in Japan*, Los Angeles County Museum of Art, Los Angeles & Agency for Cultural Affairs, Government of Japan, 2002

Takemoto Mikio. *Kan'ami – Zeami jidai no nōgaku*, Meiji Shoin, Tokyo, 1999
Tokuda Rinchū. *Rinchū hishō*, vol 2 of *Nōgaku shiryō*, Sakamoto Setchō (ed), Wan'ya Shoten, Tokyo, 1967

Tyler, Royall. *Japanese nō dramas*, Penguin Classics, London, 1992

Yasuda, Kenneth. *Masterworks of the nō theater*, Indiana University Press, Bloomington, 1989

Zeami Motokiyo. *Zeami performance notes*, Tom Hare (trans), Translations from the Asian Classics, Columbia University Press, New York, 2008

WEBSITES

'An introduction to Noh and Kyogen', Japan Arts Council
www2.ntj.jac.go.jp/unesco/noh/en

www.the-noh.com/en/plays/index.html

digital.library.pitt.edu/k/kogyo/index.html

www.theatrenohgaku.org

Acknowledgments

Theatre of dreams, theatre of play presents for the first time in Australia a comprehensive overview of the rich visual delights of Japan's oldest performance art – the nō theatre. Such an ambitious project would not have been possible without the dedication and generosity of numerous individuals and institutions in Sydney and beyond. My deepest gratitude to the staff members of the Agency for Cultural Affairs of Japan and the National Noh Theatre, Tokyo for their expertise and professionalism in the seamless organisation of the exhibition. My heartfelt thanks go to my committed and talented colleagues at the Art Gallery of New South Wales who have contributed in many and various ways to the realisation of this exhibition and the accompanying publication.

The beautiful design of the book is equalled by the high level of scholarship of the main essays and I am indebted to authors Monica Bethe, Eric Rath, Thomas Rimer and Takemoto Mikio who have supported the project with great enthusiasm and expertise. The challenge of writing concise but informative entries to the works has been achieved with aplomb by Kadowaki Yukie and Kobayashi Ayako with excellent translations of the Japanese texts into English by Chiaki Ajioka and Amy Reigle Newland. To all I offer my sincere appreciation and admiration.

Further, I wish to specially acknowledge Higuchi Kazutaka, Ikeda Fumi, Kadowaki Yukie, Katsumori Noriko, Kobayashi Ayako, Ann MacArthur, Marco Pompili, Rachel Saunders, Natalie Seiz, Tazawa Hiroyoshi and Elise Tipton for their assistance, guidance and ongoing encouragement throughout this wonderful journey.

Khanh Trinh

Contributors

ESSAY AUTHORS

Monica Bethe is director of the Medieval Japanese Studies Institute in Kyoto, Japan and has taught for many years at the Kyoto Consortium for Japanese Studies at Columbia University. A specialist in nō, she has written many books, including *Miracles and mischief: noh and kyōgen theater in Japan* (with Sharon Sadako Takeda, LACMA, 2002).

Eric C Rath is professor of history at the University of Kansas and a specialist in early modern Japanese culture. His writings on the traditional performing arts include *The ethos of noh: actors and their art* (2004). His most recent focus is on Japanese culinary history with publications including *Food and fantasy in early modern Japan* (2010).

J Thomas Rimer is professor emeritus of Japanese literature and theatre at the University of Pittsburgh. He has written widely on aspects of Japanese theatre of all periods, as well as on modern Japanese literature, cultural history and the visual arts. His latest publication, edited with Mitsuya Mori and M Cody Poulton, is *The Columbia anthology of modern Japanese drama* (forthcoming 2014).

Takemoto Mikio is professor of Japanese literature at Waseda University, Tokyo. Since 2004 he has been the director of the Tsubouchi Memorial Theatre Museum, Waseda University. He has published widely on the history of the nō theatre and has translated many nō plays into modern Japanese.

Khanh Trinh is curator of Japanese and Korean art at the Art Gallery of New South Wales. She has curated numerous exhibitions and edited and contributed to their publications, including *Kamisaka Sekka: dawn of modern Japanese design* (2012); *Hymn to beauty: the art of Utamaro* (2010) and *Genji: the world of the shining prince* (2009).

SECTION INTRODUCTIONS AND ENTRY AUTHORS

Kobayashi Ayako (KA)
Agency for Cultural Affairs of Japan (Bunkachō)

Kadowaki Yukie (KY)
National Noh Theatre, Tokyo

Natalie Seiz (NS)
Art Gallery of New South Wales, Sydney

Khanh Trinh (KT)
Art Gallery of New South Wales, Sydney

Published by the
Art Gallery of New South Wales
Art Gallery Road, The Domain
Sydney 2000, Australia
artgallery.nsw.gov.au

in association with the exhibition
*Theatre of dreams, theatre of play:
nō and kyōgen in Japan*
Art Gallery of New South Wales
14 June – 14 September 2014

The exhibition has been organised by the
Art Gallery of New South Wales, the Agency
for Cultural Affairs of the Government
of Japan and the Japan Arts Council
(National Noh Theatre)

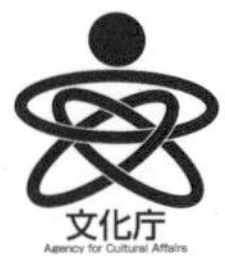

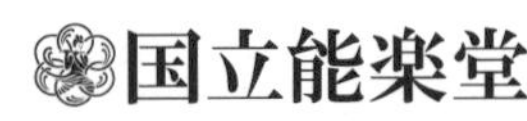

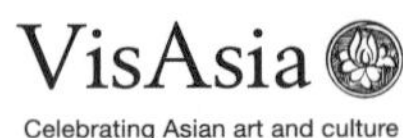

IMAGE CREDITS

Scenes from plays courtesy National Noh
Theatre, Tokyo:

p 16: Performed 15 September 2013.
Sanbasō: Yamamoto Tōjirō; nō flute: Fujita
Rokurobyoue; shoulder drum: Ōkura Genjirō,
Iitomi Akihiro, Koga Hiromi; hip drum:
Yasufuku Mitsuo; assistants: Kizuki Takayuki,
Kanze Yoshinobu

p 21: Performed November 21, 2011.
Shite: Takeda Naohiro; shite tsure: Fujinami
Shigehiko; nō flute: Issō Hisayuki; shoulder
drum: Kō Sejirō; hip drum: Kamei Tadao;
assistants: Takeda Munekazu, Ueda Kimitake

p 24: Performed 18 June 2012 (evening
session). Shite: Umewaka Naoyoshi;
nō flute: Hattanda Tomoko; shoulder drum:
Toriyama Naoya

p 29: Performed 18 June 2012 (morning
session). Shite: Umewaka Kishō; nō flute:
Hattanda Tomoko; shoulder drum:
Toriyama Naoya

p 34: Performed 25 December 2010. Shite:
Umewaka Genshō; nō flute: Issō Hisayuki

p 36: Performed 3 June 2009.
Shite: Nomura Shirō

p 39: Performed 13 June 2009.
Shite: Udaka Michishige

p 42: Performed 14 January 2012. Shite:
Matsuda Takayoshi; ado: Okutsu Kentarō,
Nomura Matasaburō

p 49 (both photos): Performed 26 December
1998. Shite: Umewaka Rokurō; waki:
Hōshō Kan; waki tsure: Hōshō Kinya,
Tonoda Kenkichi; nō flute: Matsuda Hiroyuki;
shoulder drum: Ōkura Genjirō; hip drum:
Kamei Hirotada; taiko: Kanze Motonori;
assistants: Umewaka Yasuyuki, Yamazaki
Eitarō, Hirai Toshiyuki; jiutai: Kakutō
Naotaka, Tsuchida Kiyoshi, Matsuyama
Takao, Umewaka Yasunori, Shibata
Minoru, Yamazaki Masamichi, Inoue Ryōji,
Washikawa Jun; assistants for bell: Umewaka
Shiya, Odagiri Yasuharu, Kakutō Naotaka,
Yamanaka Takahiro, Matsuyama Takayuki

pp 62/67: Performed 16 October 2009.
Shite: Kanze Kiyokazu; shite tsure:
Sakaguchi Taknobu, Takeda Munemori

pp 124/29: Performed 7 November 2012.
Shite: Ogasawara Tadashi; ado: Nomura
Senjō, Nomura Taichirō

pp 152/55: Performed 18 June 2012
(morning session). Shite: Umewaka Kishō;
nō flute: Hattanda Tomoko; shoulder drum:
Toriyama Naoya; hip drum: Ōkura Keinosuke;
taiko: Hayashi Yūchirō

Art Gallery of New South Wales
Cataloguing-in-publication

Theatre of dreams, theatre of play: nō and
kyōgen in Japan / edited by Khanh Trinh;
with essays by Monica Bethe ... [et al]
Includes bibliographical references.
ISBN: 9781741741063
1. Arts, Japanese – Exhibitions.
2. Costumes – Japan – Exhibitions.
3. Kyōgen – Exhibitions. 4. Kyōgen –
Costumes – Exhibitions. 5. Nō – Exhibitions.
6. Nō – Costumes – Exhibitions.
7. Nō in art – Exhibitions. I. Khanh, Trinh.
II. Bethe, Monica. III. Art Gallery of New
South Wales. IV. Japan Arts Council.
V. Nihon Geijutsu Bunka Shinkōkai.
VI. Japan. Bunkachō.

Managing editor: Julie Donaldson
Text editor: Amy Reigle Newland
Translation: Chiaki Ajioka,
Amy Reigle Newland
Rights and permissions: Donna Brett,
Megan Young

Design: Karen Hancock
Production: Cara Hickman
Colour reproduction: Spitting Image, Sydney
Printing and binding:
1010 Printing International, China

DISTRIBUTION

Thames & Hudson Australia
11 Central Boulevard, Portside Business Park,
Fishermans Bend, Melbourne 3207
T: 03 9646 7788
E: enquiries@thaust.com.au

Thames & Hudson UK
181A High Holborn, London WC1V7QX
T: 44 20 7845 5000
E: sales@thameshudson.co.uk
www.thameshudson.co.uk

The Art Gallery of New South Wales is a
statutory body of the NSW State Government

cover: *Atsumori* mask (see cat 20, p 82)
front cover flap: *Aka (red) hannya* mask
(see cat 33, p 91)
back cover: *Oto* mask (see cat 93, p 136)
back cover flap: *Usofuki* mask
(see cat 91, p 134)
inside cover, pp 10, 61,198, 231: adapted
from *Surihaku* with design of triangular scales
on white ground (see cat 81–82, p 122)
pp 1–8, 233–36: Details from *Compendium
of nō pictures* (see cat 141, pp 178)

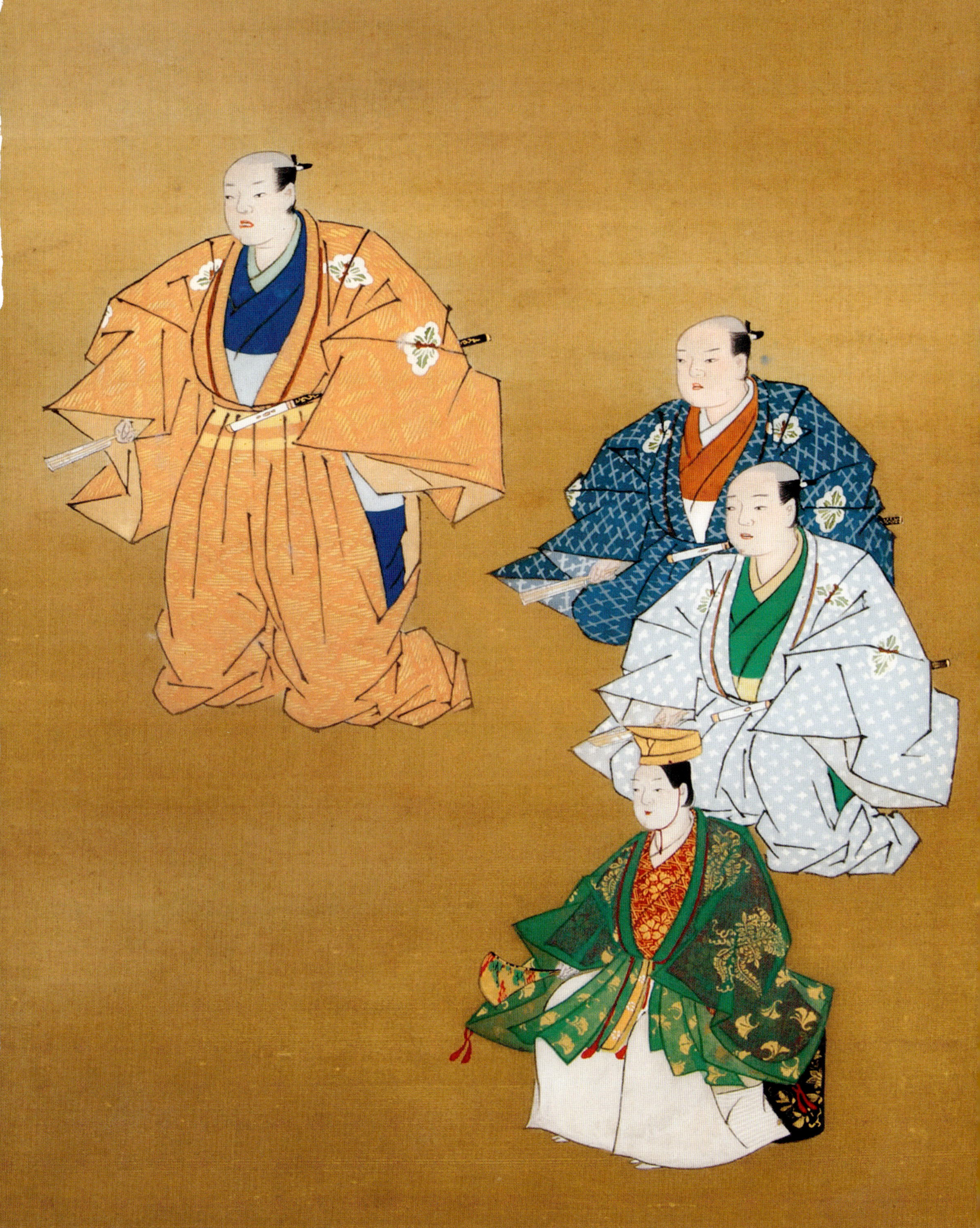

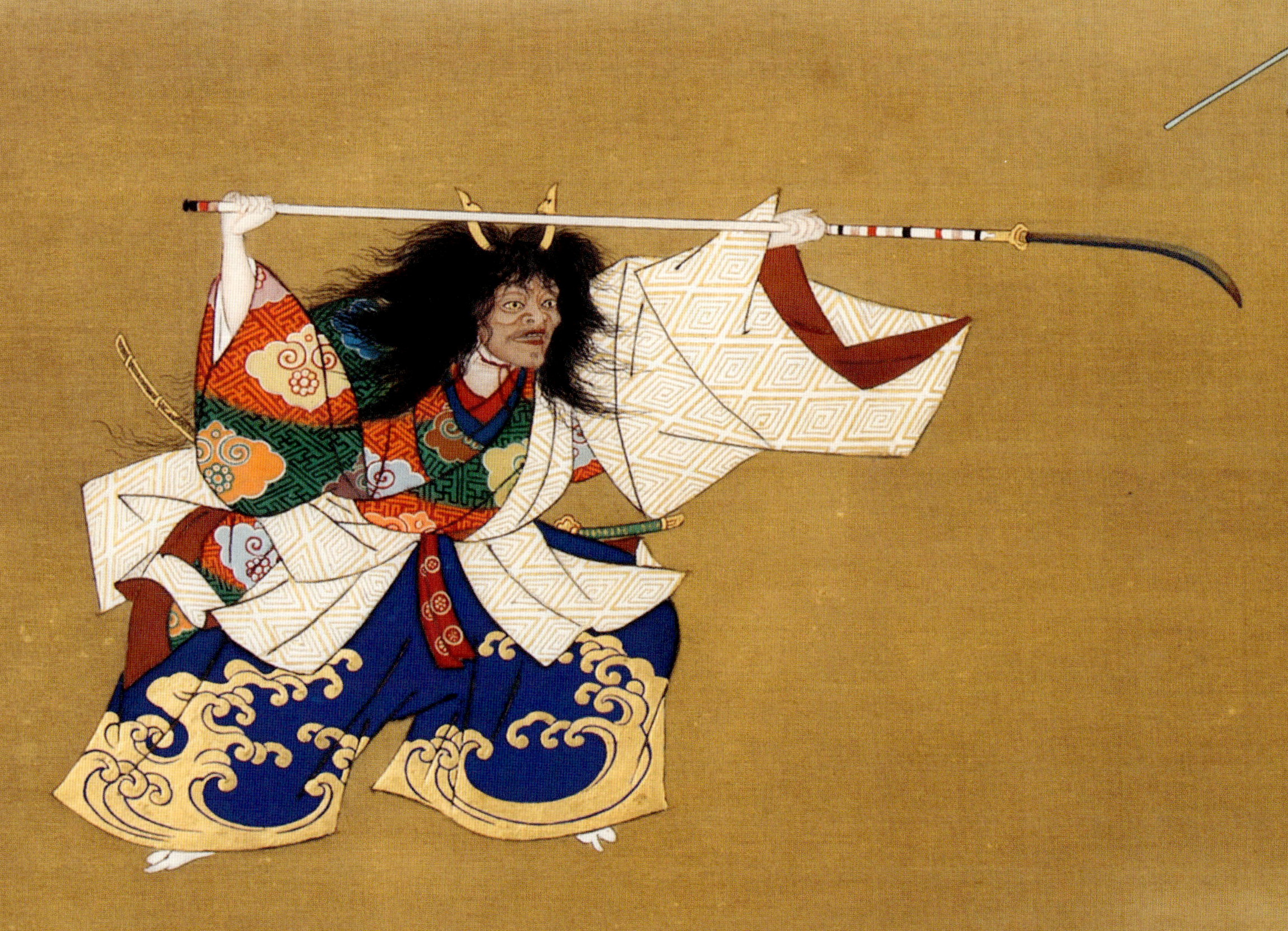

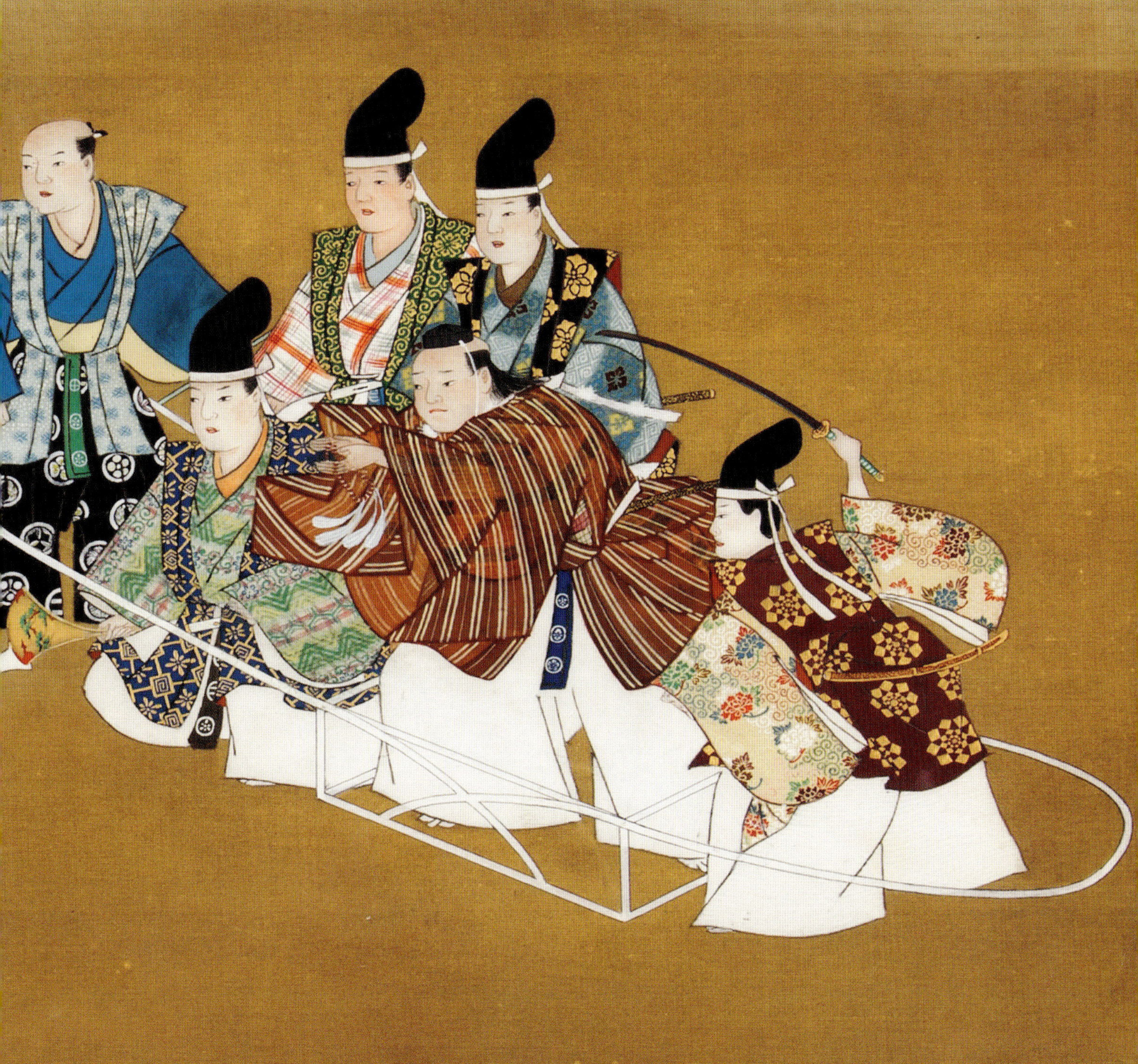

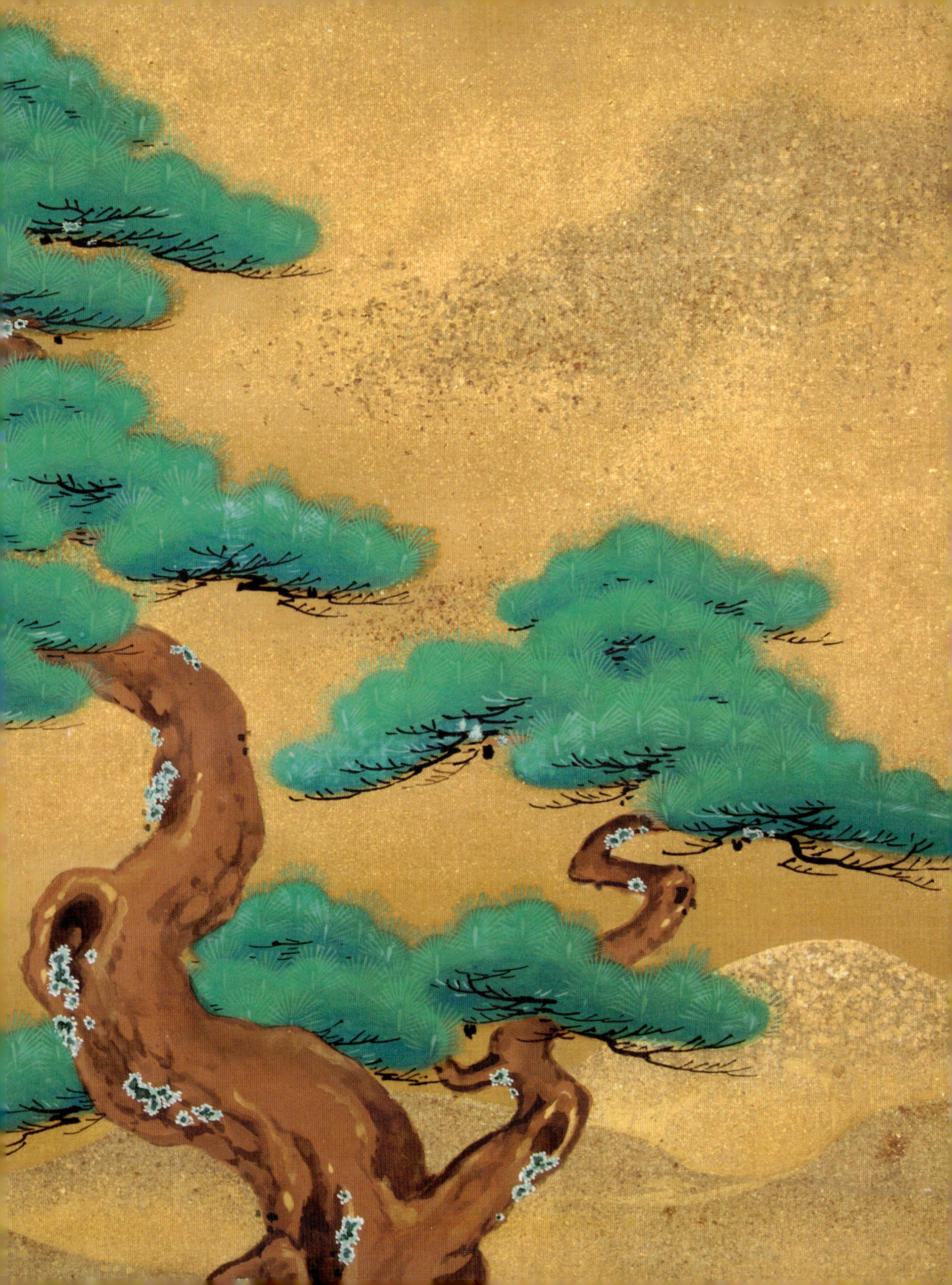